Understanding Theology
Volume Three

Understanding Theology Volume Three

RT Kendall

Christian Focus

© R.T. Kendall
ISBN 1 85792 581 5

Published in 2001 by
Christian Focus Publications
Geanies House, Fearn, Ross-shire
IV20 1TW, Great Britain

Cover design by Owen Daily

CONTENTS

Faith in Action

PREFACE

I have expressed in the previous two volumes of *Understanding Theology* my amazement that these volumes ever came into being at all. And now comes a third. All I can say is that I give all the honour and praise to God that he would use my feeble efforts to help people who have a desire to know God better via a theological understanding.

I want to thank Malcolm Maclean for his continued encouragement as well as that of William MacKenzie who never ceases to amaze me with his graciousness.

I pray the blessing of God Almighty upon those who read this volume and those that have preceded it.

Dr R T Kendall
Westminster Chapel, London
February 2001

to
Richard and Debbie

Books by R.T. Kendall
published by Christian Focus

Meekness and Majesty (an exposition of Philippians 2:5–11)

Are You Stone Deaf to the Spirit or Rediscovering God? (an exposition of Hebrews 6)

When God says 'Well Done!' (a consideration of what the judgment seat of Christ will mean for believers)

A Vision of Jesus (John's vision of Jesus in Revelation 1)

Just Love (an exposition of 1 Corinthians 13)

Higher Ground (based on Psalms 121–134)

A Man After God's Own Heart (the life of David)

Understanding Theology, Volume 1

Understanding Theology, Volume 2

1

IS THE BIBLE INFALLIBLE?

A. An assumption in historic Protestant Evangelicalism has been that the Bible is the Word of God.

  1. *The emergence of neo-orthodoxy earlier in the twentieth century side-stepped the issue, claiming:*

   a. The Bible 'contains' the Word of God.

   b. The problem: no-one knew for sure which part of the Bible was being referred to.

    (1) There was a feeling that God 'spoke' through the Bible.

    (2) But the question 'which part of the Bible actually is the Word of God?' could never be answered.

   c. Neo-orthodoxy (def.): 'new' orthodoxy, championed by men such as Karl Barth and Emil Brunner.

    (1) It came so close to orthodoxy at times that some felt it was sufficiently 'sound'.

    (2) But it allowed for the critical appraisal of the Bible, so that you were free to be selective with the Scriptures (e.g. Brunner did not believe in Christ's virgin birth).

  2. *There have been a number of people in the historic Protestant Evangelical tradition who do not want to be neo-orthodox, but who nonetheless will not affirm the infallibility of the Bible.*

   a. Historical Protestant Evangelicalism:

    (1) Protestant, as opposed to being Roman Catholic.

    (2) Evangelical, as opposed to being liberal, believing that Jesus is the God-man; we are saved by his substitutionary death on the cross; he rose physically from the dead; people need to be saved by personal faith in Christ.

    (3) Historic, as opposed to less known bodies of believers; e.g. Church of England, Baptist, Presbyterian, Methodist and reformed church.

   b. Some people from some of these churches are apparently reluctant to say that the Bible is infallible.

3. See Wayne Grudem's Systematic Theology. I have used a lot of his material in what follows below.

B. Biblical infallibility (def.): the belief that the books of the Old and New Testaments, as originally written, were without error in what they affirm.

1. Scripture in the original manuscripts does not affirm anything that is contrary to God.

2. *The Bible always tells the truth, and it always tells the truth concerning everything it talks about.*

    a. This does not mean that the Bible tells us every fact there is to know.

    b. It affirms that what it does say about any subject is true.

3. *All the words in the Bible are God's words.*

    a. To disbelieve or disobey any word in Scripture is to disbelieve or disobey God.

    b. All words in Scripture are completely true and without error in any part.

4. 'Inerrancy means that when all facts are known, the Scriptures in their original autographs and properly integrated will be shown to be totally true in everything they affirm, whether that has to do with doctrine or morality or with the social, physical or life sciences.' Michael Eaton.

5. Note: infallibility and inerrancy are interchangeable terms.

C. Why is this study important?

1. *The Bible is God's integrity put on the line.*

    a. God has magnified his word above all his name (Ps. 138:2 AV).

    b. If the Bible is not completely truthful, neither is God.

2. *The foundation of the Christian faith is at stake.*

    a. If the Bible is not true, how do we know Christianity is true?

    b. The only source for the truthfulness of the Christian faith is the Bible; all we believe about Jesus Christ stands or falls in proportion to the reliability of Scripture.

3. With esteemed men in the ministry distancing themselves from the infallibility of the Bible, many sincere Christians are likely to be confused, if not disillusioned.

4. Every Christian has a right to know what biblical infallibility is.

5. We all want to know if the infallibility of the Bible can be honestly defended.

I. WHAT THE BIBLE CLAIMS FOR ITSELF

A. In the Old Testament.

1. That God cannot lie or speak falsely. 'O Sovereign Lord, you are God! Your words are trustworthy, and you have promised these good things to your servant' (2 Sam. 7:28).

2. *That his word is true and without error in any part.*

    a. 'God is not a man, that he should lie, nor a son of man, that he should change his mind. Does he speak and then not act? Does he promise and not fulfil?' (Num. 23:19).

    b. 'And the words of the Lord are flawless, like silver refined in a furnace of clay, purified seven times' (Psalm 12:6).

    c. 'Your word, O LORD, is eternal; it stands firm in the heavens' (Ps. 119:89).

    d. 'Every word of God is flawless; he is a shield to those who take refuge in him' (Prov. 30:5).

B. In the New Testament.

1. That God cannot lie.

    a. 'A faith and knowledge resting on the hope of eternal life, which God, who does not lie, promised before the beginning of time' (Titus 1:2).

    b. 'God did this so that, by two unchangeable things in which it is impossible for God to lie, we who have fled to take hold of the hope offered to us may be greatly encouraged' (Heb. 6:18).

2. His Word is fully reliable. 'Heaven and earth will pass away, but my words will never pass away' (Matt. 24:35).

3. *His Word is the ultimate standard of truth. 'Sanctify them by the truth; your word is truth'* (John 17:17).

    a. That the Old Testament is God's Word.

        (1) 'All Scripture is God-breathed and is useful for teaching, rebuking, correcting and training in righteousness' (2 Tim. 3:16).

(2) 'Above all, you must understand that no prophecy of Scripture came about by the prophet's own interpretation. For prophecy never had its origin in the will of man, but men spoke from God as they were carried along by the Holy Spirit' (2 Pet. 1:20-21).

b. That the New Testament is God's Word.

(1) 'He writes the same way in all his letters, speaking in them of these matters. His letters contain some things that are hard to understand, which ignorant and unstable people distort, as they do the other Scriptures, to their own destruction' (2 Pet. 3:16).

(2) 'If anybody thinks he is a prophet or spiritually gifted, let him acknowledge that what I am writing to you is the Lord's command' (1 Cor. 14:37).

c. Note: when Paul said he spoke a personal word as a 'concession, not a command' (I Cor. 7:6) he proves all else he said was under the Lord's command (1 Cor. 7:10. cf. 1 Cor. 7:12,25).

4. In 1 Timothy 5:18 Paul quotes Jesus' words as found in Luke 10:7 and calls them 'Scripture'.

C. How God speaks.

1. *'Thus says the Lord' is a phrase which appears hundreds of times.*

a. When prophets say this they are claiming to be messengers from the true God.

b. They are claiming that their words are absolutely authoritative words of God.

(1) When a prophet spoke in God's name, every word he spoke had to be from God.

(2) Otherwise he would be a false prophet (Num. 22:18; Deut. 18:20; Jer. 1:9; 14:14; 23:16-22; 29:31-32; Ezek. 2:7; 13:1-16).

2. *God is often said to speak 'through' a prophet* (1 Kings 14:18; 16:12; 2 Kings 9:36; 14:25; Jer. 37:2; Zech. 7:7,12).

a. Thus what a prophet says in God's name, God says (cf. 1 Kings 13:26 with v.21; 1 Kings 21:19 with 2 Kings 9:25-26; Hag. 1:12).

b. Words that prophets spoke can equally be referred to as words God himself spoke.

c. To believe or disobey anything a prophet says is to believe or disobey God himself (Deut. 18:19; 1 Sam. 10:8; 13:13-14; 15:3, 19, 23; 1 Kings 20:35, 36).

3. Paul affirms that all of the Old Testament writings are theopneustos, 'breathed out by God' (2 Tim. 3:16).

   a. God used human agents to write them down.

   b. Peter spoke along the same line (2 Pet. 1:20-21), but:

      (1) He did not intend to deny completely human volition or personality.

      (2) He meant that the ultimate source was not a man's decision about what he wanted to write but rather the Holy Spirit's activity in the prophet's life.

II. CLARIFICATION REGARDING BIBLICAL INERRANCY

A. The Bible can be inerrant and still speak in the ordinary language of everyday speech.

   1. *This is true in 'scientific' or 'historic' descriptions of facts or events.*

      a. The Bible speaks of the sun rising and the rain falling because this is what happens from the speaker's perspective.

      b. These are perfectly true descriptions of the natural phenomena which the writer observes.

   2. *This is true with measuring or counting.*

      a. If it is said that 8,000 died it would be false to say 16,000 died.

      b. It is not false if in fact 7,823 or 8,242 died.

B. The Bible can be inerrant and still include loose or free quotations.

   1. As Michael Eaton says, there is hardly a single exact quotation of an Old Testament verse in the New Testament.

   2. Written Greek in New Testament times had no quotation marks.

   3. As long as the content was not false, the meaning was conveyed and true to the context.

C. One can believe in inerrancy and have unusual or uncommon grammatical constructions in the Bible.

   1. This sometimes includes failures to follow the commonly accepted 'rules' of grammatical expression (such as the use of a plural verb where grammatical rules require a singular verb).

2. They do not affect the truthfulness of the statements; a statement can be ungrammatical but entirely true.

3. The issue: truthfulness in speech.

D. There might be errors of translation.

1. *No translator is infallible.*

   a. They are at best interpretations of the original language.

   b. Some (e.g. The Living Bible) are paraphrases.

2. *The Authorised Version is probably the most literal translation; but it does not take into account more recent discoveries of ancient copies.*

   a. There might be errors of copyists.

   b. The Bible was copied by hand before the invention of the printing press.

III. CHALLENGES TO BIBLICAL INFALLIBILITY

A. The Bible is only authoritative for 'faith and practice'.

1. This premiss seeks to avoid biblical claims for what may be 'scientific' or 'historical'.

2. *Response: all of Scripture is 'God-breathed' (2 Tim. 3:16).*

   a. The Bible does not make any restriction on the kinds of subjects to which it speaks truthfully.

   b. Every one of God's words in Scripture was deemed by him to be important for us; God does not say anything unintentionally.

B. The term 'inerrancy' is a poor term.

1. It is said that this term 'inerrancy' is too precise, is not even a biblical word; therefore it is an inappropriate term.

2. *Response: the term 'inerrancy' is easily defined and is not used to denote a kind of absolute scientific precision.*

   a. Inerrancy simply means total truthfulness in language.

   b. Note: the words 'trinity' and 'incarnation' are not biblical terms either.

C. Since we have no inerrant manuscripts, talk about an inerrant Bible is misleading.

   1. Since no original copies of the biblical documents survive, why place importance on a doctrine that applies to documents no-one has?

   2. *Response: in over ninety-nine percent of the words of the Bible we know what the original manuscript said.*

   a. In the small percentage of cases where there is significant uncertainty about what the original text said, the general sense of the sentence is usually quite clear from the context.

   b. Our present manuscripts are for most purposes the same as the original manuscripts, and the doctrine of inerrancy therefore directly concerns our present manuscripts as well.

   3. *It is extremely important to affirm the inerrancy of the original documents, for the subsequent copies were made by men with no claim or guarantee by God that these copies would be perfect.*

   a. Therefore the original manuscripts are those to which the claims to be God's very words apply.

   b. Thus any mistakes in the copies are but the mistakes of men.

D. Inerrancy overemphasises the divine aspect of Scripture and neglects the human aspect.

   1. It is claimed that the human aspect is downplayed.

   2. *Response: it is agreed that Scripture has both a human and divine aspect, but those who make this objection almost invariably say that the human aspect of Scripture must include some errors in Scripture.*

   a. God overruled the writing of Scripture so that it does not include error.

   b. After all, human beings can make statements all the time that are completely true.

E. 'There are some clear errors in the Bible,' it is said.

   1. This is presumably why those who deny biblical infallibility stick to their guns.

   2. *Response: those who make this claim usually have little or no idea where the specific errors are, but believe there are errors because others have told them so.*

a. When there is a specific problem raised, a close inspection will show there to be no error at all.

b. It is surprising how often it turns out that a careful reading merely of the English text in question will bring to light one or more possible solutions to the difficulty.

c. There are many Bible scholars today who will say that they do not presently know of any problem texts for which there is no satisfactory solution. See W Grudem, op. cit. p.99.

IV. THE CONSEQUENCES OF DENYING BIBLICAL INFALLIBILITY

A. A serious moral problem confronts us: may we imitate God and intentionally lie in small matters also?

1. We are told to be imitators of God (Eph. 5:1).

2. A denial of inerrancy that nonetheless claims that Scripture is God-breathed implies that God intentionally spoke falsely to us in some things.

B. We begin to wonder if we can really trust God in anything he says.

1. Since we become convinced that God has not always told the truth in some matters (even minor) in Scripture, we then realise that God is capable of speaking falsely to us.

2. *This will have a determined effect on our ability to take God at his word.*

    a. Why should we trust him completely?

    b. Why obey him in the rest of Scripture?

C. We essentially make our own human minds a higher standard of truth than God's Word itself.

1. We use our minds to pass judgment on some sections of God's Word and pronounce them to be in error.

2. This is saying, in effect, that we know truth more certainly and accurately than God's Word does (or than God does), at least in some cases.

3. Note: this is the root of all intellectual sin.

D. We must also say that the Bible is wrong, not only in minor details but in some of its doctrine as well.

1. A denial of inerrancy means that we say that the Bible's teaching about the nature of Scripture and about the truthfulness and reliability of God's words is also false.
2. These are not minor details but major doctrinal concerns in Scripture.

V. HOW DO WE COME TO BELIEVE THE ABOVE IN OUR HEART OF HEARTS?

A. There are two ways by which we come to believe that the Bible is the Word of God.

1. *The objective witness.*
   a. There are at least four ways this can be explained:
      (1) What the Bible says about itself.
      (2) Archaeological confirmation.
      (3) The testimony of people who have been blessed by the Bible.
      (4) Deductive reasoning, as we have attempted to do in this lesson.
   b. But these will fail at the end of the day unless there is a further witness.
      (1) What the Bible says about itself is in a sense circular reasoning (def.): using as evidence for its conclusions the very thing that it is trying to prove. Note: Everyone either implicitly or explicitly uses some kind of circular argument when defending ultimate authority for his belief.
      (2) Archaeological confirmations are limited at best.
      (3) Testimonies have limited appeal.
      (4) After the clearest possible reasoning, 'a man convinced against his will is of the same opinion still'.

2. *The internal witness of the Holy Spirit.*
   a. At the end of the day this alone will persuade and hold us firmly in our conviction that the Bible is God's Word.
   b. The same Holy Spirit who wrote the Bible is in us and testifies to its total reliability.

B. The inner testimony of the Holy Spirit is stronger than all the 'proofs'.

1. We must seek our conviction in a higher place than human reason, judgment, testimonies or conjectures.

2. *It is in 'the secret testimony of the Holy Spirit.' John Calvin, Institutes, I:vii:4.*

   a. Faith is the principal work of the Holy Spirit (Eph. 1:13; 2 Thess. 2:13).

     (1) 'Faith is a firm and certain knowledge of God's kindness toward us, founded upon the truth of the freely given promise in Christ, both revealed to our minds and sealed upon our hearts by the Holy Spirit' (Calvin, op. cit., III:ii:7).

     (2) This faith is so strong that, in Luther's words, 'we could stake our life upon it a thousand times'.

3. *This has been called the analogy of faith* (Rom. 12:6). (Gr. *analogia*: 'proportion'.) This is two things:

   a. Comparing Scripture with Scripture (2 Tim. 2:15).

   b. Keeping in step with the Spirit (Gal. 5:25).

     (1) The best way of discovering the Bible's reliability is to get to know it and trust it.

     (2) It proves itself as you go along.

CONCLUSION

Those who really want to believe in the infallibility of the Bible discover its total trustworthiness. The most powerful and faithful testimony is the inner witness of the Holy Spirit to the Bible being the Word of God.

Who is Jesus?

2

IS JESUS GOD?

INTRODUCTION

A. The Millennium Challenge: who is Jesus?
  1. *Most people sadly did not grasp the implications of the new millennium.*
  a. The year is numbered 2000 because of the birth of Jesus two thousand years ago.
  b. AD stands for *anno domini*: the year of our Lord.
    (1) Granted: Jesus may have been born in 6 BC, or 4 BC (six or four years before Christ); this would mean we entered the new millennium a few years ago!
    (2) None the less; by the way we now understand the calendar, the year 2000 has direct reference to the coming of Jesus Christ into the world – approximately 2000 years ago.
    (3) It is a reminder to Jews who rejected Jesus as Messiah.
    (4) It may be an offence to Muslims.
    (5) It may be that others are unaware of the significance of the date.
      (a) We are proud of the year 2000.
      (b) It was a point of witness to one's faith.

B. At the end of the day the ultimate issue regarding the person of Jesus is whether or not he was – and is – God.
  1. He was God or he wasn't – and the answer to the question, 'Is Jesus God?' is crucial.
  2. If we are Christians, we affirm that Jesus is God, that is, the God-man.
  3. *If he is less than God – in our estimation – we are not Christians.*
    a. A Christian is one who claims that Jesus is God.
    b. There is such a thing as 'damning with faint praise':
      (1) Saying that Jesus was a prophet – but not the Son of

God (as Muslims claim) – is undermining Jesus.

(2) Saying that he was a good man – a good teacher, a good example and one who did not deserve to be crucified – but that he was not God – is to undermine Jesus.

C. The purpose of this study is to examine the following:

1. *What the Bible claims about the Deity of Jesus Christ.*
   a. Deity (def.): God-hood, God-ship; fully Divine.
   b. The Deity of Christ means that Christ was – and is – fully God.
2. *What Jesus himself claimed as to his own Deity.*
   a. What was Jesus conscious of pertaining to himself?
   b. When did he know who he was?
   c. Did he ever say, 'I am God'? If not, can we say that he claimed Deity for himself?
3. *Certain important Christological heresies in church history.*
   a. Christological (def.): any teaching that pertains to Christ's person.
   b. Heresy (def.): false doctrine or teaching, that is, according to the historic consensus of the Church.

D. Why is this lesson important?

1. If the Millennium Challenge is 'Who is Jesus?' the most important question that must ultimately be answered is whether or not he is God.
2. *Many Christians affirm his Deity, but would be in difficulty if asked to defend it or prove it.*
   a. This lesson will help us see why the Church claims that Jesus is God.
   b. You should be able to help another to see this after absorbing this important lesson.
3. *The most offensive claim of the Christian faith is that Jesus is God. and that the only way to Heaven is by Jesus Christ.*
   a. Jesus said, 'I am the way and the truth and the life. No one comes to the Father except through me' (John 14:6).
   b. We need to see why this is true.
4. *If Jesus is not God, the claim of the Christian faith and of the Church is not only false; it would mean that Christianity is a sham and that we are all deceived.*

a. It is high time we got to the bottom of this matter.

b. If Jesus is not God, we should close down all churches.

5. *The inspiration and reliability of the Bible hangs on this question.*

    a. All we shall say is based on Holy Scripture.

    b. We have no other source.

I. WHAT THE BIBLE CLAIMS CONCERNING CHRIST'S DEITY

A. The Virgin Birth.

1. *Note: The Virgin Birth for some may not prove Christ's deity.*

    a. Arianism (see below) holds to the Virgin Birth, as do Jehovah's Witnesses, but not Christ's deity.

    b. Ironically, Emil Brunner (neo-orthodox theologian) believed in Christ's deity but not his Virgin Birth.

    c. In the next chapter we will show how the Virgin Birth is essential to Christ's humanity.

    d. The Virgin Birth implies that Jesus is the Son of God, which implies deity; therefore Virgin Birth implies deity.

2. *Jesus did not have an earthly father.*

    a. Mary's reaction to the promise of the angel Gabriel that she would become pregnant: "'How will this be," Mary asked the angel, "since I am a virgin?"' (Luke 1:34).

      (1) Gabriel said she would give birth to a son and his name would be Jesus (Luke 1:31).

      (2) Gabriel added: 'He will be great and will be called the Son of the Most High. . . So the holy one to be born will be called the Son of God' (Luke 1:32-35).

    b. This would take place by the Holy Spirit who 'will come upon you, and the power of the Most High will overshadow you' (Luke 1:35).

      (1) This means that Mary was impregnated by the Holy Spirit.

      (2) 'For nothing is impossible with God' (Luke 1:37).

3. *The birth of a son without a human father – but rather the Most High God – could only mean that Jesus is God's Son.*

    a. Note: this is a useful tool in witnessing to a Muslim since the Qur'an (the Muslim Bible) teaches Christ's virgin birth.

    b. Sheer common sense would conclude that this means Jesus is the Son of God.

B. The Son of God.

  1. *Using the term 'Son of God' is the same as saying Jesus is God.*
   a. The New Testament makes no distinction between the terms.
   b. By Son of God we equally mean God the Son.
  2. *The Jews saw it this way.*
   a. The claim to be the Son of God was the same as the claim to deity.
    (1) Jesus' testimony to being the Son of God was the ammunition the Jews needed to justify their crucifying him.
    (2) 'They all asked, "Are you then the Son of God?" He replied, "You are right in saying I am." Then they said, "Why do we need any more testimony? We have heard it from his own lips"' (Luke 22:70-71. Cf. Mark 14:61-64).
   b. The purpose of the Gospel of John is summed up: 'But these are written that you may believe that Jesus is the Christ, the Son of God, and that by believing you may have life in his name' (John 20:31).
    (1) The contents of his Gospel included: 'In the beginning was the Word, and the Word was with God, and the Word was God' (John 1:1).
    (2) '"We are not stoning you for any of these," replied the Jews, "but for blasphemy, because you, a mere man, claim to be God"' (John 10:33).
   c. 'For this reason the Jews tried all the harder to kill him; not only was he breaking the Sabbath, but he was even calling God his own Father, making himself equal with God' (John 5:18).
    (1) The New Testament, as well as the ancient Jews, made no distinction between the two terms.
    (2) 'Son of God' meant the same as being God, that is, God the Son.

C. Explicit references to the Deity of Jesus.

  1. *'In the beginning was the Word, and the Word was with God, and the Word was God'* (John 1:1).
   a. There is no way that we can get around this verse with integrity.

b. It shows Christ's relationship with the Father; the Word (Gr. *logos*) was 'with God'.

c. It shows the pre-existence of the Word: 'In the beginning', that is, before the Word became flesh. 'The Word became flesh and made his dwelling among us. We have seen his glory, the glory of the One and Only, who came from the Father, full of grace and truth' (John 1:14).

d. Athanasius (296-393) held fast to this verse in an atmosphere that was charged with making Jesus 'like' God.

   (1) The Greek *homoousios* (the same nature as) and *homoiousios* (like) gave rise to the phrase 'one *iota* of difference'; but that *iota* was a crucial difference.

   (2) Athanasius won the day over Arius (d.336) and his view has been regarded as orthodox (sound) ever since.

2. *'No one has ever seen God, but God the One and Only, who is at the Father's side, has made him known'* (John 1:18).

  a. This is an unpacking of John 1:1 and John 1:14.

  b. John 1:18 is perhaps best translated 'the unique one, who is himself God.'

3. 'Thomas said to him, "My Lord and my God!"' (John 20:28).

4. 'Theirs are the patriarchs, and from them is traced the human ancestry of Christ, who is God over all, forever praised! Amen' (Romans 9:5).

5. 'While we wait for the blessed hope – the glorious appearing of our great God and Saviour, Jesus Christ' (Titus 2:13).

6. 'But about the Son he says, "Your throne, O God, will last for ever and ever, and righteousness will be the sceptre of your kingdom' (Heb. 1:8).

7. 'Simon Peter, a servant and apostle of Jesus Christ, To those who through the righteousness of our God and Saviour Jesus Christ have received a faith as precious as ours' (2 Pet. 1:1).

8. 'We know also that the Son of God has come and has given us understanding, so that we may know him who is true. And we are in him who is true – even in his Son Jesus Christ. He is the true God and eternal life' (1 John 5:20). Note: this further shows that being the Son of God is the same as being God.

9. This is also brought out by the words that God 'appeared in a body' (1 Tim. 3:16).

10. Philippians 2:6: 'Who, being in very nature God, did not consider equality with God something to be grasped.' 'Form' (Gr. *morpho*), means what a thing really is inwardly and outwardly. 'In the form of God' is as strong a statement of Christ's deity as could possibly be made.

11. 'For in Christ all the fullness of the Deity lives in bodily form' (Col. 2:9). 'For by him all things were created: things in heaven and on earth, visible and invisible, whether thrones or powers or rulers or authorities; all things were created by him and for him. He is before all things, and in him all things hold together' (Col. 1:16-17).

12. He is Creator (John 1:3).

13. His name is Immanuel, 'God with us' (Matt. 1:23).

14. Isaiah applies the name God to the coming Messiah. 'For to us a child is born, to us a son is given, and the government will be on his shoulders. And he will be called Wonderful Counsellor, Mighty God, Everlasting Father, Prince of Peace' (Isa. 9:6).

15. 'He is the image of the invisible God, the firstborn over all creation' (Col. 1:15). 'The Son is the radiance of God's glory and the exact representation of his being, sustaining all things by his powerful word. After he had provided purification for sins, he sat down at the right hand of the Majesty in heaven' (Heb. 1:3). If Christ is the mirror-image of the Father, what do you see in a mirror? A replica. The Son is the divine mirror-image of the Father.

D. Jesus as Lord.

1. Sometimes the word Lord (Gr. *kyrios*) is used simply as a polite address to a superior, roughly equivalent to 'sir' (Matt. 13:27; 21:30; 27:63; John 4:11).

2. *The same word however is used in the LXX (Septuagint, the Greek translation of the Hebrew Old Testament) for Yahweh – translated 'Lord'.*

   a. *Kyrios* translates the name of the Lord 6,814 times in the Old Testament.

   b. Anyone with knowledge of that at the time would know that 'Lord' was used to mean the Creator – the omnipotent God.

      (1) 'Today in the town of David a Saviour has been born to you; he is Christ the Lord' (Luke 2:11).

(2) 'But why am I so favoured, that the mother of my Lord should come to me?' (Luke 1:43).

(3) Referring to Jesus, John the Baptist cried, 'Prepare the way for the Lord' (Matt. 3:3).

(4) 'Yet for us there is but one God, the Father, from whom all things came and for whom we live; and there is but one Lord, Jesus Christ, through whom all things came and through whom we live' (1 Cor. 8:6).

(5) 'Therefore I tell you that no one who is speaking by the Spirit of God says, "Jesus be cursed," and no one can say, "Jesus is Lord," except by the Holy Spirit' (1 Cor. 12:3).

II. JESUS' OWN CLAIM TO DEITY

A. When was Jesus conscious of his true identity?

1. *In some sense he was aware of this after his bar mitzvah, when a Hebrew boy becomes a man – aged 12, in Jerusalem.*

   a. He said to his parents, 'Didn't you know I had to be in my Father's house?' (Luke 2:49).

   b. This may well be the first witness to Jesus' self-awareness of being God's Son.

2. *The full awareness of his deity was probably at his baptism.*

   a. He was obviously aware of his mission when he said to John the Baptist – inviting John to baptise him, 'It is proper for us to do this to fulfil all righteousness' (Matt. 3:15).

   b. But the full awareness came immediately after he was baptised. 'And a voice from heaven said, "This is my Son, whom I love; with him I am well pleased"' (Matt. 3:17).

B. Jesus asked Peter, 'Who do you say I am?' (Matt. 16:15).

1. Peter answered, 'You are the Christ, the Son of the living God' (Matt. 16:16).

2. Jesus affirmed Peter's testimony. 'Jesus replied, "Blessed are you, Simon son of Jonah, for this was not revealed to you by man, but by my Father in heaven"' (Matt. 16:17).

3. This was later recognised by the Father's voice when Jesus was transfigured (Matt. 17:5).

C. Jesus' reference to his origin and pre-existence.

1. 'I am the bread that came down from heaven' (John 6:41,51).
2. 'The Father who sent me has himself testified concerning me' (John 5:37).
3. 'No one has seen the Father except the one who is from God; only he has seen the Father' (John 6:46).
4. 'I am from above. You are of this world; I am not of this world' (John 8:23).
5. *'"I tell you the truth," Jesus answered, "before Abraham was born, I am!"'* (John 8:58).
   a. Note: whenever Jesus said, 'I am,' he was repeating the very words God used when he identified himself to Moses as 'I am who I am' (Ex. 3:14).
   b. Jesus was claiming for himself the title, 'I am,' by which God designates himself as the eternal existing one.
   c. The Jews got the point! 'At this, they picked up stones to stone him, but Jesus hid himself, slipping away from the temple grounds' (John 8:59).
6. 'Anyone who has seen me has seen the Father' (John 14:9).
7. 'And now, Father, glorify me in your presence with the glory I had with you before the world began' (John 17:5).

D. Jesus referring to himself as the Son of Man.

1. This title is used 84 times in the four gospels, but only by Jesus and only to speak of himself.
2. *This expression refers not to his humility or humanity but to deity.*
   a. This unique term has as its background the vision in Daniel 7.
   b. The Son of Man was given 'authority, glory and sovereign power; all peoples, nations and men of every language worshipped him. His dominion is an everlasting dominion that will not pass away' (Dan. 7:14).
   c. This speaks of one who had a heavenly origin and who was given an eternal rule over the whole world.
3. *The high priest did not miss the point when Jesus said, answering the high priest, that he was the Son of God and Son of Man.*
   a. The high priest said, 'I charge you under oath by the living God: Tell us if you are the Christ, the Son of God.'

b. "'Yes, it is as you say,'" Jesus replied. "But I say to all of you: In the future you will see the Son of Man sitting at the right hand of the Mighty One and coming on the clouds of heaven'" (Matt. 26:64).

c. 'Then the high priest tore his clothes and said, "He has spoken blasphemy! Why do we need any more witnesses? Look, now you have heard the blasphemy'" (Matt. 26:65).

III. EVIDENCE OF JESUS' DEITY

A. Demonstration of omnipotence.

1. When Jesus stilled the storm with a word (Matt. 8:26-27).

2. When Jesus multiplied the loaves and fish (Matt. 14:19).

3. *When Jesus changed the water into wine* (John 2:1-11).

    a. It is true that the above demonstrated the power of the Holy Spirit and Jesus' faith.

    b. However, John says by turning the water into wine he *revealed* his 'glory' (John 2:11).

B. His eternity

1. 'Before Abraham was born, I am' (John 8:58).

2. 'I am the Alpha and the Omega' (Rev. 22:13).

C. His omniscience

1. Knowing people's thoughts (Mark 2:8).

2. Seeing Nathaniel under the fig tree from far away (John 1:48).

3. Knowing who would betray him (John 6:64).

4. The disciples said to him, 'Now we can see that you know all things' (John 16:30. Cf. John 21:17).

D. His sovereignty

1. He could forgive sins (Mark 2:5-7).

2. The Old Testament prophets would say, 'Thus saith the Lord,' but Jesus said, 'But I say unto you' (Matt. 5:22,28,32,34,39,44).

3. He had the authority to reveal the Father to whomsoever he chose (Matt. 11:25-27).

E. His immortality (cf. 1 Tim. 6:16): only God has immortality.

1. 'Jesus answered them, "Destroy this temple, and I will raise it again in three days'" (John 2:19).

2. 'The reason my Father loves me is that I lay down my life – only to take it up again. No one takes it from me, but I lay it down of my own accord. I have authority to lay it down and authority to take it up again. This command I received from my Father' (John 10:17-18).

3. He has the power of an 'indestructible life' (Heb. 7:16).

F. Worship of Jesus commended and commanded.

1. The Magi came to worship him (Matt. 2:11; cf. Matt. 8:2).

2. The angels were told to worship him (Heb. 1:6).

3. 'Therefore God exalted him to the highest place and gave him the name that is above every name, that at the name of Jesus every knee should bow, in heaven and on earth and under the earth, and every tongue confess that Jesus Christ is Lord, to the glory of God the Father' (Phil. 2:9-11. Cf. Rev. 5:12-13).

G. Why are the words, 'Jesus is God,' not to be found?

1. 'God' is a technical word for the Father.

2. Had the New Testament said, 'Jesus is God,' it would imply that Jesus is the Father, which would be an anti-Trinitarian heresy.

3. It would imply that 'God is Jesus,' which is a somewhat misleading statement.

4. *The facts of the matter are:*

  a. The New Testament uses the word 'God' for the Father.

  b. 'Lord' *equally* implies deity, and it is 'Lord' which is the technical word for the Lord Jesus Christ.

  c. Paul confirmed this: 'Therefore God exalted him to the highest place and gave him the name that is above every name, that at the name of Jesus every knee should bow, in heaven and on earth and under the earth, and every tongue confess that Jesus Christ is Lord, to the glory of God the Father' (Phil. 2:9-11).

IV. EMERGING HERESIES IN CHURCH HISTORY

A. The Ebionites (first century).

1. These were Jews who 'solved' a Christological problem by denying the Deity of Christ altogether; they said Jesus was an inspired prophet but only a man.

2. They rejected the Virgin Birth, regarding Jesus as born normally from Joseph and Mary; and yet they claimed he was the predestined Messiah and would return to reign on earth.

B. Arianism (fourth century).

   1. *Arius (d.336), bishop of Alexandria, taught that Jesus was at one point created by God the Father.*

   a. Before that time the Son did not exist.

   b. Before that time the Holy Spirit did not exist.

   2. *The Son however existed before the rest of creation and is far greater than all the rest of creation.*

   a. He is still not equal to the Father in all his attributes.

   b. He is 'like' (*homoiousios*) the Father but not 'of the same nature' (*homoousios*) with the Father.

   3. The Nicene Creed, owing to the influence of Athanasius, condemned Arianism, and affirmed that the Lord Jesus Christ was the Son of God, 'begotten of the Father, only-begotten, that is, of the substance of the Father, God of God, Light of Light, true God of true God, begotten not made, of one substance with the Father, through whom all things were made.'

   4. Note: Jehovah's Witnesses are modern day Arians.

C. Apollinarianism (fourth century).

   1. *Appollinarius (d.392), bishop of Laodicea, opposed Arianism but embraced the divinity of Jesus without accepting his full manhood.*

   a. The teaching was that the body and soul of Jesus were human but his natural spirit was replaced by the Divine *logos*.

   b. The idea was that Jesus' personality was replaced by the *logos*.

   c. In a word: Jesus had a human body but not a human mind.

   2. *Apollinarianism was rejected by the Council of Constantinople in 381.*

   a. They recognised that it was not just our human body that needed salvation but our minds and spirits as well.

   b. Therefore Jesus had to be fully and truly man if he were to represent us, be our substitute and save us.

   c. In a word: Apollinarian Christology failed to meet the essential conditions of redemption.

D. Nestorianism (fifth century).

1. Nestorius, bishop of Constantinople from 428, was a popular preacher; whether he himself taught the heretical view that goes by his name is doubtful, since he later affirmed the findings of Chalcedon (below).

2. *Nestorianism is the doctrine that there were two separate persons in Christ: two persons in one body.*

   a. The idea was that there was a human person and a divine person.

   b. This is different from the biblical view that Jesus is one person.

3. *Nestorius opposed the use of the term theotakos (Mother of God).*

   a. He said this was an inappropriate term for the mother of Jesus.

   b. His reasoning was that Mary was the mother of the man Jesus only and not the divine *logos*.

4. This view was condemned at a council in Ephesus in 431, where the views of Bishop Cyril of Alexandria prevailed: the *logos* was so bound up with Jesus' complete human nature as to constitute a natural unity.

E. Eutychianism (fifth century), also known as monophysitism (Christ has one nature only).

1. *Eutyches (378-454) was a leader of a monastery at Constantinople.*

   a. He taught the opposite error to Nestorianism.

   b. He denied that the human nature of Christ remained fully human.

      (1) The human nature was taken up and absorbed into the divine nature.

      (2) Both natures were changed somewhat and a *third* kind of nature resulted!

2. *By this teaching Christ was neither truly God nor truly man.*

   a. He could not represent us as man.

   b. He could not be God and earn our salvation.

3. The solution: the Chalcedon definition of AD 451.

F. The Chalcedon statement that dealt with all the above.

1. At a city called Chalcedon (near Constantinople) bishops gathered in 451 to guard against the aforementioned heresies.

2. Christ was acknowledged to be one person 'in two natures, inconfusedly, unchangeably, indivisibly, inseparably; the distinction of natures being by no means taken away by the union, but rather the property of each nature being preserved, and concurring in one Person and one Subsistence, not parting or divided into two persons, but one and the same Son. . .'

3. This statement has been taken as the standard, orthodox definition of the biblical teaching on the person of Christ since that day by Catholic, Protestant and Orthodox branches of Christianity.

4. In a word: the union of Christ's human and divine nature in one being.

CONCLUSION

We must remember that in ancient times there was no transport or communication system such as there is today; no telephones, jets, faxes or e-mails. It took many years for the best minds to formulate a doctrine of Christ that was biblical and understandable. We may find accounts of the process tedious. But we are all the better for the hard work that preceded us and we should thank God for what has been handed on to us.

3

HOW HUMAN WAS JESUS?

A. Having dealt with the question, 'Is Jesus God?' (Yes), there follows another important question: 'Is Jesus man?' (Yes).

1. It is as essential to believe in Jesus' humanity as it is to believe in Jesus' Deity.

2. *Some people believe that if they believe in Jesus' Deity, that is enough.*

   a. Wrong: the earliest major heresy in the church was called Gnosticism.

   (1) Gnosticism (from the Greek *gnossis* – 'knowledge') held that the Christian faith was good as far as it went; but it did not go far enough.

   (2) The Gnostics claimed that they had a new way of 'knowing'; that they would make Christianity better.

   b. One part of Gnosticism was called *docetism* (from the Greek *dokeo* – what 'appeared' or 'seemed').

   (1) Their proponents argued that Jesus only appeared or seemed to have a body.

   (2) They insisted that God could not truly indwell human flesh – for the human body or human flesh was too sinful.

   (3) God truly and literally indwelling human flesh was out of the question.

   c. Gnosticism was on the horizon toward the latter half of the first century, and certain New Testament epistles as well as the Gospel of John dealt with this.

   (1) 'Dear friends, although I was very eager to write to you about the salvation we share, I felt I had to write and urge you to contend for the faith that was once for all entrusted to the saints' (Jude 1:3).

   (2) 'Dear friends, do not believe every spirit, but test the spirits to see whether they are from God, because many false prophets have gone out into the world. This is how you can recognise the Spirit of God: Every spirit that acknowledges that Jesus Christ has come in the flesh is from God' (1 John 4:1-2).

    (3) 'The Word became flesh and made his dwelling among us. We have seen his glory, the glory of the One and Only, who came from the Father, full of grace and truth' (John 1:14).

3. *The Apostles' Creed (2nd century) was drawn up not so much to attack opponents to the Deity of Christ, but to argue against those who didn't believe that God really indwelt human flesh.*

    a. The better known form is this:

        (1) I believe in God the Father Almighty, maker of heaven and earth.

        (2) And in Jesus Christ his only Son our Lord.

        (3) Who was conceived by the Holy Spirit, born of the Virgin Mary.

        (4) Who suffered under Pontius Pilate; was crucified, died and buried; he descended into hell.

        (5) He rose again on the third day.

        (6) He ascended into heaven.

        (7) Where he sat down at the right hand of the Father.

        (8) Thence he will come to judge the living and the dead.

        (9) I believe in the Holy Ghost.

        (10) The holy catholic church, the communion of the saints.

        (11) The forgiveness of sins.

        (12) The resurrection of the dead and life eternal.

    b. It used to be thought that each of the Apostles had a hand in the formulation, hence the twelve sections.

    c. What is noteworthy however:

        (1) The reference to the Virgin birth was inserted to prove the humanity of Jesus.

        (2) The original statement referred to the 'resurrection of the flesh' rather than just resurrection of the dead.

B. The purpose of the aforementioned verses (and others to be seen below) from John, Jude, and 1 John was to show how important it is to believe in Jesus' humanity.

    1. Because of Arianism and the need for the Nicene Creed, the church has often tended to forget that the earlier threat to the faith was undermining Jesus' humanity.

2. To deny that Jesus is in the 'flesh' is to reveal that one has a spirit of error behind him or her.

C. Our subject 'How human was Jesus?' refers to his days on earth.

    1. *To ask 'How human is Jesus?' is not quite the point that must be faced.*

        a. He is in the flesh – now, this is true.

            (1) He did not pass behind the clouds (Acts 1:9ff) and become a spirit, like the Logos was before he came to earth.

            (2) 'For there is one God and one mediator between God and men, the man Christ Jesus' (1 Tim. 2:5).

        b. Now that he is in glory he is not beset with the temptations and challenges he met on earth, which can be called 'days of his flesh' (Heb. 5:7 AV).

    2. *We want to look at the human Jesus – as though he were not God – and ask, 'How human?'*

        a. Never forget:

            (1) Jesus was God as though he were not man.

            (2) Jesus was man as though he were not God.

        b. The main New Testament books which most demonstrate his deity (John and Hebrews) equally most demonstrate his humanity.

            (1) When we see his deity, it seems incomprehensible that he could be man!

            (2) When we see his humanity, it seems incomprehensible that he could be God!

            (3) This is why we call him the God-man.

        c. It is an antinomy (def.): parallel principles that seem irreconcilable but both being equally true.

            (1) Jesus was not fifty percent God and fifty percent man.

            (2) He was one hundred percent God and one hundred percent man.

D. Why is this lesson important?

    1. To believe in Christ's deity is only one half of the battle; we need to believe equally in his humanity.

    2. *If Jesus were not fully man he could not be our substitute.*

    a. He was our substitute by his sinless life and life of faith prior to the cross.

    b. He was our substitute when he died on the cross.

3. Many Christians claim with their lips that they believe Jesus was fully man but are taken aback when they see how human he was!

4. There are sadly many 'docetic' Christians who don't realise how impoverished they are!

5. This lesson should give us a greater love for Jesus and also appreciation for all he went through on our behalf.

I. CERTAIN BIBLICAL FACTS ABOUT THE HUMANITY OF JESUS

A. The Virgin Birth.

    1. This is proof of his Deity.

    2. *It is equally proof of his humanity; he was the son of Mary.*

        a. Jesus was conceived in her womb by a miraculous work of the Holy Spirit.

            (1) Mary was 'found to be with child through the Holy Spirit' (Matt. 1:18).

            (2) That which was conceived 'in her is from the Holy Spirit' (Matt. 1:20).

            (3) The child would be 'holy' (Luke 1:35).

        b. When he was born he was a human baby.

            (1) The line of a hymn which says, 'No crying he makes,' is probably false.

            (2) It is more likely, 'Tears and smiles like us he knew.'

    3. *Note three important areas:*

        a. Salvation comes through the 'offspring' of the woman (Gen. 3:15) and not through human effort; it is the work of God himself.

        b. The Virgin Birth made possible the uniting of the full deity and full humanity in one person.

            (1) Jesus came into the world as a man (Gal. 4:4).

            (2) Jesus was a complete human being.

        c. The Virgin Birth makes possible the full humanity of Jesus without inherited sin.

            (1) Human beings have inherited legal guilt and a corrupt moral nature from their first father – Adam.

(2) This is sometimes called 'inherited' or 'original' sin.

(3) The fact that Jesus did not have a human father meant that the line of descent from Adam was partially interrupted.

(4) Jesus did not descend from Adam in exactly the same way in which every other human being descended from Adam.

(5) This is why the legal guilt and moral corruption which belongs to other human beings did not belong to Christ.

(6) The Holy Spirit's work prevented not only the transmission of sin through Joseph but also, in a miraculous way, the transmission of sin from Mary. '*So the holy one to be born will be called the Son of God*' (Luke 1:35).

B. Human weaknesses and limitations.

1. *Jesus had a human body.*

    a. He was born as all human babies are born (Luke 2:7).

    b. He grew through childhood just like other children grow. 'And the child grew and became strong; he was filled with wisdom, and the grace of God was upon him' (Luke 2:40).

    c. He grew 'in wisdom and stature, and in favour with God and man' (Luke 2:52).

2. He got tired as we do (John 4:6).

3. He became thirsty (John 19:28).

4. He became hungry (Matt. 4:2).

5. His fast in the desert would have made him physically weak; at that time the angels ministered to him (Matt. 4:11).

6. On his way to be crucified, the soldiers forced Simon of Cyrene to carry his cross (Luke 23:26).

7. *The culmination of his limitations is seen in his succumbing to death on a cross* (Luke 23:46).

    a. His human body ceased to function, just as ours do when we die.

    b. Paul said he was crucified 'in weakness' (2 Cor. 13:4).

C. His resurrected body.

1. Although our chief focus is on Jesus' humanity before his resurrection, an examination of his humanity afterwards is revealing.

How Human Was Jesus?

2. *Although he was no longer subject to weakness or death, Jesus himself demonstrated that he still had a real physical body.*

    a. 'Look at my hands and my feet. It is I myself! Touch me and see; a ghost does not have flesh and bones, as you see I have' (Luke 24:39).

        (1) This shows he has flesh and bones.

        (2) He was not merely a spirit without a body.

    b. 'When he had said this, he showed them his hands and feet. And while they still did not believe it because of joy and amazement, he asked them, "Do you have anything here to eat?" They gave him a piece of broiled fish, and he took it and ate it in their presence' (Luke 24:40-43).

3. *The way in which Jesus ascended to heaven was calculated to demonstrate the continuity between his existence in a physical body below and his continuing existence in that same body in heaven.*

    a. There is a man in glory!

    b. There is one mediator – the 'man Christ Jesus' (1 Tim. 2:5).

D. Jesus had a human mind.

1. The fact that he 'increased in wisdom' tells us that he went through a learning process just as all children do.

2. *He had to learn to read and write, how to walk and talk.*

    a. He had to learn his ABC – or the equivalent!

    b. He had to learn his multiplication tables – or the equivalent!

    c. He had to read the Old Testament in order to quote it and show mastery of it.

3. He leaned obedience (Heb. 5:8) and continued this even after his bar mitzvah. 'Then he went down to Nazareth with them and was obedient to them. But his mother treasured all these things in her heart' (Luke 2:51).

4. When the disciples, having been told to buy swords, replied, 'See, Lord, here are two swords,' Jesus replied as though he had not known they had them. 'That is enough,' he replied, (Luke 22:36-38).

E. He had a human soul and emotions.

1. 'Now my heart is *troubled*' (John 12:27).

2. *'After he had said this, Jesus was troubled in spirit'* (John 13:21).

a. Gr. *tarasso*, troubled, is a word that is often used of people when they are anxious or suddenly surprised by danger.

  (1) Herod was 'disturbed' when he heard from the Magi (Matt. 2:3).

  (2) The disciples were 'terrified' when they saw Jesus walking on the sea and thought he was a ghost (Matt. 14:26).

  (3) Zechariah was 'startled and gripped with fear' when he saw an angel in the temple (Luke 1:12).

  (4) The disciples were 'troubled' when Jesus appeared after his resurrection (Luke 24:38).

b. When Jesus was troubled we must not think there was any lack of faith or sin involved.

3. He was 'astonished' at the faith of the centurion (Matt. 8:10).

4. He wept with sorrow at the death of Lazarus (John 11:35).

5. He could be angry (Mark 3:5. Cf. John 2:15ff; Mark 11:11ff).

6. *He prayed with deep emotion.*

a. 'During the days of Jesus' life on earth, he offered up prayers and petitions with loud cries and tears to the one who could save him from death, and he was heard because of his reverent submission' (Heb. 5:7).

b. 'And being in anguish, he prayed more earnestly, and his sweat was like drops of blood falling to the ground' (Luke 22:44).

7. *Possibly the most extraordinary revelation is that Jesus was perfected by way of suffering!*

a. He was made 'perfect through suffering' (Heb. 2:10).

b. 'Although he was a son, he learned obedience from what he suffered' (Heb. 5:8).

  (1) The older he became the more demands his parents could place on him.

  (2) The more difficult also were the tasks that his heavenly Father could assign to him – the worst being the last week, last hours of his earthly life.

8. *He was tempted 'in every way' like us and yet without sin* (Heb. 4:15. Cf. Heb. 2:18).

a. We won't know until we get to Heaven how fierce his temptations were.

b. I predict: they were worse than what you and I experience, and would have included every kind of temptation, with particular reference to pride and sex.

9. *People saw Jesus only as a man.*

  a. There was nothing spectacular about his appearance (Is. 53:2).

  b. Judas gave a signal by which the chief priests would recognise Jesus, which shows there was nothing extraordinary about his appearance (Matt. 26:48).

  c. For the first thirty years of his life Jesus' life was so ordinary that the people of Nazareth who knew him best were amazed that he could teach and work miracles.

    (1) He was the 'carpenter's son' (Matt. 13:55).

    (2) He was 'the carpenter' (Mark 6:3).

    (3) Even his brothers did not believe in him (John 7:5).

    (4) 'They said, "Is this not Jesus, the son of Joseph, whose father and mother we know? How can he now say, 'I came down from heaven'?"' (John 6:42).

II. JESUS' FAITH AND PRAYER LIFE

A. There are at least three further matters of Jesus' life and mission that spring from his being a man.

  1. Jesus as a man of faith.

  2. Jesus as a man of prayer.

  3. Jesus and his relationship to the Holy Spirit.

B. Jesus was said to be 'full of the Holy Spirit' (Luke 4:1).

  1. *He was said also to be led by the Spirit* (Luke 4:1).

    a. We may therefore take it that all he did was under the leadership of the Spirit in his life.

    b. He went so far as to say:

      (1) 'The Son can do nothing by himself' (John 5:19).

      (2) 'By myself I can do nothing; I judge only as I hear, and my judgement is just, for I seek not to please myself but him who sent me' (John 5:30).

  2. *At what point Jesus became full of the Holy Spirit is uncertain.*

    a. If John the Baptist was filled with the Spirit from his mother's womb (Luke 1:15), could we expect less of God's Son?

    b. There was a degree of Messianic self-consciousness at his bar mitzvah (Luke 2:49-50).

c. It is likely that this came to its fullest measure at his baptism, for 'At that moment heaven was opened, and he saw the Spirit of God descending like a dove and lighting on him. And a voice from heaven said, "This is my Son, whom I love; with him I am well pleased"' (Matt. 3:16-17).

3. *John the Baptist said that Jesus had the Spirit 'without limit'* (John 3:34).

  a. By contrast, we have the Spirit with a certain measure, or limit (Rom. 12:3); that is why we are urged to be filled with the Spirit (Eph. 5:18).

  b. But Jesus had all of God that there is, all of the Holy Spirit that it is possible for a person to have.

C. The Spirit without limit enabled Jesus to have faith without limit.

1. His faith in God was foreseen by Isaiah (Isa. 8:17).

2. The writer of Hebrews affirms Jesus as a man of faith: 'I will put my trust in him' (Heb. 2:13).

3. His tormentors and accusers at the cross said of him: 'He trusts in God. Let God rescue him now if he wants him, for he said, "I am the Son of God"' (Matt. 27:43).

D. Jesus' faith had no fewer than two purposes:

1. *It enabled him to heal, to perform miracles, pray, keep his eyes on the Father and maintain perfect obedience.*

  a. Faith is what produces obedience.

  b. Jesus' perfect faith resulted in perfect obedience.

  c. Whereas it can be argued cogently that Jesus' miracles demonstrate his deity, it may be equally argued that such came as a result of his perfect faith in the Father.

2. *It enabled him to be our perfect substitute.*

  a. He was obedient to the Law for us because of his perfect faith.

  b. His perfect faith was vicarious as well; he believed for us, showing a total trust in God that we are unable to have.

  c. This is why the Gospel is revealed 'from faith to faith' (Rom. 1:17 AV).

    (1) It is by Jesus' faith that he accomplished all that he did – in life and death.

(2) But unless we too believe we cannot be saved. 'Even the righteousness of God which is by faith of Jesus Christ unto all and upon all them that believe: for there is no difference' Romans 3:22 (AV). Cf. 'Knowing that a man is not justified by the works of the law, but by the faith of Jesus Christ, even we have believed in Jesus Christ, that we might be justified by the faith of Christ, and not by the works of the law: for by the works of the law shall no flesh be justified' (Gal. 2:16 AV).

d. His intercession at God's right hand is with a perfect faith. Hebrews 7:25; Galatians 2:20 where Paul says he lives 'by the faith of the Son of God' (AV).

E. Jesus was a man of prayer.

1. *He did not pray because he was God but because he was a man.*

   a. He obviously felt the need to pray.

   b. He prayed at all times.

      (1) Morning. 'Very early in the morning, while it was still dark, Jesus got up, left the house and went off to a solitary place, where he prayed' (Mark 1:35).

      (2) Evening. 'After he had dismissed them, he went up on a mountainside by himself to pray. When evening came, he was there alone' (Matt. 14:23).

      (3) All night. 'One of those days Jesus went out to a mountainside to pray, and spent the night praying to God. When morning came, he called his disciples to him and chose twelve of them, whom he also designated apostles' (Luke 6:12-13).

2. *Why did Jesus feel the need to pray?*

   a. Communion with the Father. 'You always hear me' (John 11:42).

      (1) He needed to get away from the crowds; he dismissed them, as well as the disciples, to be alone (Matt. 14:22-23).

      (2) He wanted no distraction, nothing to compete with his attention and communion with God.

   b. Further guidance.

      (1) As seen above, Jesus' praying all night preceded his

> > choice of the Twelve.
> > **(2)** He wanted final clarification of his mission in Gethsemane (Matt. 26:36-44).
> > **c.** When he anticipated an extraordinary miracle.
> > > **(1)** Just before he walked on water (Mark 6:46-51).
> > > **(2)** Just before feeding the five thousand with the loaves and fish (Matt. 14:13ff).
> > > **(3)** Just before raising Lazarus from the dead (John 11:41-44).
> > > **(4)** Just before being transfigured (Luke 9:29).

3. He prayed for the coming of the Holy Spirit. 'And I will ask the Father, and he will give you another Counsellor to be with you forever' (John 14:16).

4. *His high priestly prayer in John 17 included:*
  a. Praying for himself (John 17:1-5,19).
  b. Praying for the disciples (John 17:6-19).
  c. Praying for all of us (John 17:20-26).

5. His communion with the Father was apparently broken on the cross, this being the only time he addressed the Father as 'God'. 'About the ninth hour Jesus cried out in a loud voice, "Eloi, Eloi, lama sabachthani?" – which means, "My God, my God, why have you forsaken me?"' (Matt. 27:46).

CONCLUSION

Jesus was very human indeed. If he had not been so, he could not have truly represented us, thus being our Substitute. Hallelujah, what a Saviour!

4

WHAT DID JESUS TEACH US?

A. No series on the person of Jesus, or Christology, would be complete without a lesson on his teachings.

1. *Jesus was a preacher and a teacher.*
   a. Preaching (def.): proclaiming and applying God's Word.
      (1) Gr. *kerygma* refers both to the message and method. 'For since in the wisdom of God the world through its wisdom did not know him, God was pleased through the foolishness of what was preached to save those who believe' (1 Cor. 1:21).
      (2) 'From that time on Jesus began to preach, "Repent, for the kingdom of heaven is near"' (Matt. 4:17. Cf. Matt. 4:23).
   b. Teaching (def.): explaining the Word of God:
      (1) Gr. *didasko* refers to the passing on of knowledge, or imparting information.
      (2) 'Now when he saw the crowds, he went up on a mountainside and sat down. His disciples came to him, and he began to teach them' (Matt. 5:1-2. Cf. Mark 6:34).
   c. The two ways are linked together in Acts 5:42: 'Day after day, in the temple courts and from house to house, they never stopped teaching and proclaiming the good news that Jesus is the Christ.'

2. *It is wonderful that the Son of God came equipped to teach and preach.*
   a. While it is a great mistake to isolate Jesus' teachings from the rest of the New Testament, it is none the less interesting to read Jesus' teaching by itself. Why?
   b. This helps us to see how Jesus spoon-fed his hearers before his death and how he laid the foundation for the faith delivered to the saints (Jude 3).

B. 'No one ever spoke the way this man does' (John 7:46).

   1. These words were uttered in amazement by temple guards who had been ordered to arrest Jesus.

   2. *These guards were not prepared for what they heard.*

      a. Their minds had been made up – until they heard Jesus.

      b. 'Finally the temple guards went back to the chief priests and Pharisees, who asked them, "Why didn't you bring him in?" "No one ever spoke the way this man does," the guards declared' (John 7:45-46).

   3. *Matthew tells us about the grassroots reaction to Jesus' Sermon on the Mount: 'When Jesus had finished saying these things, the crowds were amazed at his teaching, because he taught as one who had authority, and not as their teachers of the law'* (Matt. 7:28-29).

      a. This reaction was not limited to the Sermon on the Mount.

      b. Matthew tells us of the reaction to Jesus' silencing the Sadducees: 'When the crowds heard this, they were astonished at his teaching' (Matt. 22:33).

         (1) The Greek word *ekplesso*, translated 'amazed' or 'astonished' is also used when Jesus cast out demons (Luke 9:43).

         (2) This tells us that Jesus could astonish with his word as easily as he could astonish with miracles.

C. In this lesson we will necessarily have to be selective with what we can go into.

   1. After all, John said, 'Jesus did many other things as well. If every one of them were written down, I suppose that even the whole world would not have room for the books that would be written' (John 21:25).

   2. *While this may refer to the miraculous, it almost certainly could describe the volume of Jesus' teachings.*

      a. There are references to Jesus' teaching in the New Testament which cannot be found in the Gospels.

         (1) The words 'It is more blessed to give than to receive' (Acts 20:35) are a quotation from Jesus which cannot be found in the Gospels.

         (2) Such may also refer to passages like 1 Thessalonians 4:15.

b. The Gospel writers were obviously selective in what they reported.

D. In this lesson, drawn largely from the Sermon on the Mount and Jesus' parables, we will restrict ourselves to four categories:

   1. Jesus' teaching on the Kingdom of Heaven.

   2. Jesus' teaching on the Law.

   3. Jesus' teaching on prayer.

   4. Jesus' teaching on humility.

   5. Note: obviously we will take a very brief look at each.

E. Why is this lesson important?

   1. Many people claim to admire Jesus as a good teacher but often don't have a clue as to what he taught.

   2. Jesus' teachings were addressed to those who did not realise he would end up dying on a cross; we therefore need to keep a pre-crucifixion perspective while at the same time observing how this coheres with all that followed.

   3. We must remember that, though people were amazed at Jesus' 'authority', they probably didn't grasp very much of what they heard at the time.

   4. The teachings of Jesus cannot be fully understood apart from the cross and the coming of the Holy Spirit.

   5. The teachings of Jesus are totally relevant for all of us today.

I. THE KINGDOM OF HEAVEN (OR KINGDOM OF GOD)

A. First John the Baptist, then Jesus, preached the Kingdom of Heaven and both said that it was 'near' (Matt. 3:2; 4:17).

   1. *Jesus credited John with saying this first. 'From the days of John the Baptist until now, the kingdom of heaven has been forcefully advancing, and forceful men lay hold of it'* (Matt. 11:12. Cf. Luke 16:16).

   a. The AV says, 'The kingdom of heaven suffereth violence, and the violent take it by force.'

   b. Some have interpreted this to mean that Jesus commanded this; that we too must take the Kingdom by force.

   (1) I rather think that Jesus was describing a scenario that took place in his time and has been repeated many times since.

(2) This is not a good thing after all; overly zealous people have always rushed in and spoiled what was beautiful and precious.

2. *The Kingdom being 'near' meant two things:*

   a. The unfolding of it was at hand.

   b. It is not something to be observed – like a political regime or structure; it is in the heart. 'Once, having been asked by the Pharisees when the kingdom of God would come, Jesus replied, "The kingdom of God does not come with your careful observation, nor will people say, 'Here it is,' or 'There it is,' because the kingdom of God is within you"' (Luke 17:20-21).

B. Kingdom of Heaven (def.): the reign of the Holy Spirit.

1. *This concept would only become clear after the Holy Spirit came down at Pentecost (Acts 2:1-4) and applied all that Jesus had taught.*

   a. The central theme of the Sermon on the Mount is the Kingdom of Heaven.

      (1) The Holy Spirit however is not mentioned in the Sermon on the Mount.

      (2) God is not mentioned in Esther – a God-centred book.

   b. The Kingdom of Heaven makes no sense without the Holy Spirit.

      (1) The Holy Spirit was explicitly explained by Jesus later.

      (2) But with that explanation, the Sermon on the Mount opens up.

2. *'Kingdom' refers to a realm, a monarchy; it presupposes a monarch.*

   a. In the Old Testament God made it clear: he is King (1 Sam. 8:7).

   b. The hasty desire for an earthly king was not God's idea (Hos. 13:11).

3. *Since the Kingdom of Heaven is within us, it has to refer to the Holy Spirit; it is actually another term for 'anointing'.*

   a. This is why it is not visible; it is also the key to understanding Jesus' parables.

b. But this is why it was at hand; for it would all come home once Jesus died, ascended and sent the Holy Spirit.

c. All that Jesus taught concerning the Kingdom is perhaps best summed up by the apostle Paul: 'For the kingdom of God is not a matter of eating and drinking, but of righteousness, peace and joy in the Holy Spirit' (Rom. 14:17).

II. The Law

A. Fairly early in the Sermon on the Mount Jesus said, 'Do not think that I have come to abolish the Law or the Prophets; I have not come to abolish them but to fulfil them' (Matt. 5:17).

1. This was his first recorded reference to the Mosaic Law.

2. *It seems to have come out of the blue.*

  a. Why did Jesus says, 'Do not think that I have come to abolish the Law. . .'?

    (1) Were the people thinking he would?

    (2) If so, why would they think that?

    (3) Had he said something already in the Sermon on the Mount that would make them wonder this?

  b. There were those at the time who hoped Jesus would abolish the Law.

    (1) There were those of a 'revolutionary' mind-set who would be glad if Messiah would overthrow the Law and start all over again with something else.

    (2) There were legalists (like the Pharisees) who were suspicious of Jesus and surmised that he would abolish the Law.

  c. Jesus put any rumours to rest: 'Do not think that I have come to abolish the Law or the Prophets; I have not come to abolish them but to fulfil them' (Matt. 5:17).

    (1) Martyn Lloyd-Jones reckoned this was the most stupendous statement Jesus ever made.

    (2) He was thus saying: I am the fulfilment of the Old Testament.

  d. The promise to fulfil the Law was an extraordinary prophecy.

    (1) No one had ever made such a claim; much less carried it out.

(2) Jesus virtually said: I will fulfil it – every one of those 2,000 verses of legislation in Exodus, Leviticus, Numbers and Deuteronomy.

B. Jesus' view of the Law and the Kingdom of Heaven are inseparably connected.

1. *For once the Kingdom had come, the Law would be fulfilled.*

   a. Pentecost – fifty days after Passover – was also the annual commemoration of the Law given at Sinai.

   b. Once the Spirit came down, the Law was fulfilled.

   (1) This is why Paul later said, 'But if you are led by the Spirit, you are not under law' (Gal. 5:18).

   (2) This further explains Galatians 3:25: 'Now that faith has come, we are no longer under the supervision of the law.'

2. *The Law is generally thought to be in three parts:*

   a. Moral Law: the Ten Commandments.

   b. Civil Law: how the people of Israel should govern themselves.

   c. Ceremonial Law: how the people of Israel should worship the true God.

3. *The Kingdom of Heaven replaced the Law.*

   a. The Holy Spirit did what the law could not do:

   (1) The Spirit produced brokenness (Matt. 5:2-6).

   (2) The Spirit produced graciousness (Matt. 5:7-9).

   (3) The Spirit produced stalwartness (Matt. 5:10-12).

   b. The Holy Spirit produced a righteousness that surpassed that of the teachers of the Law and the Pharisees.

   (1) Jesus said that if one did not surpass the righteousness of the Pharisees one could not enter the Kingdom of Heaven. 'For I tell you that unless your righteousness surpasses that of the Pharisees and the teachers of the law, you will certainly not enter the kingdom of heaven' (Matt. 5:20).

   (2) Paul later showed the difference between what the Law couldn't do and what walking in the Spirit does. 'For what the law was powerless to do in that it was weakened by the sinful nature, God did by sending his own Son in the likeness of sinful man to be a sin offering. And so

he condemned sin in sinful man, in order that the righteous requirements of the law might be fully met in us, who do not live according to the sinful nature but according to the Spirit' (Rom. 8:3-4).

C. Nobody ever heard teaching on the Law like this.

1. *Until then the common consensus was that the teachers of the Law and the Pharisees had 'the corner on the market' when it came to lawful living.*

   a. They were seen as beyond reproach.

   b. The average Israelite living in Galilee or Jerusalem never dreamed of coming *up* to the standard of the teachers of the Law, much less *surpassing* it!

2. *Jesus' brief statement on the Law in the Sermon on the Mount (Matt. 5:17-20 – four verses) must have shocked his hearers, even though they did not grasp the depth of the meaning at the time.*

   a. It was a statement that pleased nobody.

   (1) It offended the Pharisees.

   (2) It offended those who would do away with the Law altogether.

   b. It showed both continuity and discontinuity with the Mosaic Law:

   (1) Continuity: Jesus would fulfil it.

   (2) Discontinuity: once it was fulfilled people were no longer under it.

D. How could any ordinary person surpass the righteousness of the teachers of the Law and the Pharisees?

1. *By an inward righteousness as opposed to an external righteousness.*

   a. All the Pharisees ever did was for people to see. 'Everything they do is done for men to see: They make their phylacteries wide and the tassels on their garments long; they love the place of honour at banquets and the most important seats in the synagogues; they love to be greeted in the marketplaces and to have men call them, " Rabbi"' (Matt. 23:5-7).

   b. When the glory that comes from people was taken away, their motivation was gone!

    c. In a word: the righteousness of the Pharisees was an outward righteousness.

2. *Jesus taught a righteousness of the heart:*

    a. Anger in the heart was murder in the Kingdom of Heaven (Matt. 5:21-23).

    b. Lust in the heart was adultery in the Kingdom of Heaven (Matt. 5:27-30).

    c. Swearing by God's name abused his name in the Kingdom of Heaven (Matt. 5:33-37).

3. *Jesus' standard of righteousness even surpassed what the Law itself encouraged.*

    a. Personal vengeance was out of the question (Matt. 5:38-42).

    b. Loving your enemies is true godliness (Matt. 5:43-48).

    c. Righteousness which God alone knows about would be the standard of the Kingdom of Heaven (Matt. 6:1-18).

III. PRAYER

A. Jesus' addressing God as Father in prayer, then teaching us to do so, was as astonishing as his teaching on the Law and the Kingdom.

1. *It was one thing for Jesus to call God Father; quite another for him to say: 'This, then, is how you should pray: Our Father in heaven'* (Matt. 6:9).

    a. Jesus was uniquely the Son of God, and God was uniquely his Father.

    b. But when he told us to pray, 'Our Father' (note plural):

      (1) It would make us equal to himself as sons of God.

      (2) It put us all equal in the Father's love as a family.

      (3) It anticipated Paul's teaching on adoption (Rom. 8:14ff; Gal. 4:6; Eph. 1:5).

2. *This means that we have access to the Father as Jesus had; we are loved by the Father as Jesus was loved.*

    a. It demonstrates our security in the family.

      (1) There is no possibility of Jesus being dislodged from the Trinity – or from the Godhead.

      (2) You and I have the same security.

    b. The 'Lord's Prayer' (although it is ours – not a prayer he himself would pray – see Matthew 6:12) is a complete prayer.

(1) It shows the pattern of prayer: beginning with worship, ending with petition.

(2) All we should ask for is included in this prayer.

B. All our praying should be for God's glory only.

1. *The Pharisees prayed to be 'seen by men'* (Matt. 6:5).

   a. Take away people noticing them, and they would never pray.

   b. This is one more way we exceed the righteousness of the Pharisees: 'But when you pray, go into your room, close the door and pray to your Father, who is unseen. Then your Father, who sees what is done in secret, will reward you' (Matt. 6:6).

2. *The entire principle of Jesus' teaching concerning religious righteousness is underscored by John 5:44: 'How can you believe if you accept praise from one another, yet make no effort to obtain the praise that comes from the only God?'*

   a. By nature we seek the praise and approval of men; that was the essence of Pharisaical righteousness.

   b. After we are gripped by seeking the honour that comes from God alone, our entire perspective changes.

C. We should never tire of praying or give up praying. Luke 18:1: 'Then Jesus told his disciples a parable to show them that they should always pray and not give up.'

1. Jesus gave us the parable of the widow who daily begged the cruel judge for vengeance over her adversary.

2. *The judge finally gave in – for one reason: 'Yet because this widow keeps bothering me, I will see that she gets justice, so that she won't eventually wear me out with her coming!'* (Luke 18:5).

   a. Jesus ordered us to take note – and be like this widow.

   b. How much more will a loving Father step in and rescue? 'And will not God bring about justice for his chosen ones, who cry out to him day and night? Will he keep putting them off?' (Luke 18:7).

3. *This is brought home by a similar parable:* 'Then he said to them, "Suppose one of you has a friend, and he goes to him at

midnight and says, 'Friend, lend me three loaves of bread, because a friend of mine on a journey has come to me, and I have nothing to set before him.' Then the one inside answers, 'Don't bother me. The door is already locked, and my children are with me in bed. I can't get up and give you anything.' I tell you, though he will not get up and give him the bread because he is his friend, yet because of the man's boldness he will get up and give him as much as he needs' (Luke 11:5-8).

a. Jesus concluded: 'So I say to you: Ask and it will be given to you; seek and you will find; knock and the door will be opened to you. For everyone who asks receives; he who seeks finds; and to him who knocks, the door will be opened' (Luke 11:9-10. Cf. Matt. 7:7).

b. Note the comparison between Matthew 7:11 and Luke 11:13:

   (1) 'If you, then, though you are evil, know how to give good gifts to your children, how much more will your Father in heaven give good gifts to those who ask him!' (Matt. 7:11).

   (2) 'If you then, though you are evil, know how to give good gifts to your children, how much more will your Father in heaven give the Holy Spirit to those who ask him!' (Luke 11:13).

c. In a word: never, never, never give up!

IV. HUMILITY

A. Jesus' teaching summed up: become vulnerable, never exalt yourself. 'For everyone who exalts himself will be humbled, and he who humbles himself will be exalted' (Luke 14:11).

  1. *It was also put like this:* 'I tell you the truth, unless a kernel of wheat falls to the ground and dies, it remains only a single seed. But if it dies, it produces many seeds. The man who loves his life will lose it, while the man who hates his life in this world will keep it for eternal life' (John 12:24-25).

   a. Note the practical if not pragmatic implications:

    (1) If we don't live this way, we lose.

    (2) If we live this way, we win.

   b. What is more: we bless others, producing 'many seeds'.

  2. *Jesus gave a very practical suggestion by a parable:* 'When someone invites you to a wedding feast, do not take the place of honour, for a person more distinguished than you may have been invited. If so, the host who invited both of you will come and say to you, "Give this man your seat." Then, humiliated, you will have to take the least important place. But when you are invited, take the lowest place, so that when your host comes, he will say to you, "Friend, move up to a better place." Then you will be honoured in the presence of all your fellow guests. For everyone who exalts himself will be humbled, and he who humbles himself will be exalted' (Luke 14:8-11).

  a. It will save us all a lot of embarrassment if we don't take ourselves too seriously – by presuming our importance.

  b. If we do not take ourselves seriously, God can use us and exalt us. Peter later put it this way: 'Humble yourselves, therefore, under God's mighty hand, that he may lift you up [AV – 'exalt you'] in due time' (1 Peter 5:6).

B. This teaching applies to all personal relationships.

1. Jesus called it 'turning the other cheek'. 'But I tell you, Do not resist an evil person. If someone strikes you on the right cheek, turn to him the other also' (Matt. 5:39).

2. Jesus called it 'going the second mile'. 'If someone forces you to go one mile, go with him two miles' (Matt. 5:41).

3. *Jesus called it 'praying for your enemies'.* 'But I tell you: Love your enemies and pray for those who persecute you' (Matt. 5:44).

  a. He told us to forgive those who have sinned against us (Matt. 6:14).

  b. He told us not to judge others (Matt. 7:1).

  c. The ultimate proof we have forgiven and not judged others is when we pray as Jesus himself later did: 'Jesus said, "Father, forgive them, for they do not know what they are doing"' (Luke 23:34).

    (1) He did not say, 'I forgive you,' (almost always a big mistake!). He asked the Father to forgive them.

  d. The greatest evidence of humility is to pray sincerely for your enemies or those who have hurt you.

    (1) We do not pray, 'O Lord, judge them – punish them!'

    (2) We sincerely petition God to *overlook* what they did.

C. This teaching extends to our love for the advancement of the Kingdom.

   1. *We are told not to resist those who come in at the last hour and get what we have worked for for years* (Matt. 20:1-16).

   a. We must recognise God's blessing of others we feel don't deserve it.

   b. This means accepting those who have been forgiven and who may not have paid the price we feel we paid!

   2. *We must not see greatness in terms of high profile, but in serving.* (Mark 10:35-45).

   a. James and John wanted exaltation and admiration.

   b. Jesus said that greatness is being a 'slave of all' (Mark 10:44).

CONCLUSION

Jesus practised what he preached. He never grieved the Holy Spirit. He fulfilled the Law – as he promised. He was the greatest man of prayer that ever was. He became nothing, when he became obedient to the death on a cross. May God grant that what Jesus taught us may grip us!

5

JESUS AND THE HOLY SPIRIT

INTRODUCTION

A. A few years ago a Christian publisher said to me that there were over fifty books in print on the Holy Spirit but only three on Jesus.
   1. This is because of an ever-increasing interest in the Holy Spirit which emerged from the arrival of the charismatic movement.
   2. *People were keenly interested in 'baptism of the Holy Spirit', 'speaking in tongues' and the gifts of the Spirit.*
      a. There is nothing particularly wrong in being interested in the Holy Spirit.
      b. But there is surely something wrong when we are not interested in Jesus.

B. This lesson focuses on Jesus' teaching regarding the Holy Spirit.
   1. *This teaching can be said to be two-fold.*
      a. Jesus' implicit teaching of the Holy Spirit – when the Spirit is not actually mentioned but must be implied.
      b. His explicit teaching of the Holy Spirit, when there is explicit reference to the Holy Spirit.
   2. *Jesus himself added*: 'I have much more to say to you, more than you can now bear' (John 16:12).
      a. This is in the context of the teaching of the Holy Spirit.
      b. It is therefore fair for us to unpack what Jesus meant by this – at least in part – in order to be clear on what he himself wants us to understand.

C. Why is this lesson important?
   1. *As our theme is 'Who is Jesus?' it follows:*
      a. We cannot really know who Jesus is but by the Holy Spirit.
         (1) It would be the Spirit who would testify about Jesus.

'When the Counsellor comes, whom I will send to you from the Father, the Spirit of truth who goes out from the Father, he will testify about me' (John 15:26).

    (2) 'No one can say, "Jesus is Lord," except by the Holy Spirit' (1 Cor. 12:3).

  b. A crucial segment of Jesus' teaching generally is about the Holy Spirit.

2. *It is good to approach a subject we tend to think we know so well with a view of presuming nothing.*

  a. What if you had to explain the Holy Spirit to another who knew nothing about the Spirit; where would you begin?

  b. This lesson will introduce the Spirit to one who knows nothing.

3. *It is good to put ourselves in the place of the disciples who were not prepared for Jesus' words: 'It is for your good that I am going away'* (John 16:7).

  a. This however did not make them happy.

  b. Can you feel what the disciples felt at that time?

4. In an era when many focus on the gifts of the Spirit – or manifestations – sometimes the bigger picture is lost; this lesson will focus on the bigger picture.

5. There is nothing more edifying than a true perspective of how we should view the Spirit; after all, what was true (and possible) then is true and relevant today.

I. JESUS' IMPLICIT TEACHING OF THE SPIRIT

A. The synoptic Gospels: Matthew, Mark and Luke.

  1. *The Kingdom of Heaven is the realm of the Holy Spirit.*

    a. Although the Holy Spirit is not mentioned in the Sermon on the Mount, it is inexplicable apart from the Holy Spirit – as the book of Esther (which contains no reference to God) is inexplicable apart from God.

    b. When Jesus said that the 'kingdom of God is within you' (Luke 17:21), it had to refer to the Holy Spirit.

      (1) The kingdom does not come by 'observation' that is, it does not come visibly (Luke 17:20).

      (2) It happens in our hearts.

  2. *It is the Holy Spirit who makes sense of the Beatitudes, for example:*

    a. We are made poor in spirit only by the Spirit (Matt. 5:3).

    b. We do not hunger and thirst for righteousness, much less to be 'filled', except by the Spirit (Matt. 5:6).

3. *Jesus' interpretation of the Law and its application presupposes conviction of sin – which the Pharisees knew nothing about – by the Spirit.*

    a. Our awareness of hate and how we grieve the Spirit by name-calling. (Matt. 5:21ff).

    b. Our awareness and feeling convicted of lust – and causing another to lust – is possible only by the Spirit. (Matt. 5:27ff).

4. *Understanding the parables of Jesus is for the family of God only, and this is made possible only by the Spirit.*

    a. Those outside the family are not heirs: 'In them is fulfilled the prophecy of Isaiah: "You will be ever hearing but never understanding; you will be ever seeing but never perceiving."' (Matt. 13:14).

    b. The saying 'He who has ears, let him hear,' shows the need for the Spirit to unstop spiritual deafness. (Matt. 13:43).

5. *What is 'revealed' comes only by the Spirit.*

    a. 'At that time Jesus said, "I praise you, Father, Lord of heaven and earth, because you have hidden these things from the wise and learned, and revealed them to little children."' (Matt. 11:25).

    b. 'Jesus replied, "Blessed are you, Simon son of Jonah, for this was not revealed to you by man, but by my Father in heaven"' (Matt. 16:17).

6. Unusual power to heal shows the manifestation of the Spirit: 'The power of the Lord was present for him to heal the sick' (Luke 5:17).

7. Believing that you *have* received what you pray for could only come by the immediate work of the Holy Spirit (Mark 11:24).

8. *Note: Explicit references to the Holy Spirit by Jesus in the synoptics are rare:*

    a. He spoke of blaspheming the Spirit (Matt. 12:31-32. Cf. Mark 3:29).

    b. He spoke of divine inspiration of the psalmist: 'David, speaking by the Spirit' (Matt. 22:43. Cf. Mark 12:36).

    c. He motivated to prayer by promising the Holy Spirit. 'If you then, though you are evil, know how to give good gifts to your children, how much more will your Father in heaven give the Holy Spirit to those who ask him!' (Luke 11:13).

B. The Gospel of John

1. *The reference to water from within a person.*
   a. 'But whoever drinks the water I give him will never thirst. Indeed, the water I give him will become in him a spring of water welling up to eternal life' (John 4:14).
   b. 'Whoever believes in me, as the Scripture has said, streams of living water will flow from within him' (John 7:38). Note: John added, 'By this he meant the Spirit, whom those who believed in him were later to receive. Up to that time the Spirit had not been given, since Jesus had not yet been glorified' (John 7:39).
2. *The Son giving life.*
   a. 'For just as the Father raises the dead and gives them life, even so the Son gives life to whom he is pleased to give it' (John 5:21).
   b. 'I tell you the truth, a time is coming and has now come when the dead will hear the voice of the Son of God and those who hear will live' (John 5:25).
3. *The drawing power of the Father.*
   a. 'No one can come to me unless the Father who sent me draws him, and I will raise him up at the last day' (John 6:44).
   b. 'He went on to say, "This is why I told you that no one can come to me unless the Father has enabled him"' (John 6:65).
4. *Knowing Jesus' voice.*
   a. 'I have other sheep that are not of this sheep pen. I must bring them also. They too will listen to my voice, and there shall be one flock and one shepherd' (John 10:16).
   b. 'My sheep listen to my voice; I know them, and they follow me' (John 10:27).
5. *Note: there are a few explicit references to the Holy Spirit by Jesus in John's Gospel before he openly announced the coming of the Spirit:*
   a. To Nicodemus:
      (1) 'Jesus answered, "I tell you the truth, no one can enter the kingdom of God unless he is born of water and the Spirit"' (John 3:5).

(2) 'The wind blows wherever it pleases. You hear its sound, but you cannot tell where it comes from or where it is going. So it is with everyone born of the Spirit' (John 3:8).

b. To the Samaritan woman: 'God is spirit, and his worshippers must worship in spirit and in truth' (John 4:24).

c. When so many were deserting him: 'The Spirit gives life; the flesh counts for nothing. The words I have spoken to you are spirit and they are life' (John 6:63).

II. JESUS' EXPLICIT INTRODUCTION OF THE HOLY SPIRIT

A. Jesus waited until just before the end of his earthly ministry to introduce the Holy Spirit in a definite and explicit way.

1. He spoon-fed the disciples as gently as possible, because he knew they would not be thrilled at first; they were 'filled with grief' (John 16:6).

2. *His aim: to help them make the adjustment from the level of nature to the level of the Spirit.*

   a. Level of nature: seeing Jesus in the flesh, knowing the sound of his voice, having him with them at all times – physically.

   b. Level of the Spirit: seeing Jesus in the Spirit or by faith, getting to know his voice by the Spirit's impulse, having him with them at all times – but by the presence of the Spirit.

B. His opening line: 'I will ask the Father, and he will give you another Counsellor to be with you forever' (John 14:16).

1. This verse is loaded with information, none of which was welcome.

2. *Note: how often do we resist what God is saying at first?*

   a. We all must – in varying degrees and from time to time – make the transition from what seems natural to what is higher and spiritual. 'And we, who with unveiled faces all reflect the Lord's glory, are being transformed into his likeness with ever-increasing glory, which comes from the Lord, who is the Spirit' (2 Cor. 3:18).

   b. Often our first reaction is negative; later, having made the adjustment, we see how it was for our good.

   c. Jesus had to say, 'It is for your good' (John 16:7).

C. Jesus' introductory statement says three things:

1. *He will put a petition to the Father:*

    a. This prayer is described in part in John 17.

    b. His prayer was heard, for he said just before his ascension: 'I am going to send you what my Father has promised; but stay in the city until you have been clothed with power from on high' (Luke 24:49).

    c. In Acts 1:4 he tells the disciples to wait for the gift 'my Father promised'.

    d. When he took his place at God's right hand, Jesus fully carried out this promise. 'Exalted to the right hand of God, he has received from the Father the promised Holy Spirit and has poured out what you now see and hear' (Acts 2:33).

2. *The Father would give 'another Counsellor'.*

    a. Both words are important:

        (1) Another – meaning one like Jesus himself.

        (2) Counsellor – one who comes alongside, Gr. *paracletos*.

    b. Jesus had been a *Paraclete* for some three years.

        (1) He had come alongside – physically.

        (2) They had him all to themselves.

        (3) This was physical; at the natural level.

    c. Another Paraclete would come from the Father – but invisible.

        (1) He would however be as real to them as Jesus himself had been.

        (2) He would even make Jesus as real at the spiritual level as he had been to them at the natural level.

    d. Later Jesus put it like this to them: 'In a little while you will see me no more, and then after a little while you will see me' (John 16:16).

        (1) They had no idea what that meant and began discussing it among themselves (John 16:17-20).

        (2) Jesus assured them that, at the end of the day, they would have no complaints. 'A woman giving birth to a child has pain because her time has come; but when her baby is born she forgets the anguish because of her joy that a child is born into the world. So with you: Now is your time of grief, but I will see you again and you will rejoice, and no one will take away your joy' (John 16:21-22).

(3) Note: this helps explain why Peter quoted Psalm 16:8-11 in Acts 2:25-28, especially, 'I saw the Lord always before me.'

    e. Note also: an ancient controversy that helped divide Eastern Christianity from Western Christianity is at stake here:

        (1) Did the Holy Spirit come from the Father and the Son? Western Christianity.

        (2) Did the Holy Spirit come from the Father through the Son? Eastern Christianity.

        (3) Talk about splitting theological hairs!

3. *This Counsellor would be with us forever.*

    a. The person of Jesus was on earth for only thirty-three years.

    b. This is what Hebrews meant by the 'days of his flesh' (AV), that is, the days of Jesus' life on earth (Heb. 5:7).

    c. The Counsellor who would be coming would be with them 'forever'.

    d. There would be no fear of being deserted.

        (1) He later said, 'I will not leave you as orphans; I will come to you' (John 14:18).

        (2) But his coming in this instance was not physical but by the Holy Spirit – which means they got Jesus back again!

        (3) That is the meaning of John 16:16: 'In a little while you will see me no more, and then after a little while you will see me.'

    e. This statement upholds the teaching of 'Once saved, always saved'.

        (1) 'I give them eternal life, and they shall never perish; no one can snatch them out of my hand' (John 10:28).

        (2) 'Who shall separate us from the love of Christ?' (Rom. 8:35).

        (3) 'God has said, "Never will I leave you; never will I forsake you"' (Heb. 13:5).

III. THE CHARACTER AND PURPOSE OF THE HOLY SPIRIT

A. He is 'the Spirit of truth' (John 14:17).

    1. Jesus is the truth (John 14:6).

    2. It is impossible for God to lie (Titus 1:2; Heb. 6:18).

    3. The Holy Spirit cannot lie or deceive, and can only witness to the truth.

B. He will be our teacher (Cf. 1 John 2:27).

  1. Jesus had been a teacher; likewise the Holy Spirit will be a teacher.

  2. *What would Jesus teach? 'But the Counsellor, the Holy Spirit, whom the Father will send in my name, will teach you all things and will remind you of everything I have said to you'* (John 14:26).

    a. Everything that is true that Jesus did not share.

      (1) Jesus admitted, 'I have much more to say to you, more than you can now bear' (John 16:12).

      (2) What would the Spirit teach? 'All things.'

    b. Everything Jesus had already taught. He 'will remind you of everything I have said to you'.

      (1) They may have had a poor ability to remember!

      (2) Not to worry; the Holy Spirit would gently bring to their minds what they had been taught.

      (3) Note: if there isn't teaching in our minds already, we should not expect the Holy Spirit to make up for our lack of discipline; for those who are taught 'all things' are those who had *learned* first.

C. He is unknown to the world.

  1. *'The world cannot accept him, because it neither sees him nor knows him. But you know him, for he lives with you and will be in you'* (John 14:17).

    a. A particular operation of the Spirit would have to come to unsaved people before they would accept the Spirit.

    b. But the disciples were not totally ignorant of the Spirit.

      (1) They had Jesus with them, hence the Spirit.

      (2) Indeed, a measure of the Spirit in them would be required for them to accept Jesus in the first place.

      (3) Some manuscripts read, 'is in you' (John 14:17).

  2. *What would be needed for the world's acceptance of the Holy Spirit is three things:*

    a. Conviction of sin. 'He will convict the world of guilt in regard to sin' (John 16:8).

      (1) This is the essential work of the Spirit – to make people see they are sinners; 'because men do not believe in me' (John 16:9).

      (2) Apart from the Spirit, people will never see themselves this way.

   b. Conviction of righteousness.

      (1) This refers to the righteousness of Christ, because he went on to say, 'I am going to my Father, where you can see me no longer.'

      (2) Jesus is already referring to himself, that he would have to be received by faith.

      (3) Faith counts for righteousness; it is the imputed righteousness of Christ – that is, righteousness put to our credit.

   c. Conviction of judgement.

      (1) This refers to Christ's victory over Satan at the cross – but also to Christ's second coming. 'Just as man is destined to die once, and after that to face judgement, so Christ was sacrificed once to take away the sins of many people; and he will appear a second time, not to bear sin, but to bring salvation to those who are waiting for him' (Heb. 9:27-28).

      (2) This means the accuser of the brothers has been judged; his accusations are covered by Christ's blood (Rev. 12:10-11).

      (3) This indirectly refers to assurance of salvation.

D. The Holy Spirit, like Jesus, only does what he is told. 'But when he, the Spirit of truth, comes, he will guide you into all truth. He will not speak on his own; he will speak only what he hears, and he will tell you what is yet to come' (John 16:13).

1. *He is our guide.*

   a. If we try to guide ourselves, we will fail to see what is there.

   b. Why do we need a guide? 'The man without the Spirit does not accept the things that come from the Spirit of God, for they are foolishness to him, and he cannot understand them, because they are spiritually discerned' (1 Cor. 2:14).

2. *As he is the Spirit of truth, he only guides into* 'all *truth':*

   a. He will show us what is in God's Word.

   b. After all, he wrote it! (2 Tim. 3:16; 2 Peter 1:20-21).

   c. If you want to understand theology that is *truth* be on good terms with the Holy Spirit!

3. *He does what he is told.*
  a. This is another indication that the Spirit is 'another Counsellor', just like Jesus.
    (1) Jesus was not 'his own man'.
    (2) 'Jesus gave them this answer: "I tell you the truth, the Son can do nothing by himself; he can do only what he sees his Father doing, because whatever the Father does the Son also does"' (John 5:19).
    (3) 'By myself I can do nothing; I judge only as I hear, and my judgement is just, for I seek not to please myself but him who sent me' (John 5:30).
  b. In exactly the same way, the Holy Spirit has no agenda of his own; he is obedient to the Father and the Son as the Son was to the Father.
  c. Like Jesus, he speaks 'what he hears'.
4. *He guides into 'all truth'.*
  a. Jesus gave us much truth, but not all. 'I have much more to say to you, more than you can now bear' (John 16:12).
  b. There were some truths to be revealed later.

E. The departure of Jesus and the coming of the Spirit is for our good.
1. 'But I tell you the truth: It is for your good that I am going away. Unless I go away, the Counsellor will not come to you; but if I go, I will send him to you' (John 16:7).
2. *The real purpose of Christ's coming and death would not be known until:*
  a. Jesus died, rose and ascended.
  b. The Holy Spirit came down to make things plain.
3. *What we now call the Gospel is made plain by the Holy Spirit applying:*
  a. What Jesus taught.
  b. What the original disciples learned.
  c. What the rest of the New Testament revealed.
4. *The purpose of the Holy Spirit, summed up:*
  a. He took Jesus' place but makes him real.
  b. He applies the Gospel.
  c. He guides into all truth.

F. Note: some of the things Jesus could have had in mind that the disciples could not bear at the time are:
    1. *The sensitivity to the Spirit that is required* (Eph. 4:30; 1 Thess. 5:19).
        a. If we grieve the Spirit, he cannot be himself in us.
        b. If we grieve the Spirit, we will not be led to all truth.
    2. The gifts of the Holy Spirit. (1 Cor. 12).

CONCLUSION

Though filled with grief when they heard these teachings, there were no complaints from the apostles on the Day of Pentecost. If we know the Holy Spirit ungrieved and unquenched, all Jesus promised will be as true for us as with his first disciples.

6

FROM THE CROSS TO THE ASCENSION

INTRODUCTION

A. Discussing 'Who is Jesus?' would not be complete without a look at what he did, as well as who he is.
  1. The old theologians spoke of the 'Person and work of Christ'.
  2. *The work of Christ is generally seen as Jesus' accomplishment on the cross.*
   a. There are basically two ways of looking at Jesus' death on the cross.
    (1) Historically – when it is called crucifixion.
    (2) Theologically – when it is called atonement.
   b. The question this study will raise is: how is Christ's atonement to be applied?

B. Scope of study and definition of terms:
  1. The cross: the event of Jesus' death.
  2. The resurrection: the event of Jesus being raised physically from the dead.
  3. The ascension: the event of Jesus being taken up to Heaven.
  4. The intercession: the priestly work of Christ interceding on our behalf.
  5. The reign: the kingship of Christ at God's right hand.

C. Why is this lesson important?
  1. Who Jesus was and is must never be separated from what he did, and what he accomplished on our behalf.
  2. An overview of the essential things Jesus did and continues to do enables a new Christian to be introduced to the key things in this connection.
  3. We must never forget how these final events hang together with regard to our salvation.
  4. The work of Christ is a 'finished work' and yet he had a lot more to do after he died.

5. The work of Christ continues to this day – until he comes again; we need to be reminded of what exactly he is doing now.

I. THE CROSS – JESUS' FINEST HOUR

A. Historically: the crucifixion.

1. *The Jews, especially the Pharisees and teachers of the Law, had been aiming to do away with Jesus for a long time* (Cf. John 10:33-39).

   a. They resented his power and popularity.

   b. Instead of embracing him they wanted to get rid of him.

2. *The first hint that he should be crucified came from Caiaphas, the high priest at the time* (John 11:49-53).

   a. Jesus himself prophesied to his disciples that he would be crucified (Matt. 20:19).

   b. This was not what they wanted to hear (Cf. Matt. 16:22).

3. *Crucifixion was the Roman form of capital punishment.*

   a. The Jews did not have authority to crucify; they could only request this of the Roman Governor – which they did (Matt. 27:23).

   b. Although Pontius Pilate the Governor found no just cause to crucify Jesus, he acquiesced (Matt. 27:24-26).

4. *Jesus was crucified about 9 o'clock in the morning on Good Friday between two criminals.*

   a. 'The written notice of the charge against him read: the king of the Jews' (Mark 15:26).

   b. He gave a pardon to one of the criminals. 'Jesus answered him, "I tell you the truth, today you will be with me in paradise"' (Luke 23:43).

5. *Jesus' last words before he died were:*

   a. According to John, 'It is finished' (John 19:30).

   b. According to Luke, 'Father, into your hands I commit my spirit' (Luke 23:46).

B. Theologically: atonement.

1. *Atonement (def.): to make amends, to make up for some error or deficiency.*

   a. Jesus atoned for our sins by his death.

   b. In a word: he paid our debt by his own blood.

73

2. *There are three notable events at the cross which have profound theological implications.*

  a. From noon until 3 o'clock darkness came over the land.

    (1) This was not an eclipse of the sun; it was the cloud of glory, which demonstrated that atonement was taking place.

    (2) God said long before that he would appear 'in the cloud over the atonement cover' (Lev. 16:2).

    (3) Solomon witnessed this phenomenon when the Ark of the Covenant was brought to the temple. 'And the priests could not perform their service because of the cloud, for the glory of the LORD filled his temple. Then Solomon said, "The LORD has said that he would dwell in a dark cloud"' (1 Kings 8:11-12).

  b. At about 3 o'clock 'Jesus cried out in a loud voice, "Eloi, Eloi, lama sabachthani?" – which means, "My God, my God, why have you forsaken me?"' (Matt. 27:46).

    (1) This was the moment the Lord laid on Jesus our iniquity (Is. 53:6).

    (2) This was the moment Paul speaks of: 'God made him who had no sin to be sin for us, so that in him we might become the righteousness of God' (2 Cor. 5:21).

    (3) A transaction took place between God and Jesus, between God and the world: the price of sin was paid.

  c. Jesus' words, 'It is finished' (John 19:30).

    (1) All he came to do on earth was now done. '"My food," said Jesus, "is to do the will of him who sent me and to finish his work"' (John 4:34).

    (2) The Greek which translates, 'It is finished,' is *tetelestai*, which was also a colloquial expression that meant 'paid in full'.

    (3) This means that all we need to do now in order that our salvation is assured is to trust Christ's work on the cross.

3. *The blood Jesus shed was a fulfilment of the ancient sacrificial system.*

  a. The Passover Lamb was a type of Christ; it prefigured how God saw the cross: 'When I see the blood, I will pass over you' (Ex. 12:13).

  b. The Day of Atonement anticipated Christ's death; the

shedding of blood preceded the high priest's entry into the Most Holy Place (Lev. 16).

c. As a consequence, the blood did basically two things:

(1) It satisfied God's justice (Rom. 3:22-26).

(2) It washed away our sins (Rom. 3:22-26).

II. THE RESURRECTION: THE VINDICATION OF THE CROSS

A. Historically: it was a fact.

1. *Three of Jesus' close followers went to anoint Jesus' body on the first day of the week.*

a. On the way to the tomb they panicked, 'Who will roll the stone away from the entrance of the tomb?' (Mark 16:3).

b. They need not have worried! 'But when they looked up, they saw that the stone, which was very large, had been rolled away' (Mark 16:4).

2. *There were no BBC cameras stationed at the tomb.*

a. Nobody saw the actual event; when we get to Heaven we will all get a video replay of the event – or its equivalent!

b. The nearest anybody came to seeing the event was the guards who were paid 'hush money'.

(1) 'While the women were on their way, some of the guards went into the city and reported to the chief priests everything that had happened' (Matt. 28:11).

(2) The solution was simple: 'When the chief priests had met with the elders and devised a plan, they gave the soldiers a large sum of money, telling them, "You are to say, 'His disciples came during the night and stole him away while we were asleep.' If this report gets to the governor, we will satisfy him and keep you out of trouble." So the soldiers took the money and did as they were instructed. And this story has been widely circulated among the Jews to this very day' (Matt. 28:12-15).

(3) The guards have a lot to answer for; they saw the angel who rolled the stone away. 'His appearance was like lightning, and his clothes were white as snow. The guards were so afraid of him that they shook and became like dead men' (Matt. 28:3-4).

3. *The angel announced Jesus' resurrection to the women. 'He is not here; he has risen, just as he said. Come and see the place where he lay'* (Matt. 28:6).

    a. 'So the women hurried away from the tomb, afraid yet filled with joy, and ran to tell his disciples' (Matt. 28:8).

    b. 'Suddenly Jesus met them. "Greetings," he said. They came to him, clasped his feet and worshiped him' (Matt. 28:9).

4. *Jesus made several appearances to the Eleven.*

    a. Jesus said, 'Look at my hands and my feet. It is I myself! Touch me and see; a ghost does not have flesh and bones, as you see I have' (Luke 24:39).

    b. He said to Thomas, '"Put your finger here; see my hands. Reach out your hand and put it into my side. Stop doubting and believe." Thomas said to him, "My Lord and my God!"' (John 20:27-28).

5. *Before his ascension five hundred saw Jesus after he was raised* (1 Cor. 15:6).

    a. Luke says that Jesus gave 'many convincing proofs that he was alive' (Acts 1:3).

    b. The point: we are talking about an historical fact.

B. Theologically: it vindicates the cross and also assures us of being saved.

1. *Had Jesus not been raised from the dead, it follows:*

    a. His teachings cease to be very weighty.

    b. The charge at the Cross, 'He saved others, but he can't save himself,' would be valid.

    c. He shed his blood for nothing.

    d. There is no hope of Heaven.

    e. The Christian faith is false. 'And if Christ has not been raised, your faith is futile; you are still in your sins' (1 Cor. 15:17).

2. *Everything that the Christian message claims hinges on the Resurrection.*

    a. If Jesus was not raised from the dead, there is no message for us to present.

    b. If he was not raised from the dead, the church should not exist.

    c. Note: those who are church leaders yet deny the Resurrection should resign their posts.

3. *The Resurrection proves at least two things:*
    a. That God accepted the sacrifice of his Son.
        (1) This was obvious because the veil (curtain) of the Temple was torn in two from top to bottom (Matt. 27:51).
        (2) But the Resurrection was the open and ultimate proof that all Christ came to do by dying on a cross was done!
    b. That we too will be raised from the dead.
        (1) Jesus' resurrection is called 'the firstfruits' of those who are dead (1 Cor. 15:20).
        (2) All people will be raised from the dead by virtue of Christ's own resurrection. 'For as in Adam all die, so in Christ all will be made alive' (1 Cor. 15:22).
    c. This will happen at Jesus' Second Coming. 'Listen, I tell you a mystery: We will not all sleep, but we will all be changed – in a flash, in the twinkling of an eye, at the last trumpet. For the trumpet will sound, the dead will be raised imperishable, and we will be changed' (1 Cor. 15:51-52).

III. THE ASCENSION: CHRIST'S WELCOME BACK TO HEAVEN

A. After the Resurrection Christ lingered for forty days (Acts 1:3).
    1. *This must have been a frustrating time for the disciples.*
        a. They never knew when Jesus would appear.
        b. He would apparently appear, then disappear.
        c. At one time Peter said, 'I'm going out to fish' (John 21:3).
    2. *There is no way for us to know why Jesus did not stay with the disciples continually during those forty days.*
        a. A good guess is that they needed to get used to his absence.
        b. Perhaps total continuity of his being with them would have resulted in:
            (1) Their getting too used to having him around.
            (2) People finding out about his Resurrection who were not supposed to know about it yet.

B. The disciples still didn't know why Jesus died or rose from the dead.
    1. During the forty days we are told that he did some teaching about the Kingdom of God (Acts 1:3).

2. *But the disciples still had a wrong mind-set as to the role of the Messiah.*

    a. They still thought in old Jewish terms: that Messiah would overthrow Rome and restore the Kingdom.

    b. They wanted to get the answer to this burning question. 'So when they met together, they asked him, "Lord, are you at this time going to restore the kingdom to Israel?"' (Acts 1:6).

3. *They were not prepared for this mystery, but they should have been.*

    a. Jesus told them that the kingdom is not visible but inside their hearts (Luke 17:20-21).

    b. He had prepared them for the Holy Spirit.

    c. His answer: 'It is not for you to know the times or dates the Father has set by his own authority. But you will receive power when the Holy Spirit comes on you; and you will be my witnesses in Jerusalem, and in all Judea and Samaria, and to the ends of the earth' (Acts 1:7-8).

C. At that point Jesus ascended to Heaven.

1. 'After he said this, he was taken up before their very eyes, and a cloud hid him from their sight' (Acts 1:9).

2. No one has seen him since with the naked eye.

D. What happened then?

1. *While the disciples entered into prayer in the upper room (Acts 1:13ff), a great celebration was taking place in Heaven.*

    a. The Father welcomed Jesus back to Heaven.

        (1) Jesus left Heaven 33 years before as the Logos – to enter Mary's womb.

        (2) He returned in the flesh.

2. *The Father said to Jesus, 'Sit at my right hand until I make your enemies a footstool for your feet'* (Ps. 110:1).

    a. Therefore when people ask, 'Where is Jesus?' the answer is: 'Exalted to the right hand of God, he has received from the Father the promised Holy Spirit and has poured out what you now see and hear' (Acts 2:33).

    b. There is a man in glory – the Lord Jesus Christ – at God's right hand.

**IV. THE INTERCESSION – THE PRIESTLY WORK OF CHRIST AT GOD'S
RIGHT HAND**

A. What is Jesus doing at God's right hand? Interceding for us.
  1. *Intercede (def.): to interpose, intervene or plead on behalf of
     another person.*
     a. 'Who is he that condemns? Christ Jesus, who died – more
        than that, who was raised to life – is at the right hand of
        God and is also interceding for us' (Rom. 8:34).
     b. 'Therefore he is able to save completely those who come to
        God through him, because he always lives to intercede for
        them' (Heb. 7:25).
  2. *Christ's intercession consists of two things:*
     a. Interposing his blood.
     b. Praying.
     c. These two activities come to this: Christ beckons the attention
        of the Father to himself to keep the Father's gaze away
        from our sins.

**B. There are two Old Testament truths that anticipate Christ's
intercession.**
  1. *That there should be a priest after the order of Melchizedek.*
     a. This is based on Psalm 110:4: 'The LORD has sworn and
        will not change his mind: "You are a priest forever, in the
        order of Melchizedek."'
        (1) This passage probably made little sense at the time.
        (2) But there it was – it had to be fulfilled.
     b. Melchizedek is a mysterious character to whom Abraham
        gave his tithe after a spectacular victory (Gen. 14:20).
     c. The writer of Hebrews explains:
        (1) Jesus was that person (Heb. 7).
        (2) But this presented a problem; the priesthood came only
           from the tribe of Levi and Jesus was of the tribe of Judah
           (Heb. 7:14).
        (3) No problem; Jesus fulfilled this role by ascending to
           God's right hand and from there he became a priest 'in
           the order of Melchizedek' (Heb. 7:17-22).
  2. *That the Levitical priesthood be fulfilled.*
     a. All that took place in ancient times was 'only a shadow' of
        what was to come (Heb. 10:1).

(1) The sacrifices of animals did not cleanse the consciences of the worshippers (Heb. 10:3).

(2) It was impossible for the blood of bulls and goats to take away sins (Heb. 10:4).

b. Christ fulfilled the ceremonial Law in two ways:

(1) He was the perfect lamb who shed his blood.

(2) He then entered the Most Holy Place 'by his own blood' (Heb. 9:12).

c. Note: behind this teaching lies the Day of Atonement (Lev. 16; Heb. 9:1-10).

(1) The animal was sacrificed openly on the altar.

(2) The high priest took the blood behind the curtain and sprinkled it on the mercy seat in the Most Holy Place.

d. Jesus fulfilled both of these:

(1) He died on the cross – openly for all.

(2) He entered the Most Holy Place by his own blood – behind the curtain where nobody could see – for believers (John 17:9).

C. This intercession continues: 'Exalted above the heavens' (Heb. 7:26).

1. 'Unlike the other high priests, he does not need to offer sacrifices day after day, first for his own sins, and then for the sins of the people. He sacrificed for their sins once for all when he offered himself' (Heb. 7:27).

2. This intercession – which applies the atonement of Christ – is effectual for 'those who come to God through him' (Heb. 7:25).

V. THE REIGN: THE KINGSHIP OF CHRIST AT GOD'S RIGHT HAND

A. Pontius Pilate asked Jesus, 'Are you the king of the Jews?' (John 18:33).

1. Jesus replied that he was, adding, 'My kingdom is not of this world' (John 18:36).

2. *Over the cross was written the charge: Jesus of Nazareth, the King of the Jews'* (John 19:19).

a. The truth is, he was born king of the Jews (Matt. 2:2).

b. His kingship was never recognised here below (John 19:20-21).

B. When the Father said, 'Sit at my right hand,' it meant that Jesus was given the place of equal authority and power with the Father.

1. It was then that he began his reign in Heaven.

2. *It was recognised by the Holy Spirit and by those who are led by the Spirit.* 'Therefore let all Israel be assured of this: God has made this Jesus, whom you crucified, both Lord and Christ' (Acts 2:36).

    a. To those in the family he is the Mighty King Jesus.

    b. 'Therefore God exalted him to the highest place and gave him the name that is above every name, that at the name of Jesus every knee should bow, in heaven and on earth and under the earth, and every tongue confess that Jesus Christ is Lord, to the glory of God the Father' (Phil. 2:9-11).

        (1) One day every knee will bow to him. 'It is written: "As surely as I live," says the Lord, "every knee will bow before me; every tongue will confess to God"' (Rom. 14:11).

        (2) Those who do it now will one day reign with him (Rev. 5:10).

C. His reign will continue at God's right hand. 'For he must reign until he has put all his enemies under his feet' (1 Cor. 15:25).

1. *Speaking of the coming kingship of Messiah, David said,* 'You made him a little lower than the heavenly beings and crowned him with glory and honour. You made him ruler over the works of your hands; you put everything under his feet' (Ps. 8:5-6).

    a. Quoting this, the writer of Hebrews added, 'In putting everything under him, God left nothing that is not subject to him' (Heb. 2:8).

    b. But the writer took notice of the obvious: 'Yet at present we do not see everything subject to him' (Heb. 2:8).

    c. Why is this so obvious?

        (1) People still hate God and don't acknowledge his Son.

        (2) Wars continue; suffering continues; evil thrives.

        (3) People still die.

2. *What then does it mean that Christ must reign until God has put everything under his feet? Answer:*

    a. God is waiting for a particular day and hour, a predestined time. 'No one knows about that day or hour, not even the angels in heaven, nor the Son, but only the Father' (Matt. 24:36).

b. Jesus is King over his chosen people who gladly submit to him.

c. He will leave his present position – God's right hand – when 'he has destroyed all dominion, authority and power' (1 Cor. 15:24).

    (1) 'The last enemy to be destroyed is death' (1 Cor. 15:26).

    (2) 'When he has done this, then the Son himself will be made subject to him who put everything under him, so that God may be all in all' (1 Cor. 15:28).

    (3) This happens at Christ's Second Coming; he will appear 'a second time' (Heb. 9:28).

D. A day will come when the whole world will recognise what is true now; Jesus will be seen as 'King of kings and Lord of lords' (Rev. 19:16).

  1. 'Look, he is coming with the clouds, and every eye will see him, even those who pierced him; and all the peoples of the earth will mourn because of him. So shall it be! Amen' (Rev. 1:7).

  2. This is the ultimate victory of the Cross.

CONCLUSION

The atonement of Jesus on the Cross was vindicated by the Resurrection. His Ascension prepared the way for his priestly intercession (the intercession of Jesus applies the benefits of the blood he shed). One day the whole world will see this!

7

THE SECOND COMING OF JESUS

INTRODUCTION

A. Some people asked themselves if Jesus would return on January 1, 2000?
    1. *That question was partly serious; mostly facetious.*
        a. Serious: because Jesus could come back any day.
        b. Facetious: because some all but predicted this!
            (1) Some take an eschatological view that the year 2000 marks the end of the world's 6000 year history; the last one thousand years would be the Millennium.
            (2) As there is a six day working week, the seventh being the day of rest (and a day with the Lord is like a thousand years and a thousand years a day – 2 Peter 3:8), so there are to be 6,000 years of toil and sorrow followed by a thousand years of rest.
            (3) This view is based on Archbishop Ussher's opinion that the earth was created in 4000 BC.
        c. Illustration: 'Elijah' who predicted the Rapture on October 11, 1957.
    2. *The millennium reminds us of 2000 years of Christianity and brings us face to face with one important part of Jesus' teaching: his Second Coming.*
        a. 'After he said this, he was taken up before their very eyes, and a cloud hid him from their sight. They were looking intently up into the sky as he was going, when suddenly two men dressed in white stood beside them. "Men of Galilee," they said, "why do you stand here looking into the sky? This same Jesus, who has been taken from you into heaven, will come back in the same way you have seen him go into heaven"' (Acts 1:9-11).
        b. 'Just as man is destined to die once, and after that to face judgement, so Christ was sacrificed once to take away the

sins of many people; and he will appear a second time, not
to bear sin, but to bring salvation to those who are waiting
for him' (Heb. 9:27-28).

B. Definitions:
1. *Second Coming: the personal return of Jesus to the earth.*
   a. Now at God's right hand, he will leave this to return to the
      earth.
   b. Note: 'This same Jesus. . . . will come back in the same way
      as you have seen him go into heaven.'
      (1) A cloud hid him from their sight as he was taken up.
      (2) Many references indicate that he will come back with
          clouds.

'Look, he is coming with the clouds, and every eye will see him,
even those who pierced him; and all the peoples of the earth will
mourn because of him. So shall it be! Amen' (Rev. 1:7).

'At that time the sign of the Son of Man will appear in the sky,
and all the nations of the earth will mourn. They will see the Son
of Man coming on the clouds of the sky, with power and great
glory' (Matt. 24:30).

'For the Lord himself will come down from heaven, with a
loud command, with the voice of the archangel and with the
trumpet call of God, and the dead in Christ will rise first. After
that, we who are still alive and are left will be caught up together
with them in the clouds to meet the Lord in the air. And so we
will be with the Lord for ever' (1 Thes. 4:16-17).

2. Eschatology: doctrine of 'last things', such as the Second
   Coming, judgement, the 'signs of the times', prophecies of the
   'last days'.
3. The Final Judgement: the awesome day in which God will judge
   the world with justice by Jesus Christ himself (Acts 17:31).
4. *Views about the one thousand year reign, called the Millennium.*
   a. Note: the word millennium means 'one thousand years'.
   b. This emerges from how one interprets these verses:

'And I saw an angel coming down out of heaven, having the key
to the Abyss and holding in his hand a great chain. He seized the
dragon, that ancient serpent, who is the devil, or Satan, and bound

him for a thousand years. He threw him into the Abyss, and locked and sealed it over him, to keep him from deceiving the nations any more until the thousand years were ended. After that, he must be set free for a short time. I saw thrones on which were seated those who had been given authority to judge. And I saw the souls of those who had been beheaded because of their testimony for Jesus and because of the word of God. They had not worshipped the beast or his image and had not received his mark on their foreheads or their hands. They came to life and reigned with Christ for a thousand years. (The rest of the dead did not come to life until the thousand years were ended.) This is the first resurrection. Blessed and holy are those who have part in the first resurrection. The second death has no power over them, but they will be priests of God and of Christ and will reign with him for a thousand years. When the thousand years are over, Satan will be released from his prison' (Rev. 20:1-7).

    c. There are generally three views as to the meaning (to be explained further below):
        (1) Pre-millennialism: the Second Coming precedes the Millennium, that is, Jesus comes before the thousand years begin.
        (2) Post-millennialism: the Second Coming follows the Millennium.
        (3) A-millennialism: the thousand years are not to be taken literally at all but rather spiritually or even metaphorically.
  5. The Rapture: the view that Christians will be 'caught up' secretly in advance of the visible Second Coming.

C. Why is this lesson important?
  1. The Second Coming of Jesus, promised in the New Testament, is often neglected and deserves careful examination at any time.
  2. The Second Coming will be a fact in history; it is only a matter of time before it takes place.
  3. *All of us will see it happen – dead or alive.*
    a. The 'dead in Christ' will rise first (1 Thess. 4:16).
    b. All the dead in any case will be raised (1 Cor. 15:22; Rev. 20:12-13).

c. Those that remain who are saved will be caught up with the rest of the saved to meet the Lord in the air (1 Thess. 4:17).

d. The bottom line: 'Look, he is coming with the clouds, and every eye will see him, even those who pierced him; and all the peoples of the earth will mourn because of him. So shall it be! Amen' (Rev. 1:7).

4. There is no better time than now to study the Second Coming.

5. God has used the preaching and teaching of this matter to bring many to Christ.

6. It gives us an opportunity to focus on the most important question of all: are we ready to meet God were Jesus to come today? Are we?

I. Basic facts regarding Jesus' Second Coming. Note: I am indebted again to Wayne Grudem's *Systematic Theology* and have found so much agreement and help with his manner of outlining these things.

A. There will be a sudden, personal, visible and bodily return of Jesus.

1. 'So you also must be ready, because the Son of Man will come at an hour when you do not expect him' (Matt. 24:44).

2. 'And if I go and prepare a place for you, I will come back and take you to be with me that you also may be where I am' (John 14:3).

3. 'For the Lord himself will come down from heaven, with a loud command, with the voice of the archangel and with the trumpet call of God, and the dead in Christ will rise first' (1 Thess. 4:16).

4. 'But the day of the Lord will come like a thief. The heavens will disappear with a roar; the elements will be destroyed by fire, and the earth and everything in it will be laid bare' (2 Peter 3:10).

5. 'Dear friends, now we are children of God, and what we will be has not yet been made known. But we know that when he appears, we shall be like him, for we shall see him as he is' (1 John 3:2).

6. 'Listen, I tell you a mystery: We will not all sleep, but we will all be changed – in a flash, in the twinkling of an eye, at the last trumpet. For the trumpet will sound, the dead will be raised imperishable, and we will be changed. For the perishable must clothe itself with the imperishable, and the mortal with immortality. When the perishable has been clothed with the imperishable, and the mortal with immortality, then the saying that is written will come true: "Death has been swallowed up in victory." "Where, O death, is your victory? Where, O death, is your sting?"' (1 Cor. 15:51-55).

    a. We are talking about 'this same Jesus' (Acts 1:10-11).

    b. We are talking about 'the Lord himself' (1 Thess. 4:16).

B. We should eagerly long for Jesus' return.

    1. John's response at the end of the book of Revelation should be ours as well: 'Amen. Come, Lord Jesus!' (Rev. 22:20).

    2. It is called a 'blessed hope', not a dreaded fear (Tit. 2:13).

    3. *To 'be ready' for Christ's return means:*

        a. That you know you are saved (Eph. 2:8).

        b. That you are faithfully walking in the light (1 John 1:7).

C. We do not know when Christ will return.

    1. He will come at an hour we 'do not expect' (Matt. 24:44).

    2. 'You do not know when the time will come' (Mark 13:33). 'Finally, brothers, we instructed you how to live in order to please God, as in fact you are living. Now we ask you and urge you in the Lord Jesus to do this more and more. For you know what instructions we gave you by the authority of the Lord Jesus' (1 Thes. 4:1-2).

    3. *Jesus makes it clear that we cannot know when he is coming back.*

        a. He himself said that he didn't even know! 'No one knows about that day or hour, not even the angels in heaven, nor the Son, but only the Father' (Matt. 24:36).

        b. Therefore anyone who claims to know specifically when Christ is returning is at once to be considered wrong.

II. SIGNS THAT PRECEDE CHRIST'S RETURN

A. The Gospel must be preached to all nations (Mark 13:10; Matt. 24:14).

    1. Generally speaking, this prophecy has been fulfilled.

    2. On the other hand, there are towns and villages in which the name of Christ has not been heard.

B. Tribulation

1. 'When you hear of wars and rumours of wars, do not be alarmed. Such things must happen, but the end is still to come. Nation will rise against nation, and kingdom against kingdom. There will be earthquakes in various places, and famines. These are the beginning of birth-pains' (Mark 13:7-8).

2. Note: there is considerable difficulty in differentiating between those signs which may refer to the impending fall of Jerusalem (AD 70) and the last days; however, it is not unlikely that they refer to both and indeed parallel those two great events.

3. 'Because those will be days of distress unequalled from the beginning, when God created the world, until now – and never to be equalled again. If the Lord had not cut short those days, no one would survive. But for the sake of the elect, whom he has chosen, he has shortened them' (Mark 13:19-20).

4. Note also: these verses may be used by those of the pre-millennial school of thought (to be explained below) to refer to the Great Tribulation following the Rapture.

C. False prophets working signs and wonders

1. 'For false Christs and false prophets will appear and perform great signs and miracles to deceive even the elect – if that were possible' (Mark 13:22. cf. Matt. 24:23-24).

2. *Satan has long been active in masquerading as an angel of light* (2 Cor. 11:14).

   a. This may refer to false teaching like Jehovah's Witnesses.

   b. It no doubt includes many cults abroad today.

   c. It could also be that the worst is yet to come.

D. Signs in the heavens

1. 'But in those days, following that distress, "the sun will be darkened, and the moon will not give its light; the stars will fall from the sky, and the heavenly bodies will be shaken"' (Mark 13:24-25).

2. It may be worth mentioning that Joel's prophecy, that the 'sun will be turned to darkness and the moon to blood before the coming of the great and dreadful day of the LORD' (Joel 2:31), which Peter referred to on the Day of Pentecost, may not have been fulfilled then but awaits a future day. See Acts 2:16-21. Surely Luke would have mentioned this had it happened.

E. Man of lawlessness

1. It is difficult to know what all this means, but Paul was emphatic that the Second Coming cannot occur until such a person emerged. 'Don't let anyone deceive you in any way, for that day will not come until the rebellion occurs and the man of lawlessness is revealed, the man doomed to destruction. He will oppose and will exalt himself over everything that is called God or is worshipped, so that he sets himself up in God's temple, proclaiming himself to be God' (2 Thes. 2:3-4).

2. This person has been connected to the beast of Revelation 13, sometimes called the antichrist, the final and worst in a series of antichrists in 1 John 2:18: 'Dear children, this is the last hour; and as you have heard that the antichrist is coming, even now many antichrists have come. This is how we know it is the last hour.'

F. The salvation of Israel

1. *Before the end it would seem that a large number of Jews will turn to Christ.*

    a. 'But if their transgression means riches for the world, and their loss means riches for the Gentiles, how much greater riches will their fullness bring!' (Rom. 11:12).

    b. 'I do not want you to be ignorant of this mystery, brothers, so that you may not be conceited: Israel has experienced a hardening in part until the full number of the Gentiles has come in. And so all Israel will be saved, as it is written: "The deliverer will come from Zion; he will turn godlessness away from Jacob"' (Rom. 11:25-26).

2. This does not necessarily mean that every living Jew will be converted any more than every living Gentile was converted when God turned to the Gentiles after Israel rejected Christ.

G. Other signs that suggest we are near the end

1. Increase in travel. 'Many will go here and there' (Dan. 12:4).

2. Increase of knowledge (Dan. 12:4). 'Always learning but never able to acknowledge the truth' (2 Tim. 3:7).

3. Increase of greed and love for material things (2 Tim. 3:1-4).

4. Superficiality (shallowness) in the church. 'Having a form of godliness but denying its power' (2 Tim. 3:5). 'For the time will come when men will not put up with sound doctrine. Instead, to suit their own desires, they will gather around them a great number of teachers to say what their itching ears want to hear' (2 Tim. 4:3).

5. Parallel with wars and rumours of wars some will be saying 'we never had it so good'. 'While people are saying, "Peace and safety," destruction will come on them suddenly, as labour pains on a pregnant woman, and they will not escape' (1 Thes. 5:3).

III. THE ONE THOUSAND YEAR REIGN OF CHRIST

A. A-millennialism: no future millennium in a literal sense.

1. The era of the Church – the church age – from 33 AD until the time of Christ's coming.

2. *This is an age in which Satan's influence over the nations has been greatly reduced so that the Gospel can be preached to the world.*

   a. Satan is bound during this time.

   b. The one thousand years are figurative, not literal.

   c. Those who reign with Christ are Christians who have died and are reigning with Christ in heaven.

   d. In a word: the Millennium is now happening; the exact duration of the church age cannot be known.

3. When Christ returns, there will be a remnant of both believers and unbelievers, followed by the Final Judgement and the eternal state.

B. Post-millennialism: Christ will return after the Millennium.

1. *The church age, the time of the Gospel, will culminate in a more rapid growth of the Church; the population of Christians will exceed the number of unbelievers.*

   a. There are basically two types of post-millennialism:

      (1) Classic post-millennialism: the world will gradually get better and better due to the acceleration of the Gospel's influence.

      (2) Revolutionary post-millennialism: a sudden intervention of Christ's power and glory that awakens the church and results in great revival.

    b. In either case the thousand year reign is symbolic and does not mean a literal thousand year period during which Satan is bound.

2. *At the end of the Millennial period (whether brief or long), Christ will return to earth.*

    a. Believers and unbelievers will be raised.

    b. The Judgement follows, then the eternal state.

C. Pre-millennialism: Christ will return before the Millennium.

1. *The church age is followed by the return of Christ.*

    a. Some believe the return of Christ is via a secret Rapture of believers.

       (1) A period called the Great Tribulation occurs on earth.

       (2) Christ returns visibly at the end of the Great Tribulation.

    b. Some believe that the Rapture and the visible return of Christ are simultaneous, meaning they are one and the same event.

       (1) The Great Tribulation therefore precedes the Second Coming.

       (2) Those who take this view tend to believe we are in this period of tribulation at the present time.

2. *Once Christ returns he begins his literal reign on earth of a literal thousand years.*

    a. Believers will reign with Christ on earth; they will have resurrected bodies.

    b. Of those unbelievers who remain on earth, some will turn to Christ.

    c. It will be an era of total peace on earth.

    d. At the end of the thousand years Satan will be loosed and will join forces with unbelievers who submitted outwardly to Christ's reign but inwardly rebelled; but they will be defeated.

    e. Then the bodies of unbelievers will be raised to stand before the Judgement; then the eternal state follows.

D. Note: the present study is too general to put all the arguments for and against each view.

1. *What is certain:*

    a. Jesus will come again.

    b. All people will be raised.

    c. All will stand before God at the Final Judgement.

    d. The eternal state follows.

  2. The Big Question we must answer: are we ready?

IV The Final Judgement and the eternal state

A. Both the Old and New Testaments teach that there is coming a day of days in which God will judge the world with justice. (Amos 5:18; Joel 3:14ff; Matt. 10:15; 11:22,24; 12:36; Heb. 6:2; 2 Pet. 2:13; Jude 6). 'Just as man is destined to die once, and after that to face judgement, so Christ was sacrificed once to take away the sins of many people; and he will appear a second time, not to bear sin, but to bring salvation to those who are waiting for him' (Heb. 9:27-28).

  1. 'Just as man is destined to die once, and after that to face judgement, so Christ was sacrificed once to take away the sins of many people; and he will appear a second time, not to bear sin, but to bring salvation to those who are waiting for him' (Heb. 9:27-28).

  2. 'Then I saw a great white throne and him who was seated on it. Earth and sky fled from his presence, and there was no place for them. And I saw the dead, great and small, standing before the throne, and books were opened. Another book was opened, which is the book of life. The dead were judged according to what they had done as recorded in the books' (Rev. 20:11-12).

B. The Second Coming and Final Judgement are inseparably connected.

  1. 'In the presence of God and of Christ Jesus, who will judge the living and the dead, and in view of his appearing and his kingdom, I give you this charge' (2 Tim. 4:1).

  2. 'Enoch, the seventh from Adam, prophesied about these men: "See, the Lord is coming with thousands upon thousands of his holy ones to judge everyone, and to convict all the ungodly of all the ungodly acts they have done in the ungodly way, and of all the harsh words ungodly sinners have spoken against him"' (Jude 14-15).

    a. Christ will be the Judge (2 Tim. 4:1; Acts 10:42; 17:31; John 5:21-27).

b. 'Not everyone who says to me, "Lord, Lord," will enter the kingdom of heaven, but only he who does the will of my Father who is in heaven. Many will say to me on that day, "Lord, Lord, did we not prophesy in your name, and in your name drive out demons and perform many miracles?"' (Matt. 7:21-22).

C. The Judgement will reveal two conditions of people: 'For it is time for judgement to begin with the family of God; and if it begins with us, what will the outcome be for those who do not obey the gospel of God? And, "If it is hard for the righteous to be saved, what will become of the ungodly and the sinner?"' (1 Peter 4:17-18).

  1. Who are saved and who are lost. 'Then they will go away to eternal punishment, but the righteous to eternal life' (Matt. 25:46).

  2. *Who among the saved will have a reward.* 'For we must all appear before the judgement seat of Christ, that each one may receive what is due him for the things done while in the body, whether good or bad. (2 Cor. 5:10).

  a. Some will have a reward.

  (1) 'If what he has built survives, he will receive his reward' (1 Cor. 3:14).

  (2) 'No, I beat my body and make it my slave so that after I have preached to others, I myself will not be disqualified for the prize' (1 Cor. 9:27).

  b. Some will be saved by fire. 'If it is burned up, he will suffer loss; he himself will be saved, but only as one escaping through the flames' (1 Cor. 3:15).

D. Angels will be judged (2 Pet. 2:4; Jude 6; 1 Cor. 6:3).

E. Satan will be judged. 'And the devil, who deceived them, was thrown into the lake of burning sulphur, where the beast and the false prophet had been thrown. They will be tormented day and night for ever and ever' (Rev. 20:10).

F. There are moral implications of the Final Judgement.
  1. It satisfies our innate sense of a need for justice in the world.
  2. *It enables us to forgive others freely.*

    a. 'Do not take revenge, my friends, but leave room for God's wrath, for it is written: "It is mine to avenge; I will repay," says the Lord' (Rom. 12:19).

    b. Whenever we have been wronged, we can give into God's hands any desire to harm or pay back (2 Thess. 1:5-8).

  3. It provides a motive for righteous living.

  4. It provides a great motive for evangelism.

G. The eternal state consists of two final destinies: Heaven or Hell.

  1. Hell: a place of eternal conscious punishment for the wicked.

    a. 'And throw that worthless servant outside, into the darkness, where there will be weeping and gnashing of teeth' (Matt. 25:30).

    b. 'Then he will say to those on his left, "Depart from me, you who are cursed, into the eternal fire prepared for the devil and his angels"' (Matt. 25:41).

    c. 'Then they will go away to eternal punishment, but the righteous to eternal life' (Matt. 25:46).

    d. It is a place of 'unquenchable fire' (Mark 9:43,48).

    e. The smoke of torment 'goes up for ever and ever' (Rev. 14:11).

  2. *Heaven: the final abode of the saved.*

    a. 'Then the King will say to those on his right, "Come, you who are blessed by my Father; take your inheritance, the kingdom prepared for you since the creation of the world"' (Matt. 25:34).

    b. 'And I heard a loud voice from the throne saying, "Now the dwelling of God is with men, and he will live with them. They will be his people, and God himself will be with them and be their God. He will wipe every tear from their eyes. There will be no more death or mourning or crying or pain, for the old order of things has passed away"' (Rev. 21:3-4).

    c. 'Behold, I will create new heavens and a new earth. The former things will not be remembered, nor will they come to mind' (Is. 65:17).

    d. '"As the new heavens and the new earth that I make will endure before me," declares the Lord, "so will your name and descendants endure"' (Is. 66:22).

e. 'But in keeping with his promise we are looking forward to a new heaven and a new earth, the home of righteousness' (2 Pet. 3:13).

CONCLUSION

Nearly every statement mentioned in this study deserves a complete study in itself. I have only given a brief survey of eschatology and many questions remain that must be answered by further study. The essential and by far the most important questions are:

1. Do we know for sure that if we were to die today, we would go to Heaven?
2. Do we know for sure, that if Jesus were to come today, we are ready to meet him?
3. Can we say right now, 'Even so, come Lord Jesus'?

Faith

8

WHAT IS FAITH?

Introduction

A. Two thousand years ago the angel Gabriel said to Mary: 'Do not be afraid, Mary, you have found favour with God. You will be with child and give birth to a son, and you are to give him the name Jesus' (Luke 1:30-31).

   1. Mary could not figure out how this could happen. '"How will this be," Mary asked the angel, "since I am a virgin?"' (Luke 1:34).

   2. But not to worry. 'The angel answered, "The Holy Spirit will come upon you, and the power of the Most High will overshadow you. So the holy one to be born will be called the Son of God"' (Luke 1:35).

   3. *All this is because 'Nothing is impossible with God'* (Luke 1:37).

      a. The question is: did Mary believe this?

      b. Yes. '"I am the Lord's servant," Mary answered. "May it be to me as you have said." Then the angel left her' (Luke 1:38).

         (1) In a word: Mary believed God.

         (2) She believed the angel which meant that she believed God.

B. Believing God.

   1. *Nothing has changed; faith then and now is summed up in two words: believing God.*

      a. This is not only believing *in* God, and there is nothing wrong with that! The Apostle Paul could say, 'I have faith in God' (Acts 27:25). This is the same as believing God (Cf. Acts 27:25 AV).

      b. But 'believing God' puts it more strongly.

         (1) It is one thing to say you believe *in* a person.

         (2) But when you say you believe that person – whatever

he or she says – it shows an even higher level of trust in their *word*; you believe them!

    c. This is how faith was sometimes described:

        (1) 'Abram believed the LORD, and he credited it to him as righteousness' (Gen. 15:6).

        (2) 'The Ninevites believed God. They declared a fast, and all of them, from the greatest to the least, put on sackcloth' (Jonah 3:5). Note: it might have read that 'the Ninevites believed Jonah' for he had proclaimed, 'Forty more days and Nineveh will be destroyed' (Jonah 3:4).

2. *Before Mary conceived she believed; she believed God.*

    a. She did not conceive and then believe.

    b. She believed first. 'Blessed is she who has believed that what the Lord has said to her will be accomplished!' (Luke 1:45).

        (1) Her faith is seen in her response to the angel. '"I am the Lord's servant," Mary answered. "May it be to me as you have said." Then the angel left her' (Luke 1:38).

        (2) She immediately conceived; for only a day or two later she was affirmed as being pregnant by her cousin Elizabeth (Luke 1:41-45).

C. Faith is described if not defined in Hebrews 11:1: 'Now faith is being sure of what we hope for and certain of what we do not see.'

    1. *Hebrews 11:1 may be a description of faith more than a definition.*

        a. Hebrews 11:1 describes what faith is.

        b. The examples of the rest of Hebrews 11 describe what faith does.

    2. *The more succinct definition: believing God.*

        a. This includes everything implied in Hebrews 11:1.

            (1) Being sure; certain.

            (2) Believing without seeing, that is, without evidence.

        b. The carnal (fleshly) mind wants it the other way around: seeing is believing.

            (1) '"Let this Christ, this King of Israel, come down now from the cross, that we may see and believe." Those crucified with him also heaped insults on him' (Mark 15:32).

 (2) If you see and *then* believe it is no longer faith as far as the biblical understanding of faith is concerned.

 (3) Faith, to be pure faith, is not seeing but still believing.

 (4) In a word: it is believing God.

c. Faith is based upon God's integrity.

 (1) The Bible is God's integrity put on the line.

 (2) If you believe that the Bible is God's Word, believing it is to believe him.

  (a) 'All Scripture is God-breathed and is useful for teaching, rebuking, correcting and training in righteousness' (2 Tim. 3:16).

  (b) 'For prophecy never had its origin in the will of man, but men spoke from God as they were carried along by the Holy Spirit' (2 Peter 1:21).

D. I believe this is needed more than anything as we enter this new Millennium.

1. The church needs to recover its faith in the Bible.

2. The church needs to believe that God was personally involved when he gave us the Bible – it is God speaking to us.

3. *The Holy Spirit who wrote the Bible is equally present today.*

 a. He speaks in two ways:

  (1) Indirectly, that is, through the Bible.

  (2) Directly, that is, as if apart from the Bible but never contradicting or adding to the Bible.

  (3) 'The Bible was not given to replace direct revelation; it was given to correct abuses' (D Martyn Lloyd-Jones).

 b. The degree to which we are on good terms with the Holy Spirit will be the degree to which we believe God and demonstrate the kind of faith needed in these times.

E. Why else is this study important?

1. Faith is a vast subject and one all of us should explore and try to understand.

2. Faith is the only way to please God. 'And without faith it is impossible to please God, because anyone who comes to him must believe that he exists and that he rewards those who earnestly seek him' (Heb. 11:6). We therefore should seek to know how to please God.

3. There is more than one kind of faith – not only saving faith but 'achieving' faith; to grasp this is to be better able to handle the word of truth (2 Tim. 2:15).

4. This will help us better to understand the Gospel and how faith must be exercised after we are saved.

5. This study is aimed at helping us to increase our faith, to have more faith.

I. Saving faith: believing God with regard to our salvation

A. This is to believe the Gospel, that is, believing what God has said about his Son coming into the world, and knowing we are saved.

    1. John 3:16 is what Martin Luther called 'the Bible in a nutshell'. 'For God so loved the world that he gave his one and only Son, that whoever believes in him shall not perish but have eternal life.'

    2. *Keep Hebrews 11:1 in mind: 'Now faith is being sure of what we hope for and certain of what we do not see.'*

        a. It is being sure without the evidence, that is, empirical (scientific or visible) evidence.

        b. We have not seen Jesus with our physical eyes. 'And, "A stone that causes men to stumble and a rock that makes them fall." They stumble because they disobey the message – which is also what they were destined for' (1 Peter 2:8).

    3. *The Gospel is presented as righteousness from God that is revealed from 'faith to faith'.* 'For therein is the righteousness of God revealed from faith to faith: as it is written, The just shall live by faith' (Rom. 1:17 AV).

        a. Sadly, for some strange inexplicable reason the NIV chose to paraphrase (or give some scholar's odd interpretation) rather than translate. Fortunately it gives a marginal note that puts it right: 'from faith to faith'.

        b. Paul's words 'faith to faith' are crucial to an understanding of Romans generally and justifying (saving) faith particularly.

            (1) Note: justifying faith and saving faith may be used interchangeably in this lesson.

(2) To justify means to be made righteous.

c. 'Faith to faith' means (1) the faith of Jesus, and (2) our faith.

(1) The phrase 'righteousness of God' (Rom. 1:17) appears again in Romans 3:22: 'Even the righteousness of God which is by faith of Jesus Christ unto all and upon all them that believe: for there is no difference.' (Rom. 3:22 AV).

(2) Sadly the NIV chose to translate 'faith of Jesus' as 'faith in Jesus'; but the AV got it right.

(3) Only those who believe have the benefit of what Christ did for us.

(4) Had Paul said: the righteousness of God which is by 'faith of Jesus Christ unto all and upon all' – and stopped there – it would imply that all would be saved.

(5) But Paul didn't stop there; he went on to say 'upon all them that believe.'

(6) Why? If you don't believe you won't be saved, even though Jesus believed perfectly for you on your behalf.

d. What Paul means by 'faith to faith' is stated in Galatians 2:16: 'Knowing that a man is not justified by the works of the law, but by the faith of Jesus Christ, even we have believed in Jesus Christ, that we might be justified by the faith of Christ, and not by the works of the law: for by the works of the law shall no flesh be justified' (Gal. 2:16 AV). Follow this carefully:

(1) 'We have believed *in* Jesus Christ' – why?

(2) 'That we might be justified by the faith *of* Jesus Christ' – why?

(3) Because the faith *of* Jesus Christ is the meaning of the 'first faith' of 'from faith to faith'; the 'second faith' of that phrase is our faith.

(4) I promise you! Read Galatians 2:16 over and over again in the Authorised Version; compare it with Romans 3:22 and Romans 1:17 and this will become clear.

(5) All the above is based upon a literal translation of the Greek.

B. The faith of Jesus.

1. *This means just that – Jesus' own personal faith.*
    a. He was a believer. 'I will put my trust in him' (Heb. 2:13).
    b. He was a perfect believer because he was given the Holy Spirit without any limit (John 3:34).
        (1) You and I are given a 'measure of faith' (Rom. 12:3).
        (2) But not Jesus. 'For the one whom God has sent speaks the words of God, for God gives the Spirit without limit' (John 3:34).
2. *Jesus' faith was a substitutionary or vicarious faith.*
    a. This means he took our place.
    b. Everything he did was for us.
    c. He did for us what we could not do for ourselves; this includes:
        (1) Believing perfectly.
        (2) Fulfilling the Law by obeying perfectly.
        (3) Satisfying God's justice.
3. *When Paul said that the righteousness of God is revealed from 'faith to faith' he meant therefore:*
    a. The faith of Jesus – his believing perfectly on our behalf.
    b. Our faith – trusting what Jesus did for us.

C. The object of our faith is God.

1. We believe God – what he has told us in his word.
2. *He tells us to put our faith in his Son.*
    a. When we do that the righteousness of Jesus is put to our credit. 'What does the Scripture say? "Abraham believed God, and it was credited to him as righteousness"' (Rom. 4:3).
    b. This comes from transferring our trust in ourselves to what Jesus has done for us.

D. Our faith: being sure.

1. It is when we are convinced that Jesus' life and death are what save us.
2. *When we are 'sure' of that, we put our trust in the Gospel.*
    a. Faith therefore assures.
    b. It is not a perfect faith, but faith none the less in a perfect and great Saviour!

c. This is why we are sure we will go to Heaven.

   (1) Not because of works. 'For it is by grace you have been saved, through faith – and this not from yourselves, it is the gift of God – not by works, so that no one can boast' (Eph. 2:8-9).

   (2) It is faith alone in Christ alone.

d. Note: when it comes time to die, this is the only comfort that is possible.

II. ACHIEVING FAITH: BELIEVING GOD WITH REGARD TO HIS WILL

A. If believing God is the best way to die it is also the best way to live.

1. Saving faith secures a home in Heaven.

2. *Achieving faith enables us to accomplish things on the way to Heaven.*

   a. It is described throughout Hebrews 11.

   b. The faith of Hebrews 11 is not referring to how we are saved, with the possible exception of Hebrews 11:4: 'By faith Abel offered God a better sacrifice than Cain did. By faith he was commended as a righteous man, when God spoke well of his offerings. And by faith he still speaks, even though he is dead.'

   (1) It is what 'the ancients were commended for' (Heb. 11:2).

   (2) It enabled them to do things in this life.

   c. God wants us to have both kinds of faith:

   (1) Saving faith: assurance we will go to Heaven.

   (2) Achieving faith: accomplishing something here below.

3. *What if your own name were added to the list; what do you suppose might be said about you? 'By faith Mary Jones. . .'*

   a. I believe we are all called to follow in the footsteps of those stalwarts in Hebrews 11.

   b. They were ordinary people; God made them unusual by what they did by faith.

4. *What is good enough to die by, then, is good enough to live by.*

   a. This is partly what Paul meant: 'I am crucified with Christ: nevertheless I live; yet not I, but Christ liveth in me: and the life which I now live in the flesh I live by the faith of

the Son of God, who loved me, and gave himself for me'
(Gal. 2:20 AV).
- **(1)** Greek literally means: I live by faith, namely that of the
Son of God.
- **(2)** Paul continues to refer to Jesus' own faith and says he
lives by that!
- **(3)** It is not only what saves but the way we should continue
to live.
- **b.** Living by the faith of Christ achieves things; what God has
in mind for each of us.
- **(1)** He has a will for each of us – just as he had a will for
Abraham, Moses and Samuel.
- **(2)** The degree to which we live by the faith of Christ will
be the degree to which we accomplish what God had in
mind for us.
- **c.** Note: Christ is now at the right hand of God interceding for
us. What level of faith do you suppose Jesus exercises there?
- **(1)** 'Who is he that condemns? Christ Jesus, who died –
more than that, who was raised to life – is at the right
hand of God and is also interceding for us' (Rom. 8:34).
- **(2)** 'He always lives to intercede for us (Heb. 7:25).
- **(3)** He intercedes with a perfect faith! No wonder, then, that
Paul says, 'I live by the faith of the Son of God'!

B. Habakkuk's vision: 'the righteous will live by his faith' (Hab. 2:4. Cf. Rom. 1:17; Gal. 3:11; Heb. 10:38).

- **1.** The Hebrew is best translated 'faithfulness' in Habakkuk 2:4,
which is why the NIV says so in the footnote.
- **2.** The greater issue however: what does 'his' mean; who does
'his' refer to?
- **a.** If 'his' means the person's own faithfulness, this could lead
to trusting our own ability to endure.
- **b.** But if 'his' means God's faithfulness it means we are trusting
God and not ourselves to be faithful.
- **c.** Answer: it means God's faithfulness.
- **3.** *Context of Habakkuk's word that the just would live by God's faithfulness:*
- **a.** God told Habakkuk to write down the revelation he had
been given (Hab. 2:2).

b. This revelation, however, awaited an appointed time (Hab. 2:3).

  (1) It refers to the end; not Habakkuk's day.

  (2) It won't be coming in a day or two. 'Though it linger, wait for it; it will certainly come and will not delay' (Hab. 2:3).

c. What, then, is a person to do? Answer: live by the faithfulness of God who promised all this.

  (1) Do not trust ourselves or our own faithfulness.

  (2) Live by his faithfulness, 'for he who promised is faithful' (Heb. 10:23).

d. This is precisely how Hebrews 10:35-39 (which introduces the achieving faith of Hebrews 11) is to be understood:

'For in just a very little while,
"He who is coming will come and will not delay.
But my righteous one will live by faith.
And if he shrinks back,
I will not be pleased with him"' (Heb. 10:37-38).

  (1) Those discouraged Hebrew Christians were exhorted to trust God's faithfulness regarding the future!

  (2) This is why the writer refers to Habakkuk! They were to wait. How long? 'In just a little while.'

C. It is at this point that the writer brings in the 'faith chapter' of the Bible.

1. Hebrews 11 is in a sense a long parenthesis (brackets).

2. You could go from Hebrews 10:39, 'But we are not of those who shrink back and are destroyed, but of those who believe and are saved,' to Hebrews 12:1b, 'Let us throw off everything that hinders. . .' and not lose the writer's meaning.

3. *Hebrews 11 is given to encourage us.*

  a. We learn what they did by believing God.

  b. What they did we can do, that is, achieve in our day the purpose for which God made us as they achieved God's purposes for them in their day.

4. *One important observation: no person mentioned repeated what was done before.*

    a. Each faith was an 'original' faith; there were no imitations; each had to achieve on his own what God led him to do.

    b. Noah was not allowed to do what Enoch did; Abraham was not allowed to build an ark!

    c. So it is with you and me; we cannot look over our shoulders and do what others have done; we fix our eyes on Christ. 'Let us fix our eyes on Jesus, the author and perfecter of our faith, who for the joy set before him endured the cross, scorning its shame, and sat down at the right hand of the throne of God' (Heb. 12:2).

CONCLUSION

Saving faith is believing God; achieving faith is believing God. We must experience both; and if we do we can turn the world upside down for God in this new and exciting day!

9

FAITH AND CREATION

INTRODUCTION

A. Harrison Matthews, a leading scientist and evolutionist, writing in the Introduction to the 100th anniversary Everyman's Library Edition of Charles Darwin's *Origin of Species* said:
   1. Belief in the theory of evolution is thus exactly parallel to belief in special creation.
   2. *It is a faith that lies behind one's embracing the theory of evolution.*
      a. Any number of evolutionary writers concur, that evolution is a matter of faith on the part of biologists:
         (1) That biogenesis did occur.
         (2) That living cells came into existence.
      b. Dr Arthur Field said that evolution is based upon belief in the reality of the unseen, belief in fossils that cannot be produced, belief in embryological evidence that does not exist.
      c. Dr John Howitt: evolution is based and accepted on faith alone, for three quarters of the record is non-existent and there are systematic gaps that cannot be covered.
   3. *However, there are two kinds of evolution:*
      a. Microevolution.
         (1) It is possible for a scientist to produce thousands of generations of insects (whose life-span is sometimes only a few hours) and demonstrate in a laboratory the possibility of some kind of small-scale evolution.
         (2) But this does not involve the production of any new species.
      b. Macroevolution: evolution from one species to another.
         (1) This is what the present study means by the term evolution.
         (2) The evidence of this is lacking; scientists cannot solve

the problem of 'missing links' – despite a century of searching.

    c. Note: what scientists call species the Bible calls 'kinds'.

        (1) 'So God created the great creatures of the sea and every living and moving thing with which the water teems, according to their kinds, and every winged bird according to its kind. And God saw that it was good' (Gen. 1:21).

        (2) 'And God said, "Let the land produce living creatures according to their kinds: livestock, creatures that move along the ground, and wild animals, each according to its kind." And it was so' (Gen. 1:24).

B. 'By faith we understand that the universe was formed at God's command, so that what is seen was not made out of what was visible' (Heb. 11:3).

  1. This means creation by God *ex nihilo* (out of nothing).

  2. *The issue: will we believe God as a consequence of what he has said in the Bible – God's integrity put on the line – or whether we follow so-called empirical proofs at the level of nature.*

    a. Do we believe the Word of God for its own sake?

    b. Must we pay homage to the empirical method of science before we can trust the Lord?

  3. *When all the facts are rightly understood, there will be no final conflict between Scripture and natural science.*

    a. Francis Schaeffer, *No Final Conflict* (1975), lists several areas where, in his judgement, there is room for disagreement among Christians who believe in the total truthfulness of the Bible:

        (1) There is a possibility that God created a 'grown up' universe.

        (2) There is a possibility of a break between Genesis 1:1 and 1:2 or between Genesis 1:2 and 1:3.

        (3) There is a possibility of a long day in Genesis 1.

        (4) There is a possibility that the flood (of Noah's day) affected the geological data.

        (5) The use of the word 'kinds' in Genesis 1 may be quite broad.

(6) There is a possibility of the death of animals before the Fall.

(7) Where the Hebrew word *bara* is not used there is the possibility of sequence from previously existing things.

b. Schaeffer is not saying any of the above positions is his own, only that they are theoretically possible; our understanding of the natural world and of Scripture, he says, is not perfect.

C. I, too, have a theory: every generation of Christianity has its own stigma by which the believer's faith is severely tested.

1. In the first century: saying that Jesus of Nazareth is the fulfilment of the Old Testament.

2. In the fourth century: affirming that Jesus Christ is co-eternal and co-substantial with God Almighty.

3. *In the sixteenth century: trusting that faith alone in what Jesus did for us on the cross saves us – without works.*

  a. The most hotly contested issue of any day is that which is true but which also makes the minority view look foolish and the believer appear to be a fool.

  b. The issue is whether the internal witness of the Spirit that the Bible is true has priority over the external witness.

   (1) The internal witness: affirming the Scriptures by faith without the need of further evidence.

   (2) The external witness: affirming the Scriptures because we have amassed sufficient evidence that the Bible is true and reliable; therefore we believe it.

4. *The stigma of our generation is to believe God's account of creation without the empirical evidence.*

  a. The irony: nobody has proved that real empirical evidence for evolution is available.

  b. One, therefore, must make a choice between two positions:

   (1) Faith in evolution.

   (2) Faith in creation.

  c. But to affirm creation is to look like a fool!

  d. Why? Because of a godless conspiracy against the Christian faith; it is an innate bias – another word for what we may wish to call 'original sin'.

   (1) Sir Julian Huxley, who in his day was probably the

premier evolutionist in the world and President of United Nations Educational, Scientific, Cultural Organisation (UNESCO), said, 'It is clear that the doctrine of evolution is directly antagonistic to that of Creation. . . Evolution, if consistently accepted, makes it impossible to believe the Bible.'

(2) Jacque Monod, Nobel prize-winning scientist from France, said he is appalled that any Christian would try to embrace evolution.

(3) H G Wells: 'If all animals and man evolved. . . then there were no first parents, no Eden, no Fall. And if there had been no Fall, then the entire historic fabric of Christianity. . . the story of the first sin and the reason for the Atonement – collapses like a house of cards.'

(4) Sir Julian Huxley was asked, 'Why do you think that evolution caught on so quickly?' He replied, 'We all jumped at the *Origin* [Darwin's *Origin of Species*] because the idea of God interfered with our sexual mores.' Note: you could say that 'mores' is the secular version of 'morals'; mores are simply what people are doing, not what God says they ought to do. Therefore translate 'sexual mores' as 'sexual immorality' and you discover Huxley's reason for the acceptance of evolution.

(5) Philosopher Bertrand Russell, a devout evolutionist, said that getting rid of the idea of God, which evolution enabled him to do, 'freed me up to my erotic desires'.

D. Why is this lesson important?

1. It is essential to remember that acceptance of creation as described in Genesis is by *faith* – not by sight or scientific evidence.

2. *To embrace theistic evolution is taking one's cue from certain scientists, not from Scripture.*

   a. Theistic evolution (def.): the view that evolution was God's chosen way of creating what is.

   (1) This view claims to uphold Scripture, that it does not necessarily conflict with the Genesis account.

   (2) God could have created the world apart from the

evolutionary process but chose evolution as the way things came to be.
- **b.** No-one who believes in theistic evolution would have thought to embrace this had not some scientist first come up with evolutionary theory.
  - **(1)** It is based upon principles that are imported into Christianity.
  - **(2)** According to Louis Berkhof, 'theistic evolution is really a child of embarrassment which calls God in at periodic intervals to help nature over the chasms that yawn at her feet. It is neither the biblical doctrine of creation, nor a consistent theory of evolution.'
- **c.** This means that science has priority over Scripture when it comes to belief in creation.
  - **(1)** No doubt some would say they are only trying to square the Bible with science.
  - **(2)** But theistic evolution contradicts Hebrews 11:3.
3. *We must be willing to accept whatever stigma God requires of us.*
- **a.** To affirm creation as the Bible describes it is to be seen as foolish.
- **b.** Martin Luther says we need to fight where the battle is hottest.
4. *The very Gospel is ultimately at stake in this matter.*
- **a.** The infallibility and reliability of the Bible is at stake.
- **b.** If evolution is true there would be no Adam and Eve as first parents; hence no Fall.
5. Although we do not take our cue from science (which is always changing), it is interesting to note the inconsistencies in the scientific community when it comes to evolution.

I. UNFOLDING OF THE BIBLICAL POSITION

A. Hebrews 11:3 is worded very carefully:
1. 'By faith we understand that the universe was formed at God's command, so that what is seen was not made out of what was visible' (Heb. 11:3).
2. *'Through faith we understand that the worlds [ages] were framed by the word of God, so that things which are seen were*

not made of things which do appear' (Heb. 11:3 AV).

   a. We cannot hold to creation *ex nihilo* (out of nothing) and evolution at the same time.

   b. Creation means there was a time when there was *nothing* – but God.

   c. Evolution assumes that matter always existed.

3. *The writer does not state that by faith we 'prove' that the worlds or ages were created by the Word of God.*

   a. Some make the mistake of trying to prove certain things to be true first – before they can believe; this would mean faith isn't truly faith.

   b. The biblical view is that by faith – believing God without proof – we 'understand'.

4. *It does not say that by 'science' we understand.*

   a. Many assume that science must be right.

      (1) Scientists are people, many of whom specialise to such an extent that each is often ignorant of what is going on outside his or her own field.

      (2) Scientists are not only human but often with biases against God and therefore have no difficulty in accepting the theory of evolution.

   b. Science in any case is always changing.

      (1) Yesterday's text books are largely out of date.

      (2) Today's text books will shortly be out of date.

B. By 'faith' – believing God – we understand.

1. *'The fear of the Lord is the beginning of wisdom, and knowledge of the Holy One is understanding'* (Prov. 9:10).

   a. By believing God there is a breakthrough to knowledge.

   b. By believing God we understand that time and space were created by the Word of God.

   c. Note: it could be that one day scientists will affirm creation by empirical knowledge.

      (1) If that were true it would still not be the reason you and I accept the biblical account.

      (2) However, let us thank God for those Christians who are scientists and who are involved in this area.

      (3) It is by 'faith' we believe in creation in the first place.

2. *Faith in creation is the family secret: 'We' understand.*
  a. Who are the 'we'? Answer: the family of God.
    (1) The world may not understand.
    (2) Scientists may not understand.
    (3) But the Bible never said they would!
  b. 'We' do; creation was never meant to be understood by those outside the family.
    (1) It is not a matter of believing in creation first, and then being adopted into the family.
    (2) We become Christians first – by faith in Christ's blood – and then we discover the truth about creation.

C. Creation 'out of nothing'.

  1. *This means that the things which 'appear' – time and space and all matter – were not made of things that are visible, or already existed.*
    a. Time, space, matter, were brought into being by the Word of God.
      (1) Until God *spoke* – 'let there be light' (Gen. 1:3), time, space and matter had no existence at all.
      (2) Before God chose to speak there was nothing at all – but the triune God.
    b. Things which are *there* were *put there* from nothing by the very voice of God.
      (1) What Hebrews 11:3 calls the Word of God was indeed the Word (*logos*) that was with God from the beginning (John 1:1).
      (2) 'He was with God in the beginning' (John 1:2). He, then, is the Word. Hence, 'Through him all things were made; without him nothing was made that has been made' (John 1:3. cf. Col. 1:17).
    c. Note: those who subscribe to theistic evolution take their cue not from Scripture but from nature and 'science'.
      (1) They assume that, since so many scientists believe in evolution, there must be something to it.
      (2) They begin with the assumption that evolution is probably true – but so is the Bible, that is, up to a point.
      (3) Any view of evolution takes it for granted that what now appears, or is there, has *evolved* to its present state, and evolved from what already existed.

115

(4) To superimpose the name of God upon a system of thought – namely, evolution – that never intended to cohere with Scripture, is not only to dignify atheism but to show that one does not begin with the simple statement of the inspired Word of God.

2. *Hebrews 11:3 says that what is seen was not made out of what is visible. This denies theistic evolution.*

  a. What is 'seen' (Gr. *phainomenon* – literally 'what is being seen') at one point did not exist.

  b. What now exists or is seen was brought into being (Gr. *gegonenai*) but not from what now exists or appears (Gr. *blepomenon*, 'what is visible').

  c. In a word: creation *ex nihilo*. Had the writer of Hebrews wanted to make a statement that would categorically refute any view of evolution, he could not have worded it better.

  d. Anybody who holds to theistic evolution has to run slipshod over Hebrews 11:3.

II. THE DANGER OF TAKING ONE'S CUE FROM NATURE OR SCIENCE

A. Nature is cursed by the Fall.

  1. *To take one's cue only from nature is necessarily to assume the utter reliability of nature and of the scientist who studies it; after all, he too is a sinner.*

  a. But nature has been 'cursed'. 'To Adam he said, "Because you listened to your wife and ate from the tree about which I commanded you, 'You must not eat of it,' Cursed is the ground because of you; through painful toil you will eat of it all the days of your life"' (Gen. 3:17).

  b. This means that nature in some ways could have ceased to be a reliable instrument or mirror by which to view the age of the world, or the way in which nature came along.

  2. *We know the results of the Fall on the human race* (Gen. 3:16-19; Rom. 5:12; 6:23); *it should not be surprising that the whole of nature was adversely affected in such a way that no biased scientist can always use it as a reliable instrument.*

  a. It is true that some physical laws have been derived from nature, and this is part of God's common grace.

  b. But a biased scientist can be selective with the evidence.

B. Some scientists *do* have sufficient integrity to admit their own inconsistencies.

   1. *Some acknowledge that evolutionists have continually failed to face up to the fact that the theory of evolution flies in the face of some of the best established laws in the scientific world.*

   a. It violates the first and second laws of thermodynamics.

   b. It violates the laws of probability.

       (1) A group of the world's leading mathematicians met with fifty-two of the greatest evolutionary biologists at the Witsar Institute in Philadelphia and presented to them the mathematical problems that were showing up concerning evolution.

       (2) With a digital computer they began to examine the mathematical problems concerning evolution and concluded that evolution was mathematically impossible.

   c. Dr Murray Eden, from the Massachusetts Institute of Technology, noted that before there could be any viable theory of evolution there would have to be the discovery and elucidation of entirely new natural laws; chemical, chemico-physical and biological. This means:

       (1) They will either have to throw out all the known laws of science or wait for a new set of natural laws.

       (2) There would have to be an entirely different universe before evolution can be true.

   2. *Dr Calvin Patterson, who was senior palaeontologist at the Natural History Museum of London (which has the largest collection of fossils in the world) and author of Evolution actually stated that he came to realise that there was not a single thing he knew for sure about evolution!*

   a. He asked a group of scientists at the Field Museum if they could name one thing they knew for sure about evolution. Silence.

   b. Dr Patterson said evolution is an 'anti-theory' that not only produces no knowledge; it produces positive 'anti-knowledge' (Quoted by Dr D James Kennedy, 'Creationism: science or religion?' p.7).

   3. Dr Paul Lemoine, a prestigious French scientist, said that evolution is a 'fairy tale for grown-ups'.

4. *Dr Francis Crick, the co-discoverer of DNA, received the Nobel Prize for that discovery. He decided later to apply probability analysis to the possibility of just one DNA molecule coming into existence by random chance in the entire history of the earth.*

   a. DNA is the master control of all of our genetic development; it is the most complex molecule known to man, so tiny that it fits inside the microscopic nucleus of a microscopic cell.

   b. Dr Crick discovered that there was *no possibility* that the DNA molecule could ever in the entire history of the earth have originated by chance.

5. *Sir Fred Hoyle, former professor at Cambridge, and Chandra Wickramasinghe, a mathematician from India, decided to find out what were the probabilities of an entire cell – the simplest living cell – coming into existence in the entire history of the universe, now estimated to be roughly 15 to 20 billion years.*

   a. They concluded that the chance of this would be 10 to the 40,000th power years.

   b. They said that the chances of a tornado blowing through a junkyard and creating a Boeing 747 are vastly greater.

   c. Sir Fred Hoyle said that to suppose that somewhere on this earth, by purely natural spontaneous random causes, the entire complexity of a living cell with all of its amazing and unbelievable complexity could have arisen by chance 'is evidently nonsense of a high order.'

   d. Evolutionary theory makes it difficult to be an atheist and should in a sense make it easier than ever to accept the Bible's account of creation!

CONCLUSION

The Bible only uses the word 'create' with God as the subject. 'Create' means 'to bring into existence without using pre-existing material'.

To affirm creation 'out of nothing' is to affirm what is perhaps the profoundest thing that can be said about God – that he always was. He became Creator because he chose to create.

Even if the majority of scientists affirmed the Genesis account, we would still need faith. Scientists affirming creation will not fill churches. Lives must be changed, but by the gospel of Christ.

10

FAITH AND RIGHTEOUSNESS

By faith Abel offered God a better sacrifice than Cain did. By faith he was commended as a righteous man, when God spoke well of his offerings. And by faith he still speaks, even though he is dead' (Heb. 11:4).

INTRODUCTION

A. **As we proceed in this series of studies on Faith, based largely on Hebrews 11, we conclude:**
   1. The writer followed the order of the Old Testament – he moved from creation to Cain and Abel; then to Enoch.
   2. *The writer assumes the historicity of the book of Genesis.*
      a. That Genesis 1 and 2 describe what happened regarding the creation of the world generally and man particularly.
      b. That the Garden of Eden was literally a place on the map.

B. **The account of Cain and Abel assumes more: the Fall.**
   1. *The Garden of Eden was not only a place on the map but the Fall was a date in history.*
      a. The writer of Hebrews does not refer to the Fall.
      b. He is looking for examples of faith – when people believed God.
         (1) Did Adam and Eve believe God?
         (2) There is no explicit proof that they did, only implicit; since God clothed them with garments of skin. (Gen. 3:21).
            (a) This is a fairly strong indication that they were saved and forgiven – that they will be in Heaven.
            (b) This would strongly suggest therefore that they believed God, that is, all he said to them after they were found out (Gen. 3:9-19).
   2. *After the Fall of Adam and Eve, sin emerged upon the whole of the human race.*
      a. All God prophesied came true.
         (1) 'And the LORD God commanded the man, "You are free

to eat from any tree in the garden; but you must not eat from the tree of the knowledge of good and evil, for when you eat of it you will surely die"' (Gen. 2:16-17).

(2) Adam and Eve died spiritually the day they sinned; they died physically after that. Adam lived 930 years, 'and then he died' (Gen. 5:5).

b. All mankind is born into the condition of spiritual death into which Adam and Eve fell.

(1) We are not born as Adam was created before the Fall but as he became after the Fall. 'Therefore, just as sin entered the world through one man, and death through sin, and in this way death came to all men, because all sinned' (Rom. 5:12).

(2) This is why we too will die physically (Rom. 6:23).

c. Note: St Augustine's four stages; man was:

(1) Able to sin – as he was before the Fall.

(2) Not able not to sin – as we are born with a sinful nature. (Ps. 51:5).

(3) Able not to sin – after we are converted.

(4) Not able to sin – when we get to Heaven.

3. The account of Cain and Abel is an example of how deeply we fell – and what any of us is capable of.

4. This account is equally an example of how we are saved – what happens by the sheer grace of God.

C. Why is this lesson important?

1. *It shows what is the only solid hope (and basis of assurance) of going to Heaven.*

a. The issue is: which would we want to trust when it comes time to die – or when we stand before the Judgement Seat of Christ:

(1) Our own righteousness, even if by God's help.

(2) Another's righteousness, namely, what is put to our credit.

b. We will show that the only sound and comforting basis of salvation is when the righteousness of another, that is, Jesus Christ, is put to our credit – as though we were as righteous as Jesus.

2. *It shows the awfulness and heaviness of sin.*
  a. That spiritual death led to jealousy and murder.
  b. What Cain did we all could do – save by the goodness of God.
3. *It shows the importance of a sound doctrine of sin.*
  a. A faulty teaching of salvation is traceable to a faulty view of sin.
  b. Man is depraved by nature and incapable of being saved unless given faith (Eph. 2:1-10).
4. *It brings us face to face with the very teaching that turned the world upside down in the sixteenth century: justification by faith alone.*
  a. For some (sadly) this is as alien as it was to Christendom then.
  b. A sound doctrine of justification is essential to a solid theology generally.
5. *It brings us to the heart of the teaching of justification: imputation.*
  a. Imputation (def.): put to the credit of.
  b. We will show that the person who transfers his or her trust to what Jesus did on the cross:
    (1) Is justified (def.: declared righteous) before God.
    (2) This is forensic (def.: legal – the way God sees you, not the way people see you).

I. WHAT HAPPENED CONCERNING CAIN AND ABEL? (GEN. 4:1-16).

A. Cain and Abel, brothers, each brought an offering to the Lord.
  1. Cain brought some of the fruits of the soil (Gen. 4:3).
  2. Abel brought 'fat portions from some of the firstborn of his flock' (Gen. 4:4).

B. God did not regard those offerings with equal estimation.
  1. He looked with favour on Abel and his offering (Gen. 4:4).
  2. He did not look with favour on Cain and his offering (Gen. 4:5).

C. Cain's reaction to God was not a happy one.
  1. Cain was 'very angry, and his face was downcast' (Gen. 4:5).

2. *But God seems to have given Cain a second chance:*
  a. 'Then the LORD said to Cain, "Why are you angry? Why is
  your face downcast? If you do what is right, will you not
  be accepted? But if you do not do what is right, sin is
  crouching at your door; it desires to have you, but you must
  master it"' (Gen. 4:6-7).
  b. This indicates that Cain had a choice.
    (1) He had an opportunity to be accepted; it was clear what
    that was: the sacrifice of an animal.
    (2) He could choose not to do what was right, which meant
    sin crouching at his door.
  c. Note: we too have a choice to make; which will it be for us:
    (1) A substitute – God's lamb.
    (2) What we can do – our own efforts.

D. Cain made a deliberate choice not to submit to God's righteousness.

  1. This was the mistake Israel would make thousands of years
  later: 'Since they did not know the righteousness that comes
  from God and sought to establish their own, they did not submit
  to God's righteousness' (Rom. 10:3).
  2. *Instead of submitting to God's righteousness Cain killed the
  one who in fact had already submitted to God's righteousness.*
  a. 'Now Cain said to his brother Abel, "Let's go out to the
  field." And while they were in the field, Cain attacked his
  brother Abel and killed him' (Gen. 4:8).
  b. 'Do not be like Cain, who belonged to the evil one and
  murdered his brother. And why did he murder him? Because
  his own actions were evil and his brother's were righteous.
  Do not be surprised, my brothers, if the world hates you' (1
  John 3:12-13).
  c. Cain did not get away with this; God punished him.
    (1) 'The LORD said, "What have you done? Listen! Your
    brother's blood cries out to me from the ground"' (Gen.
    4:10).
    (2) To this day this is true: those who perceive the choice
    between God's righteousness and their own righteous-
    ness – and choose the latter – incur a punishment on
    themselves which is unbearable.

II. Abel's 'better' sacrifice

A. **Why did Abel offer a blood sacrifice? How did he know to do this? Was he 'lucky' – and Cain 'unlucky'?**
  1. *There are at least two possible answers:*
    a. Both Cain and Abel were taught this by their parents.
      (1) After Adam and Eve sinned they were given garments of skin by God (Gen. 3:21).
      (2) This was the beginning of the Old Testament sacrificial system.
    b. God spoke to Cain and Abel as they grew older.
      (1) God gives sufficient witness to every generation.
      (2) It took no more faith for either Cain or Abel to believe the voice of the Spirit than it does for us to believe the Scriptures.
  2. *God offered his grace equally to both Cain and Abel.*
    a. Abel's offering was no leap in the dark.
    b. Faith is believing God; Abel did what he did by faith (Heb. 11:4).

B. **Abel's offering prefigured atonement by substitution.**
  1. Cain's offering – the fruit of the ground – corresponded to the third day of creation. 'Then God said, "Let the land produce vegetation: seed-bearing plants and trees on the land that bear fruit with seed in it, according to their various kinds." And it was so' (Gen. 1:11).
  2. *Abel's offering corresponded to the sixth day of creation in which both men and animals were created* (Gen. 1:24-31).
    a. Abel's offering therefore prefigured a substitute; the blood of an animal taking the place of man's sin.
      (1) Without the shedding of blood there would be no remission (Lev. 17:11; Heb. 9:22).
      (2) What God required was not vegetation substituting for man but a slain animal doing this.
    b. Vegetation is not an analogy to man, but an animal is; whether it be a lamb, goat or bull.
      (1) A beast is the nearest likeness to man, both having blood.
      (2) God would always demand a sacrifice of blood for sin.

3. *Cain did not wish to dignify God's method regarding how he was to be appeased.*

    a. He preferred to bring the labours of his own hands.

    b. He tried to upstage God's requirements, foolishly by works.

C. Abel did what he did 'by faith': believing God.

    1. He made a choice – to do things God's way.

    2. The result: a 'better' (AV: more excellent) sacrifice than Cain's choice to appease God by works.

III. ABEL WAS COMMENDED AS A RIGHTEOUS MAN BY FAITH 'HE'. . .

A. This means he was declared righteous.

    1. It is not that Abel was righteous in himself.

    2. *It was not the labour of his hands.*

        a. If what Abel did was righteous, then faith becomes a work.

        b. Faith is not a work, only the instrument by which we rely on God.

            (1) God does not accept our efforts as meriting favour.

            (2) He accepts the sacrifice that we *point* to – namely, Jesus' death on the cross.

        c. Abel presented a lamb – the object of his faith.

'I need no other argument,
I need no other plea;
It is enough that Jesus died
And that he died for me.'

B. The result: Abel is seen as righteous.

    1. *This is where 'imputation' comes into the picture.*

        a. The moment Abel put his faith in a lamb not his own efforts, here is what happened:

            (1) Abel's sins were forgiven.

            (2) Righteousness was put to Abel's credit, therefore he is seen as righteous.

        b. This prefigures the way in which you and I are saved; the moment we transfer our trust (what we rely on) from our own efforts to what God's lamb has done for us:

            (1) Our sins are forgiven.

(2) Christ's righteousness is put to our credit; from that moment we are regarded as righteous as Jesus.

2. *Imputation is used in two ways by Paul:*
    a. What is *not* imputed to us, namely, sin.
    b. What is imputed to us – namely righteousness.
        (1) 'Blessed are they whose transgressions are forgiven, whose sins are covered. Blessed is the man whose sin the Lord will never count against him' (Rom. 4:7-8).
        (2) This means we are righteous in God's eyes; that is the way he sees us (and does anybody else's opinion matter?).

C. The place of works.

1. *Before justification.* 'For it is by grace you have been saved, through faith – and this not from yourselves, it is the gift of God – not by works, so that no one can boast' (Eph. 2:8-9).
    a. God does not accept our works as meriting anything towards being justified.
        (1) Any righteousness prior to Christ's righteousness being put to our credit is filthy rags (Is. 64:6).
        (2) All we can do before we rely on a sinless substitute is of no value in God's sight.
    b. God does not therefore regard our 'good' works prior to our justification with favour.
        (1) There is no preparation for justification insofar as our efforts to appease God.
        (2) Nothing counts but God's lamb and our reliance upon him.

'Nothing in my hand I bring,
Simply to Thy cross I cling;
Naked, come to Thee for dress;
Helpless, look to Thee for grace;
Foul, I to the fountain fly;
Wash me, Saviour, or I die.'
Augustus Toplady (1740-78)

2. *After justification.* 'For we are God's workmanship, created in Christ Jesus to do good works, which God prepared in advance for us to do' (Eph. 2:10).

a. God calls us to good works after we have put our trust in his Son, also called:

(1) Righteousness (Rom. 6:16).

(2) Holiness (Rom. 6:19).

(3) Living by the Spirit (Rom. 8:4; Gal. 5:25).

(4) Offering our bodies as living sacrifices (Rom. 12:1).

(5) Walking in love (1 Cor. 13).

(6) Living worthy of God (1 Thess. 2:12).

(7) Walking in the light (1 John 1:7).

(8) Sanctification (1 Thess. 4:3).

b. Works following justification are done out of gratitude.

(1) They are not manifest to stay justified; the righteousness of Christ is put to our credit forever.

(2) Works are manifested by us as a way of saying, 'Thank you Lord'; like a P.S. at the end of a letter.

3. *The question follows: in which do we want to put our trust: Christ's imputed righteousness or the righteousness or sanctification that flows from being justified?*

a. In death, which would we trust? Two choices:

(1) That we have been faithful.

(2) That God is faithful – still looking to his Son.

b. At the Judgement Seat of Christ, which would we trust?

(1) What we have done for the Lord since being saved? That we haven't backslidden? Note: this is to trust our faithfulness not Christ's atonement at the end of the day.

(2) Would we still cling to Christ's blood?

'My hope is built on nothing less
Than Jesus' blood and righteousness;
I dare not trust the sweetest frame,
But wholly lean on Jesus' name.'

Edward More (1797-1874)

IV. GOD SPOKE WELL OF ABEL'S OFFERING

A. What matters: God's opinion.

1. If he says it, nothing else matters!

2. *It is not what people say*

a. We may not appear to be righteous in others' eyes.
b. It is not appearance that matters.

B. Abel knew he was accepted.

1. God witnessed to him.
2. It is true also with us. 'Anyone who believes in the Son of God has this testimony in his heart' (1 John 5:10a).

C. When our faith is focussed on God's Son, and not on our works, we *know* him.

1. *However, there are basically two levels of assurance:*
   a. By simple reasoning:
      (1) All who trust in Christ's blood are saved.
      (2) I trust only in Christ's blood.
      (3) Therefore I am saved.
   b. By the immediate and direct witness of the Spirit.
      (1) This is usually preceded by the above reasoning process; most Christians normally come to assurance of faith by reasoning as above.
      (2) Sometimes God's Spirit comes down in power and eliminates the need for any reasoning; it is the Spirit's own testimony (Eph. 1:13).
2. *Works after justification that are done in obedience and out of gratitude:*
   a. Do not become the main basis of assurance of salvation.
      (1) For our obedience can vary.
      (2) We will feel 'more saved' some days and 'less saved' on other days.
   b. They do however erect a superstructure of gold, silver, precious stones (1 Cor. 3:12).
      (1) Those who fail in this are still saved but lose a reward (1 Cor. 3:15).
      (2) Those who are faithful receive a reward – in addition to being saved (1 Cor. 3:14).

CONCLUSION

Our justification is by faith – before God. It is his righteousness, the only righteousness which matters.

11

FAITH AND PLEASING GOD

A. Pleasing God is the greatest privilege a human being can have on earth.
  1. There is a way this can be done on earth but not in Heaven.
  2. *In a word: by faith.*
     a. There will be no faith in Heaven, that is, as defined by Hebrews 11:1: 'Now faith is being sure of what we hope for and certain of what we do not see.'
     b. Only on earth can we believe God without the empirical evidence.
        (1) No faith will be required in Heaven.
        (2) It is only possible here below.
  3. Recall our definition of faith: believing God.

B. Believing God is pleasing God.
  1. *Pleasing God (def.): making him happy, giving him pleasure; satisfying him.*
     a. The blood of Jesus satisfies divine justice.
     b. When we transfer our trust from our good works to what Jesus has done for us we may know that we have pleased God. This is called saving faith.
  2. *Achieving faith is pleasing God by believing him in difficult circumstances.*
     a. This is what we can do now which we cannot do in Heaven.
     b. There will be no difficult circumstances in Heaven. 'He will wipe every tear from their eyes. There will be no more death or mourning or crying or pain, for the old order of things has passed away' (Rev. 21:4).
     c. A reward which comes at the Judgement Seat of Christ will be the result of pleasing God by achieving faith.

(1) Saving faith assures us of Heaven but not necessarily a reward in Heaven. 'No, I beat my body and make it my slave so that after I have preached to others, I myself will not be disqualified for the prize' (1 Cor. 9:27).

(2) Achieving faith – pleasing God in difficult circumstances – is honoured at the Judgement Seat of Christ. 'For we must all appear before the judgment seat of Christ, that each one may receive what is due to him for the things done while in the body, whether good or bad' (2 Cor. 5:10).

C. Hebrews 11 contains two references to pleasing God by faith.
1. A person: Enoch. 'By faith Enoch was taken from this life, so that he did not experience death; he could not be found, because God had taken him away. For before he was taken, he was commended as one who pleased God' (Heb. 11:5).
2. A principle: diligent faith. 'And without faith it is impossible to please God, because anyone who comes to him must believe that he exists and that he rewards those who earnestly seek him' (Heb. 11:6).

D. Why is this lesson important?
1. *It elaborates the distinction between saving faith and achieving faith.*
    a. This is a distinction never to be underestimated.
    b. Many sincere Christians confuse the two and consequently think we can lose our salvation (or new birth) if we don't have achieving faith.
        (1) Saving faith *saves*: Heaven is assured.
        (2) Achieving faith *achieves*: not only a reward in Heaven but the witness here below that we please God.
2. *It shows how an individual can know that he or she pleases God.*
    a. We do not have to wait until we get to Heaven to learn that we please God.
    b. What Enoch did we too can do, without being taken to glory before everybody else.
3. *It shows that unbelief displeases God.*
    a. A Christian can temporarily give in to unbelief.

    b. When that happens we may be sure we do not please God; we displease him indeed.

  4. *We will have a deeper look at the kind of faith that pleases God – which is two-fold:*

    a. First, believing 'that he exists'.

    b. Second, that he 'rewards those who earnestly seek him.'

  5. *This lesson should stimulate us to please God more than ever.*

    a. This will come by a greater faith.

    b. This kind of faith is born in difficult circumstances in which we believe God *all the more* – and don't give up!

I. ENOCH

A. Certain facts about him:

  1. His father Jared outlived Enoch by 435 years.

  2. His son Methuselah became the oldest man in human history, living 969 years.

  3. He 'walked with God' for 300 years, something that seems to have started at age 65 (Gen. 5:22).

  4. He had other sons and daughters as well as Methuselah.

  5. At the age of 365 he disappeared from the earth. 'He was no more, for God took him away' (Gen. 5:24).

  6. During his lifetime he prophesied of the Second Coming of Christ (Jude 14).

  7. The writer of Hebrews says that Enoch achieved what he did 'by faith' (Heb. 11:5).

  8. He became a legendary figure in Israel; he is referred to in the Apocrypha (Wisdom of Solomon 4:10 and Ecclesiasticus 44:6), and Jude quotes from the Book of Enoch 1:9.

  9. He pleased God.

B. The key to all Enoch achieved was his faith.

  1. *If faith is believing God, what had God said to Enoch that he believed? Answer: that he would not die.*

    a. AV: 'By faith Enoch was translated that he should not see death.'

    b. NIV: 'By faith Enoch was taken from this life, so that he should not experience death.'

2. *In order for this verse to be true it follows that Enoch had been given a promise. . . which he believed.*

    a. He could not have merely said to himself, 'Today I am going to believe myself to be translated to Heaven without dying.' No.

    b. His faith was preceded by a word from God – that he would not die – which he actually believed!

      (1) There was no precedent for this.

      (2) What pleased God: Enoch believed God.

    c. God promised Enoch he would not die; otherwise this verse makes no sense.

      (1) Enoch was not translated in order to believe.

      (2) He believed this first – without any evidence save God's promise to him that he would not die.

C. Pleasing God.

1. *We are told that this was true before his translation.*

    a. 'Before he was taken, he was commended as one who pleased God.' (AV: 'Before his translation he had this testimony, that he pleased God.')

2. *Enoch knew that he pleased God.*

    a. The writer does not say that everybody else knew this; how could they?

    b. He had the testimony – witness – that he pleased God.

      (1) 'Anyone who believes in the Son of God has this testimony in his heart. Anyone who does not believe God has made him out to be a liar, because he has not believed the testimony God has given about his Son' (1 John 5:10).

      (2) This is the testimony (or witness) of the Spirit. 'We are witnesses of these things, and so is the Holy Spirit, whom God has given to those who obey him' (Acts 5:32).

3. *There is no greater witness on earth.*

    a. It does not say that Enoch pleased people.

    b. It does not say that Enoch pleased his friends.

    c. He pleased God – and knew it.

      (1) This meant more to him than anything.

      (2) This is how he got his joy – walking with God and knowing he pleased God.

D. Enoch was a product of what was almost certainly the first Great Awakening.

    1. The world's first Great Awakening is recorded in Genesis 4:26: 'At that time men began to call on the name of the LORD.'

    2. *Enoch was a product of this phenomenon.*

        a. This created an atmosphere that led to Enoch's walk with God; he had a thirst for God.

        b. We can only pray for an awakening in our own day that will cause a longing for more of God and will hopefully produce many Enochs.

    3. *Enoch was a testimony to people far better known at the time: Jabal, Jubal and Tubal-Cain* (Gen. 4:20-22).

        a. They were Cain's heirs and famous then.

            (1) Jabal might be called the father of the construction business.

            (2) Jubal might be called the father of music.

            (3) Tubal-Cain might be called the father of the hardware business.

        b. These were examples of 'common grace' of their day.

            (1) Common grace: 'special grace in nature' (Calvin).

            (2) It means giftedness but not necessarily salvation.

            (3) There is no evidence that these three men were believers.

    4. The man even better known then was also called Enoch, Cain's son; a city was named after him (Gen. 4:17).

    5. But the Enoch who pleased God is the one remembered for all time.

II. THE KIND OF FAITH THAT PLEASES GOD: DILIGENT FAITH

'And without faith it is impossible to please God, because anyone who comes to him must believe that he exists and that he rewards those who earnestly seek him' (Heb. 11:6).

A. Why is it impossible to please God without faith?

    1. *Faith is our response to God's Word.*

        a. Faith – believing God – presupposes that God has spoken.

        b. Believing God is believing his Word, what he has said.

        c. God's Word is his integrity put on the line.

        d. He wants us to believe in his integrity.

        e. We do this by faith.

(1) He has magnified his Word above all his name (Ps. 138:2 AV).

(2) Faith is trusting that Word.

2. *Faith is the work of God – the Holy Spirit.*

  a. We could not believe had not God enabled us to do so.

  b. We need the Spirit in order to believe God.

  c. God supplies the ability to believe.

    (1) This is why faith is a gift of God. 'For it is by grace you have been saved, through faith – and this not from yourselves, it is the gift of God' (Eph. 2:8).

    (2) We therefore can take no credit for believing.

3. *The flesh cannot believe, only miss the mark.*

  a. Flesh (def.): our fallen nature.

  b. This means we cannot do anything, even accidentally, that pleases God.

    (1) This is why people think they can be saved by good works.

    (2) By nature we all try to offer God the best of our hands – as Cain did.

B. The faith that pleases God is two-fold.

1. *Believing that he exists. AV: that he 'is'; that he is there.*

  a. The awareness that God 'is' may come to man as a shock, even though we know he is there (Rom. 1:21).

  b. Some theologians speak of the 'ontological shock' – why is there 'something' and not 'nothing'?

    (1) Ontology is the philosophy of being.

    (2) It is an ontological shock when I am aware that I *am*, that I have being.

  c. The greater shock is the *theological* shock – that God is, that he is Creator and that I have sinned against him.

  d. Believing that God is, however, is not enough.

    (1) After all, the devil believes that too. 'You believe that there is one God. Good! Even the demons believe that – and shudder' (Jas. 2:19).

    (2) Therefore believing that God exists only matches the devil's faith.

  e. And yet believing that he is there is still essential.

    (1) Sometimes a Christian can fall into unbelief.

     (2) Such a person must rise above this if he or she is to please God.

     (3) Believing that God exists is a beginning and a necessary one.

2. *That God rewards those who diligently seek him.*

   a. Note: 'and'.

     (1) It is essential but not enough to believe God is there.

     (2) There is more: 'And that he rewards those who earnestly seek him.'

   b. The concept of reward, sadly, puts some people off.

     (1) They want to believe they seek God without any concept of being rewarded for doing so.

     (2) This is nonsense; why else would we seek God if there would be no positive benefit – or reward, or whatever you may wish to call it?

   c. The idea of reward is a prominent New Testament teaching.

     (1) It is not something one earns prior to faith; we are not saved by works but by faith alone (Eph. 2:8-9).

     (2) It is what is promised to believers only:

       (a) 'Blessed are you when people insult you, persecute you and falsely say all kinds of evil against you because of me. Rejoice and be glad, because great is your reward in heaven, for in the same way they persecuted the prophets who were before you' (Matt. 5:11-12).

       (b) 'Anyone who receives a prophet because he is a prophet will receive a prophet's reward, and anyone who receives a righteous man because he is a righteous man will receive a righteous man's reward. And if anyone gives even a cup of cold water to one of these little ones because he is my disciple, I tell you the truth, he will certainly not lose his reward' (Matt. 10:41-42).

       (c) 'If what he has built survives, he will receive his reward' (1 Cor. 3:14).

       (d) 'No, I beat my body and make it my slave so that after I have preached to others, I myself will not be disqualified for the prize' (1 Cor. 9:27).

       (e) 'He regarded disgrace for the sake of Christ as of

greater value than the treasures of Egypt, because he was looking ahead to his reward' (Heb. 11:26).

f. The rewarding that is promised in Hebrews 11:6 however is not limited to what comes at the Judgement Seat of Christ.

(1) It certainly points to that.

(2) It mainly means God rewarding us in this life.

C. How God rewards:

1. *Help.*

a. When tempted (Heb. 2:18).

b. In time of need (Heb. 4:16).

2. *Hearing God's voice* (Heb. 3:7).

a. Being hard of hearing spiritually is a danger sign (Heb. 5:11).

b. When we can no longer hear God's voice we can no longer be renewed to repentance (Heb. 6:6).

3. *Entering God's rest* (Heb. 4:1-11).

a. This is the main thing God wants us to inherit, what the Epistle to the Hebrews is largely about.

b. It is called by other names.

(1) The oath (Heb. 6:9-20).

(2) Confidence being rewarded by the Lord stepping in (Heb. 10:34).

c. The context of Hebrews 11:6 is with particular reference to God revealing himself to discouraged Christians.

(1) 'So do not throw away your confidence; it will be richly rewarded. You need to persevere so that when you have done the will of God, you will receive what he has promised. For in just a very little while, "He who is coming will come and will not delay. But my righteous one will live by faith. And if he shrinks back, I will not be pleased with him"' (Heb. 10:35-38).

(2) This is what led to Hebrews 11 in the first place, with Hebrews 11:6 focussing on the real concern.

4. *Apart from Hebrews, we may add:*

a. A greater anointing. 'If you then, though you are evil, know how to give good gifts to your children, how much more will your Father in heaven give the Holy Spirit to those who ask him!' (Luke 11:13).

b. Anything that comes under the category of answered prayer.

D. Seeking God.
   1. *Seeking means time and effort.*
      a. We seek because we expect it to take time.
      b. We do not seek if we already know where what we are looking for is; we just go and get!
      c. Seeking implies a search that may or may not result in success.
   2. *But the Bible tells us such seeking is not in vain.*
      a. 'You will seek me and find me when you seek me with all your heart' (Jer. 29:13. Cf. Deut. 4:29).
      b. Jesus said, 'So I say to you: Ask and it will be given to you; seek and you will find; knock and the door will be opened to you. For everyone who asks receives; he who seeks finds; and to him who knocks, the door will be opened' (Luke 11:9-10).
      c. Hence Hebrews 11:6: God rewards those who earnestly seek him.

E. Diligent faith: earnestness in all circumstances. Not giving up:
   1. In prayer (Luke 18:1-8).
   2. In extreme suffering (Job 13:15).
   3. When challenged to compromise (Dan. 3:17-18; 6:10).
   4. When God hides his face (Ps. 13).
   5. When you stand alone (2 Tim. 4:16).
   6. When it is 'out of season' (2 Tim. 4:2).
   7. When almost in despair (2 Cor. 1:8-9).
   8. When people are judging you (1 Cor. 4:3).
   9. When friendship turns sour (Gal. 4:15-16).
   10. When under financial pressure (Phil. 4:12-19).

CONCLUSION

Pleasing God by faith will not be possible after we die and when we are in Heaven. We please God now when we still believe him although he may not answer our prayers, when we still seek him at the times when he is not showering us with blessing, and when we maintain a daily seeking of his face although we may not feel his presence.

12

FAITH AND THE UNPRECEDENTED

'By faith Noah, when warned about things not yet seen, in holy fear built an ark to save his family. By his faith he condemned the world and became heir of the righteousness that comes by faith' (Heb. 11:7).

INTRODUCTION

A. Unprecedented (def.): that for which there is no previous case as an example to be followed.
  1. *Most of us like the luxury of repeating what has been done before.*
    a. It is safe; it gives us a feeling of security.
    b. It is a comfort zone.
  2. *The apostle Paul was different from most of us.* 'It has always been my ambition to preach the gospel where Christ was not known, so that I would not be building on someone else's foundation' (Rom. 15:20).
    a. Some church leaders and ministers I know would prefer to go where there has been a start, and build on what preceded.
    b. Not Paul; he wanted the opposite.

B. There are at least two things each person described in Hebrews 11 had in common:
  1. They accomplished what they did by faith. . . believing God.
  2. *They were not allowed the luxury of repeating what had been done before.*
    a. Noah was not allowed to be translated as Enoch was.
    b. Abraham did not build an ark.
    c. Sarah gave birth to a child in her old age.
    d. Abraham was told to sacrifice their child.
    e. The list goes on and on; not a single person was allowed to do what had been done previously.
  3. *In a word: each had to move outside his or her comfort zone.*

    a. Comfort zone (def.): where we feel at home.

    b. Moving outside our comfort zone: taking risks.

        (1) Samuel had to do this (1 Sam. 16:1-7).

        (2) Joseph had to do this when he stayed with Mary, his pregnant fiancée (Matt. 1:18-25).

        (3) Ananias had to do this when he went to pray for Saul of Tarsus (Acts 9:11-19).

        (4) Peter had to do this by visiting a Gentile (Acts 10).

        (5) The early church had to do this by accepting Gentiles who had not been circumcised (Acts 15).

C. There is a sense in which Hebrews 11 is an unfinished chapter.

    1. We are challenged to do what they did. 'Therefore, since we are surrounded by such a great cloud of witnesses, let us throw off everything that hinders and the sin that so easily entangles, and let us run with perseverance the race marked out for us. Let us fix our eyes on Jesus, the author and perfecter of our faith, who for the joy set before him endured the cross, scorning its shame, and sat down at the right hand of the throne of God' (Heb. 12:1-2).

    2. *Question: what are you and I accomplishing by faith?*

        a. Are we comfortable and secure with the familiar?

        b. Have we moved outside our comfort zone?

D. Conversion is the first move outside our comfort zone.

    1. It is scary when a person initially comes to Christ in faith. 'Therefore, if anyone is *in* Christ, he is a new creation; the old has gone, the new has come!' (2 Cor. 5:17).

    2. This crossover from death to life is no small journey!

    3. Therefore all of us have – at least once – moved outside our comfort zone.

E. The question is: have we done it since?

F. Why is this lesson important?

    1. The purpose of theology is not merely to stimulate the mind, but to change lives.

    2. It is not enough to grasp what the people of Hebrews 11 did; it needs to happen to us too.

    3. *The 'new and different' is always a part of faith.*

    a. 'Now faith is being sure of what we hope for and certain of what we do not see' (Heb. 11:1).

    b. God provides fresh challenges to each of us in proportion to our walking in the light (1 John 1:7).

    c. Walking in the light partly means:

        (1) Moving outside our comfort zone.

        (2) Being granted fresh repentance (Cf. Heb. 6:6).

        (3) Being changed from glory to glory (2 Cor. 3:17ff).

4. *The glory of God is seldom manifested in a manner that keeps us in our comfort zone.*

    a. Illustration: our Prayer Covenant.

    b. The 'glory' is almost always moving us from where we are to where we've never been. 'In all the travels of the Israelites, whenever the cloud lifted from above the tabernacle, they would set out; but if the cloud did not lift, they did not set out – until the day it lifted. So the cloud of the LORD was over the tabernacle by day, and fire was in the cloud by night, in the sight of all the house of Israel during all their travels' (Ex. 40:36-38).

5. *We are challenged to fill out Hebrews 11 by doing in our day the equivalent of what they did in theirs.*

    a. Jesus said, 'Whoever can be trusted with very little can also be trusted with much, and whoever is dishonest with very little will also be dishonest with much' (Luke 16:10).

    b. If we are faithful to the light God entrusts to us, we will be the equivalent of those people described in Hebrews 11; and we will receive a reward in Heaven (2 Cor. 5:10).

G. A prime example of all the above: Noah.

I. NOAH: MOVING OUTSIDE HIS COMFORT ZONE

A. Note: there is nothing necessarily wrong with living in our comfort zone.

1. We thank God for valid traditions handed down to us.

2. What is outside our comfort zone today may become a comfort zone tomorrow.

3. But Noah bore the stigma (offence) of his own generation with such dignity that we must stand in awe of him.

B. The situation in Noah's day.

1. There were no architects who knew about arks.
2. *There were no weather forecasters who knew about rain.*
   a. But God said:
      (1) 'So make yourself an ark of cypress wood; make rooms in it and coat it with pitch inside and out. This is how you are to build it: The ark is to be 450 feet long, 75 feet wide and 45 feet high. Make a roof for it and finish the ark to within 18 inches of the top. Put a door in the side of the ark and make lower, middle and upper decks' (Gen. 6:14-16).
      (2) 'I am going to bring floodwaters on the earth to destroy all life under the heavens, every creature that has the breath of life in it. Everything on earth will perish' (Gen. 6:17).
   b. There was no precedent for a boat, or even rain since, prior to this, water came from below: 'But streams came up from the earth and watered the whole surface of the ground' (Gen. 2:6).
3. *It was a time of violence, unrestrained sexual activity and pleasure.* 'The LORD saw how great man's wickedness on the earth had become, and that every inclination of the thoughts of his heart was only evil all the time. The LORD was grieved that he had made man on the earth, and his heart was filled with pain' (Gen. 6:5-6).
   a. Jesus said, 'For in the days before the flood, people were eating and drinking, marrying and giving in marriage, up to the day Noah entered the ark' (Matt. 24:38).
   b. Morality alone made Noah unique in his day.

C. Noah seems to have started out as Enoch did.

1. We know that Enoch 'walked with God' (Gen. 5:24).
2. For all we know Noah grew up hearing about the legendary Enoch; he not only walked with God but was suddenly translated to Heaven so that he did not experience death (Heb. 11:5).
3. Noah may have surmised that if he too walked with God he also would be taken up to Heaven!
4. *But no; God had other plans for Noah.*

a. We may imitate godly people who have preceded us. 'Remember your leaders, who spoke the word of God to you. Consider the outcome of their way of life and imitate their faith' (Heb. 13:7).

b. It does not follow that we can do the exact same thing that they were called to do.

c. This is what makes faith scary; it leads us to do what those before us were not called to do.

    (1) Our critics will say: 'So and so would never have done this or that.'

    (2) But chances are their critics said the same thing to *them* as well!

D. Noah had to be faithful in what was 'least' before he could be faithful in the 'much', namely building the ark.

    1. *That which was 'least' for Noah: breaking out of his own father's mould.*

        a. Noah had a father who had high expectations of his son.

        b. His father Lamech said, 'He will comfort us in the labour and painful toil of our hands caused by the ground the LORD has cursed' (Gen. 5:29).

            (1) Lamech wasn't thinking of Noah but himself.

            (2) Noah grew up under pressures of what was expected of him.

        c. Many parents want to relive their own lives through their children in order to compensate for their own failures or unfulfilled dreams.

    2. *Building an ark wasn't exactly what Noah's father had in mind.*

        a. Obeying God in small things precedes obeying him in big things.

        b. Many times our first major test has to do with obeying the Lord rather than pleasing our parents (after we are grown up). Illustration: Luther.

II. NOAH: GIVEN GRACE TO BE DIFFERENT 'BUT NOAH FOUND FAVOUR IN THE EYES OF THE LORD' (GEN. 6:8).

A. This is the first time the word 'grace' is used in the Bible. 'But Noah found grace in the eyes of the LORD' (Gen 6:8 AV).

1. One would have to say grace was given to Abel, also to Enoch.

2. *But the writer of Genesis shows the contrast between Noah and what was prevalent in Noah's day.* 'Now the earth was corrupt in God's sight and was full of violence' (Gen. 6:11).

    a. Wickedness prevailed. 'So the LORD said, "I will wipe mankind, whom I have created, from the face of the earth – men and animals, and creatures that move along the ground, and birds of the air – for I am grieved that I have made them"' (Gen. 6:7).

    b. Then follows: 'But Noah'.

        (1) God was gracious to Noah.

        (2) Noah consequently was indebted to God.

B. Grace – unmerited favour which God bestowed – lay at the bottom of what made Noah different.

1. This grace produced a righteousness and desire to walk with God. 'Noah was a righteous man, blameless among the people of his time, and he walked with God' (Gen. 6:9).

2. *Noah did what he did because of God's grace.*

    a. That is always the only hope anybody has.

    b. Noah could therefore take no personal credit for what he did in his day.

        (1) He did what was unprecedented, yes; but God enabled him.

        (2) So with us; we must never be inflated with pride if we are called and enabled to move outside our comfort zone – it is by grace.

C. Hebrews 11:7 says Noah did what he did by faith; Genesis 6:8 says it is by grace.

1. *This is not a contradiction but an explanation of how any of us ever achieves something.*

    a. It is how we are saved. 'For it is by grace you have been saved, through faith – and this not from yourselves, it is the gift of God' (Eph. 2:8).

    b. It is how we achieve things for God.

        (1) Grace is the underlying cause.

        (2) Faith is what makes things happen; in that order!

2. *God's grace enabled Noah to believe him and want to walk with him.*

a. Noah stands out as unique in his day.

b. So will we – if we like Noah are faithful.

c. But we will always know that God's grace is at the bottom of it all.

III. NOAH: DOING THE UNPRECEDENTED

A. He was warned of 'things not yet seen'.

1. This coheres with Hebrews 11:1; that faith is being certain of what we 'do not see'.

2. *This calling separates him from his own generation and history as well.*

    a. He had no historical precedent to which he could point.

    b. This increased the stigma; how could he convince his contemporaries that he was on the right track?

      (1) There was no tradition of rain at all.

      (2) No ark had previously been built.

3. *We are told he was 'warned'.*

    a. But who would believe such a warning?

    b. Had Noah not found favour with God he too would have scoffed at a warning that all life was going to be destroyed by rain (Gen. 6:17).

    c. But Noah believed the warning; he believed God.

B. When we stand for something unprecedented we will always look foolish – or appear arrogant.

1. This could relate to any discovery or invention.

2. *At the spiritual level it could pertain to new insights in theology – not that they are truly new.*

    a. What Luther fought for was not really new; it was a rediscovery of what had been lost.

    b. But theological insight that has not been taught or preached for a while may seem strange.

C. Noah's faith produced a godly fear.

1. *He did what he did in 'holy fear'.*

    a. Gr. *eulabetheis* – moved in godly fear.

    b. Often when the word *phobos* (fear) is used it too means godly fear (Cf. Luke 5:26; Acts 2:43; 5:5).

    2. *Noah wasn't trying to be clever or unique.*
        a. He was running scared because he had a vision from the Most High God.
        b. He was authentically motivated; God had spoken, Noah knew this to his fingertips and was never the same again.
    3. *When you and I have a vision from the Lord like this it would seem impossible not to be catapulted from our comfort zone.*
        a. Those who stay in their comfort zones surely could not do so had they felt what Noah felt.
        b. On the other hand, some appear to choose not to believe in a warning from God.

D. The ark was built for all to see.
    1. This took courage.
    2. *Imagine this: building in front of your friends and everybody else what had never been thought of in order to prepare for rain that never before had come.*
        a. People may well have laughed and scoffed.
        b. And yet when a person is moving with holy reverence it is no laughing matter.
        c. What is missing today: the fear of God.

IV. NOAH'S SUCCESS: HE SAVED HIS FAMILY

A. Noah moving with fear did not save millions or even thousands.
    1. By today's standards Noah was hardly a great success.
    2. By comparison with Peter's success at Pentecost Noah was not much of a success (Cf. Acts 2:41).

B. He only saved his family.
    1. But this is surely a remarkable accomplishment.
    2. When anyone is led by faith to save their family it is a wonderful, productive faith indeed.
        a. Noah saved his family; when a person saves his or her household, it tells us a lot about that person.
        b. It tells us that those who were closest to him believed in him the most.
            (1) It is one thing to win thousands.
            (2) It is another to win the respect of one's wife and children.

C. How did Noah save his family?
1. By example. He walked with God.
2. By teaching them. He is called 'a preacher of righteousness' (2 Pet. 2:5).
3. He warned everybody of the approaching flood but succeeded only with his wife, his children and their wives – 'eight in all' (1 Pet. 3:20).

V. NOAH'S WITNESS; HE LEFT THE WORLD WITHOUT EXCUSE: 'By faith he condemned the world' (Heb.11:7).

A. The world was warned by Noah's preaching.
1. The ark was proof that Noah believed a flood was coming.
2. Had people believed Noah they could have built arks too.

B. Our responsibility at the end of the day is not to save the world but to be faithful.
1. When William C. Burns was leaving Scotland for China someone said, 'I suppose you are going to China to convert the Chinese.' His reply: 'I am going to China to glorify God.'
2. *'When the pure Gospel is preached to men as they are it will save some and condemn others, but it will accomplish God's purpose' (Henry Mahan).*
   a. 'For we are to God the aroma of Christ among those who are being saved and those who are perishing. To the one we are the smell of death; to the other, the fragrance of life. And who is equal to such a task?' (2 Cor. 2:15-16).
   b. This is why we witness to all we can.

CONCLUSION

In addition to saving his family, Noah received a reward – he became 'heir of the righteousness that comes by faith'. Achieving faith achieves two things: (1) accomplishments here below; (2) a reward – inheritance – at the judgment Seat of Christ (2 Cor. 5:10). Living by faith can be scary, but the results are gratifying. How would you like to be in Noah's shoes at the Judgement Seat of Christ? Yet we can all be like Noah by being faithful to God in our day as Noah was in his.

13

FAITH AND MOTIVATION

'By faith Abraham, when called to go to a place he would later receive as his inheritance, obeyed and went, even though he did not know where he was going. By faith he made his home in the promised land like a stranger in a foreign country; he lived in tents, as did Isaac and Jacob, who were heirs with him of the same promise. For he was looking forward to the city with foundations, whose architect and builder is God' (Heb. 11:8-10).

INTRODUCTION

A. It is sometimes said, 'Some people are so heavenly minded that they are no earthly use.'
  1. *The idea is sometimes advanced that:*
      a. People who pray a lot never get things done.
      b. People who have visions never live in the present.
      c. People who think about Heaven care little about what is going on here.
  2. *No doubt this has been true with some people.*
      a. I knew of a lady who always felt led to pray when it was time to do the washing up.
      b. Some people daydream and are lazy.
  3. *This, however, was not the case with Abraham.*
      a. He is one of the most important figures of the Old Testament.
      b. He became known as the father of all who believe (Rom. 4:11).
      c. Few people, if any, have made a greater impact on this earth than Abraham.
          (1) But he did it because he was looking forward to Heaven.
          (2) That produced a very powerful motivation.

B. Motivation (def.): an inward inspiration and incentive to do things; the power to get things done.
  1. Some would say that is what wisdom is: the ability to get things done.

2. Wisdom is also discernment and no doubt carries with it the incentive to get things done.

3. *Believing God – which is what faith is – produces the motivation needed to make a lively impact here below.*

    a. It issues in the wisdom necessary to do what God wants us to do.

    b. By believing God we find our individual calling; as a consequence we will be motivated to fulfil that calling.

C. Abraham is the first great patriarch of the Old Testament.

1. He is second only to Moses in stature.

2. *He occupies nearly one-third of the eleventh chapter of the epistle to the Hebrews.*

    a. He is mentioned no fewer than 74 times in the New Testament.

    b. He is Paul's chief example of justification by faith (how we are declared righteous before God); James's chief example of justification by works (how faith is vindicated before men).

    c. He is called God's friend (Is. 41:8; Jas. 2:23).

    d. The Jews regarded him as their father at the level of nature (John 8:33).

    e. Paul claimed Abraham is our father at the level of the Spirit (Gal. 3:7,29).

3. He did what he did because he was 'looking forward to the city with foundations, whose architect and builder is God' (Heb. 11:10).

D. Why is this lesson important?

1. *Most of us need help in being motivated.*

    a. We would like to 'get things done'.

    b. We would like to accomplish more than we do.

2. *We are put here for a purpose; how many find any purpose and meaning to life?*

    a. Abraham was Paul's main example for his teaching of justification by faith.

    b. He can be our example regarding being properly motivated.

3. *This lesson will show that motivation is within the reach of all of us.*

    a. Some are naturally gifted with motivation.

    b. But all of us can be like Abraham – who did what he did 'by faith' – believing God.

4. Abraham shows that we accomplish more on earth to the degree we have our eyes on Heaven.

5. It is a reminder: we are all going to Heaven!

I. Obedience without knowing full directions at first.

A. It began with Abraham's being 'called'.

1. God called him. 'The Lord had said to Abram, "Leave your country, your people and your father's household and go to the land I will show you"' (Gen. 12:1).

2. God led him one step at a time; he did not know 'where he was going' (Heb. 11:8).

B. God however promised an unexpected motivation. 'I will make you into a great nation and I will bless you; I will make your name great, and you will be a blessing. I will bless those who bless you, and whoever curses you I will curse; and all peoples on earth will be blessed through you' (Gen. 12:2-3).

1. *The motivation was seven-fold:*

a. He would become a great nation.

b. He would be blessed.

c. He would have a great name – that is, be famous.

d. He would be a blessing.

e. Those who blessed him would be blessed.

f. Those who cursed him would be cursed.

g. Through him all people on earth would be blessed.

2. *Does it surprise us that God would motivate us like that?*

a. He appeals to our self-interest.

b. He appeals to our sense of satisfaction.

c. He appeals to our need for protection.

3. *God motivates us by appealing to our self-interest:*

a. 'Do not judge, and you will not be judged. Do not condemn, and you will not be condemned. Forgive, and you will be forgiven. Give, and it will be given to you. A good measure, pressed down, shaken together and running over, will be poured into your lap. For with the measure you use, it will be measured to you' (Luke 6:37-38).

b. 'Remember this: Whoever sows sparingly will also reap sparingly, and whoever sows generously will also reap generously' (2 Cor. 9:6).

    c. 'Let us not become weary in doing good, for at the proper time we will reap a harvest if we do not give up' (Gal. 6:9).

4. *All that is required: to believe this; believing God.*

    a. God does not despise our being great – as long as he is the architect of it.

    b. If we are intent on making ourselves great, we will be fighting against God.

5. Abraham obeyed and went!

C. God promised to make Abraham's name great, but not before he was ready.

1. 'The worst thing that can happen to a man is to succeed before he is ready.' Dr Martyn Lloyd-Jones.

2. *Abraham had much to go through before he was ready.*

    a. He was a 'nobody' when God called him.

    b. God loves to take people from nothing and make them something.

    c. Only requirement: we obey.

      (1) But Abraham had to believe God.

      (2) Faith produces obedience.

3. *Abraham had to leave his own country.*

    a. The first step of a believer: cutting loose from the familiar – our comfort zone.

    b. Abraham went out!

      (1) He had to leave home. 'Leave your country' (Gen. 12:1).

      (2) He had to leave family. 'Your father's household' (Gen. 12:1).

    c. He had no way of proving to another person that he had got it right. This is part of the stigma.

II. At home in a foreign country: 'By faith he made his home in the promised land like a stranger in a foreign country; he lived in tents, as did Isaac and Jacob, who were heirs with him of the same promise' (Heb. 11:9).

A. Abraham was a man of great suffering.

1. Many of us may claim to want Abraham's faith; how many of us are willing to accept the suffering that seemed to go with it?

2. *Abraham's faith was not immediately met with great reward.*

    a. His faith led to a need for yet more faith.

    b. Not only did he not know where he was going when he started out, but also there was no great fanfare when he arrived at the place God intended.

      (1) Hebrews calls it 'the promised land'.

      (2) But there was no welcoming committee waiting for Abraham.

    c. This might have diminished his motivation.

B. By faith he was at home in a strange country.

    1. *'Home' is a good word for 'comfort zone'.*

      a. Most of us can look back to former days – childhood, old surroundings – with some nostalgia.

      b. When things remind us of 'home' it is probably because of a feeling of security.

    2. *But what could remind Abraham of home in this strange land?*

      a. He had left his old surroundings.

      b. Canaan may have been the Promised Land, but there was not a lot there to make Abraham feel 'at home'.

    3. *But he made himself at home – by faith.*

      a. What is our land of promise? It may be elsewhere or where we are right now.

      b. If God keeps you where you are, it may well be that the very absence of what appears promising is God's opportunity to show his power.

C. God motivated Abraham by his word: 'He took him outside and said, "Look up at the heavens and count the stars – if indeed you can count them." Then he said to him, "So shall your offspring be"' (Gen. 15:5).

    1. *Abraham might have argued with God.*

      a. He was childless and Sarah was advancing in years.

      b. Many of us argue with God when he comes with an extraordinary word.

    2. *But Abraham didn't argue; he believed.* 'Abram believed the LORD, and he credited it to him as righteousness' (Gen. 15:6).

      a. It was this kind of faith that motivated him to carry on in a strange land.

      b. His faith pleased God; knowing this motivated Abraham to trust more than ever.

(1) Note: God has a way of encouraging us with a timely word when we need it.

(2) A renewal of the old promise is like hearing the preaching of the Gospel; it confirms our faith.

D. Although Abraham was at home he never fully 'settled in'; he was like a stranger in a foreign country.

1. He was always a stranger there; not because of where he came from but because of where he was going.

2. *This is what lay at the bottom of Abraham's faith and motivation.*

   a. The irony, if not the secret, of life is this: when we see the changing nature of life, we make the greatest contribution to the world.

   b. When we are most detached from the world, we can make the most contribution to it.

3. *Abraham lived in tents.*

   a. What a way to live – not exactly staying in five-star hotels.

   b. But because he was detached from earthly things God made him wealthy.

   (1) But that meant little to him.

   (2) His eyes were focussed beyond this life.

III. MOTIVATED BELOW BECAUSE OF WHAT WAS BEYOND: 'For he was looking forward to the city with foundations, whose architect and builder is God' (Heb. 11:10).

A. In a word: Abraham was on his way to Heaven – and knew it.

1. *As Abraham's hope of Heaven was his underlying motivation, so is the genius of Christianity precisely this: hope of Heaven.*

   a. As Christians we never forget: we are going to Heaven.

   b. If we lose this motivation, it follows:

   (1) We cease to uphold authentic Christianity.

   (2) We make Christianity into something it was never meant to be.

2. *The genius of Christianity is the message of Heaven – and Hell.*

   a. Many today confuse 'cause' and 'effects'. For example:

   (1) A change of life is the effect; the hope of Heaven is the cause.

   (2) A rise of living standards (at home or abroad) is frequently the effect of being converted; the cause was trusting Christ who died to save us from God's wrath (Rom. 5:9).

b. The purpose of the gospel is not to raise living standards; it is to make us fit for Heaven.

(1) The 'effects' follow: happiness; marriages put back together; decrease in crime.

(2) The 'cause' was the purpose of the Gospel, namely, to fit us for Heaven.

3. *So much of contemporary Christianity centres on 'what it does for me'. I fear it is a part of the 'me' generation.*

a. Nothing is more self-defeating for the Christian faith than primarily seeking to achieve certain effects in men and women.

b. It is seeking the fruit without the root.

(1) A hundred years ago returning missionaries spoke of glorious conversions.

(2) Today they often speak of glorious hospitals, high-crop agricultural improvements, overcoming cultural barriers.

c. Some say, 'If there were no Heaven or Hell I'd still be a Christian.'

(1) Not Paul. 'If only for this life we have hope in Christ, we are to be pitied more than all men' (1 Cor. 15:19).

(2) Hebrews 11 forces us to see what produces real faith and motivation: the hope of Heaven.

B. Abraham therefore did not mind living in tents.

1. *With all his wealth he could have lived in luxury.*

a. He could have purchased real estate from the Canaanites.

b. He could have made a palace for himself.

(1) His wealth was incidental to him.

(2) He was looking for a city – beyond this life.

2. *Abraham passed this lifestyle down to his son and grandson.* 'He lived in tents, as did Isaac and Jacob, who were heirs with him of the same promise' (Heb. 11:9).

a. Abraham may have wished that his sons could have seen the countryside of Ur – and be brought up in the kind of atmosphere he enjoyed as a child.

b. All of us who are parents probably wish we could do more for our children than we are able to do.

(1) Do you ever say: 'What a pity that I must pass on to my children this way of life'?

(2) Abraham passed on to Isaac a lifestyle of living in tents.

(2) What do you suppose Isaac did with it? He passed this way of life on to Jacob.

   c. Note: if we pass on to our children the promise of eternal life, we give them the greatest inheritance of all.

C. Abraham, Isaac and Jacob were different but had in common being heirs of the same promise.

1. Isaac was different from Abraham; Jacob was no Isaac.
2. *But they were heirs of the same promise.*
   a. One of the great things about the promise is that we are not required to be what we are not.
   b. We don't have to pretend.
      (1) Some of us have lesser abilities.
      (2) The Christian faith is unique also in that it alone lets people become what they are.

D. What kept these patriarchs going? They were looking forward to a city.

1. Consider how magnanimous and gracious Abraham was with Lot. See Genesis 13: 8-9. Why? Abraham was looking forward to a city.
2. Why did Abraham refuse to take anything from the king of Sodom? See Genesis 14:22-24. He was looking forward to a city.
3. What kept him motivated even though he did not understand all he perceived to be from the Lord? He was looking forward to a city.
4. *Christianity only turns the world upside down when it has that city in view.*
   a. When did Abraham look forward to that city? All the time.
   b. Where did Abraham expect to find that city? Not in Canaan.
      (1) He could have erected his own city. He had the money and 318 slaves (Gen. 14:14).
      (2) He had a different kind of city in mind; a city which had foundations (unlike tents).
      (3) Only God could build such a city; Abraham knew he could not be the architect or builder of such an enterprise.

CONCLUSION

John the apostle got a close look at the heavenly city: 'I saw the Holy City, the new Jerusalem, coming down out of heaven from God, prepared as a bride beautifully dressed for her husband' (Rev. 21:2). What a city! But Abraham seems to have seen it first. He saw it from a distance; one glimpse kept him going. Abraham knew it was worth waiting for. Because of that city he did more on earth than anybody of his day or before him.

14

FAITH AND TRIAL

INTRODUCTION

A. According to Peter the 'trial of your faith' is more precious than gold: 'That the trial of your faith, being much more precious than of gold that perisheth, though it be tried with fire, might be found unto praise and honour and glory at the appearing of Jesus Christ' (1 Pet. 1:7 AV).

1. We can understand that our faith is more precious than gold.

2. But do we regard the trial of that faith as precious too?

B. Nobody particularly likes trials.

1. *Paul was concerned that we would not be 'unsettled' by trials, especially since we are destined for them.*

    a. This means that trials are predestined.

    b. Paul said, 'For it has been granted to you on behalf of Christ not only to believe on him, but also to suffer for him' (Phil. 1:29).

2. *Trials are essential to our growth.*

    a. We grow in proportion to the measure of the Spirit in us, yes.

    b. But the measure of the Spirit in us is partly determined by the way we respond to trials.

C. Trial (def.): a time of severe testing allowed by God.

1. *There is more than one meaning in the Greek, however.*

    a. *Peirasmos* can either mean trial or temptation.

    b. The context determines which is meant.

        (1) 'Trial' is probably meant in James 1:2: 'Consider it pure joy, my brothers, whenever you face trials of many kinds.'

        (2) 'Temptation' is certainly meant in James 1:13-15: 'When tempted, no one should say, "God is tempting me." For God cannot be tempted by evil, nor does he tempt anyone; but each one is tempted when, by his own evil desire, he is dragged away and enticed. Then, after desire has conceived, it gives birth to sin; and sin, when it is full-grown, gives birth to death.'

(3) Either word could be used in 1 Corinthians 10:13: 'No temptation has seized you except what is common to man. And God is faithful; he will not let you be tempted beyond what you can bear. But when you are tempted, he will also provide a way out so that you can stand up under it.'

2. *How we respond to trial determines whether we grow and thereby receive a greater measure of the Spirit.*

a. We can dignify the trial, which pleases God; this means:
  (1) Not complaining while it lasts.
  (2) Not trying to hasten its conclusion by manipulation.
  (3) Learning all we can from it.

b. We can show contempt for the trial by:
  (1) Murmuring during the whole time of the trial.
  (2) Not seeing it as from God and trying to hasten its end.
  (3) Making no attempt to learn.

c. Note: all trials have a built-in time scale and eventually end.
  (1) While it is going on we may think it will never end.
  (2) But God knows how much we can bear and will ensure that it comes to an end.
  (3) When it is over, it is over; the question follows: Did we dignify it or show contempt for it?
  (4) We may not have another trial quite like the one that passed; we should therefore take every trial from God with both hands – we will be glad we did.
  (5) If we fail, rather than pass, God may send another to see if we really want to grow in grace.

d. One trial which may not end – a thorn in the flesh: 'To keep me from becoming conceited because of these surpassingly great revelations, there was given me a thorn in my flesh, a messenger of Satan, to torment me' (2 Cor. 12:7).
  (1) This may be permanent, or at least much longer than an ordinary trial. 'Three times I pleaded with the Lord to take it away from me' (2 Cor. 12:8).
  (2) It too is for our good. 'But he said to me, "My grace is sufficient for you, for my power is made perfect in

weakness." Therefore I will boast all the more gladly about my weaknesses, so that Christ's power may rest on me' (2 Cor. 12:9).

D. No person in history (other than Jesus) has been tried more than Abraham.
   1. He is the father of all who have faith (Rom. 4:12).
   2. This applies primarily to justification by faith, but Abraham's life as a whole is also one to be imitated and admired.

E. Why is this lesson important?
   1. Trials in this life are inevitable. 'I have told you these things, so that in me you may have peace. In this world you will have trouble. But take heart! I have overcome the world' (John 16:33).
   2. Trials come from God.
   3. They help us to grow – both in knowledge of God's ways and also in receiving more of the Spirit. 'I ask you, therefore, not to be discouraged because of my sufferings for you, which are your glory' (Eph. 3:13).
   4. This lesson should teach us not to complain when God brings us to a time of trial, but to accept it with grace and dignity.
   5. We will increase in faith to the degree we learn to dignify every trial, whether great or small.

I. GROWING OLDER AND SEEING LITTLE HAPPEN: 'By faith Abraham, even though he was past age – and Sarah herself was barren – was enabled to become a father because he considered him faithful who had made the promise. And so from this one man, and he as good as dead, came descendants as numerous as the stars in the sky and as countless as the sand on the seashore' (Heb. 11:11-12).

A. Abraham had been told that his seed would be as numerous as the stars in the heavens (Gen. 15:5) and the dust of the earth (Gen. 13:16).
   1. He believed that – and was declared righteous (Gen. 15:6).
   2. *But there was no evidence for this.* 'Now faith is being sure of what we hope for and certain of what we do not see' (Heb. 11:1).
      a. Abraham was 'past age' – getting old.
      b. His wife Sarah was barren.

B. Both Abraham and Sarah apparently began to think that they had misunderstood God's promise, or perhaps miscalculated it.

   1. Abraham began to surmise that his offspring must come through his servant Eliezer (Gen. 15:2).

   2. *Sarah had another idea; her solution was to nudge the arm of God's providence and made her servant Hagar the way for Abraham to become a father* (Gen. 16:2).

   a. Was this faith? Surely not.

   b. Manipulating prophecy and providence shows:

   (1) A bit of faith in God's word generally.

   (2) Unbelief that God will keep his promise particularly.

   3. *Sarah's solution brought grief both to herself and Abraham.*

   a. Ishmael was born (Gen. 16:15).

   b. Abraham eventually had to give him up (Gen. 21:14).

C. For thirteen years Abraham sincerely thought that Ishmael was the promised child.

   1. To this day, when we elbow in on what God wants to do in his own way and time, we tend to justify our efforts.

   2. *But unexpectedly God told Abraham that Sarah would conceive.* 'God also said to Abraham, "As for Sarai your wife, you are no longer to call her Sarai; her name will be Sarah. I will bless her and will surely give you a son by her. I will bless her so that she will be the mother of nations; kings of peoples will come from her"' (Gen. 17:15-16).

   a. Abraham's reaction: he laughed (Gen. 17:17).

   b. Sarah had the same reaction when she was told (Gen. 18:12).

   3. *But eventually both of them believed. They 'considered him faithful who had made the promise'.*

   a. Isaac was born, his name means 'laughter' (Gen. 21:3).

   b. Shakespeare: 'He who laughs last laughs best.' 'Sarah said, "God has brought me laughter, and everyone who hears about this will laugh with me"' (Gen. 21:6).

II. BEING TRIED TO THE HILT: 'By faith Abraham, when God tested him, offered Isaac as a sacrifice. He who had received the promises was about to sacrifice his one and only son, even though God had said to him, "It is through Isaac that your offspring will be reckoned"' (Heb. 11:17-18).

A. Some people suffer more than others, some are tested more than others.

1. *Why? I can only conclude that the matter of suffering is a sovereign invitation to receive two things:*

    a. A greater anointing here below.

        (1) The greater the suffering, the greater the anointing.

        (2) It is probably also true: the greater the anointing, the greater the suffering.

    b. A greater Reward in Heaven.

        (1) Not all Christians necessarily receive a Reward in Heaven; some (who knows what percentage?) will be saved by fire (1 Cor. 3:15).

        (2) It seems that a Reward is based somewhat on going beyond the call of duty. For example, Paul said, 'What then is my reward? Just this: that in preaching the gospel I may offer it free of charge, and so not make use of my rights in preaching it' (1 Cor. 9:18).

2. *I know some who seem to suffer all the time. I have observed two reactions:*

    a. Some never seem to grow but always complain.

    b. Some take it as God's will – and dignify the trial.

    c. 'I have served the Lord for so long now that I find it almost impossible to tell the difference between a blessing and a trial.' Anonymous.

3. *Abraham suffered to the hilt.*

    a. This does not appear to include physical or financial suffering – but spiritual and emotional.

        (1) The emotional aspect was concerning his own flesh and blood – Isaac – in being called to sacrifice him.

        (2) The spiritual aspect was concerning Isaac as the child of promise.

        (3) Which was harder for Abraham is not possible for us to know.

    b. The essence of Abraham's suffering consisted in the trial of his faith.

        (1) The irony is, faith is what Abraham is best known for.

        (2) And yet his faith was tried to the hilt.

B. The height of Abraham's spiritual suffering was with reference to God's request to sacrifice his son Isaac. 'Then God said, "Take your son, your only son, Isaac, whom you love, and go to the region of Moriah. Sacrifice him there as a burnt offering on one of the mountains I will tell you about"' (Gen. 22:2).

1. *This made no sense at all.*

    a. God required that Abraham let Ishmael go.

    b. God had said that his seed would issue through Isaac.

        (1) 'Then God said, "Yes, but your wife Sarah will bear you a son, and you will call him Isaac. I will establish my covenant with him as an everlasting covenant for his descendants after him' (Gen. 17:19).

        (2) 'But my covenant I will establish with Isaac, whom Sarah will bear to you by this time next year' (Gen. 17:21).

    c. And now Abraham is told to sacrifice the only link between himself and God's own promise.

2. *Abraham was 'tested'* (Gen. 22:1).

    a. The AV says God tempted Abraham, which is sadly misleading (Cf. Jas. 1:13ff).

    b. And yet what is the difference between being tested and being tempted?

        (1) Testing is what God does directly; he causes the test.

        (2) Tempting is what God allows and uses in our lives; he allows us to be tempted.

        (3) In either case, 1 Corinthians 10:13 is true: 'No temptation has seized you except what is common to man. And God is faithful; he will not let you be tempted beyond what you can bear. But when you are tempted, he will also provide a way out so that you can stand up under it.'

        (4) God allowed Joseph to be tempted (Gen. 39), and yet this too must be seen as a test; Joseph passed with flying colours.

        (5) God allowed the devil to test Job – with God initiating the entire matter (Job 1:8-12).

C. What can we learn from this ordeal Abraham was put through?

1. *What God asks of us often makes no sense at the time.*

    a. Had it made complete sense, no faith would have been needed.

    b. God tests us to see whether we will believe him alone.

2. *Faith is never brought to maturity without suffering.*

    a. James uses this same incident as an illustration of justification by works. 'You see that his faith and his actions were working together, and his faith was made complete by what he did' (Jas. 2:22).

    b. Even Jesus needed to be made perfect through suffering (Heb. 5:8-9).

    c. We must go through many hardships to enter the kingdom of God (Acts 14:22).

3. *We must obey the Holy Spirit without knowing all of the details or implications of his will.*

    a. Abraham was only told to go to 'one of the mountains I *will tell you about*'.

    b. He was not allowed to strike a bargain with God or ask: 'Tell me what this is leading to first.'

        (1) We all would like to know the details of what is in the package in advance.

        (2) True faith is in a willingness not to know the end from the beginning – as God does.

        (3) 'Whoever can be trusted with very little can also be trusted with much, and whoever is dishonest with very little will also be dishonest with much' (Luke 16:10).

        (4) Sometimes God gives us a general idea what he is doing but keeps the details in reserve in order to test our obedience one moment at a time.

4. *We may not be permitted to let anyone else know what God is doing with us.*

    a. 'He said to his servants, "Stay here with the donkey while I and the boy go over there. We will worship and then we will come back to you"' (Gen. 22:5).

    b. It is often a severe temptation to share at least with one other person what God is doing in our lives.

        (1) Sometimes this is perfectly legitimate.

        (2) Sometimes however we must keep quiet.

    c. Abraham told neither his servants nor Isaac what he was doing.

    d. This principle is seen in Psalm 25:14: 'The LORD confides in those who fear him; he makes his covenant known to them.'

5. *The worst suffering may still be in the future.*

    a. We all love the expression, 'The best is yet to come'.

    b. In the kind of trial Abraham went through the worst was yet to come: 'Isaac spoke up and said to his father Abraham, "Father?" "Yes, my son?" Abraham replied. "The fire and wood are here," Isaac said, "but where is the lamb for the burnt offering?"' (Gen. 22:7).

        (1) How could Abraham cope at this moment?

        (2) But God gives the necessary strength – or words – as needed. 'Abraham answered, "God himself will provide the lamb for the burnt offering, my son." And the two of them went on together' (Gen. 22:8).

    c. Jesus was tested to the hilt right to the end of his life.

D. Abraham was utterly committed to this act of obedience.

    1. As far as Abraham was concerned, Isaac was 'as good as dead' (Heb. 11:12).

        a. Abraham was committed to carrying through outwardly what he had committed himself to inwardly.

        b. In his heart Abraham had said, 'Good-bye' to Isaac.

        c. But he still had to do it! 'When they reached the place God had told him about, Abraham built an altar there and arranged the wood on it. He bound his son Isaac and laid him on the altar, on top of the wood. Then he reached out his hand and took the knife to slay his son' (Gen. 22:9-10).

    2. *When Abraham reached out his hand to slay Isaac, there was not the remotest thought that God would stop him.*

        a. He simply thought God would raise Isaac from the dead (Heb. 11:19).

        b. God had a different idea. 'But the angel of the LORD called out to him from heaven, "Abraham! Abraham!" "Here I am," he replied. "Do not lay a hand on the boy," he said. "Do not do anything to him. Now I know that you fear God, because you have not withheld from me your son, your only son"' (Gen. 22:11-12).

III. WHEN THE TRIAL IS OVER: 'Abraham reasoned that God could raise the dead, and figuratively speaking, he did receive Isaac back from death' (Heb. 11:19).

A. Full and total obedience are worth all the effort.

1. God loves to reward obedience.
2. He rewarded Abraham with the oath – the greatest spiritual reward this side of Heaven:

'The angel of the LORD called to Abraham from heaven a second time and said, "I swear by myself, declares the LORD, that because you have done this and have not withheld your son, your only son, I will surely bless you and make your descendants as numerous as the stars in the sky and as the sand on the seashore. Your descendants will take possession of the cities of their enemies, and through your offspring all nations on earth will be blessed, because you have obeyed me"' (Gen. 22:15-18).

3. *This is why James said, 'Perseverance must finish its work so that you may be mature and complete, not lacking anything'* (Jas. 1:4).
   a. Every trial has its built-in purpose and time scale.
   b. The end is worth waiting for.

B. The purpose of God's trials in our lives is to:

1. Make us stronger than ever.
2. Increase our faith and anointing.
3. Make God more real to us.
4. Make us more godly.
5. *Teach us more about God.*
   a. We might wish we could come to these things without trial.
   b. God's way of perfecting us is – sooner or later – by testing our faith.

C. What did Abraham learn?

1. *He needed a lesson in how to make the transition from the level of nature to the level of the Spirit.*
   a. That was part of the purpose of the ordeal in having to sacrifice Isaac.
   b. When God said, 'Through Isaac your offspring will be reckoned' (Gen. 21:12), far more was meant than Abraham could have known at that time.
   (1) Without further enlightenment Abraham might have

assumed that meant that all of Isaac's posterity were the people of God.

(2) He could have assumed it merely meant Isaac's seed rather than Ishmael's.

c. Abraham needed to be taught *how* the offspring of Isaac would be incorporated into the family of God.

(1) He would have assumed this was continued by procreation.

(2) He was to learn that the seed of Isaac would be *spiritual* – those called by the Holy Spirit.

d. That is what Hebrews 11:19 means by Abraham getting Isaac back 'figuratively speaking'.

(1) This meant that God would be responsible for the continuing people of God.

(2) The continuity of Isaac's seed would be at the spiritual level – regeneration not procreation.

2. *That all the promises he had received were now replaced by God's oath – which meant that the promise of the seed like the sand of the seashore was as good as done.*

a. The oath 'puts an end to all argument' (Heb. 6:16).

(1) Until the oath is taken, we aren't totally sure that the promise is infallible.

(2) The oath removes all doubt.

b. So real was God to Abraham by the swearing of the oath that he knew without any doubt it would happen.

(1) The promise was believable – and Abraham believed God.

(2) The oath was greater; Abraham would never need the reassurance of that promise again.

CONCLUSION

The promise of the oath of God is what Hebrews offers to discouraged Christians: 'So do not throw away your confidence; it will be richly rewarded' (Heb. 10:35). It would be worth waiting for. In the meantime God would hide his face – perhaps the main ingredient in Hebrews 12:6: 'Because the Lord disciplines those he loves, and he punishes everyone he accepts as a son.' But the greater the suffering, the greater the anointing. The greater the suffering, the greater the reward.

15

FAITH AND UNWORTHINESS

INTRODUCTION

A. All of us are unworthy.
  1. *There is not a single person who is worthy of God's grace.*
    a. We should endeavour to live lives 'worthy of God' (1 Thess. 2:12).
    b. But none of us is worthy.
      (1) John the apostle 'wept and wept' because no one was found worthy to open the scroll.
      (2) A mighty angel had proclaimed, 'Who is worthy to break the seals and open the scroll?' (Rev. 5:2).
    c. Only Jesus Christ is worthy.

'Then one of the elders said to me, "Do not weep! See, the Lion of the tribe of Judah, the Root of David, has triumphed. He is able to open the scroll and its seven seals"' (Rev. 5:5).

  2. *One of the more difficult passages in the New Testament is with reference to the Lord's Supper:*
    a. 'Therefore, whoever eats the bread or drinks the cup of the Lord in an unworthy manner will be guilty of sinning against the body and blood of the Lord' (1 Cor. 11:27).
      (1) This passage has bewildered not a few Christians.
      (2) Some people will not partake of Holy Communion because of the fear of damnation over unworthiness.
    b. The irony is: the feeling of unworthiness is an essential ingredient in being worthy.
      (1) If you feel worthy because you have made the grade, you are probably unworthy.
      (2) Worthiness consists in your need to be covered by the blood of Christ.
  3. *Unworthiness is part of the qualification for becoming a Christian.*
    a. Christ came into the world to save sinners. 'Here is a

165

trustworthy saying that deserves full acceptance: Christ Jesus came into the world to save sinners – of whom I am the worst' (1 Tim. 1:15).

   b. 'It is not the healthy who need a doctor,' said Jesus, 'but the sick. . . For I have not come to call the righteous, but sinners' (Matt. 9:12-13).

    (1) God 'justifies the wicked' (Rom. 4:5).

    (2) 'But God demonstrates his own love for us in this: While we were still sinners, Christ died for us' (Rom. 5:8).

    (3) Where then is boasting? 'It is excluded' (Rom. 3:27).

B. No person in human history demonstrates unworthiness like Jacob.

   1. *Jacob was so unworthy that the writer to the Hebrews probably had a hard time finding a single event in his life that extolled the virtues of faith.*

    a. No person in the Old Testament is referred to more often in the Bible.

    b. Only one verse in Hebrews 11 refers to Jacob's faith, and that was at the end of his life. 'By faith Jacob, when he was dying, blessed each of Joseph's sons, and worshipped as he leaned on the top of his staff' (Heb. 11:21).

   2. *One of the most lack-lustre persons in all Holy Writ was Isaac.*

    a. Looking for faith in Isaac isn't an easy thing to do.

    b. Yet the writer came up with one incident: 'By faith Isaac blessed Jacob and Esau in regard to their future' (Heb. 11:20).

C. Why is this lesson important?

   1. *Abraham is regarded as the father of the faithful, but his son and grandson did not prove to be mighty men of faith like himself.*

    a. Must our heroes always be like Abraham?

    b. Isn't it encouraging that unworthy men – like Isaac and Jacob – can be included in the great Faith Chapter of the Bible – Hebrews 11?

   2. This shows that we don't have to be perfect to be men and women of faith – achieving faith.

   3. Because all of us are unworthy – and know it – it is thrilling to see unworthiness made clear before our eyes and to know here were God's chosen!

4. Jacob was arguably the worst in the Bible for doubting and self-pity yet he finished a tempestuous life with the famous words, 'All's well that ends well.'

5. Both Isaac and Jacob would blush to think that what they did – and graced with the title 'faith' – earned them a place with the great people of God in the Old Testament. Surely nothing is more encouraging than that!

I. THE FAITH OF ISAAC

A. As an historical individual.

1. He repeated his father's sin by telling his wife Rebekah to lie to Abimelech by saying that she was his sister (Gen. 26:7ff; cf. Gen. 20:2).

2. *He repeated his father's financial success* (Gen. 26:12ff).

    a. This, however, was only a continuation of a powerful father's influence.

    b. He had a strong father, a protective mother (cf. Gen. 21:9ff) and a domineering wife.

3. The whole of his life was largely characterised by reopening old wells (Gen. 26:17-33).

B. His act of achieving faith: sticking to his guns after he realised he had unwittingly blessed Jacob.

1. *All that Isaac was ultimately called to do, he did.*

    a. This was to continue Abraham's seed.

    b. Abraham's seed was to come through Isaac, not Ishmael.

2. *Before Jacob and Esau were born, Rebekah was given a prophetic word.* 'The LORD said to her, "Two nations are in your womb, and two peoples from within you will be separated; one people will be stronger than the other, and the older will serve the younger"' (Gen. 25:23).

    a. Esau and Jacob were born – in that order.

        (1) Esau was the clever brother who pleased his father.

        (2) Jacob was a 'mummy's boy'.

    c. 'Isaac, who had a taste for wild game, loved Esau, but Rebekah loved Jacob' (Gen. 25:28).

3. *One day Esau came in from hunting, exhausted and hungry.*

    a. Esau asked to eat some of Jacob's freshly cooked stew.

    b. Jacob agreed – upon one condition: that Esau sell his birthright. He did (Gen. 25:33-34).

4. *There is more: through Rebekah's manipulation, Jacob deceived his father Isaac – and received the coveted patriarchal blessing.*

    a. Pretending to be Esau, Jacob persuaded his father Isaac to bestow the blessing on him.

    b. Isaac did it.

    c. Moments later Esau himself emerged and asked for the same blessing.

        (1) Isaac was horrified that he had been tricked. 'Isaac answered Esau, "I have made him lord over you and have made all his relatives his servants, and I have sustained him with grain and new wine. So what can I possibly do for you, my son?"' (Gen. 27:37).

        (2) His historic and decisive reply: 'I blessed [Jacob] – and indeed he will be blessed.'

6. *That was Isaac's faith.*

    a. He stood by the blessing he gave to Jacob.

    b. It was not what he wanted, but it was his finest hour.

C. What do we learn from Isaac's faith?

    1. We don't have to do anything sensational to please God.

    2. Achieving faith is sometimes in 'letting things be'; in this case letting the blessing of Jacob stand.

    3. Achieving faith is pleasing God rather than those we love; Isaac loved Esau.

II. THE FAITH OF JACOB

A. The world's greatest manipulator, the world's worst parent and the man whose name (which is interchangeable with 'Israel') is mentioned most in the Bible was – in a word: unworthy.

    1. Hardly the most loveable or likeable character in the Bible.

    2. If his equivalent were on T.V. today he would be like J.R. Ewing, the man you love to hate.

    3. *But, like it or not, God said, 'I have loved Jacob'* (Mal. 1:2).

a. He became an example to Paul for biblical support of the doctrine of election.

'Yet, before the twins were born or had done anything good or bad – in order that God's purpose in election might stand: not by works but by him who calls – she was told, "The older will serve the younger." Just as it is written: "Jacob I loved, but Esau I hated"' (Rom. 9:11-13).

b. The relevance of this for us is, if God could love Jacob, he could love anybody – including you or me!

B. Jacob's early unworthiness can be summed up thus:
1. He took advantage of the vulnerable state of his brother Esau and got the latter's birthright.
2. *He tricked his own dad and achieved the patriarchal blessing – which put him in good stead for the rest of his life.*
   a. Esau nursed a grudge against Jacob. 'Esau held a grudge against Jacob because of the blessing his father had given him. He said to himself, "The days of mourning for my father are near; then I will kill my brother Jacob"' (Gen. 27:41).
   b. Running scared as a consequence, Jacob left home and started life on his own.
      (1) Ridden with guilt, Jacob never felt worthy.
      (2) Despite spectacular revelations from God, his faith was far from extraordinary.
      (3) He is the quintessence of an unworthy person loved by God.

C. Bethel.
1. *Out in the wilderness on his own, Jacob came to 'a certain place'* (Gen. 28:11).
   a. Little did he know that it would become very special to him.
   b. He gave this place its name – Bethel (Gen. 28:19).
2. *While there, a dream enabled Jacob to discover God for himself.*
   a. It was no longer a hand-me-down religion; Jacob came to know the God of his grandparents and father.
   b. His guilt was so deep and vast that he must have been overwhelmed that God would reveal himself as he did.

'He had a dream in which he saw a stairway resting on the earth, with its top reaching to heaven, and the angels of God were ascending and descending on it. There above it stood the LORD, and he said: "I am the LORD, the God of your father Abraham and the God of Isaac. I will give you and your descendants the land on which you are lying. Your descendants will be like the dust of the earth, and you will spread out to the west and to the east, to the north and to the south. All peoples on earth will be blessed through you and your offspring. I am with you and will watch over you wherever you go, and I will bring you back to this land. I will not leave you until I have done what I have promised you"' (Gen. 28:12-15).

c. Like his grandfather he chose to be a tither! (Gen. 28:22).

D. Husband and father.
  1. *Jacob fell in love with Rachel, his uncle Laban's daughter.*
    a. He agreed to work for Laban seven years in exchange for Rachel.
    b. But on the morning after the wedding, there in the tent with him was not beautiful Rachel but her plain sister Leah. 'When morning came, there was Leah! So Jacob said to Laban, "What is this you have done to me? I served you for Rachel, didn't I? Why have you deceived me?"' (Gen. 29:25).
      (1) Laban replied, as it were, 'Sorry about that. I forgot to tell you that we have a custom here that the oldest daughter must marry first' (Gen. 29:26).
      (2) But Jacob was assured he could have Rachel for seven years further work for Laban.
  2. *Jacob never loved or appreciated Leah.*
    a. Rachel was beautiful but barren.
    b. Leah was plain but bore him children.
    c. The irony is, two of Leah's children meant more to the Kingdom of God than all the others:
      (1) Levi – who gave us the priesthood.
      (2) Judah – through whom Jesus was born.
  3. *Rachel eventually gave Jacob two children: Joseph and Benjamin.*

    a. Joseph was spoiled rotten and was virtually given the rights of the firstborn.

    b. Jacob's playing favourites did Joseph no favour and served to cause great jealousy.

4. *Jacob had a daughter, Dinah, who went the way of the world.*

    a. Jacob's older sons brought vengeance upon the family that wanted to make Dinah theirs.

    b. Instead of caring about Dinah and her feelings, Jacob only thought of himself (Gen. 34:30).

5. *After Joseph went missing (presumed dead), Jacob treated the other sons (except Benjamin) as if they didn't exist.*

    a. Looking at his ten sons, Jacob referred to Benjamin as 'the only one left' (Gen. 42:38).

    b. How do you suppose that made these men feel? It didn't seem to bother Jacob at all.

E. Continued weak faith in spite of one deliverance after another.

1. *Jacob had served Laban for 20 years.*

    a. At long last he was set free – by God. 'I am the God of Bethel, where you anointed a pillar and where you made a vow to me. Now leave this land at once and go back to your native land' (Gen. 31:13).

    b. The God of Bethel is one who sees and remembers!

    c. Jacob made his great escape from Laban, eventually!

2. *The dread of Esau gripped Jacob after he was free from Laban.*

    a. His worst nightmare was having to face Esau.

        (1) He made all kinds of prior arrangements in anticipation of what Esau might do (Gen. 32:7ff).

        (2) Jacob prayed to God with all his heart (Gen. 32:9-12).

    b. On the night prior to meeting Esau, Jacob had his greatest experience with God.

        (1) It began as a wrestling match with an angel.

        (2) At some stage Jacob realised this angel was not a foe but a friend. 'I will not let you go until you bless me,' he said (Gen. 32:26).

        (3) Then came the peak experience: 'Then the man said, "Your name will no longer be Jacob, but Israel, because you have struggled with God and with men and have overcome"' (Gen. 32:28).

    c. That experience ought to have sealed Jacob's faith once and for all time. But no.

        (1) He still feared for his life when facing Esau (Gen. 33:1).

        (2) But there was no need to worry; something had happened inwardly to Esau! 'But Esau ran to meet Jacob and embraced him; he threw his arms around his neck and kissed him. And they wept' (Gen. 33:4).

        (3) Yet still after that Jacob did not trust Esau and headed in the opposite direction to the way he had promised (Gen. 33:17).

3. *The account of Dinah shows Jacob's family in disarray.*

    a. Despite the wonderful deliverance from Laban and Esau – and revelations – Jacob's faith was weak. 'Then Jacob said to Simeon and Levi, "You have brought trouble on me by making me a stench to the Canaanites and Perizzites, the people living in this land. We are few in number, and if they join forces against me and attack me, I and my household will be destroyed" (Gen. 34:30).

    b. God intervened. 'Then God said to Jacob, "Go up to Bethel and settle there, and build an altar there to God, who appeared to you when you were fleeing from your brother Esau" (Gen. 35:1).

        (1) Things began to happen for Jacob; he sought to get his family right with God (Gen. 35:2).

        (2) God put his seal on Jacob. 'Then they set out, and the terror of God fell upon the towns all around them so that no one pursued them' (Gen. 35:5).

        (3) God renewed the promise (Gen. 35:10).

    c. However, that would be the last time God spoke like that for a long while.

F. Losing Joseph.

    1. *All the suffering Jacob experienced under Laban, his fear of Esau and disarray in his family would be eclipsed by the greatest trial of all.*

    a. After sending out Joseph to check on his brothers, they brought back a bad report to Jacob.

        (1) Jacob had given Joseph a coat of many colours. NIV: 'Richly ornamented robe'.

(2) The brothers dipped the coat in blood and took it to Jacob – hoping he would take the bait.

(3) He did. 'He recognized it and said, "It is my son's robe! Some ferocious animal has devoured him. Joseph has surely been torn to pieces"' (Gen. 37:33).

    b. Neither Jacob nor his sons ever expected to see Joseph again.

       (1) But the Lord was with Joseph; he was eventually made Prime Minister of Egypt.

       (2) Famine in that part of the world sent Jacob's sons to Egypt to beg for food; they had to face Joseph who eventually revealed his identity to them – and totally forgave them (Gen. 45:1-11).

    c. The sons reported to Jacob that Joseph was alive and well – and was now Prime Minister of Egypt – and that they were invited to live in Egypt (Gen. 45:25-28).

2. *God revealed himself to Jacob for the first time in over 22 years.* 'And God spoke to Israel in a vision at night and said, "Jacob! Jacob!" "Here I am," he replied. "I am God, the God of your father," he said. "Do not be afraid to go down to Egypt, for I will make you into a great nation there. I will go down to Egypt with you, and I will surely bring you back again. And Joseph's own hand will close your eyes"' (Gen. 46:2-4).

    a. Jacob, 130 years old, was having to experience the new and different.

    b. But God appearing to him put him at ease and made him know that going to Egypt was right.

G. Seeing Joseph again.

1. It was a tearful moment. Joseph threw his arms around his father and they 'wept for a long time' (Gen. 46:29).

2. 'Israel said to Joseph, "Now I am ready to die, since I have seen for myself that you are still alive"' (Gen. 46:30).

3. Joseph introduced his father to the Pharaoh; he and his family were allowed to live in the best part of Egypt, the land of Goshen (Gen. 47:5-6).

H. Jacob worshipping. 'By faith Jacob, when he was dying, blessed each of Joseph's sons, and worshipped as he leaned on the top of his staff' (Heb. 11:21).

1. It is not easy to know the exact event from Genesis to which the writer of Hebrews refers.

2. *What is known is this:*

   a. It was at the end of his life.

   b. All his family were totally reunited.

   c. God had kept every promise – first made at Bethel, then renewed again and again.

   d. Jacob worshipped – he was so grateful to God. 'All's well that ends well.'

   e. At last – he believed!

CONCLUSION

You don't get much more unworthy than Jacob! But Jacob was loved by God. The God of Jacob is our God as well. By this we may know there is hope for us all.

16

FAITH AND GREATNESS

'By faith Joseph, when his end was near, spoke about the exodus of the Israelites from Egypt and gave instructions about his bones' (Heb. 11:22).

'By faith Moses, when he had grown up, refused to be known as the son of Pharaoh's daughter. He chose to be illtreated along with the people of God rather than to enjoy the pleasures of sin for a short time. He regarded disgrace for the sake of Christ as of greater value than the treasures of Egypt, because he was looking ahead to his reward' (Heb. 11:24-26).

INTRODUCTION

A. We are living in an era in which there seems to be a dearth of greatness.
  1. Where are the Winston Churchills of this world? The John Wesleys?
  2. Instead, by and large we have the pitiful sight of small men scrambling for power and attention.

B. Faith is partly designed to make us great in some way.
  1. Not necessarily in the eyes of men and women; but before God and the angels.
  2. *Achieving faith is in some way achieving greatness.*
     a. We are all called to 'glory' (Heb. 2:10).
     b. God will not share his glory with another (Is. 42:8).
        (1) At the same time, he wants to exalt us.
        (2) On this condition: 'Humble yourselves, therefore, under God's mighty hand, that he may lift you up in due time' (1 Pet. 5:6).

C. We will look at two examples of greatness:
  1. *Joseph, who became Prime Minister of Egypt.*
     a. Off to a bad start, he none the less achieved true greatness.
     b. His secret: totally forgiving those who hurt him.

175

2. *Moses, the greatest man of the Old Testament.*

　　a. Surviving the Pharaoh's wrath due to the faith of his parents, he was brought up in Pharaoh's palace (Ex. 2:1-10).

　　b. His greatness is seen in two ways:

　　　　(1) What he gave up because of seeing what had true value – the honour of God.

　　　　(2) His intercession for those who misunderstood him.

D. Why is this lesson important?

1. It shows how each of us can attain true greatness – if we want to.

2. It shows that true greatness comes by following God, listening to him and obeying him.

3. It shows that true greatness is graciousness.

4. We do not achieve greatness by trying to be great, but by walking in the light.

5. *Greatness does not come easily or soon but by responsibly submitting to God's preparation for us.*

　　a. 'If I knew I had twenty-five years left to live I'd spend twenty of them in preparation' (C.H. Spurgeon).

　　b. 'The price of greatness is responsibility' (Winston Churchill).

I. THE FAITH OF JOSEPH

A. Off to a bad start.

1. *He was preferred by his father* (Gen. 37:3).

　　a. He was treated as a first-born.

　　b. He was given a richly ornamented robe.

2. *He made his brothers jealous.*

　　a. He flaunted his gift of interpretation of dreams.

　　b. He did everything wrong, insofar as creating a good relationship with them was concerned.

3. *Note: there was nothing wrong with Joseph's gift, but there was a lot wrong with Joseph.*

　　a. Before he could be used by God he – not his gift – needed sorting out.

　　b. He was earmarked for greatness; but he had a long, long way to go.

4. *Overnight he went from 'riches to rags'.*

　　a. He was thrown by his brothers into a cistern to die; only some Ishmaelites turning up on the scene saved his life; his brothers sold him to the Ishmaelites.

b. His brothers took that coat, dipped it in blood, laid it before Jacob who took the bait. 'He recognized it and said, "It is my son's robe! Some ferocious animal has devoured him. Joseph has surely been torn to pieces"' (Gen. 37:33).

c. Meanwhile Joseph was a slave of an Egyptian officer, Potiphar.

   (1) But God was with Joseph (Gen. 39:2).

   (2) Joseph was put in charge of everything in Potiphar's household.

B. A new kind of trial – in three phases:

1. *Sexual temptation.*

   a. Potiphar's wife tried to get Joseph to sleep with her (Gen. 39:7).

   b. He refused. 'No one is greater in this house than I am. My master has withheld nothing from me except you, because you are his wife. How then could I do such a wicked thing and sin against God?' (Gen. 39:9).

   c. 'The devil seems to get 75% of God's best through sexual temptation.' Billy Graham.

2. *Punished for doing the right thing.*

   a. The thanks Joseph got for resisting temptation: he was accused of attempted rape (Gen. 39:16-19).

   b. He was slammed into prison (Gen. 39:20).

   c. He had three things to be bitter about:

      (1) His brothers' treatment of him.

      (2) Being punished for false accusation.

      (3) That God allowed all this.

   d. Note:

      (1) 'If you should suffer for what is right, you are blessed' (1 Pet. 3:14).

      (2) 'It is better, if it is God's will, to suffer for doing good than for doing evil' (1 Pet. 3:17).

      (3) The greater the anointing, the greater the suffering; the greater the suffering, the greater the anointing.

3. *Having to get over bitterness.*

   a. Joseph tried to shorten his time in prison by begging the cupbearer to intercede before Pharaoh.

Understanding Theology

b. It didn't work; trying to twist the arm of providence delays God's plans for us.

    (1) Love is not self-seeking (1 Cor. 13:5).

    (2) Joseph's bitterness had to go before God could use him.

c. His time came when there was no earthly hope.

    (1) But the Pharaoh had a dream which no one could interpret.

    (2) The cupbearer remembered Joseph.

    (3) Joseph was ushered into Pharaoh's presence.

    (4) Joseph interpreted the dream.

    (5) Joseph was made Prime Minister overnight.

d. Note: Joseph's vindication came overnight – when God began to work, just as he went from riches to rags overnight!

C. Joseph became an entirely different man.

1. No doubt he fantasised about how he would one day throw the book at his brothers.

2. *But by the time his dreams were fulfilled he was a different person.*

a. Instead of punishing his brothers he forgave them.

b. This came after he became Prime Minister and his brothers came begging for food – not knowing at first that the Prime Minister was their brother.

D. Greatness is graciousness; here are six proofs that Joseph had totally forgiven his brothers; how we too know we have so done:

1. *We let nobody know 'what they did' to us* (Gen. 45:1).

a. Joseph did not want anybody in Egypt to know what his brothers had done; he wanted them to be loved.

b. This is the way God forgives us (Eph. 4:32).

2. We will not let those who hurt us be afraid of us (Gen. 45:4).

3. We do not want them to feel guilty over what they did. 'And now, do not be distressed and do not be angry with yourselves for selling me here, because it was to save lives that God sent me ahead of you' (Gen. 45:5).

4. We let them save face. 'So then, it was not you who sent me here, but God. He made me father to Pharaoh, lord of his entire household and ruler of all Egypt' (Gen. 45:8).

5. *We protect them from their greatest fear.*

    a. The brothers' greatest fear: that Jacob would know what they themselves had really done when they laid that blood-stained robe before him.

    b. Joseph knew that; he ordered that they say certain things that precluded telling their father what they did (Gen. 45:9-13).

6. *You keep it up; total forgiveness is a life sentence.*

    a. Seventeen years later Jacob died; the brothers feared that Joseph would now punish them.

    b. No, he said; God meant it for good.

E. Hebrews 11:22 uncovers a further secret of Joseph's greatness.

    1. Joseph's heart was never in Egypt; it was in the land God swore to give to his forefathers.

    2. Therefore he required that he be finally buried in Canaan (Gen. 50:25).

II. THE FAITH OF MOSES

A. After Joseph died, the children of Israel multiplied.

    1. Once heroes in Egypt, they were now a threat to the new Pharaoh.

    2. *A new Pharaoh came on the scene who knew nothing about Joseph and felt he owed nothing to the Israelites.*

        a. He persecuted them, and made life extremely hard.

        b. All Israelite boys were ordered to be drowned, but Moses' parents saved their future leader.

    3. *However, it would be a long time before Moses would be the deliverer of the people of Israel from Egypt.*

        a. In the meantime God singled out Moses for greatness.

        b. He would need a long era of preparation, much longer than Joseph needed.

B. Moses' first step toward greatness: coming to terms with his true identity. 'By faith Moses, when he had grown up, refused to be known as the son of Pharaoh's daughter' (Heb. 11:24).

    1. *Moses grew up in Egypt with an Egyptian mother and in the Egyptian culture.*

        a. How painful it must have been for his natural mother to give him up as a small baby.

179

b. But Moses had something going for him no other Egyptian had: the prayers of godly parents.

 (1) Moses had been turned loose into the same river that meant death to every other Hebrew boy.

 (2) The probability that Moses would even embrace the God of Abraham, Isaac and Jacob was made virtually nil by the pagan education he would receive. 'Moses was educated in all the wisdom of the Egyptians and was powerful in speech and action' (Acts 7:22).

c. However, Moses, like all Hebrew boys, had been circumcised; Egyptian babies were not.

 (1) Moses grew up knowing he was different from other Egyptian boys; there was no way this identity could be kept from him.

 (2) A restlessness of spirit emerged until Moses could take it no longer; 'Those are my people out there in Goshen,' he must have said.

d. 'When Moses was forty years old, he decided to visit his fellow Israelites' (Acts 7:23).

 (1) He rejected the identity that had been imposed on him.

 (2) 'By faith' he came to terms with his real identity.

C. Moses' choice in the light of his true identity: suffering.

 1. *Moses knew it wouldn't be easy; he knew great suffering lay ahead.*

  a. It must have been painful to abandon the king's palace, to dissociate himself from his Egyptian family.

  b. But he consciously chose to identify with the children of Israel. 'He chose to be illtreated along with the people of God rather than to enjoy the pleasures of sin for a short time' (Heb. 11:25).

 2. *Moses' initial suffering came not from the palace of Pharaoh but from the very people of God he came to identify with – and help!*

  a. Anxious to convince his fellow Hebrews that he was one of them, Moses killed an Egyptian.

  b. This act backfired. 'Moses thought that his own people would realize that God was using him to rescue them, but they did not' (Acts 7:25).

   c. The most painful kind of persecution is often that which comes from within the family of God.

3. *Moses was hemmed in; he couldn't go back to the palace, for they knew what he had done.*

   a. Next step: the desert – forty years in the wilderness.

   b. Moses had thought he would deliver Israel in a day or two.

      (1) Wrong; he needed further preparation.

      (2) 'The worst thing that can happen to a man is to succeed before he is ready' (Dr Martyn Lloyd-Jones).

D. The rationale for Moses' radical choice: 'He regarded disgrace for the sake of Christ as of greater value than the treasures of Egypt, because he was looking ahead to his reward' (Heb. 11:26).

1. *It was a pragmatic decision.*

   a. Moses saw that the prestige and security of Pharaoh's palace were superficial and worthless.

   b. Disgrace for the sake of Christ was of greater value.

   c. His motivation: a reward.

      (1) It was a clever decision: why try to win the battle when you can win the war?

      (2) Moses knew that his own people were the wave of the future; he saw in them what nobody else could see.

2. *Moses saw in this reward the figure of the Lord Jesus Christ!*

   a. What Peter and John would one day experience Moses did then! 'The apostles left the Sanhedrin, rejoicing because they had been counted worthy of suffering disgrace for the Name' (Acts 5:41).

   b. Disgrace for the sake of Christ issues in such joy and glory that it becomes impossible to tell the difference between a blessing and a trial.

3. *The earnest of the reward: seeing him who is invisible* (Heb. 11:27).

   a. God appeared to Moses at the burning bush (Ex. 3:1-6).

   b. Here God revealed his Name. 'I appeared to Abraham, to Isaac and to Jacob as God Almighty, but by my name the LORD I did not make myself known to them' (Ex. 6:3).

   c. This brought Moses into new dimensions:

      (1) Signs and wonders became fairly common.

      (2) He was appointed leader of his people. This time the timing was right!

E. A further example of the unprecedented: 'By faith he kept the Passover and the sprinkling of blood, so that the destroyer of the firstborn would not touch the firstborn of Israel. By faith the people passed through the Red Sea as on dry land; but when the Egyptians tried to do so, they were drowned' (Heb. 11:28-29).

1. *We have seen in a previous lesson that not one person mentioned in Hebrews 11 had the luxury of repeating what had been done before.*

   a. Everyone had to move outside their comfort zone.

   b. Moses was no exception.

      (1) What he had already done – leaving the palace of Pharaoh – was only the first step in this direction.

      (2) The emergence of signs and wonders carried with it enormous responsibility – and great faith.

2. *The Passover.*

   a. Moses went to the Pharaoh with a bold request: 'Let my people go' (Ex. 5:1).

      (1) Pharaoh said, 'No.'

      (2) This led to nine plagues on Egypt to get Pharaoh to change his mind; nothing worked.

   b. The tenth plague would be different:

      (1) The Israelites were to sprinkle blood over their doors.

      (2) 'The blood will be a sign for you on the houses where you are; and when I see the blood, I will pass over you. No destructive plague will touch you when I strike Egypt' (Ex. 12:13).

   c. It worked; Pharaoh finally let the people go.

3. *Crossing the Red Sea.*

   a. The people of Israel came to the Red Sea – and the Egyptians were now after them. 'Then the LORD said to Moses, "Why are you crying out to me? Tell the Israelites to move on. Raise your staff and stretch out your hand over the sea to divide the water so that the Israelites can go through the sea on dry ground. I will harden the hearts of the Egyptians so that they will go in after them. And I will gain glory through Pharaoh and all his army, through his chariots and his horsemen. The Egyptians will know that I am the LORD when I gain glory through Pharaoh, his chariots and his horsemen"' (Ex. 14:15-18).

b. It happened, and there followed the greatest miracle of the Old Testament: Israel crossing the Red Sea on dry land.

F. Moses' leadership challenged.

1. The first time this happened was after Pharaoh made it harder than ever on the people (Ex. 5:21).

2. *The second time was after the children of Israel were in the desert following their deliverance from Pharaoh.*

    a. God made a proposition to Moses: to destroy all the Israelites and start all over again – with Moses leading another nation (Ex. 32:9-10).

    b. 'No!' said Moses; he asked God to forgive the people instead! (Ex. 32:11-14).

CONCLUSION

Joseph and Moses became famous figures in Israelite history for this reason: they were gracious men. True greatness is graciousness. Each one of us can be great, can be gracious. It does not depend on whether we are given high profile here below! What is important is what we are promised: a reward. The reward in the future will be given to those who learn graciousness in the present. Such are great without knowing it.

17

FAITH AND THE STIGMA

INTRODUCTION

A. The word 'stigma' is a pure Greek word – *stigma.*

1. *It is found in Galatians 6:17: 'I bear in my body the marks (stigmata) of Jesus.'*

   a. It comes from *stizo*, which means 'to prick', 'tattoo' or 'mark' as well as 'a sharp instrument'.

   b. In the ancient Hellenistic world it was often a brand burned on the body with a hot iron.

      (1) This became a distinguishing mark.

      (2) A man who bore the *stigma* was everywhere regarded as dishonest.

   c. It was usually marked on slaves, for running away or stealing.

2. *Paul was unashamed of the stigmata; he applied it to the wounds or scars that came from persecution.*

   a. It means he was a slave – of Christ.

   b. He was probably not referring to some mystical phenomenon on his body but to being stoned, or beaten. 'Are they servants of Christ? (I am out of my mind to talk like this.) I am more. I have worked much harder, been in prison more frequently, been flogged more severely, and been exposed to death again and again. Five times I received from the Jews the forty lashes minus one. Three times I was beaten with rods, once I was stoned, three times I was shipwrecked, I spent a night and a day in the open sea' (2 Cor. 11:23-25).

3. *It is also somewhat synonymous with the Greek word* skandalon *(from which we get the word 'scandal'): 'offence'.*

   a. 'But we preach Christ crucified: a stumbling block to Jews and foolishness to Gentiles' (1 Cor. 1:23).

   b. 'Brothers, if I am still preaching circumcision, why am I still being persecuted? In that case the offence of the cross has been abolished' (Gal. 5:11).

B. By nature every single one of us will avoid the stigma or what causes offence.

   1. By temperament most of us want to be pleasers of people. But Paul said, 'I am confident in the Lord that you will take no other view. The one who is throwing you into confusion will pay the penalty, whoever he may be' (Gal. 5:10).

   2. By nature we avoid any kind of stigma. But not Peter and John. 'The apostles left the Sanhedrin, rejoicing because they had been counted worthy of suffering disgrace for the Name' (Acts 5:41).

C. A stigma almost always characterises either saving faith or achieving faith.

   1. It was for the faith of the Gospel that Paul used the word *skandalon* (1 Cor. 1:23; Gal. 5:11).

   2. The people who believed that God rewards those who earnestly seek him (Heb. 11:6) likewise caused offence in their day.

   3. This lesson will examine the connection between the stigma and achieving faith.

D. Why is this lesson important?

   1. As we have seen in an earlier lesson that we must be prepared to go outside our comfort zones, so too must we be prepared to bear the stigma for Christ.

   2. Achieving faith carries with it the risk of being misunderstood; that is a strong ingredient in achieving, or diligent, faith.

   3. *The stigma is a necessary part of the anointing; if we want the anointing we must accept the stigma.*

   a. The greater the suffering, the greater the anointing.

   b. The greater the stigma, the greater the anointing.

   c. And almost certainly, the greater the anointing the greater the stigma.

   4. It is such a privilege to be counted among God's 'best' – who bore the stigma; we therefore must feel honoured should God grant us this same blessing.

   5. The one who bore the greatest stigma was the greatest achiever ever – our Lord Jesus Christ; he was the most misunderstood person who ever lived, but he also achieved our salvation for us on the cross.

E. The stigma (def.): the pain and offence caused by being misunderstood.

1. *Moses' initial stigma came because he jumped the gun, trying to endear himself to his people.* 'Moses thought that his own people would realise that God was using him to rescue them, but they did not' (Acts 7:25).

   a. This shows that there can be a needless stigma. 'If you suffer, it should not be as a murderer or thief or any other kind of criminal, or even as a meddler' (1 Pet. 4:15).

   b. The stigma this lesson is about refers to what we bear for doing the right thing.

   (1) Joseph went to prison for doing what was right.

   (2) 'Therefore, prepare your minds for action; be self-controlled; set your hope fully on the grace to be given you when Jesus Christ is revealed. As obedient children, do not conform to the evil desires you had when you lived in ignorance' (1 Pet. 1:13-14).

2. *Moses' later stigma came from these genuine misunderstandings when he was in leadership:*

   a. The Pharaoh's reaction to Moses' demand, 'Let my people go,' was met with harshness. 'That same day Pharaoh gave this order to the slave drivers and foremen in charge of the people: "You are no longer to supply the people with straw for making bricks; let them go and gather their own straw. But require them to make the same number of bricks as before; don't reduce the quota. They are lazy; that is why they are crying out, 'Let us go and sacrifice to our God.' Make the work harder for the men so that they keep working and pay no attention to lies"' (Ex. 5:6-9).

   b. The Israelites' reaction moreover put pressure on Moses. 'And they said, "May the LORD look upon you and judge you! You have made us a stench to Pharaoh and his officials and have put a sword in their hand to kill us"' (Ex. 5:21).

   c. Moses found the stigma painful: 'Moses returned to the LORD and said, "O Lord, why have you brought trouble upon this people? Is this why you sent me? Ever since I went to Pharaoh to speak in your name, he has brought trouble upon this people, and you have not rescued your people at all"' (Ex. 5:22-23).

3. *This is why we have two words in our definition of 'stigma':
pain and suffering.*

   a. It hurts when we know we offend.

   b. Question: are you willing to accept the stigma that goes
with an increased anointing?

I. THE STIGMA OF BEING TODAY'S MAN OR WOMAN; E.G. SAMUEL (HEB. 11:32).

A. Overcoming disillusionment.

   1. *Samuel's hero and mentor was Eli, the priest of ancient Israel.*

      a. As a small child Samuel came to live with Eli as a result of
his mother Hannah's vow (1 Sam. 1).

      b. Samuel grew up in awe of Eli; but Eli had not been the best
example in Israel, tolerating his sons' wickedness (1 Sam.
2:12-36).

   2. *God bypassed the normal channels of divine communication
and spoke directly to Samuel* (1 Sam. 3).

      a. Samuel kept thinking he was hearing Eli when it became
obvious God wasn't speaking through Eli but directly to
Samuel.

      b. Samuel grew up seeing why God spoke straight to him.

         (1) He discovered what all of us discover; the best of men
are men at best.

         (2) Disillusionment over the imperfections of a leader cause
some to go astray; but not Samuel.

B. Standing alone and learning not to take rejection personally.

   1. Israel demanded a king; they wanted to be like other nations.

   2. This displeased Samuel and the Lord.

   3. But God told Samuel to give in and not take rejection personally.
'And the LORD told him: "Listen to all that the people are saying
to you; it is not you they have rejected, but they have rejected
me as their king"' (1 Sam. 8:7).

   4. *Samuel then went to work to find them the best man in Israel to
be king.*

      a. This showed graciousness.

      b. It was the secret of his anointing: God let none of Samuel's
words 'fall to the ground' (1 Sam. 3:19)

Understanding Theology

C. Breaking with the movement God was in yesterday.

1. 'The LORD said to Samuel, "How long will you mourn for Saul, since I have rejected him as king over Israel? Fill your horn with oil and be on your way; I am sending you to Jesse of Bethlehem. I have chosen one of his sons to be king"' (1 Sam. 16:1).

   a. Saul was Samuel's discovery.

   b. But after Saul disobeyed God, Samuel had to follow the Lord not Saul.

2. *It is no small thing to do this.*

   a. We become attached to people, places and things.

   b. But if what God was in yesterday does not move with the Spirit we must make a choice:

   (1) To stay with the old, or move on.

   (2) Jonathan Edwards taught us that the task of every generation is to discover in which direction the Sovereign Redeemer is moving, then move in that direction.

D. Moving outside our comfort zone.

1. Samuel's response to God's command was, 'How can I go? Saul will hear about it and kill me' (1 Sam. 16:2).

2. There could hardly have been a more awkward situation: anointing a man to be king when there already was a king.

3. Samuel was not able to please Jesse by choosing his firstborn; he anointed the one all would have said to be the least likely candidate (1 Sam. 16:7-13).

II. THE STIGMA OF BEING TOMORROW'S MAN OR WOMAN E.G., DAVID (HEB. 11:32).

A. Misunderstood by his family.

1. *His own father would not have included David in Samuel's visit had not Samuel insisted* (1 Sam. 16:11-12).

   a. Sometimes our own parents have little or no confidence in us.

   b. God may have his hand on us and our parents miss it.

2. *David's brothers misunderstood him; they accused him of being conceited.*

   a. David saw Goliath merely as an uncircumcised Philistine (1 Sam. 17:26).

b. This annoyed his brothers, especially the eldest: 'I know how conceited you are and how wicked your heart is; you came down only to watch the battle' (1 Sam. 17:28).

B. Underestimated by the establishment.
1. King Saul initially rejected David's offer to fight Goliath. 'Saul replied, "You are not able to go out against this Philistine and fight him; you are only a boy, and he has been a fighting man from his youth"' (1 Sam. 17:33).
2. *Sometimes leaders cannot recognise the anointing or gifting of tomorrow's man or woman.*
   a. Regent's Park College did not accept Charles Spurgeon.
   b. The Methodist Church rejected G Campbell Morgan.

C. Hated by the establishment.
1. *Killing Goliath was the best and worst thing that could have happened to David.*
   a. It gave him instant profile (1 Sam. 18:1-7).
   b. He became a threat to the king. 'What more can he get but the kingdom?' (1 Sam. 18:8).
2. *Saul became jealous of David and was more concerned about David than the real enemy – the Philistines.*
   a. 'Saul was afraid of David, because the LORD was with David but had left Saul' (1 Sam. 18:12).
   b. David spent years in continual fear of Saul.

D. Having to wait for your time to come.
1. *David was given an anointing but no crown* (1 Sam. 16:13).
   a. It was a secret anointing, known only by a few.
   b. It was an inward anointing; but there was no platform.
2. *David would wait another twenty years before he wore the crown.*
   a. God ensured that David did not succeed before he was ready.
   b. Those twenty years were God's preparation.

III. THE STIGMA OF STANDING ALONE (HEB. 11:32-38).

A. Elijah.
1. *Misunderstood by the person you blessed.*
   a. God miraculously used Elijah to bless a widow with food

during a time of famine. 'For the jar of flour was not used up and the jug of oil did not run dry, in keeping with the word of the LORD spoken by Elijah' (1 Kings 17:16).

    b. But when her son became ill and died, 'She said to Elijah, "What do you have against me, man of God? Did you come to remind me of my sin and kill my son?"' (1 Kings 17:18).

2. *Hated by wicked leadership.*

    a. Elijah challenged the prophets of Baal and eventually defeated them (1 Kings 18:18-40).

    b. But he ran for his life (1 Kings 19:1-9).

B. The three Hebrews living in Babylon (Dan. 3).

1. King Nebuchadnezzar erected an image of gold and required all to bow down and worship it.

2. *Three Jews – Shadrach, Meshach and Abednego – refused to comply.*

    a. This made the king furious, 'And Nebuchadnezzar said to them, "Is it true, Shadrach, Meshach and Abednego, that you do not serve my gods or worship the image of gold I have set up? Now when you hear the sound of the horn, flute, zither, lyre, harp, pipes and all kinds of music, if you are ready to fall down and worship the image I made, very good. But if you do not worship it, you will be thrown immediately into a blazing furnace. Then what god will be able to rescue you from my hand?"' (Dan. 3:14-15).

    b. Their reply made them legendary. 'Shadrach, Meshach and Abednego replied to the king, "O Nebuchadnezzar, we do not need to defend ourselves before you in this matter. If we are thrown into the blazing furnace, the God we serve is able to save us from it, and he will rescue us from your hand, O king. But even if he does not, we want you to know, O king, that we will not serve your gods or worship the image of gold you have set up"' (Dan. 3:16-18).

3. *Their stigma: refusing to worship any but the true God.*

    a. The thanks they got: they were thrown into the fiery furnace.

    b. They were miraculously delivered (Dan. 3:26ff).

C. Daniel (Dan. 6).

1. *He was the object of jealousy because of his excellent qualities.*

  a. Those around him tried to find grounds for charges against Daniel.

  b. 'Finally these men said, "We will never find any basis for charges against this man Daniel unless it has something to do with the law of his God"' (Dan. 6:5).

2. *They manipulated the king to sign a law that forbade anyone from praying to any god for thirty days.*

  a. Daniel's reaction: 'Now when Daniel learned that the decree had been published, he went home to his upstairs room where the windows opened towards Jerusalem. Three times a day he got down on his knees and prayed, giving thanks to his God, just as he had done before' (Dan. 6:10).

  b. He was thrown into a den of lions but miraculously delivered (Dan. 6:22).

IV. STIGMA OF AN UNPOPULAR MESSAGE

A. John the Baptist: message of repentance.

1. *To the general public.* 'In those days John the Baptist came, preaching in the Desert of Judea and saying, "Repent, for the kingdom of heaven is near"' (Matt. 3:1-2).

  a. He warned of a coming wrath (Matt. 3:7).

  b. He called for fruit 'in keeping with repentance' (Matt. 3:8).

  c. He called for radical changes of lifestyle:

    (1) The man with two tunics should share.

    (2) Tax collectors were commanded to be honest.

    (3) Soldiers were urged to be content with their pay.

2. To King Herod. 'Now Herod had arrested John and bound him and put him in prison because of Herodias, his brother Philip's wife' (Matt. 14:3).

B. Jesus: interpretation of the Law.

1. *His interpretation pleased nobody.* 'Do not think that I have come to abolish the Law or the Prophets; I have not come to abolish them but to fulfill them' (Matt. 5:17).

  a. It did not please those who may have wished he would do away with the Law – and start all over again.

  b. It did not please the Sadducees who disliked the message of the prophets (except for Moses).

      c. It did not please the Pharisees who held only to the outward letter of the Law.

    2. *He required a personal righteousness that out-classed the Law.* 'For I tell you that unless your righteousness surpasses that of the Pharisees and the teachers of the law, you will certainly not enter the kingdom of heaven' (Matt. 5:20).

      a. Hate was murder (Matt. 5:21ff).

      b. Lust was adultery (Matt. 5:27ff).

      c. Swearing (taking the oath) was taking God's name in vain. (Matt. 5:33ff).

C. The apostles: righteousness by faith alone, including for Gentiles (Acts 15:11).

    1. *Paul's defence before the Jews in Jerusalem seemed to have been tolerated until he said, 'Then the Lord said to me, "Go; I will send you far away to the Gentiles"'* (Acts 22:21).

      a. 'The crowd listened to Paul until he said this. Then they raised their voices and shouted, "Rid the earth of him! He's not fit to live!"' (Acts 22:22).

      b. The offence of the Cross to the Jews was largely two-fold:

        (1) God's Messiah would die on a cross by predestined purpose (Acts 2:23).

        (2) Gentiles could be saved by faith without becoming Jews first, that is, without being circumcised (Rom. 4:9-12).

    2. *The offence continued to upset Judaisers (Jews who made profession of faith but required circumcision for Gentiles).*

      a. The Judaisers seemed to follow Paul wherever he went. Cf. Galatians; 2 Corinthians.

      b. Paul's response summed up: 'But even if we or an angel from heaven should preach a gospel other than the one we preached to you, let him be eternally condemned! As we have already said, so now I say again: If anybody is preaching to you a gospel other than what you accepted, let him be eternally condemned!' (Gal. 1:8-9).

V. The stigma of the Cross

A. Isaiah saw this coming 600 years in advance.

    1. He saw the rejection Jesus would suffer by the Jews (Is. 53:1-3).

2. He saw that the Messiah would die on a cross as our substitute. 'We all, like sheep, have gone astray, each of us has turned to his own way; and the LORD has laid on him the iniquity of us all' (Is. 53:6).

3. He saw that there was a logical rationale for reproving Messiah: 'Surely he took up our infirmities and carried our sorrows, yet we considered him stricken by God, smitten by him, and afflicted' (Is. 53:4).

B. Note: crucifixion was the Roman manner of carrying out capital punishment.

    1. It was noteworthy for both extreme suffering (slow, painful death) and extreme shame (the lowest of criminals were normally the ones crucified).

    2. *That God's own Messiah would be subjected to crucifixion was unthinkable.*

        a. This enabled the theologians to feel a pure conscience in condoning the crucifixion of Jesus.

        b. This stigma would be felt throughout the Greco-Roman world where all knew about the type of people who were crucified.

C. Paul not only was unashamed of the stigma of the Cross but actually exploited it: 'For I resolved to know nothing while I was with you except Jesus Christ and him crucified' (1 Cor. 2:2).

    1. He knew that there is a close connection between the stigma and the anointing.

    2. He therefore knew that those who would be saved would not be ultimately put off by the message of the Cross.

CONCLUSION

The greater the stigma, the greater the anointing. The greatest stigma of all was that of Jesus, and he had more of the Spirit and more faith than any (John 3:34).

18

HOW TO INCREASE YOUR FAITH

INTRODUCTION

A. In some ways I feel like a hypocrite in bringing this study.
    1. I feel I need someone to teach me how to increase my faith!
    2. *I began to ask: Have I bitten off more than I can chew?*
        a. We all want more faith – need more faith.
        b. There are two scriptures that never cease to comfort me:
            (1) Luke 17:5 'Lord, increase our faith!'
            (2) Mark 9:24 'I do believe, help me overcome my unbelief!'

B. This is another 'practical' study.
    1. *Reminder: we want a theology that is set in warm hearts.*
        a. Theology is in the head; faith is in the heart.
        b. The 'seat' of faith: the heart (Rom. 10:9-10).
    2. The longest journey for some of us: from head to heart!

I. DEFINITION OF FAITH: BELIEVING **G**OD

A. It is more than believing *in* God.
    1. The devil is NOT an atheist (Jas. 2:19).
    2. *Belief in God can exist by 'natural' revelation* (Rom. 1:19).
        a. There is a sense in which all people believe in God.
            (1) Not that all are believers – quite the opposite!
            (2) All have a conscience – put there by God in creation.
        b. Pascal: 'There is a God-shaped blank in every man'.
        c. St Augustine: 'Thou has made us for Thyself; our hearts are restless until they find their rest in Thee'.

B. It is more than believing *about* God.
    1. *We can read the Bible and learn about God.*
        a. That he is creator (Gen. 1).

    b. That he chose Israel (Gen 17:19).

    c. That he sent his Son into the world (John 3:16).

2. *We can learn about God's character.*

    a. Holy (Lev. 11:44).

    b. Jealous (Ex. 20:5).

    c. Just; he must punish sin (Ex. 34:7).

    d. Merciful; he doesn't want to punish us (2 Pet. 3:9).

    e. Truthful (Heb. 6:18).

3. *We can learn about God's attributes.*

    a. Omnipotent – all powerful (Jer. 32:17)).

    b. Omniscient – knows everything (Ps. 139:1-6)).

    c. Omnipresent – everywhere (Ps. 139:7-8).

4. *We can know his promises.*

    a. To save us (John 5:24).

    b. To keep us (John 10:28).

    c. To protect us (Ps. 91).

    d. To make all things work out for good (Rom. 8:28).

C. All of the above may be true without actually believing him!

    1. *You may believe things:*

        a. About me – my character or my personality.

        b. What people say about me – my reputation or influence.

    2. But you may not believe *me*!

D. Faith is believing God.

    1. It is total trust that what he says is true.

    2. *It is total trust that what he says he will do, he will do.*

        a. Greek word is *pistis*.

        b. Greek word comes from *pipto* – 'to persuade'.

    3. *Faith, then, is being persuaded* (Rom. 4:20-21).

        a. Believing God is being persuaded of his promises.

        b. Believing God is being persuaded of his character.

        c. Believing God is being persuaded of his attributes.

E. Faith is believing God without any empirical proof (undoubted evidence) of what he has promised.

    1. *Seeing is not believing.*

        a. If you can see it you don't need faith.

        b. To see in order to believe is always what unbelievers demand (Mark 15:32).

2. *Faith – to be faith – is only possible when you cannot see.*

    a. If God lets us see first, we cannot believe (i.e. it wouldn't be *faith* then (John 11:14-15).

    b. God keeps us from seeing what we would like to see so that faith may develop instead (John 20:29).

3. *If God lets us see:*

    a. He has removed the possibility of faith.

      (1) All will see at the Second Coming (Rev. 1:7).

      (2) But it won't be *faith* operating.

    b. It is no credit to us.

      (1) Credit comes when it is sheer faith (Gen. 15:6).

      (2) Faith is credited for righteousness (Rom. 4:5).

II. Faith is the only way to please God

A. Without faith it is impossible to please God (Heb. 11:6).

1. *He has decreed from eternity that those who endear themselves to him will do it by faith – alone.*

    a. He might have chosen to let works please him.

    b. He might have chosen to let wisdom please him.

    c. He might have chosen to let wealth please him.

    d. He might have chosen to let culture please him.

    e. He might have chosen to let knowledge please him.

    f. He might have chosen to let being religious please him.

    g. He might have chosen to let being educated please him.

    h. He might have chosen to let sound theology please him.

    i. He might have chosen to let sincerity please him.

    j. He might have chosen to let being from a good family please him.

    k. He might have chosen to let having a good reputation please him.

    l. He might have chosen to let being talented please him.

    m. He might have chosen to let usefulness please him.

2. *All of the above are what he probably was pleased to do for us!*

    a. We cannot in turn please him initially by what is his own goodness to us in the first place.

    b. It is madness – surest folly – to think we are doing something for God because:

      (1) We are intelligent – or sincere, or

      (2) We are special – or have something he needs.

B. The only link between us and God that gives him pleasure: believing him.

   1. *All that he is is revealed in his Word.*

      a. His Word is his honour.

         (1) His integrity.

         (2) His character.

      b. The highest affirmation we can give another: to believe their word – alone.

         (1) This shows trust.

         (2) It brings mutual affirmation.

      c. The Word of God is basically two things:

         (1) His Word in person (John 1:1,14).

         (2) His Word in print (2 Tim. 3:16).

   2. *The two chief ways God has demonstrated himself: his Word and his name* (Ps. 138:2).

      a. AV (correct translation): 'Thou hast magnified thy word above all thy name.'

      b. Why would God exalt his Word above his name?

         (1) He wants to be believed by hearing rather than seeing (Rom. 10:17).

         (2) His name refers largely to signs and wonders which can be seen (Ex. 3:6; 6:3 and all that follows).

         (3) His honour and integrity (cf. Heb. 6:18) mean more to him than his reputation and vindication.

      c. In a word: his word relates to faith, his name to seeing.

   3. *When we trust his Word he is affirmed for what he is* in himself, *not for what we have come to see by his deeds.*

      a. When you say to me, 'Show me and I will believe you', I know you still have doubts about what I affirm.

      b. But when you say, 'If *you* say it, I know it is true', I know you believe me.

      c. That is the way God feels.

      d. That is why faith is believing God.

III. BELIEVING GOD IS TWO THINGS: BELIEVING THAT HE IS THERE AND THAT HE REWARDS THOSE WHO EARNESTLY SEEK HIM

A. That he is there. NIV: 'that he exists' (Heb. 11:6).

   1. *Hagar lifted her eyes through her tears: 'Thou God seest me'* (Gen. 16:13 AV).

      a. It was the greatest trial of her life.

      b. She knew two things:

         (1) God was there.

         (2) God cared.

2. *When Satan succeeds in making us doubt, he has won.*

      a. Satan's initial tactic with Eve was to get her to doubt God's word (Gen. 3:1).

      b. This is how Satan tempted Jesus (Matt. 4:3).

         (1) Do not be surprised when you are tempted to doubt – even God's very existence.

         (2) Satan tried to get Jesus to doubt he was the Son of God!

3. *The order Satan employs is this:*

      a. To get us to doubt God's Word.

      b. To get us to doubt our standing with him.

         (1) This refers to our justification (how God sees us in Christ).

         (2) Satan will try to get us to doubt that we are saved.

      c. To point us to our unworthiness.

         (1) This makes us look to ourselves, not to Christ.

         (2) If we contemplate ourselves, that is sure damnation (Calvin).

      d. To get us to doubt God's very existence.

         (1) This often comes at a time of tragedy or 'coincidence' in which God seemed to hide his face.

         (2) Unbelief will seem as the only way out.

4. *The first step, then, in increasing our faith: to know we are saved.*

      a. We look to Christ's death on the cross.

         (1) Christ's sacrifice is sufficient for all (Heb. 2:9, 2 Cor. 5:14-15).

         (2) Therefore he died for me.

      b. I know I am saved because I have put all my eggs in one basket: Christ died for me.

         (1) This assures me of heaven.

         (2) This assures me of my standing with God.

      c. With that in mind all that follows is based upon his love for me: I rely on his love (1 John 4:16).

         (1) I therefore do not begin by faith in God's existence.

         (2) I begin with Christ (see 1 Pet. 1:21)

5. *Note: Hebrews 11:6 contains this assumption, that we will be 'coming to him'.*

    a. In other words, prayer.

    b. When we pray we must believe that God is *there*.

      (1) We hang fast on Christ's death and resurrection.

      (2) The faith to believe for salvation enables us to believe that the same God who gave us that faith is there.

B. That seeking him earnestly is rewarded.

  1. *This brings us back to our study on prayer.*

    a. Remember the importunate widow (Luke 18:1-8).

    b. Remember that we must keep on asking (Luke 11:9).

  2. *This promise – like all of God's promises – puts his honour and integrity on the line.*

    a. God is not threatened by this!

      (1) Calvin: 'The best praying is when we remind God of his own word'.

      (2) My son once said, 'But Daddy you promised'.

    b. There is no greater safety than resting in God's promise!

  3. *This means breaking the 'betrayal barrier': When God seems to betray us.*

    a. It is what every believer faces sooner or later. E.g.,

      (1) Abraham (Acts 7:5; Gen. 22:1ff).

      (2) The three Hebrews (Dan. 3:14).

    b. It's my guess: Nine out of ten back off when they feel betrayed by God, e.g.,

      (1) When they are not immediately blessed.

      (2) When answered prayer is delayed.

    c. For those who break through the betrayal barrier: great blessing is in store.

      (1) It is what the greatest saints have done (Heb. 11).

      (2) It is coming to God, believing he is there *and* earnestly seeking him – no matter how long the delay.

IV. THERE ARE BASICALLY TWO KINDS OF VALID FAITH

A. Saving faith. Justifying faith.

  1. *It is the faith that saves – justifies us before God.*

    a. It is believing the Gospel.

(1) We are sinners but Jesus died for us.

(2) We recognise that we are saved by Christ alone.

b. It is when we *transfer our trust*:

   (1) From trust in ourselves/our good works.

   (2) To Jesus' death on the cross.

c. Question: have you done that?

   (1) Is it possible you are studying theology and have not been converted?

   (2) If you stood before God and he said to you, 'Why should I let you into my heaven?' what would you say?

2. *Saving faith saves us:*

a. From the penalty of our sins (Matt. 1:21).

   (1) The penalty, or punishment, for sin is death (Rom. 6:23).

   (2) The ultimate punishment is everlasting Hell (John 3:16).

   (3) We are saved from God's wrath (Rom. 5:9).

b. From the power of sin.

   (1) The power of sin is broken (Rom. 6:1-2).

   (2) It is what sets us free to live holy lives (Rom. 6:22).

   (3) We are a new creation (2 Cor. 5:17).

c. Note: this does not mean we are perfect.

   (1) We all sin in measure every day (Phil. 3:12).

   (2) But the bent of our life is God-ward (Phil. 3:12).

B. Achieving faith: accomplishing great things for God.

1. Saving faith achieves salvation, yes.

2. *But there is a faith beyond saving faith: achieving faith, which accomplishes things beyond just being saved.*

a. This is what is described in Hebrews 11.

b. Those described in Hebrews 11 were already saved.

   (1) But they did things beyond just being saved.

   (2) They achieved other things; we too must be like them.

3. *Note: the order of these two kinds of faith.*

a. We must have saving faith before we can have achieving faith.

b. It is folly to try to achieve great things in Jesus' name before we have come to trust him for salvation.

C. Wherein saving faith and achieving faith are similar:

1. Both have the same object: God, or Christ.

2. Both stem from seeing our unworthiness.

3. Both come on bended knee for God's mercy.

4. Both bring glory to God.

5. Both are seated in the heart.

6. Both are by the sheer grace and gift of God.

D. Some differences between saving faith and achieving faith.

1. *Saving faith need not be a strong faith.*

    a. It is not great faith that saves, rather it is faith in a great Saviour.

    b. Achieving faith is a strong faith, an 'increased' faith.

2. *Saving faith refers to a once for all event: Christ's death.*

    a. We have rested our case in Christ's finished work.

    b. Achieving faith refers to an ongoing quest to experience great things for God.

3. *Saving faith is what accounts for righteousness in God's sight.*

    a. That righteousness is never increased nor diminished in his sight. Why?

        (1) The righteousness of Christ is put to our credit the moment we believe.

        (2) We will not be more righteous fifty years later; because Christ's righteousness cannot be improved.

    b. Achieving faith is increased through trials and tribulation (Rom. 5:3-4).

        (1) This develops character and becomes visible before others.

        (2) This means we develop and improve and become more and more like Christ.

4. *Saving faith is what secures our entrance into heaven.*

    a. Saving faith means we are going to heaven, not hell.

    b. Achieving faith is what we do on earth after we are saved.

5. *Saving faith guarantees heaven but not necessarily a reward at the Judgement Seat of Christ.*

    a. Saving faith makes a reward in heaven possible.

    b. Achieving faith makes a reward in heaven probable.

V. WHAT DOES ACHIEVING FAITH ACCOMPLISH? WHY HAVE IT?

A. To put it another way, faith for what?

1. Answered prayer (Heb. 11:6).

2. Believing fresh promises (Rom. 4:20).

3. Overcoming the devil (Eph. 6:10-18).

4. Bringing greater anointing (1 Cor. 12:31).

5. Understanding the deep things of God (1 Cor. 2:9ff).

6. Patience in tribulation (Jas. 1:2).

7. Experiencing God's oath (Heb. 6:12ff).

B. Achieving faith prepares us to follow those great saints who accomplished great things.

1. We are no different from them (Jas. 5:17).

2. *What they did, we can (and must) do.*

    a. This takes us into the 'big league'.

    b. My goal: to produce a congregation that is *full* of people like those in Hebrews 11.

        (1) Why must it be one isolated person here or there or 'way back when'?

        (2) Why not all of us – all in our place?

VI. THE STRUGGLE TO ACHIEVE ACHIEVING FAITH

A. We have two things working against us.

1. *The flesh. This includes ourselves and others.*

    a. This is a word that refers to our human nature.

        (1) We have not been delivered from our sinful bodies.

        (2) That will only come at glorification (Rom. 8:30).

    b. What can be said about the flesh:

        (1) Weak (Gal. 5:17).

        (2) Prone to repeat mistakes of the past (Phil. 3:13).

        (3) Wants attention and glory from man (John 5:44).

2. *The devil* (Eph. 6:12ff).

    a. Satan, though a conquered foe, is still active.

        (1) He works our weaknesses.

        (2) He knows all of us backwards and forwards.

    b. Satan's aim.

        (1) To defeat us and keep us from achieving faith.

        (2) To get us to grieve the Holy Spirit.

B. We have a number of things working for us.

1. *The Holy Spirit* (1 John 4:4).

    a. He took the place of Jesus (John 14:16).

        (1) Jesus called the Holy Spirit 'another' paraclete.

(2) Paraclete: One who comes alongside.

   b. The Spirit promises to show us what we need to know.

     (1) He will remind us of what we have learned (John 14:26).

     (2) He will guide us into all truth (John 16:13).

2. *The intercessory prayers of the Spirit and Jesus.*

   a. The Holy Spirit intercedes for us (Rom. 8:26,27).

     (1) We may not always pray in God's will.

     (2) He always does.

   b. Jesus also prays for us (Rom. 8:34; Heb. 7:25).

     (1) He prays with a perfect faith (Heb. 12:2).

     (2) We can live by his faith (Gal. 2:20).

3. *The power of the blood of Jesus.*

   a. The blood shed on the cross continues to be applied.

     (1) Peter refers to the 'sprinkling' of the blood (1 Pet. 1:2).

     (2) The blood continues to 'cleanse' (1 John 1:7).

   b. All the above assumes that we have faith in the blood (Rev. 12:11).

     (1) This comes by walking in the light (1 John 1:7).

     (2) This comes by obedience (1 Pet. 1:2).

4. *The Word of God.*

   a. This is where knowing the Bible is essential (Ps. 119:11).

     (1) You ask: why memorise scripture?

     (2) I answer: the Holy Spirit reminds us of what is there (John 14:26).

   b. Jesus answered Satan with scripture. 'It is written' (Matt. 4:4,7).

     (1) We overcome by the sword of the Spirit (Eph. 6:17).

     (2) There is no adequate substitute for the knowledge of the Word of God (Ps. 119:9).

5. *The knowledge that God is for us* (Rom. 8:31).

   a. He is on our side.

   b. He wants us to do the extraordinary: it is all for his glory.

C. The initial steps to achieving faith therefore are:

1. *Trust in the Word of God.*

   a. This assumes we know a bit of the Bible.

   b. Memorise and meditate upon key passages.

2. *Lean on the intercession of Christ and the Spirit.*

   a. Put our faith in Christ's faith (Gal. 2:20; 1 John 4:16).

   b. Trust in the intercession of the Spirit (Rom. 8:26-27).

3. *Walk in the Spirit not the flesh.*
  a. This comes through knowing the Spirit is not grieved.
  b. This comes through resisting temptation.
4. *Resist the devil.*
  a. Do not take him on, resist him when he attacks.
  b. Plead the merit of Jesus' blood.

D. What remains for us to do:
  1. *Avoid any trace of bitterness* (Mark 11:25).
    a. Bitterness grieves the Holy Spirit (Eph. 4:30ff).
    b. A grieved Spirit means – for us:
      (1) Confusion – no presence of mind.
      (2) The setting in of unbelief.
  2. *Being faithful in prayer.*
    a. Time with God generates faith.
    b. Distance from God results in:
      (1) The flesh getting the upper hand.
      (2) The devil taking advantage.
  3. *Claim the promises of God for our own.*
    a. Every promise in the Bible is universal.
      (1) It may have originally been addressed to another, e.g., Moses or the early church.
      (2) But they are for all of us as well.
    b. Stand on the promise, even if we don't feel like it.
      (1) Refuse to listen to any suggestion of unbelief.
      (2) When Satan attacks we are commanded to 'stand' (Eph. 6:13-14).
  4. *Walk in the light God gives us* (1 John 1:7).
    a. This is always the way forward.
    b. Not to walk in the light is to backslide.
  5. *Keep a warm, open and sensitive heart to the Holy Spirit* (Heb. 3:12).
    a. Only the Holy Spirit can increase faith.
    b. We must therefore stay on good terms with him.
  6. *Learn what pleases/displeases the Spirit.*
    a. Inner peace testifies the Spirit is generally pleased.
    b. The lack of inner peace often indicates he is grieved.
      (1) Try to trace our lack of peace to an event that could have grieved him.
      (2) Do what makes for peace (Rom. 14:19).

7. *Lean hard on 1 John 1:9 when we realise we have sinned.*
   a. Refuse to feel guilty after we have confessed our sin from our hearts.
   b. Refusing to feel guilty shows we really do believe I John 1:9 – and proves faith!
8. *Recount God's blessing up to now* (Phil. 1:6).
   a. Consider how God has supplied our needs to date.
   b. Recall answers to prayer in the past.
9. *Read good books that show God's powerful work in others.*
   a. Read the biographies of the great saints.
   b. Read books on prayer with testimonies of answered prayer.
10. *Say yes not no to any challenge God puts to you.*
   a. It may be dignifying the present trial (Jas. 1:20).
   b. It may mean taking a step of faith (Luke 16:10).

CONCLUSION

Avoid quick solutions to a life of faith. God may sometimes graciously give a wonderful 'increment' that is like a milestone. But on the whole be content with small progress when little things are dealt with (Luke 16:10). Aim for faith to become a godly habit not a sudden or exceptional event. This way you do not appropriate faith in order to use God, instead faith becomes your way of pleasing God.

Faith in Action

19

HOW TO KNOW YOU ARE SAVED

INTRODUCTION

A. Although this subject is practical (which sometimes means a bit lighter in content) the issue is very theological indeed.
    1. See The Eternal Security of the Believer (Understanding Theology Vol 1, Ch 21, p 158).
    2. *The question is: can we know we are eternally secure?*
        a. This presupposes two things:
            (1) Knowing we are of God's elect.
            (2) Knowing we can never fall away.
        b. In other words, can we know that both of the above apply to *us*?
            (1) It is one thing to affirm the teaching as being biblical.
            (2) It is quite another to say 'I am elected'; 'I am eternally secure'.

B. The doctrine of assurance.
    1. Martin Luther turned the world upside down by his re-discovery of justification by faith alone.
    2. *John Calvin came along a generation later (he never met Luther but regarded Luther as a hero) with a number of contributions, among them:*
        a. Internal witness of the Holy Spirit (how we know the Bible is true).
        b. Refinement of the doctrine of justification by faith alone.
        c. Assurance of salvation by faith alone.
    3. Some Puritans complicated the issue so that Luther's rediscovery passed behind a cloud.

C. Assurance (defined): Knowing we are saved; we will go to heaven when we die.
    1. This means we know that we are in the number of God's chosen.
    2. This means that the glorious truth of 'once saved, always saved' applies to us!

I. HISTORICAL BACKGROUND

A. The doctrine of assurance, as defined above, was not an issue in the church until after the Reformation.

   1. *In the Middle Ages there was no clear teaching that the believer could know he would go to heaven at death.*

      a. This was because of the prevailing teaching of Roman Catholicism.

         (1) There was no salvation apart from the Church.

         (2) Confession to the priest did not guarantee fitness for heaven.

         (3) It was assumed that all Christians went to Purgatory before making it to heaven in any case.

      b. Therefore the idea of knowing you were saved and would go straight to heaven did not arise.

         (1) People saved by faith plus works.

         (2) Faith was assent to the doctrines of the Church.

         (3) It would have been regarded as pompous, if not blasphemous, to claim to be worthy to go straight to heaven without passing through Purgatory.

   2. *Martin Luther's rediscovery of justification by faith alone changed people's way of thinking.*

      a. Faith alone counts for righteousness.

      b. Faith alone satisfies God's 'passive' justice.

      c. Works do not help people to get to heaven, only faith.

      d. In addition, Luther rejected the doctrine of Purgatory.

         (1) The Pope was said to control how long a person stayed in Purgatory.

         (2) Luther said, 'If that is so, why doesn't the Pope let everybody out?'

B. John Calvin's teaching was more refined, having a generation to reflect on all that Luther taught.

   1. *Calvin said there were three 'causes' of justification:*

      a. Meritorious cause: the death of Christ.

      b. Instrumental cause: faith.

      c. Efficient cause: the Holy Spirit.

   2. *Calvin defined faith as 'a firm and certain knowledge of God's benevolence toward us, founded upon the truth of the freely*

given promise in Christ, both revealed to our minds and sealed
upon our hearts through the Holy Spirit.'

   a. This definition assumes:

      (1) Faith is knowledge.

      (2) Faith is assurance.

      (3) Faith is sealed in the heart.

   b. This definition also takes for granted that:

      (1) Christ died for all; not the elect only.

      (2) If he did not die for all we could not look to the 'freely
given promise'.

      (3) We derive assurance by looking to Christ, the 'mirror
of our election'.

3. *Calvin warned against introspection and looking to our works
'for our assurance to be firm'. According to him:*

   a. If we contemplate ourselves, that is sure damnation.

   b. The only basis of assurance is trust in the general promise
that Christ died for us.

      (1) Unsaved people could temporarily manifest some
evidences that are akin to those who are saved.

      (2) But saved people are not to look primarily to the
evidences in any case.

4. In a word: we are assured by faith in Christ alone.

**C. Puritan teaching generally departed from Calvin in this
particular matter.**

   1. *The most influential Puritan was William Perkins (1558 – 1602).*

      a. He got his main ideas from Theodore Beza, Calvin's
successor in Geneva.

      b. Beza may not have been aware that he departed from Calvin;
but here is what he taught:

         (1) We must begin with sanctification 'which we feel in
ourselves'.

         (2) Since sanctification is an effect from faith it follows
that sanctification proves that faith is there.

   2. *William Perkins gave Theodore Beza the credit for his
theological system (he may have assumed that he was getting
Calvin in the package since Beza and Calvin worked together).*

      a. Perkins followed Beza almost to the letter:

         (1) We judge whether we are elected by whether there is
sanctification.

    (2) We know there is fire when there is heat; heat is the sanctification that proves the Holy Spirit has been at work.

  b. In a word: our assurance is based upon sanctification.

    (1) With Calvin, our assurance is based on Christ.

    (2) With Perkins (following Beza) our assurance is based on whether we are sanctified.

    (3) Note: the reason Perkins could never point people directly to Christ is because Christ died only for the elect; the only way we could know he died for *us* is by whether or not we are being sanctified. But there was a problem: the reprobate by temporary faith could evidence sanctification as well!

    (4) Later Puritans, such as William Ames (d.1633), dropped the idea of temporary faith and explicitly stated that faith is seated in the will. If we *willed* to be sanctified we could know we are saved. With Calvin, if we are persuaded in our hearts that Christ died for us, we are saved.

  c. All of this is reasonably straightforward except (obviously) for one thing: their teaching of the temporary faith of the reprobate (non-elect).

    (1) Those not elected to salvation could manifest the 'fruits' of sanctification, said Perkins.

    (2) This was because the non-elect may have temporary faith that was never truly saving faith in the first place.

    (3) The problem is obvious: the most godly people of the day never knew for sure that they were saved; they feared the whole time that the sanctification they manifested was but the evidence of temporary faith; therefore they were still lost!

    (4) This sort of problem is not widespread today but it does exist, especially in Scotland and in hyper-Calvinist churches.

    (5) For this reason, some Christians will not partake of the Lord's Supper.

D. Early Methodism taught a rather different brand of assurance: a 'feeling' of being forgiven.

1. *Methodists generally did not believe in the eternal security of the believer.*

    a. They believed you could lose your salvation.

    b. They had no valid teaching therefore of assurance of salvation.

2. *What they taught however was that one could know now – today – that he is saved but he could not be sure he would know this tomorrow!*

    a. He could know the witness of the Spirit that his sins were forgiven.

        (1) This is past sins only.

        (2) There is no forgiveness, they said, for future sins unless they too were forgiven after the sins were committed.

    b. The witness of the Spirit in early Methodism was a feeling for a moment that you were saved.

        (1) But if you sinned tomorrow you could be lost.

        (2) This obviously led to trust in your own faithfulness, not in what Christ did for you on the cross.

    c. In a word: assurance was only temporary.

        (1) Perkins taught that the non-elect could have a false assurance.

        (2) Methodism taught that true Christians could have a temporary assurance – but no more!

E. Modern evangelicalism has seen a varied interpretation of assurance.

1. *Experience of forgiveness by praying at a mourner's bench.*

    a. This was popularised by the revivalistic atmosphere of nineteenth century Christianity in America, especially under the influence of Charles Finney.

    b. The issue of 'once saved, always saved' was not always relevant.

        (1) For those who believed it, the experience confirmed their eternal security.

        (2) For those who did not believe it, their assurance was but temporary (as in Methodism).

2. *Walking forward in an evangelistic meeting.*

    a. D L Moody popularised the Inquiry Room. People were given assurance of salvation – with 'no emotion' – by believing in three facts:

        (1) You are a sinner.

        (2) Christ died for you.

        (3) You trust in Christ; therefore you are saved.

    b. Billy Graham largely followed in D L Moody's footsteps.

        (1) The early Billy Graham emphasised 'making a decision for Christ'.

        (2) In later years Billy stresses 'commitment to Christ'.

3. *The more sacramental (stressing baptism and the Lord's Supper as sacraments) churches (e.g. Church of England) stress the following as evidence that you are a Christian:*

    a. Baptism (infant or adult).

    b. Confirmation (when you become committed).

    c. The Lord's Supper.

    d. Church membership.

    e. Note: the issue of whether you would go straight to heaven at death varies from church to church, sometimes depending on whether it is a 'high' church or a 'low' (evangelical) church.

        (1) The eternal security of the believer is often not an issue.

        (2) The question of assurance is raised usually by the more faithful parishioner (or vicar).

F. All of the above have seen a range of views:

    1. Looking to Christ alone (faith is seated in the heart).

    2. Looking to sanctification (faith is seated in the will).

    3. An emotional experience (albeit by the Holy Spirit).

    4. A non-emotional experience.

    5. Faith in the sacraments.

II . THERE ARE TWO VALID LEVELS OF ASSURANCE

A. Sanctified reasoning.

    1. *This used to be called the 'practical syllogism' (following Aristotle).*

        a. A major premis is followed by a minor premiss that draws a conclusion.

(1) Major premis: All who trust in Jesus Christ are saved.

(2) Minor premis: But I trust in Jesus Christ.

(3) Conclusion: Therefore I am saved.

b. This kind of reasoning was used by certain Puritans but in different ways.

(1) Major premis: All who have the fruits of sanctification are those for whom Christ died, e.g.: they keep the Sabbath; love God's ministers; have turned from every known sin.

(2) Minor premis: I have the fruits of sanctification.

(3) Conclusion: Therefore Christ died for me.

c. Only with Calvin's belief that Christ died for all can the practical syllogism prove valid.

(1) I can always look to Christ; he died for all, therefore I know he died for me.

(2) This coheres with the gospel promise as in John 3:16.

2. *A necessary clarification must be made, however:*

a. That this trust in Christ is seated in the heart.

(1) By heart we mean the fully persuaded mind.

(2) In other words, as we say, in your 'heart of hearts'.

b. This warns against two things:

(1) Mental assent – when faith is bare intellectual belief and not that which reaches the heart.

(2) Voluntaryism (faith seated in the will) – when you are looking to deeds and works which you *do* in order to feel saved.

c. Only the Holy Spirit can bring about trust in the heart (Rom. 10:9-10; 1 Thess. 2:13).

(1) You can have a counterfeit faith merely by mere believing in certain facts about Christ – or what the church teaches.

(2) You can be looking to your good works for your assurance to be firm, and never see the glory of the person and work of Christ.

(3) Only the Holy Spirit can persuade the heart that 'Christ alone is my hope of salvation'.

3. *The obvious difficulty with the teaching that our good works prove that we are saved is this: how do we ever know we have enough good works?*

     a. There is a very thin line between salvation by works (which is heresy) and assurance of salvation by works (which diverts our minds away from Christ).

     b. Those who lean on their good works (call it sanctification or godliness or what you will) for assurance that they are saved:

       (1) Always have doubts.

       (2) Their assurance vacillates with their moods and state of faithfulness.

       (3) They feel saved today, lost tomorrow.

4. *The valid application of the practical syllogism is based upon four assumptions:*

     a. Christ died for all of us.

     b. I trust in his death and resurrection with all my heart.

     c. Therefore I know I am saved, for God's Word says so (John 5:24; Rom. 10:9).

     d. The only explanation for this experience of the heart: the Holy Spirit.

5. *Question: Where does sanctification come in?*
Answer: This is the inevitable effect, though it is by degrees and varies from person to person, of saving faith.

     a. It is right to regard sanctification as proof of true conversion (Rom. 6:22).

     b. But it is for others to see in me; my own basis (or ground) of assurance: Christ alone.

B. The immediate witness of the Holy Spirit.

1. *There are two kinds of witness of the Holy Spirit.*

     a. Mediate witness – the practical syllogism.

       (1) I believe – is the work of the Holy Spirit.

       (2) Therefore I am saved – is sanctified reasoning.

     b. Immediate witness – direct to the heart.

       (1) It by-passes the need to keep on reflecting again and again on whether I have looked to Christ.

       (2) It enables me to know by instant knowledge that I am saved without having to employ the reasoning process. Note: I do not doubt that many early Methodists experienced this, despite a faulty theology.

2. *This can happen in a number of ways:*

     a. At conversion (Acts 10:44).

    b. Following conversion (Acts 19:2).

    c. Following a time of either lapse or discouragement (Heb. 10:35-37).

3. *There are a number of names for the immediate witness of the Spirit:*

    a. Baptism of the Holy Spirit (Acts 1:5).

    b. Sealing of the Spirit (Eph. 1:13).

    c. Rest of faith (Heb. 4:9-10).

    d. Full assurance (Heb. 6:11).

4. *It is my view that, more often than not, this comes to a person some time after conversion – even if he had been assured already by the practical syllogism.*

    a. It is also my suspicion that this happens less frequently than some may suppose.

    b. It is a mighty work of God that is to be desired – almost above anything else!

CONCLUSION

Any Christian can and should know that they are saved – if only by the practical syllogism. The immediate witness of the Spirit should be prayed for by those who don't have it.

20

HOW TO WORSHIP GOD

INTRODUCTION

A. This is the practical application of our previous lesson 'The Worship of God' (Understanding Theology Vol 1, ch 28, p 210).

   1. There we defined worship: the response to, and/or preparation for, the preached word.

   2. How do we do that?

B. It is not a little bit presumptuous to offer this lesson. After all:

   1. Who really worships God as he or she should?

   2. Who is qualified to teach how to worship God?

C. We will not worship God as we should until we get to heaven.

D. But we must begin somewhere and make every attempt to worship God in a right way.

   1. *We must never forget: God has his own idea how he wants to be worshipped.*

   a. We must keep in mind what our worship does for him rather than what it does for us.

   b. Otherwise our worship will be selfish and not pleasing to him.

   2. *The book of Leviticus is largely about the Ceremonial Law – how God is to be worshipped.*

   a. It does not follow that we begin with Leviticus in order to learn how to worship God.

   b. But that book shows that God tells *us* how to worship him.

   (1) We are not to worship him any old way we feel like.

   (2) We are to find out how he wants to be worshipped: in the Spirit and in Truth (John 4:24).

I. THE WORSHIP OF GOD AND THE HOLY SPIRIT CANNOT BE SEPARATED

A. We worship by the Spirit of God (Phil. 3:3).
  1. *This means that the Spirit enables us to worship.*
       a. No-one can say that Jesus is the Lord but by the Holy Spirit (1 Cor. 12:3).
       b. No-one can come to Christ except by the Holy Spirit (John 6:44).
  2. *This means we follow the impulse of the Spirit.*
       a. Impulse (def.): a push, thrust or stimulating thrust.
       b. This means without the Spirit's impulse any 'worship' is in the flesh.

B. To worship by the Spirit of God presupposes that we worship in the Truth.
  1. *Because the Holy Spirit is the Spirit of truth* (John 14:17).
       a. This means the worship of God in the Spirit is not subjective but objective.
           (1) Subjective (def.): how we feel in ourselves without reference to what is true apart from us.
           (2) Objective (def.): what is true outside of us, whether or not we feel it.
       b. Worship may be emotional but empty.
           (1) We may feel good when we worship but it does not follow that we are worshipping according to Truth.
           (2) Empty worship is devoid of Truth, even though it may be sophisticated.
  2. *The truth therefore assumes certain elementary matters:*
       a. The Triune God: the affirmation of the Trinity.
       b. The full inspiration of the Bible as the Word of God.
       c. Redemption (salvation) by the blood of Christ.
       d. The glory of God (sum total of his attributes):
           (1) Omnipotence, omniscience, omnipresence.
           (2) Holiness, love, sovereignty.
       e. In a word: sound doctrine is important in the worship of God.

C. What can never be overemphasised is that, in order to worship God in the Spirit, we should be on good terms with the Holy Spirit.

1. *A grieved Holy Spirit will mean:*
    a. The flesh will have the upper hand when we worship.
        (1) There will be confusion of mind.
        (2) Our hearts will not be truly fixed on God.
    b. Our worship will therefore be outward, like going through the motions without the heart entering in.

2. *We therefore need to be in the right frame of mind when we worship:*
    a. To sing.
    b. To listen to preaching.
    c. To pray.
    d. To hear the reading of Holy Scripture.
    e. To partake of the Lord's Supper.

3. *The chief way we grieve the Spirit is by bitterness* (Eph. 4:30ff).
    a. Anger.
    b. Speaking of others in an unflattering manner.
    c. Holding a grudge (inability to forgive).

4. *If the objective worship of God is anointed (the preaching, hymns, etc.) it does not follow that we will feel that anointing.*
    a. The Holy Spirit wrote the Bible (2 Tim. 3:16; 2 Pet. 1:21), but it does not follow that the Spirit always speaks to me when I read it.
        (1) It largely depends on me; my attitude, frame of mind.
        (2) My heart must be prepared when I read the Bible.
    b. So too with all worship:
        (1) My heart must be prepared to hear God speak.
        (2) My heart must be prepared to sing – or I will utter phrases that will mean little to me or God at the time.
    c. We therefore must stay on good terms with God's ungrieved Holy Spirit to worship by the same Spirit.

II. THE WORSHIP OF GOD AND OUR DAILY LIFESTYLE CANNOT BE SEPARATED

A. What we are individually, twenty-four hours a day, is more important than what happens in church once or twice a week.
    1. The secret of acceptable worship lies in how we are at home, or at work.
    2. *The secret of acceptable worship is traceable to what we are*

when we are alone and nobody knows what we are doing.
- **a.** Jesus said: 'Whoever can be trusted with very little can also be trusted with much, and whoever is dishonest with very little will also be dishonest with much' (Luke 16:10).
- **b.** If we don't get our act together before we come to church, we can't expect truly to worship at church.
  - **(1)** Nothing 'magical' happens once we are inside the doors.
  - **(2)** It means our lifestyle generally is of utmost importance.

B. What is needed in worship, individually and corporately, is the 'unity of the Spirit' (Eph. 4:3).
1. This means that the leadership of the Spirit in you will not contradict the leadership of the Spirit in me.
2. *If we are guided by the Spirit we will be in agreement.*
   - **a.** The ungrieved Spirit in me can detect the ungrieved Spirit in you.
   - **b.** There will be no heaviness when we meet – only peace and harmony.

C. It is like a symphony orchestra: all the instruments play their own parts.
1. But no orchestra comes together without each individual having practised alone!
2. When each member of the orchestra has practised his part at home, they all play well together – beautiful music is the result!
3. *How much more, then, ought each member of a congregation be careful to worship God – to get on the best of terms with the Holy Spirit – so that when all meet together at church, spontaneous combustion takes place!*
   - **a.** When members of the congregation aren't speaking to each other, but pretend to worship God, how do you suppose this makes God feel?
   - **b.** But this is so often the case, sadly.
     - **(1)** The result is going through the form without real worship taking place.
     - **(2)** Such 'worship' does not come by the impulse of the Holy Spirit.

III. TRUE WORSHIP CANNOT BE SEPARATED FROM A CONSCIOUSNESS OF GOD LOOKING ON

A. Are you aware that God is watching you and personally listening to you when you worship?
   1. When you listen to the preaching.
   2. When you sing hymns or choruses.
   3. When you are alone at home – reading the Bible or praying.

B. We need to develop a consciousness of his eyes looking at us – his ears listening to us; because that is *exactly* how it is.
   1. *This is true at home or at church.*
      a. Illustration: suppose Her Majesty the Queen were in church with you at this moment; who would you be thinking of mostly? The Queen.
      b. But the Lord *is* with us – the King of kings; and we should develop a consciousness of his presence.
         (1) The Queen wouldn't be thinking about you!
         (2) But the Lord is!

C. The proof of the presence of God in great measure: we are minimally conscious of each other.
   1. Many would possibly lift their hands in public worship but are too conscious of what others will think.
   2. *But if we were conscious only of God, we would dismiss any thought of self-consciousness of others around us.*
      a. And yet the Bible talks of lifting up holy hands. 'I want men everywhere to lift up holy hands in prayer, without anger or disputing' (1 Tim. 2:8).
      b. The psalms speak of lifting our hands – and the psalms were to be sung! 'O LORD, I call to you; come quickly to me. Hear my voice when I call to you. May my prayer be set before you like incense; may the lifting up of my hands be like the evening sacrifice' (Ps. 141:1-2).

D. We can learn from angels, the perfect worshippers of God (Isa. 6:1-3).
   1. And yet they don't even have salvation to be thankful for!
   2. *Angels adore God.*

   a. They are conscious only of him and his glory.

   b. They cannot be bribed or diverted from their priority to God himself.

   (1) They refuse worship (Rev. 19:10).

   (2) They only want us to worship God.

3. They never tire of worshipping God (Rev. 4:8).

4. They worship Jesus Christ (Heb. 1:6).

5. They perceive the true essence of God's character. 'Holy, holy, holy.'

6. *Though they have been worshipping God for centuries, they still show great reverence for him.*

   a. Many today develop an undue familiarity with God.

   b. We do indeed have access by the Spirit by which we cry 'Abba, Father'.

   c. But that never should lead us to take God for granted.

7. *They rejoice in the conversion of the lost. (Luke 15:10).*

   a. Do we?

   b. Are we excited to see people saved?

E. We must learn to resist the devil, who hates our worship of God (Eph. 6:10-12).

1. Satan cannot stand his arch-enemy, the Lord Jesus Christ, being exalted.

2. *The devil will try to destroy your worship.*

   a. He will look for ways to annoy you, so you will grieve the Spirit.

   b. He loves to make you upset:

   (1) Just before – or during – your quiet time.

   (2) Just before – or during – worship at church.

   c. He will try to make you lose concentration.

   d. He will remind you of all your sins.

   e. He will try to hurt your sleep.

3. A great evidence of spiritual growth is the ability to recognise, refuse and resist the devil (Jas. 4:7; 1 Pet. 5:8).

F. Consciousness of God is to be sought preeminently, no matter the manner or style of worship.

1. *Singing. 'Sing unto the Lord with thanksgiving'* (Ps. 147:7).

   a. The first reference to singing in the Bible is Exodus 15:1, when Israel had just witnessed God's wrath poured out on Egypt.

b. This tells us that singing is:

(1) A response of gratitude to God.

(2) A response of rejoicing.

(3) A response to the Lord himself.

(4) A responsibility laid on the people by Moses.

c. The art of singing was cultivated in the Old Testament.

(1) We must not underestimate the importance of singing.

(2) We should sing corporately to God, but each of us should consciously sing to God as though he were listening solely to us, as though to no-one else.

2. *Music.* '*Praise him with the sounding of the trumpet, praise him with the harp and lyre, praise him with tambourine and dancing, praise him with the strings and flute*' (Ps. 150:3-6).

a. Martin Luther said that next to theology he loved music.

b. Music is God's idea; he invented it!

c. David, the man after God's own heart, loved music.

(1) It was assumed in the Old Testament that music would be a part of worship.

(2) It never crossed their minds that important events would be celebrated without music.

d. Music was an accessory to worship.

(1) Important as the musician was, his music was not seen as an end in itself.

(2) Good musicianship, like good preaching, does not call attention to itself but brings us to focus on God.

3. *Giving.* '"*Bring the whole tithe into the storehouse, that there may be food in my house. Test me in this,*" *says the Lord Almighty, "and see if I will not throw open the floodgates of heaven and pour out so much blessing that you will not have room enough for it*"' (Mal. 3:10).

a. Giving is not only a part of worship, but constitutes a greater part than many of us have thought.

b. How we respond to the preached Word shows how much we really worship.

c. We show God how much he means to us by:

(1) Whether we give (Matt. 6:1-4).

(2) The amount we give (Lev. 27:30).

(3) The spirit in which we give (2 Cor. 9:7).

d. Withholding from God what is his is disobedience.

(1) Any area of disobedience in our lives will affect our worship.

(2) It is amazing how consistent tithing will affect the *whole* of our lives!

4. *Liturgy. 'When you come together, everyone has a hymn, or a word of instruction, a revelation, a tongue or an interpretation. All of these must be done for the strengthening of the church'* (1 Cor. 14:26).

a. There are basically two styles of worship:

(1) Liturgical – which is done in the more historic churches (Anglican, Presbyterian, Baptist).

(2) Non-liturgical – which is done in the more charismatic churches.

b. The truth is, every church has its own liturgy, even if it claims to be non-liturgical!

c. Liturgy was actually God's idea from the beginning.

(1) Gr. *leitourgos* means 'minister' or 'ministry'.

(2) It means 'serving people' or 'serving God'.

d. The Law was total liturgy, telling us how to worship God.

e. Purpose of liturgy today:

(1) It lets us know when to start and where to meet.

(2) It helps people with no Christian background.

(3) It has theological content.

(4) It helps avoid extremes; it has probably been prepared with care.

(5) It ensures that the service will end!

f. In any case, worship must be by the Spirit – which may mean willingness to break out of our traditional liturgy.

CONCLUSION

We all need help in how to worship God. It is certain that we will get our worship right in heaven! But to the extent we worship 'by the Spirit' we get it right in the here and now.

21

HOW TO RECOGNISE GOD'S VOICE

INTRODUCTION

A. This is one of the most important theological studies we have yet embarked upon.
    1. *There is always the temptation, whatever the lesson, to say, 'This is one of the most important, if not the most important.'*
        a. It is like when I am reading in the Psalms.
        b. I tend to think nearly every one I am reading is the most important and best!
    2. But this lesson must not be underestimated.

B. Why is this study on hearing God's voice so important?
    1. *It is ultimately how we know we are being guided by the Holy Spirit and we are on 'speaking terms' with God.*
        a. We have had a study on guidance: 'How to know the will of God' (see Chapter 23).
        b. This lesson is a follow-up, if not further clarification, on how to know the will of God.
            (1) Recall the acrostic PEACE.
            (2) All in this study will cohere with that.
    2. *It is a test whether or not we are truly having fellowship with the Father* (1 John 1:3).
        a. The immediate proof we are having fellowship with the Father is that we hear his voice.
            (1) It is how to know we are receiving light.
            (2) It is how to know we are walking in the light (1 John 1:7).
        b. One of the most important evidences that we are walking in the light is the fresh discovery of sin (1 John 1:8).
            (1) When we walk in the light we become more conscious of (a) fellowship with the Father, (b) the cleansing blood and (c) a fresh sense of sin.

      (2) Walking in the light results in a discovery of sin we had not been conscious of before.

   c. That we have been given a fresh sense of sin shows that we are hearing God's voice.

      (1) We are convicted, and we confess (1 John 1:9).

      (2) A typical reaction is, 'Lord, why didn't you show me that before?'

3. *Not hearing God's voice is possibly the most ominous (threatening) absence imaginable; we call it a Hebrews 6:4-6 situation.*

   a. It means we are becoming deaf (Heb. 5:11).

      (1) NIV: 'slow to learn'.

      (2) AV: 'dull of hearing', an accurate translation of the Greek.

   b. Deafness begins (usually) in stages.

      (1) At the natural level, people normally become deaf only by degrees.

      (2) This is true spiritually as well.

   c. The worst thing imaginable in this area: stone deafness.

      (1) This is when we do not hear God at all.

      (2) It is what is meant by not being able to be renewed again unto repentance (Heb. 6:4-6).

C. **We therefore want to learn for sure that:**

  1. *We hear God's voice* (Heb. 3:7ff).

   a. This means recognising his voice.

   b. This means we know the difference between God's voice and :

      (1) That of Satan.

      (2) Our own propensity to think this or that and assume such to be God's voice.

  2. *We obey God's voice.*

   a. If we don't obey what we hear God will likely discontinue speaking.

   b. The only way to keep hearing God's voice is to keep doing what he says.

  3. We know what we can do to keep an open communication with him.

  4. We know what grieves him.

I. GOD SPEAKS TO HIS PEOPLE AND HE WANTS TO BE HEARD

A. This is why he has given us his word – the Bible.
    1. *Recall: previous lesson on the will of God (ch 26 of this volume).*
        a. Revealed will: the Bible.
        b. Secret will: his own opinion on what to do in a particular circumstance.
            (1) God's revealed will is to be sought above his secret will.
            (2) The more we know God's revealed will, the easier it is to know his secret will.
            (3) God's secret will will never contradict his revealed will.
    2. *Hearing God's voice will presuppose two things (almost always in this order):*
        a. Mastery of God's revealed will (knowing the Bible).
        b. Familiarity with his ways. 'They have not known my ways,' God lamented concerning the children of Israel (Heb. 3:10).

B. There are two areas in which God has spoken and each area is characterised by a corresponding instrument of God's voice.
    1. *To our forefathers. 'In times past'* (Heb 1:1 AV).
        a. This refers to people in the Old Testament.
        b. The chief way God spoke to them: by prophets.
            (1) Canonical prophets (e.g., Isaiah, Jeremiah, etc.).
            (2) Prophets who spoke in the Spirit but did not have a book named after them (e.g. Elijah, Elisha).
    2. *The last days* (Heb 1:2).
        a. This refers to the present era.
            (1) This began with the coming of Jesus Christ.
            (2) This era continues to the present time.
        b. God speaks today through his Son.
            (1) This means the Gospel.
            (2) This means the Holy Spirit who honours the Son.

C. The way God speaks today, then, is by the Gospel, and that by the Holy Spirit.
    1. No-one can receive the Gospel but by the Spirit (John 3:27; 6:44,65).
    2. *Once a person has received the Gospel it shows three things:*
        a. He has been convicted of sin (John 16:8).

b. He has been pointed to Jesus Christ.

c. He has the Holy Spirit (Rom. 8:9).

3. *The Holy Spirit in us is our link with the Father.*

    a. He abides with us forever (John 14:16-17).

    b. He is a person who can be grieved (Eph. 4:30).

    c. We therefore must be on good terms with the Spirit to hear God's voice (Heb. 3:7-8).

4. *'We can have as much of God as we want' (A W Tozer).*

    a. When I first came across those words I had mixed feelings.

        (1) My first reaction: That is wonderful.

        (2) My second reaction: It isn't true.

    b. I have concluded that it *is* true.

        (1) We tend to overestimate at first how much of God we want.

        (2) Along the way many of us are loathe to pay the price required (e.g. self-denial) in order to have more of God.

    c. Question: how much of God do we *really* want?

D. The truth is: God wants and longs for fellowship with each of us.

1. This comes only to the degree we hear his voice.

2. If, when we are talking with someone, we stop listening we put a strain on that fellowship.

3. *The other person will stop talking with us.*

    a. God wants to be heard.

    b. The question is: do we hear him?

II. IN OUR PRE-CONVERSION STATE **G**OD SPEAKS THROUGH CONSCIENCE. (R**OM**. 1:19-20).

A. All men are born with a conscience. Speaking theologically this is called:

1. *General revelation* (John 1:9).

    a. It is sometimes called 'common grace'.

    b. This is God's goodness to all men, good or bad (Matt. 5:45).

2. *Natural revelation* (Rom. 1:19-20).

    a. Called 'natural' because all are born with a certain awareness of God.

        (1) Pascal: 'God-shaped blank in every man'.

(2) Augustine: 'Thou hast made us for Thyself; our hearts are restless until they find their rest in Thee.'

b. We do not have to be converted to experience this (Ps. 19:1).

B. Conscience is the self-conscious sense of right and wrong.

1. All are born with it.

2. *The testimony of the conscience is a way of hearing God speak even before conversion.*

    a. It is not sufficient to save.

    b. But it is sufficient to condemn.

        (1) It is what vindicates God's justice in punishing men.

        (2) Those who perish will know they *chose* evil (John 3:19-21).

III. IN CONVERSION THE CONSCIENCE IS SAID TO BE CLEANSED (HEB. 9:14).

A. The cleansed conscience is the result of two things:

1. *The Blood of Christ.*

    a. This declares us just before God.

    b. This enables us to know we are forgiven.

2. *The Holy Spirit.*

    a. The Holy Spirit applies the Blood of Christ.

    b. The Holy Spirit witnesses this reality to us.

B. The cleansed conscience, then, means two things:

1. *The carry-over of the same conscience we are born with.*

    a. We do not lose this conscience.

    b. We continue to have this same sense of right and wrong.

2. *The enabling power of the Spirit to explore two things:*

    a. The deeper understanding of the conscience.

        (1) We can get to the bottom of our feelings.

        (2) This means total honesty with ourselves, something the unregenerate (unconverted) man is afraid to do.

    b. The indwelling Spirit who does two things:

        (1) Works through the cleansed conscience.

        (2) Reveals the Word and the present voice of God.

C. Hearing God's voice therefore means:
  1. Our consciences are cleansed by the Blood of Christ.
  2. *We are tuned into God's heart.*
    a. Two things are required, then, to hear God's voice.
      (1) That we have been saved.
      (2) That we are walking in the light.
    b. This enables us to know what God is doing here and now.
      (1) We will not only know his Word – the Bible.
      (2) We will know his voice via the Holy Spirit.

IV. THOSE WHO MANIFEST THE FRUIT OF THE SPIRIT ARE SUSCEPTIBLE TO THE DIRECT AND IMMEDIATE GUIDANCE OF THE SPIRIT

A. Why? Because the ungrieved Spirit is at work in their hearts and lives already.

B. When the Spirit works ungrieved in us:
  1. We can hear his voice (positive impulse); there will be liberty to proceed (Acts 8:29).
  2. We can sense his check (negative impulse); you will have no liberty to proceed (Acts 16:6-7).

C. God wants to communicate directly with all of us.
  1. The Bible was not given to replace direct guidance, which was the common experience of the early church.
  2. *The Bible was given to correct abuses.*
    a. Any 'guidance' that is contrary to Scripture is not from heaven (Jas. 3:15-16).
    b. The Bible will verify or condemn our impulses.
  3. *What Philip experienced in Acts chapter 8 can be the experience of all who seek to witness for the glory of God.*
    a. He recognised the Spirit's impulse.
    b. He followed it; a wonderful conversion followed.

V. HOW CAN WE BE SURE IT IS GOD'S VOICE WE ARE HEARING?

A. If what we hear coheres with the Bible.
  1. Nothing God says here and now will contradict the Bible.
  2. Recall earlier study: how to know the will of God (ch 26 of this volume).
  3. Recall acrostic PEACE (ch 26 of this volume).

B. When we are gripped by sound preaching/teaching.

1. *God continues to speak through preaching/teaching* (1 Cor. 1:21).
    a. This is how we were converted (Rom. 10:14).
    b. It is equally what saves those who 'believe' (present tense) (1 Cor. 1:21).
2. *Note two things:*
    a. That the teaching is sound.
        (1) This requires that we know our Bible.
    b. That we are 'gripped'.
        (1) That means stirred within; or warmed (Luke 24:32).
        (2) It is when our hearts warm to the Word.

C. When an inner conviction of 'oughtness' seizes us which leaves us with no peace until we obey.

1. *It is when we* know *what we have to do.*
    a. But is this not highly subjective and vulnerable to vain imagination?
    b. Answer: Not if it is set in the context of what is clearly revealed in the Bible.
        (1) Personal witnessing.
        (2) Tithing.
        (3) Absence of worldliness – that which cools our love for the things of God.
        (4) Absence of sensuality – that which dominates our thinking with regard to sexual sin.
        (5) Dignifying the trial.
        (6) Total forgiveness.
        (7) Commitment to and involvement with the church.
2. *When that sense of duty is embraced:*
    a. We will feel peace within.
    b. The presence of God will be real.
    c. Inner liberty will be felt.
    d. The person of Jesus will be real.
    e. Greater confidence in life generally will follow.

D. When by following that feeling of 'oughtness' there actually comes a sweet inner peace and ease (Rom. 14:19).

1. The fruit of the Spirit is always love, joy and peace (Gal. 5:22; cf. Jas. 3:17).

2. *If that sweet peace is absent after following the feeling of 'oughtness' we must be willing to back up and reassess what we did.*

  a. Sometimes 'oughtness' is motivated by pseudo-guilt.

   (1) Pseudo-guilt is false guilt.

   (2) Sometimes an 'overly scrupulous' conscience is taking something (or someone) more seriously than God requires.

  b. When we are driven by pseudo-guilt there will not be a lasting peace as a result.

   (1) A temporary relief may result.

   (2) But eventually an uneasiness sets in.

  c. It shows we were not being true to ourselves.

   (1) 'To thine own self be true' (Shakespeare).

   (2) God will never lead us to do that which is not true to ourselves.

E. When lasting peace follows (Col. 3:15)

  1. *Temporary peace may come from giving in to feelings of guilt not put there by God.*

   a. People may make us feel guilty.

   b. Satan may make us feel guilty (Rev. 12:10).

  2. *The peace that God gives stands the test of time.*

   a. Going against what God shows us will result in a loss of peace.

   b. The only way for that peace to return is to do what we know in our heart of hearts God said: 'This do.'

   c. Sometimes trial and error must be experienced before we are completely and finally sure.

F. When, by following all of the above, we are 'renewed again' to repentance.

  1. Repentance: change of mind.

  2. *The Christian life is one of continual change of mind.*

   a. It is grace upon grace: one blessing after another (John 1:16).

   b. It is being transformed into his likeness with ever increasing glory (2 Cor. 3:18).

  3. When God continues to reveal himself to us by fresh conviction of sin and new spiritual insight we are in pretty good shape!

VI. HOW DOES **G**OD SPEAK TO US AFTER WE HAVE DEVELOPED FURTHER SPIRITUAL MATURITY?

A. The Bible.
1. *We never outgrow the Bible.*
    a. 'The unfolding of your words gives light' (Ps. 119:130).
    b. 'How sweet are your words to my taste, sweeter than honey to my mouth!' (Ps. 119:103).
2. *Any impression, 'prophetic word', 'word of knowledge' or utterance by any person – even if he or she is a church leader – that diminishes your respect for, or need to lean on, the Bible is not of God.*
    a. The maturer you are the more you will love the Bible.
    b. The maturer you are the more you will need the Bible.
3. *When you are found walking in the light you will discover how often:*
    a. God quickens a verse to you – making its truth shine like letters of gold.
    b. This is a sign of the immediate witness of the Spirit.

B. Worship at church.
1. *God may break through to your heart through the singing.*
    a. It may come through an old hymn.
    b. It may come through a contemporary song.
2. It may come through the public reading of Scripture.
3. It may come through the public prayers.
4. It may come through the preached Word.

C. A prophetic word or word of knowledge (not necessarily *to* or *from* a spiritually mature person). (1 Thess. 5:20).
1. God may use someone to speak directly to you.
2. *How can we know such is truly from God?* See 1 Thessalonains 5:21: 'Test everything. Hold on to the good.'
    a. If it coheres with Holy Scripture.
    b. If it rings true.
    c. If you have every reason to trust the person giving you this word.
    d. If it gives genuine confidence.
    e. If it brings peace.
    f. If it makes you want to be more like Jesus.

D. Worship alone.

1. Through your own quiet time you can develop a genuine, unfeigned (you won't be deceived) sensitivity to the Holy Spirit.

2. *There is more than one way it may emerge:*
   a. A feeling of 'oughtness'.
   b. A sweet peace.
   c. A burden for someone.
   d. A spirit of sublime worship and intense gratitude to God.
   e. A sense of God's presence so real you hardly want to move or speak.
   f. An impression to turn to a verse in the Bible.
   g. (Rarely) a vision or an immediate word.
      (1) In this case share it with your pastor before acting hastily or talking a lot about it.
      (2) Never by-pass your leadership or develop a feeling you are more 'spiritual' than most.
   h. Note: any sense of spirituality that does not result in humility and meekness must be suspect; you should develop sufficient objectivity about yourself to see this!

VII. HOW TO DEVELOP A SHARPER SENSITIVITY TO RECOGNISING GOD'S VOICE

A. Stay grateful (Phil. 4:6; 1 Thess. 5:16-18).

1. *A negative, complaining spirit grieves God.*
   a. Learn to dignify every trial and adverse circumstance.
   b. God allowed this as a test (2 Chron. 32:31).

2. *There is nothing that God likes more than a heart which is continually grateful and thankful.*
   a. This keeps the devil at bay.
   b. This keeps the ungrieved Spirit on speaking terms!

B. Keep a warm heart (Heb. 3:12). Stay teachable.

1. *A cold heart will never do.*
   a. A critical, cynical spirit.
   b. A heart that hasn't heard from God lately.

2. *Proof of a warm heart:*
   a. You are approachable; people will not be intimidated by you or walk on eggshells round you.

   b. You are open to the direct and immediate ways of God.
      (1) If you do not believe God speaks like this you have already quenched the Spirit.
      (2) It is highly unlikely therefore that God will be intimate with you.

C. Learn to recognise and resist the devil.

   1. *The devil's ways usually appear in this order:*
      a. Doubt or unbelief.
      b. Accusing you.
      c. Irritability and a cross spirit.
      d. Speaking in a way that makes another upset.
      e. A self-justifying attitude, a desire to blame others.
   2. *How do we resist the devil?*
      a. We 'stand' (Eph. 6:11ff).
         (1) Don't fall – or run.
         (2) Don't go backwards or even try to make a lot of progress.
      b. We refuse to speak or give in to the sudden negative impulse.
         (1) When we speak when we are agitated we probably will be sorry.
         (2) Learn to do or say nothing in the evil day.
      c. The devil will eventually give up for a time (Jas. 4:7; 1 Pet. 5:8).

D. Remember the elementary lessons regarding grieving the Spirit.

   1. Refuse to be bitter (Eph. 4:30).
   2. Never hold a grudge; totally forgive.
   3. Do not say anything that diminishes anyone's credibility.

CONCLUSION

All of the above is designed to keep us from grieving the Holy Spirit. When the Spirit is himself (ungrieved), who knows in what manner or how often he will speak intimately and powerfully to you!

22

HOW TO IMPROVE YOUR PRAYER LIFE

INTRODUCTION

A. This is our first 'practical' lesson in theology.

    1. *Reminder: we are looking at two sides of theology.*

        a. Doctrinal – the more intellectual and abstract side.

        b. Practical – the concrete; how it is applied in our lives.

B. The best remedy against dry intellectualism: prayer.

    1. *The issue: knowing God himself or merely knowing 'about' God.*

        a. Prayer leads us directly to the heart of God.

        b. Theology without prayer will but teach us 'about' him.

            (1) You can look at pictures of the Grand Canyon or the Swiss Alps.

            (2) Or you can visit these places and see for yourself.

    2. *Prayer enables us to experience God directly.*

        a. Doctrine without prayer is like knowing God second hand.

        b. Prayer brings us face to face with the living God.

C. There are two Greek words worth examining, from Philippians 4:6.

    1. proseche, *the general term for prayer.*

        a. It is addressed to God.

        b. Used 36 times in the New Testament, e.g., Matthew 17:21; Luke 6:12; Acts 2:42.

    2. deesei, *'petition', 'supplication' or 'prayer'.*

        a. It may be addressed to man, as when one would present a petition to the Prime Minister or City Hall.

        b. Used 19 times in the New Testament, e.g., Luke 1:13, Philippians 1:4, and is often translated 'prayer'.

I. PRAYER: ONE OF THE GREAT 'FRINGE BENEFITS' OF BEING A CHRISTIAN

A. We do not become Christians primarily to get the fringe benefits.

1. To have his guidance, to help with our problems.
2. *To have the fellowship of his people.*
   a. Note: The main thing about being a Christian is heaven to come.
      (1) We must never forget this (John 3:16).
      (2) Jesus died to save us from God's wrath (Rom. 5:9).
   b. But God did not congratulate us at conversion: 'See you in heaven!'
      (1) Conversion is the beginning of a personal relationship with God himself.
      (2) Prayer is a chief way by which we get to know God.

B. Two of the greatest fringe benefits: the Bible and prayer.

1. *The Bible: God's infallible Word.*
   a. We will be looking at doctrine that emerges from the Bible.
   b. But the Bible should be read *every day*. We should have a plan.
2. *Prayer: talking with God.*
   a. There are other valid definitions of prayer.
      (1) Communion (fellowship) with God.
      (2) Asking God to act.
      (3) Seeking his face.
      (4) Listening to God.
   b. For our purposes at this stage: prayer is essentially talking with God.
      (1) Not talking *to* God (monologue).
      (2) Rather, talking *with* God (two-way conversation).

C. Fellowship with God was cut short after the Fall of Adam and Eve in the Garden of Eden.

1. Prior to the Fall there was no shame (Gen. 2:25).
2. *After the Fall they felt shame* (Gen. 3:7).
   a. God clothed them with garments of skin (Gen. 3:21).
      (1) This presupposes the shedding of blood.
      (2) Ever since, we have needed the sacrifice of blood to go between God and us.

b. God drove them out of the Garden of Eden.

    (1) Cherubim *kept* them out of the Garden (Gen. 3:24).

    (2) A return to fellowship is by invitation only (Matt. 11:28).

II. PRAYER IS ONLY POSSIBLE BY A MEDIATOR

A. Mediator (definition): One who acts as a go-between or peace-maker between opposing sides. Note: God is holy, we are sinners; approaching God on our own without a mediator is not only unthinkable, it is impossible.

    1. *After the Fall God and man became 'mutual enemies'.*

        a. Man from birth lives under God's wrath (Eph. 2:3).

            (1) God hates sin (whatever comes short of his glory).

            (2) God is angry with the wicked every day (Ps. 7:11).

        b. Man from birth is alienated from God (Eph. 4:18).

            (1) Man hates God (i.e., the God of the Bible).

            (2) Man by nature does not seek him (Rom. 3:11).

    2. *God was under no obligation to seek or save man* (Rom. 9:15).

        a. God might have let the whole human race perish.

        b. But he took the decision to show mercy!

            (1) This became clear immediately after the Fall (Gen. 3:15).

            (2) Jesus Christ moreover is the lamb chosen before creation (1 Pet. 1:20).

B. God provided a Mediator: his one and only Son (1 Tim. 2:5).

    1. *All praying under the Old Testament anticipated this Mediator.*

        a. The sacrificial system of the Old Testament pointed to the Lord Jesus Christ (Heb. 10:1).

        b. God sees the end from the beginning (Isa. 46:10).

            (1) He ordained that Jesus would die on a cross.

            (2) He accepted ancient sacrifices as tokens of his Son's death.

    2. *The gift of God's Son made prayer possible.*

        a. The first prayer we have a right to pray is for mercy.

            (1) 'God, have mercy on me, a sinner' (Luke 18:13).

            (2) Contained in the Greek: the idea of propitiation.

        b. In other words, the 'sinner's prayer' brings salvation.

            (1) We know we have no bargaining power with God.

            (2) All we can do is to ask for mercy that is based on Jesus' shed blood.

C. All prayer must presuppose the blood of Jesus.

1. *There are certain things we never out-grow as Christians:*
   a. The need of a Mediator.
   b. The blood of Jesus.
   c. Pleading for mercy (Heb. 4:16).
2. *No matter how godly or obedient, we come by his blood.*
   a. The more we are conscious of this when we pray, the better.
   b. The more we mention this when we pray, the better.

D. Conclusion: The first thing we can do to improve our prayer life is to ask for mercy.

1. *Mercy, to be sheer mercy, means that we have nothing to give in exchange.*
   a. We cannot 'snap our fingers' at God.
   b. Mercy can be given or withheld and justice be done either way.
2. *This puts us on bended knee.*
   a. We are conscious that God owes us nothing.
   b. This puts him on the throne; us in a begging position.
3. *Question: Have you been guilty of rushing into God's presence?*
   a. Perhaps this is why your prayers are not answered.
   b. Perhaps this is why you feel no sense of his presence.
4. *Note: never forget that we are talking about the God of the Bible.*
   a. I fear that our generation has lost sight of the sovereignty of God.
   b. I fear that our generation has lost sight of the holiness of God.
      (1) The leper said to Jesus, 'If you are *willing*, you can make me clean' (Matt. 8:2).
      (2) We never outgrow this attitude toward God.

III. THE PURPOSE OF PRAYER

A. Why pray?

1. *If we desire intimacy with God.*
   a. If we want to know God personally.
      (1) To know his ways (Heb. 3:10).
      (2) To recognise his voice (Heb. 3:7).

b. Two Old Testament men were called God's 'friend'.

(1) Moses (Ex. 33:11).

(2) Abraham (Is. 41:8, Jas. 2:23).

c. The 'rule of thumb' – seek his face, not his hand (Ps. 27:8).

(1) To seek his hand is to ask him to work for us.

(2) To seek his face is to want to know what he is feeling.

2. *If we desire guidance* (Prov. 3:6).

a. We ask for guidance when we don't know the way.

b. God *knows* the way.

(1) He is willing to show us the way.

(2) Prayer puts us in touch with him who knows the way.

3. *If we need help* (Ps. 46:1).

a. In this case prayer is (defined): asking God to act.

b. This presupposes: things are out of our hands.

(1) We are asking *him* to do what we cannot do.

(2) We are asking because he is *able* to do what we cannot do.

4. *If we want more power.*

a. This may refer to gifts, or anointings, of the Spirit (1 Cor. 12:31).

b. We are encouraged by Jesus himself to pray along these lines (Matt. 7:11; Luke 11:13).

5. *God wants us to pray*! (Luke 18:1).

a. This is the most encouraging thing of all.

b. God himself wants us to turn to him.

(1) Jesus' illustration (Luke 18:1-8) encourages us to pray about anything that concerns us.

(2) We are to pray and not give up.

6. *God answers prayer*! (Luke 11:9).

a. God would not mock us by asking us to pray (Gal. 6:7).

b. He asks us to pray for good reasons:

(1) That we might get to know him intimately.

(2) That we might see him act.

7. *Prayer is a sign of faith* (Heb. 11:6).

a. That we turn to him means we believe he is there.

b. That we keep on praying means his honour is at stake: he *promises* to reward those who diligently seek him.

B. Those God has used most in church history have been those who prayed most!

1. *Is this a coincidence? Certainly not.*

  a. Do we want to be used by God?

  b. How important is this to us?

2. *Martin Luther: 'I have a very long day, I must spend not two but three hours in prayer today.'*

3. We show how important another person is to us by how much time we give them!

C. There will be no praying in heaven.

1. *Worship, yes; prayer and petition, no.*

  a. We are on our way to heaven.

  b. No regrets – when we get to heaven – over how much time we spent in prayer here below.

    (1) I put stress on the amount of *time* spent in prayer.

    (2) Prayer is never wasted time!

IV PRAYER AS A DISCIPLINE

A. 95% perspiration, 5% inspiration.

1. So with all of God's work; all great men say the same thing.

2. If prayer were always 95% inspiration, 5% discipline, we wouldn't need this lesson.

B. What is wrong with the old Spiritual, 'Every time I feel the Spirit I'll pray'?

1. Certainly we should do that! But how often does that happen?

  a. The point is that we do that to which we are called, with or without inspiration.

  b. How many of us are inspired to be at work every day at 9 a.m.?

2. *Compare tithing: 90% goes as far as 100%, if not further.*

  a. So with prayer: we get more done the more we pray.

  b. We cannot afford NOT to tithe; we cannot afford NOT to pray.

C. Eventually the discipline becomes a delight.

1. *Discipline means making prayer time a priority, cf. tithing.*

  a. We thus determine God alone has 30 minutes of our time, no matter what.

  b. In most cases this will be the same time each day.

2. *The day will come that those 30 minutes are the most special time of our day.*

  a. No-one will argue if we decide to increase that time.

  b. Talking with God, knowing he's listening, becomes sheer delight.

V. PRAYER AND CONCENTRATION

A. We all wrestle with the problem of our minds wandering. John Newton said:

"Often at the mercy-seat, while calling on thy name
Swarms of evil thoughts I meet, which fill my soul with shame
Agitated in my mind, like a feather in the air
Can I thus a blessing find? My soul, can this be prayer?"

B. What has helped me: Psalm 16:8 and Philippians 4:5.

1. David: what he did and what is true anyway.

2. *When we know he is there, we begin talking to him.*

  a. It is hard to concentrate when we are not sure we are being heard.

  b. Being convinced he listens to every word, we proceed to talk.

C. Here is my own procedure (for what it's worth):

1. I immediately pray for the blood of Jesus to cleanse me.

2. *I hang fast on two scriptures – both chapter 4 verse 16 – in the New Testament.*

  a. Hebrews 4:16 – asking for mercy.

  b. 1 John 4:16 – I rely on his love.

   (1) If I feel unworthy, or condemned in my heart, I plead the blood of Christ.

   (2) If our own heart condemns us, God is greater; the blood of Christ satisfies him (1 John 3:20).

3. *I set the Lord before me.*

  a. I pray for the presence of the mind of the Spirit – to be filled with love.

b. I pray to be emptied of any competing thought. Why?
  (1) As much as possible, I want him to set the agenda.
  (2) I want my requests to be in the Spirit.
c. I commit the day ahead to the Lord (if at night, no problem).
  (1) I recount everything I am thankful for over the previous 24 hours. NB: the Lord's Prayer begins with praise.
  (2) I try to miss nothing, taking Philippians 4:6 literally.
4. *I eventually go to my prayer list (same every day).*
  a. I don't do it straight away; I see if I pick up on something that may not be on the prayer list.
    (1) I have learned to try to pray in the Spirit (only those prayers in God's will are answered (1 John 5:13-14).
    (2) I get to the place where I 'follow peace' (this is hard to articulate).
  b. Eventually I turn to my list – to be sure I miss nothing.
    (1) I'm adding to it all the time, and revise it every year or two.
    (2) It includes mostly names of people; also things I want God to do.
5. *Note: I do not omit the smallest details; the more specific, the better.*
  a. Prayer is a great mystery, e.g.,
    (1) Why some prayers are answered immediately, others take years.
    (2) Which comes first, the idea, or God putting the request there?
  b. Prayer, combined with Bible reading, is the ABC of getting to know God.
    (1) We get to know his ways and develop a sense of 'light' (I John 1:7).
    (2) We get ten times more out of a sermon than the next person.
  c. Until God says no, keep on asking.
    (1) Special reward to those who are found asking when prayer is answered.
    (2) Any prayer prayed in the will of God will be answered (Dan. 10:12).
  d. Challenge: Aim to pray for a complete hour at least once a week.

– Learn to follow the Spirit as we pray.
– Learn to feel certain impulses when we pray.

VI. Prayer and the will of God

A. Any prayer prayed in the will of God will be answered (1 John 5:14-15).

1. *We may not know at the time that we prayed according to his will.*
   a. John said, 'If we know.......' (we don't always know!)
   b. Paul did not always know (Rom. 8:26).
2. *Sometimes we do know it will be answered* (Mark 11:24).
   a. This does not always happen.
   b. I suspect, in fact, it is not common.
3. *What do we do when we don't know we are praying according to God's will? Pray on.*
   a. Until God says a definite, undoubted 'No,' keep on praying.
   b. This is the lesson from Luke 18:1-8.

B. The shape answered prayer takes is determined by our readiness at the time God answers.

1. The example of Zechariah (Luke 1:20).
2. *The example of Israel* (Luke 19:41-44).
   a. Neither of the above examples were ready when God answered.
   b. Far better, to fulfil (Is. 25:9).
      (1) There is no greater joy than to be ready for answered prayer.
      (2) This happens when two things coalesce: expectancy and readiness.

CONCLUSION

If the Lord Jesus needed a healthy prayer life, how much more do we. Yet there are few areas of Christian living in which we are less disciplined. Prayer is spending time in the presence of the One who loves us more than any other. So what's the problem?

23

HOW TO KNOW THE WILL OF GOD

INTRODUCTION

A. Perhaps the most common question I get in the vestry is 'How can I know the will of God?'

    1. Sooner or later every Christian, young or old, comes across this.

    2. *However, most of the concerns that lie behind this question are:*

        a. Should I take this job offer?

        b. What should I do with my life?

        c. How can I know what gift I have?

        d. Should I get married?

        e. Should I move into this or that flat?

        f. Should I go out with this person?

        g. Where should I go on holiday?

        h. Should I ask for a rise in pay?

        i. Should I get baptised?

        j. Should I go to a local church or Westminster Chapel?

        k. Should I tithe? If so, is it gross or nett of my pay?

            (1) What if I am a student?

            (2) Should I tithe my pension?

        l. Who is the anti-christ? Will the church go through the Tribulation?

        m. How do I deal with my noisy neighbour?

        n. Should I go on a ship with Operation Mobilisation?

        o. How will I know if I am called to preach?

B. Will of God (definition): his opinion.

I. IT IS **G**OD'S WILL THAT WE SHOULD KNOW HIS WILL **(E**PH. **5:17)**

A. According to Ephesians 5:17 four observations can be made:

    1. God has a will.

2. God's will is knowable.

3. We should know what his will is.

4. It is foolish not to know God's will.

B. It is encouraging to know that God wants us to know his will as much as we want to know his will.

  1. We so often think that we are the ones in the dark, and that we are isolated from the knowledge that is so important for us.

  2. *The truth is: God is seeking us and is, if anything, far more willing to show his will than we are to seek it.*

    a. Many times we only *think* we want to know his will.

    b. Many times we are afraid to know what his will is.

      (1) Sometimes it is fear that keeps us from knowing.

      (2) Sometimes it is pride that keeps us from knowing.

      (3) Sometimes it is rebellion that keeps us from knowing.

      (4) Sometimes it is unbelief that keeps us from knowing.

C. Let us consider the four observations above.

  1. *God has a will.*

    a. This is thrilling and sobering.

    b. Why is it thrilling?

      (1) God cares for us; he has already planned for us.

      (2) There *is* a way forward.

    c. Why is this sobering?

      (1) We may not like it if we really knew his will.

      (2) We may have to make some changes!

    d. Note: God does have a will, that is, an opinion.

      (1) On any subject we can raise.

      (2) On any issue in our lives.

      (3) What we ought to do in the next five seconds.

  2. *God's will is knowable.*

    a. He not only has an opinion, it is an opinion that he is willing to share with us.

    b. It does not follow however that *all* that he thinks is for us to know in the next five seconds.

    c. But what *is* knowable can be known in the next five seconds to the depth we are able to accept it.

  3. *We should know what his will is.*

    a. This does not mean we are responsible for knowing all we wish to know.

      b. It does mean we are responsible for knowing all that is knowable for us now – and for the next five seconds.

4. *It is foolish not to know God's will. AV: 'unwise'.*

      a. This by itself strongly hints that God's will is not only knowable but that it is imprudent not to know it.

      b. Why is it wrong not to know his will?

          (1) We are moving without direction or definite purpose.

          (2) We may well be moving backward not forward.

          (3) We will make avoidable mistakes.

          (4) We will be subject to anxiety.

          (5) We can't help others if we don't have direction ourselves.

II. TO KNOW GOD'S WILL IS TO SEE HIS GLORY

A. The glory of God is unveiled basically two ways:

1. *The dignity of his person and power.*

      a. This is how his glory is often seen in the Old Testament.

      b. Moses asked: 'Show me your glory' (Ex. 33:18).

          (1) Moses really meant by that: to see God.

          (2) We know that because God said in reply: 'You cannot see my face, for no-one may see me and live' (Ex. 33:20).

      c. This therefore coheres with what God said to Moses in reply to his request to see his glory: 'I *will* have mercy on whom I *will* have mercy, and I *will* have compassion on whom I *will* have compassion' (Ex. 33:19).

B. Moses therefore was confronted with the glory of God in a way for which he was not prepared.

1. What could not be seen – lest Moses die.

2. What could be known – something of God's will.

C. This brings us to the next but more profound stage in our quest to know the will of God.

III. THE WILL OF GOD IS TO BE UNDERSTOOD AS HAVING TWO ASPECTS: REVEALED WILL AND SECRET WILL

A. These two aspects of God's will can be briefly summed up:

1. Revealed will: the Bible.

2. Secret will: his sovereign purpose.

B. These two aspects of God's will fit perfectly with each other but there is a definite order by which we come to understand each of them.

    1. We must seek to know God's revealed will before we should ask to know his secret will.

    2. *It is wrong for us to enquire of his secret will when we show contempt for what he has clearly revealed to us.*

        a. 'What more can he say than to you he hath said?'

        b. Recall the saying: 'If I give my son a watch I don't expect him to keep asking me the time.'

C. What are some biblical examples of God's secret will?

    1. *His secret purposes:*

        a. Predestination (Eph. 1:11).

        b. Who will be saved, who will be lost (John 6:37).

            (1) We don't know whom God has chosen (Rom. 9:11).

            (2) We don't know absolutely who is saved (2 Tim. 2:19).

    2. *His future timing* (Eph. 1:10-11).

        a. The Second Coming (Mark 13:32).

        b. The events of the Book of Revelation.

            (1) I doubt even John himself understood all he saw.

            (2) The Old Testament prophets wanted to know (1 Pet. 1:10-11. cf. Dan. 8:13).

    3. *The role of the Old Testament priests.*

        a. Urim and Thummim (Ex. 28:30; Lev. 8:8).

        b. Ephod (1 Sam. 30:7-8).

    4. *The role of the Old Testament prophet.*

        a. 1 Kings 17:1; 18:1.

        b. Jer. 29:10.

    5. *The mystery of Old Testament prophets.*

        a. 2 Kings 20:1-6.

        b. Jonah 3:4,10.

        c. 1 Kings 21:24,27-29.

D. What are theological/philosophical examples of God's secret will?

    1. *The problem of evil.*

        a. How can a just God who is all-powerful and all-loving allow evil?

      b. Why did God create man knowing he would suffer?

      c. Why did God create man knowing he would sin?

  2. *How providence works* (Rom. 11:33).

      a. Providence: the mystery of God's overruling will and power.

      b. How is it that in God's incredible timing things happen which coalesce with external and internal events?

  3. *How will God clear his name?*

      a. Will he do it at the time of the Second Coming?

      b. Will he do it at the Judgement?

      c. Will he do it before or after Satan is punished?

  4. *How is the Book of Revelation to be understood?*

      a. Are there literal streets of gold? (Rev. 21:21).

      b. Who is the woman clothed with the sun? (Rev. 12:1ff).

      c. Is the fire of hell literal?

  5. *How will those who never heard the Gospel be dealt with?*

      a. Is there a chance they will be saved?

      b. Will their punishment be the same as all others?

E. What are the practical examples of God's secret will?

  1. Where will I be in three years' time? When shall I retire? Will we return to America before revival comes?

  2. How does this book fit in with God's overall scheme of things?

  3. Will healings and miracles really come to our church?

  4. (See the questions put in the Introduction above.)

F. Note these observations:

  1. Most of us are far more interested in the secret will of God than we are in the revealed will of God.

  2. God is more interested that we know his revealed will than his secret will.

  3. The more we are interested in his revealed will, the more we will come to know his secret will.

G. The secret will of God is in a word: mystery.

  1. *It is what the prophets of the Old Testament foresaw but didn't completely understand themselves.*

      a. How could the Messiah be brought up in Nazareth when he was to be born in Bethlehem?

      b. When would these events occur?

2. *There are two ways of understanding mystery:*

   a. *a priori*: it is completely hidden.

   b. *a posteriori*: it is completely revealed.

3. *The secret will of God must remain precisely that – secret – until God is pleased to make it absolutely clear.*

   a. It is made clear three ways:

     (1) In time.

     (2) By circumstances.

     (3) By immediate revelation of the Spirit (should God be pleased to do so).

   b. Until then, do not delve into it; be content to know God's revealed will backwards and forwards!

   c. Note: some of God's knowable opinions cannot be shared with us because of where we are in our pilgrimage at the present time (John 16:12).

     (1) What Jesus knew was knowable.

     (2) But the disciples had to wait a while.

     (3) We are all like that in one way or another.

IV. THE REVEALED WILL OF GOD GENERALLY IS TO BE CHERISHED ABOVE HIS SECRET WILL

A. The revealed will is the Bible.

   1. God has told us all we need to know.

   2. *What is not in the Bible is not worth knowing – at least not now.*

     a. 'Where the scriptures speak, we speak; where the scriptures are silent, we are silent.'

       (1) Details of the boyhood of Jesus.

       (2) What did Jesus actually look like?

     b. We must treasure his words much more than food (Job 23:12).

     c. Mark Twain: 'It is not those passages in the Bible that I don't understand that worry me; it is those I understand all too well.'

B. The Ten Commandments are a beginning in knowing how we should live our lives.

   1. A more detailed lesson on God's Law is to be found in Understanding Theology I, Chapter 10, page 75.

2. *In the meantime, here is a rule of thumb: the Ten Commandments are God's instructions as to how we should order our personal lives*

    a. It is God's will that we understand what sin is (Rom. 7:7).

    b. It is God's will that we should be holy (Lev. 11:44; 1 Pet. 1:16).

C. It is God's will that people are saved.

  1. 2 Peter 3:9.

  2. 1 Timothy 2:4.

  3. John 3:16.

  4. *Note: these verses give us every right:*

    a. To pray for anyone's salvation (Rom. 10:1).

    b. To evangelise all men and women (Matt. 28:19; 2 Cor. 5:20).

    c. Rule of thumb: an assurance that you are in God's will is when you are attempting to win the lost to Christ.

D. It is God's will for us to be holy.

  1. Hebrews 12:14.

  2. 1 Thessalonians 4:3.

  3. Galatians 5:16.

E. It is God's will that we are like Jesus.

  1. We won't be perfectly like Jesus until we get to heaven (Rom. 8:30; 1 John 3:2).

  2. *But we must be like Jesus in the meantime.*

    a. Delighting to do the will of God (Heb. 10:7).

      (1) This was the will of our Lord (John 5:30).

      (2) There is a subsidiary benefit in this, namely getting our doctrine straightened out! (John 7:17).

    b. Suffering for the shame of his name (Acts 5:41).

      (1) There is no higher honour than this in the present life.

      (2) Becoming a pilot light may hasten this experience!

    c. Indiscriminate involvement.

      (1) Jesus treated all men the same; he was no respecter of persons (Matt. 22:16).

      (2) A hint whether or not we are approaching Jesus' standard is whether or not we attract the kind of people he attracted.

    d. Passive mistreatment (1 Pet. 2:23).
        (1) We are not allowed to retort in the slightest way when men speak unkindly to us (Matt. 5:39).
        (2) Living like this all the time (at home, in college, in the office) will make this easy when we are witnessing for Jesus.

V. THE REVEALED WILL OF GOD PARTICULARLY: TO BE OBEYED BEFORE GOD'S SECRET WILL CAN BE MADE KNOWN

A. God is not opposed to sharing his secret will with us (Ps. 25:14).
    1. *It is knowable, however, to the degree we fear him.*
        a. Fear means reverence or respect, as a child should feel toward a parent.
        b. Fear really comes to love when it is used with reference to God.
    2. *There is a sense in which fear and love, when it comes to our relationship with God, are used interchangeably.*
        a. Psalm 37:4 has to do with our love for God.
        b. Psalm 145:19 has to do with our fear of God.

B. The degree to which we revere God's revealed will will be the degree to which his secret will is unveiled.
    1. This is the main principle we should learn from the present study.
    2. *We must not get the cart before the horse!*
        a. Rule of thumb:
            (1) Seek the secret will of God apart from the revealed will of God and we are likely to end in confusion.
            (2) Revere the revealed will of God *as though* there were no secret will, and you are likely to understand his secret will after all!
        b. Treasure the 'words of his mouth' more than we do our daily food (Job 23:12).

C. Here is God's particular will for all of us.
    1. *To affirm his love for us* (1 John 4:16).
        a. We may feel we should be sure we love God instead of God loving us.
        b. The way forward is 'not that we love God but that he loves us' (1 John 4:10).

2. *Walk in the light* (1 John 1:7).

    a. Do not try to advance from A to Z but from A to B.

    b. Seize upon any insight, opportunity for further obedience, fresh disclosure of sin, or whatever comes from the Holy Spirit as a way forward.

3. *Dignify any trial* (Jas. 1:2; 1 Thess. 5:16-18).

    a. Do not murmur or complain when any trial, large or small, comes your way.

    b. See any trial as a test as to how we are doing spiritually.

    c. One way to know we are in God's will: to give thanks in all circumstances!

4. *Totally forgive those who have hurt us* (Matt. 6:15).

    a. We do not have any choice in this matter.

    b. Any grudge we hold, however justified it seems, will be grieving to the Holy Spirit and counter-productive to knowing God's will.

5. *Find our niche in the church.*

    a. It will not do for any of us to be on the outside – or even on the fence – when it comes to church involvement.

    b. Be willing to do any job for which we are qualified – including the possibility that we are over-qualified!

6. *Esteem a word of God in print (the Bible) more than we do a prophetic word.*

    a. A prophetic word usually gives immediate access to God's secret will, this is why so many people love them.

    b. But the test of our love for Christ will be our esteeming the Bible above a word of prophecy.

VI. HOW WILL WE THEN KNOW THE WILL OF GOD?

A. The Holy Spirit, following the above, will be in us ungrieved.

1. This means he is at ease – himself.

2. *The consequence is, we have immediate access to his will for us.*

    a. It does not follow that we will know everything we *wanted* to know.

    b. But we will know exactly what we *need* to know.

        (1) We will know what to do.

        (2) We will know what not to do.

    c. The result: peace.

B. There is an acrostic (a word in which each letter forms the first letter of another word) that can easily be memorised – PEACE – and will help you through our quest to know the will of God. Ask these questions:

1. *Is it Providential?*
   a. Do we have to push a door open?
   b. Or does it open by itself?
2. *What do we suppose the Enemy would want us to do?*
   a. Imagine what we sincerely think the devil would wish us to do in a given circumstance.
   b. Do the very opposite and we are very likely to get it right!
3. *What is our Authority?*
   a. In other words, what does the Bible say?
   b. God will never, never, never lead us contrary to his Word.
4. *Does this give us more or less Confidence?*
   a. When we are in the will of God our confidence increases.
   b. We lose confidence when we are out of the will of God.
5. *Ease. Do you have inner ease?*
   a. Shakespeare said, 'To thine own self be true'.
   b. Do what makes for peace (Rom. 14:19).

C. Note: All five of the above acrostic must coalesce. If they do, I predict you will not fall into error or grave mistake.

1. The will of God will be plain enough.
2. You will have great inner peace.

CONCLUSION

Remember that God's will is best. The greatest folly on earth is to try to improve upon God's will.

24

HOW TO DISCOVER OUR OWN GIFT

INTRODUCTION

A. Of all the practical studies we have had so far, surely none is more practical than this.
1. Perhaps there is an over-abundance of 'how to' books on the market; people generally are more interested in the 'how' than the 'what'.
2. But this is a needful lesson.

B. Behind the promise of 'Discovering our own gift' lies an assumption: that we *do* have a gift!
1. Some may want to say, 'But I don't have a gift'.
2. *Wrong. According to these verses, they do:*
   a. 1 Corinthians 1:7. 'Therefore you do not lack any spiritual gift as you eagerly wait for our Lord Jesus Christ to be revealed.'
   b. 1 Corinthians 12:6. 'There are different kinds of working, but the same God works all of them in *all* men.'
   c. Romans 12:3. 'For by the grace given me I say to every one of you: Do not think of yourself more highly than you ought, but rather think of yourself with sober judgement, in accordance with the measure of faith *God has given you.*'

C. Why is this study important?
1. *We all need to find our niche in God's church.*
   a. Many join a church and, even after years, do not find their niche.
   b. Surely there is a better way forward!
2. *It builds self-confidence.*
   a. A proof we are in God's will is a personal sense of confidence.
   b. Nothing increases confidence more than discovering what our gift is. Recall the acrostic PEACE (see chapter on 'How to know the will of God).

3. *Discovering our gift is God's 'hint', says Dr Clyde Narramore, about what we should do with our lives.*

　a. Some Christians are always asking, 'What does God want me to do in life?'

　b. A discovery of what our gift is may well be the answer!

4. *God wants us to discover our gift (or gifts)* (Rom. 12:2-3).

　a. We must learn not to think *more* highly of ourselves than we ought to think.

　b. It stands to reason, therefore, that we should not think *less* of ourselves than we ought to think.

5. *Many good Christians have a sense of unworth (feelings of inferiority) and honestly do not know what their gift is.*

　a. Some fear they have no gift at all.

　b. But we all *do* have a gift, as the aforementioned verses show.

6. *It is important for the functioning of the church.*

　a. The church functions because of the members of the body.

　b. Every member of the body of Christ is like a member of the physical body (1 Cor. 12:14-27).

7. *It is important for the unity of the body.*

　a. God has placed gifts in the body just as he has given us eyes, hands, etc..

　b. But there would be no unity if there was competition between the eye and the hand.

8. *It brings glory to God.*

　a. God made us the way we are and it is he who gave us the gifts we have.

　b. When we come to terms with our gift – however great or modest it máy be – it glorifies him.

9. *It helps us to know ourselves. This is sometimes called 'self-image'.*

　a. Socrates' ancient axiom 'know thyself' has a lot of merit.

　b. Discovering our gift enables us to know ourselves a little better.

10. *It helps us accept our limitations.*

　a. God never promotes us to the level of our incompetence (Peter Principle).

　b. It can be humbling to accept ourselves as we are – to admit to our limitations.

　　(1) Some of us have more than one gift.

　　(2) This is suggested in Matthew 25:14-30.

I. THERE ARE FOUR KINDS, OR LEVELS, OF GIFTS

A. Natural gifts
  1. *This is what we have without the saving work of the Holy Spirit.*
    a. We sometimes call it 'common grace'.
    b. Calvin called it 'special grace within nature'.
  2. *Natural gifts stem from these factors:*
    a. Heredity: taking after our parents
      (1) Natural intelligence.
      (2) Certain abilities.
    b. Environment.
      (1) Input of parents, relatives, friends.
      (2) We are all a part of those we have known.
    c. Training or education.
      (1) This comes from choice of subjects.
      (2) How well we do in what we learn helps mould our gifts.
  3. *Aptitude. This refers mainly to:*
    a. Intelligence, intellectual interests, ability or skill.
    b. What it is we like to do – or are 'good at'.
  4. *Never underestimate the natural factor in determining our gift.*
    a. It is how God made us.
    b. We were chosen before we were born; God knew what he was doing when he:
      (1) Chose our parents.
      (2) Chose the time of our births.
      (3) Chose the place of our births.
      (4) Chose the time of our conversion.
    c. Our natural skill or interest will have a lot to do in:
      (1) Discovering our gift.
      (2) Knowing God's will for our lives.

B. Vocational gift
  1. *This refers to God's calling in terms of what we do generally with our lives.*
    a. Will I be a dentist? Typist? Blue collar worker?
    b. Will I get married? If so, will this change my vocation?
  2. *God's vocation, or calling, may fall into these categories:*
    a. What we do in terms of secular work.
    b. What we do in terms of church work.

3. *Those whose chief calling is to be in the secular realm should never question that they are as called to be there as a preacher is called to do what he does.*

   a. A person called to be a housewife will be as definitely in the will of God being a housewife as a minister of the Gospel is when he preaches.

   b. A person who is employed as a secretary, nurse, doctor or lorry driver can have the anointing of God that is as glorifying to him as anybody in full time Christian work.

4. *For those in Christian work, there are a number of options, according to Ephesians 4:11ff or 1 Corinthians 12:28ff.*

   a. Not all are apostles or teachers.

   b. We must come to terms with our particular vocation, even if we are in 'church' work.

C. Motivational gifts (Rom. 12:6-8).

1. *According to some, every Christian (every member of the body of Christ) has one of these seven 'motivational' gifts:*

   a. Prophet. This does not necessarily refer to the gift of prophecy as much as it refers to a natural tendency to 'see through things' and give a fairly shrewd judgement. It is not unlike having a 'woman's intuition'!

   b. Servant. This refers to one whose obvious gift or style is doing things for people. The person who is like this wants to help, doesn't mind being taken advantage of; considers it an opportunity to help others.

   c. Teaching. This may or may not refer to teaching the Bible. It refers to a rather natural ability to teach things, that is, make something clear to another at a verbal level. A salesman may be a teacher in that he explains the advantages of a product.

   d. Encouraging. AV: exhorting. Some people have a natural ability to exhort (not necessarily publicly – this does not really mean public speaking), that is, to cheer people up. You go to them feeling low; you come away feeling better! It is a lovely gift.

   e. Giving. NIV: 'contributions to the needs of others'. This probably assumes that the person is better off financially than most – but not necessarily. A person with this gift has an eye out for those who are in need, and manages to come up with a way to give others relief.

f. Leadership. AV: 'he that ruleth'. A person like this could never be Number Two to anybody. In a team of horses there is one who must be out in front. God equips some with a capacity to take the lead and motivate others to do what needs to be done. It could be the president of a company or the pastor.

g. Mercy. A person like this is by nature full of compassion. This is the typical Good Samaritan (Luke 10:33). He or she will stop what they are doing to show a feeling of care. This person is naturally sympathetic and attracts people to himself or herself because a feeling of care exists.

2. *If we discover ourselves in one of the above, we should be careful to see what Paul says we must remember:*

a. The prophet must be guided by faith and know his limitations.

b. The servant must know he will be taken advantage of.

c. The teacher must be prepared to fulfil his calling.

d. The encourager must do this, even when he may not feel like it!

e. The giver must be generous but keep quiet about it.

f. The leader must be firm and not sentimental.

g. The person with mercy must show mercy with cheerfulness.

D. Spiritual gifts (1 Cor. 12:8-10; 28-30).

1. *Here is a list of Spiritual gifts.*

a. Wisdom.

b. Word of knowledge.

c. Faith.

d. Healing.

e. Miracles.

f. Prophecy.

g. Discerning of spirits.

h. Tongues.

i. Interpretation of tongues.

j. Helping others.

k. Leadership.

2. *Although we are encouraged to covet, or desire earnestly, the 'greater' gifts (whatever that may be), they are sovereignly given* (1 Cor. 12:11,18).

a. This means they cannot be 'worked up'.

b. Note: we may indeed try to work up, say, the gift of tongues, but will it be genuine?

II . DISCOVERING OUR ANOINTING

A. Perhaps the best way to understand gifts is with this word: anointing.
   1. *It comes from (Gr.):* chrio – *to smear as with an ointment.*
      a. It is not the same as *charisma* or *charismata.*
      b. *Chrio* is the root word for Christ, the Anointed One.
   2. *As all of us are in him, we all have an anointing* (1 John 2:20,27).
      a. It is a word that includes *charismata* (spiritual gift) but not necessarily.
      b. It includes *charisma* (grace-gift) but that does not tell the whole story.

B. Anointing (def.): an ability that comes easily.
   1. *When we look for our gift we must be honest with ourselves and ask: what comes with ease?*
      a. What can I do without much effort?
      b. What can I do without much fatigue?
      c. What can I do without getting panicky or nervous?
   2. *The Holy Spirit never promotes us to the level of our incompetence.*
      a. If I have to work very, very hard at something, chances are that is *not* my anointing, or gift.
      b. There are some things (speaking personally) I know I cannot do: algebra, physics, speak Chinese, perform gall bladder surgery, work on your teeth, write a book on architecture, play a violin, do a miracle or give an interpretation of tongues. At least so far!
      c. The same is true with spiritual gifts; if there is not the special presence of the Lord, we cannot make things happen – even if we, say, had the gift of wisdom yesterday.
   3. *We must take several things into consideration before we determine our gift:*
      a. Our natural gift, whether it is hereditary or by training.
      b. Our motivational gift, that is, what comes to us with relative ease. Be honest!
      c. What spiritual gift God may have sovereignly bestowed upon us. Does it come easily?
      d. What we are asked to do very often. For example:
         (1) Do people ask us to preach?
         (2) If not, chances are we are not called to preach.

    e. Where we happen to be.

        (1) Where we are means where we are needed.

        (2) We must keep our eyes open, and be willing to be used.

4. *Note: be willing to be 'over-qualified' for what you may be asked to do at church* (cf. Gen. 39:2-3).

    a. A barrister may be asked to be a steward.

    b. A nurse may be asked to help in the kitchen.

5. *Note also: our anointing may not necessarily be your talent.*

    a. We may be a musician and God not be pleased to use that gift at the present time.

        (1) It may be we are not ready.

        (2) It may be we are not very spiritual at the present time.

    b. Joseph was over-qualified to work for Potiphar; but eventually he was made Prime Minister of Egypt.

Conclusion

The anointing is a composite picture of three things: (1) our natural ability, (2) motivation and (3) what is needed around us. We are never to underestimate the connection between grace and gift. When we are truly spiritual, we will not mind being the eye in the secular world and the kidney at church! (1 Cor. 12:21ff). The proof of finding our anointing is peace (Rom. 14:19).

25

HOW TO BE AN EFFECTIVE EVANGELIST

A. Why deal with a subject like this?

1. *This is obviously one of our practical studies.*
    a. We need to keep warm hearts.
    b. We must always be on our guard against cold hearts.
2. *Nothing warms the heart more than a heart for lost souls.*
    a. When a person has a passion for the lost – and is doing something about it – there probably isn't much that is seriously wrong with him (speaking spiritually).
    b. Nothing is more corrective to our spiritual defects than a renewal of concern for those not yet saved.
3. *It is right in line with the reason God sent his Son to die on the cross.*
    a. We can be experts on the atonement but be failures in pointing men and women to the cross.
    b. When we are sticking our necks out where evangelism is concerned we get God's attention.
4. *Too many evangelists have minimal doctrinal understanding.*
    a. Some are not theologically-minded at all.
    b. Many have a defective theology in any case.
        (1) They have little sense of sin and man's helplessness.
        (2) They have virtually no concept of the sovereignty of God.
5. *My aim is to produce disciples of the Lord Jesus who have the rare combination of zeal and sound theology.*
    a. Many have zeal but no theology (speaking generally).
    b. Some who are theologically sound (I fear):
        (1) Don't have a burden for the unsaved.
        (2) Don't really know how to lead a soul to Christ.
    c. Note: have *you* ever led a soul to Jesus Christ? Lately?

B. The importance of this subject.

1. *Predestination and free will – a dangerous subject.*

   a. It has diminished zeal for prayer and holy living in some.

   b. It has also done the same with respect to evangelism.

      (1) This does not need to happen.

      (2) I want to avoid it!

2. *A robust view of the sovereignty of God should lead us to be more evangelistic, not less evangelistic!*

   a. As J I Packer says, we are all Calvinists on our knees!

   b. Many of the great evangelists in history were those who upheld the sovereignty of God to the hilt – like George Whitefield and Jonathan Edwards.

3. Evangelism and the sovereignty of God are not contradictory but complementary. The best book on this subject is J I Packer's *Evangelism and the Sovereignty of God.*

4. *It is because we believe in predestination and election that we are evangelistic.*

   a. God will save his people.

   b. If we don't go into the world, he will raise up those who will – whatever their theology.

5. *I long to see history repeat itself: that those who are most eager to win the lost are those who believe most in the sovereignty of God.*

   a. This defies a natural explanation; people who look on from the outside say, 'It doesn't add up.'

   b. Let us dazzle the world by the simultaneous combination of:

      (1) The Word and the Spirit.

      (2) Evangelism and the sovereignty of God.

I. Understanding the Gospel

A. The first thing required of the soul-winner is that he understands the Gospel.

1. *The word Gospel means 'good news'.*

   a. *Evaggelion* (Gr.) is not a theological term.

   b. It is a secular word that referred to the ancient herald who announced good news.

2. *The early church, following Jesus, incorporated this word as the best available to summarise our message.*

a. Christ died for sinners and was raised from the dead.

b. We are saved by believing that message.

3. *Being 'saved' means basically two things:*

   a. Saved from our sins (Matt. 1:21).

     (1) From the penalty of sin (death).

     (2) From the power of sin (its grip on us).

   b. Fit for heaven (Rom. 5:9).

     (1) The blood of Jesus makes us fit.

     (2) We will go to heaven, not hell, when we die.

B. Good news presupposes (takes for granted) bad news, namely:

1. We are sinners (Rom. 3:23).

2. We are helpless (John 6:44).

3. We are under God's wrath (Eph. 2:3).

4. God's wrath ultimately means hell (1 Thess. 1:10).

5. *Note: Good news does not really become good news until we perceive what the bad news is.*

   a. Bad news: we are lost, helpless, heading for hell.

   b. Good news: Jesus died to change all this.

C. What is it that must be perceived, sooner or later, before we can know we are saved?

1. *Who Jesus is; the God-man.*

   a. He was God as though he were not man (John 1:1).

   b. He was man as though he were not God (Heb. 5:8).

2. *What he did. He saved us.*

   a. He fulfilled the Law, i.e. he never sinned (Matt. 5:17; Heb. 4:15).

   b. He died on the cross, satisfying God's justice (Rom. 3:26).

3. *We are guilty before God* (Rom. 3:19-20).

   a. Our righteousness is filthy rags (Is. 64:6).

   b. We are vile before God (Jer. 17:9).

4. *All that Jesus did for us is transferred to our credit the moment we believe.*

   a. It is called 'imputed righteousness' (Rom. 4:5).

     (1) Imputed means 'put to our credit'.

     (2) Righteousness is thus put to our credit.

   b. This can be done two ways:

     (1) The righteousness of Christ is put to our credit (Rom. 5:10).

(2) It is as though we had never sinned (Rom. 4:8).

5. *Saving faith is two things:*

    a. Persuasion of the heart (Rom. 10:9-10).

        (1) The word for faith is *pistis* (Gr.).

        (2) This comes from *pipto*, 'to persuade'.

    b. Repentance (Rom. 2:4).

        (1) The word for repentance is *metanoia* (Gr.).

        (2) This means 'change of mind'.

    c. Which comes first – faith or repentance? Answer: it depends on how you define repentance.

        (1) If repentance means 'change of mind', it may well precede faith since change of mind is what leads to being persuaded.

        (2) If repentance is (wrongly) defined (as it sometimes is) as 'turning away from every known sin', then it obviously *follows* faith – for who can ever know for sure he has done that?

6. *Saving faith is assurance.*

    a. Some say faith only *leads to* assurance.

    b. But surely faith *is* assurance, for:

        (1) I know whether my faith is in Christ alone (2 Tim. 1:12).

        (2) If it is, I need never look beyond Christ for my assurance! (Heb. 2:9).

7. *Two questions summarise all the above and precede all below:*

    a. Do we know for certain, were we to die today, that we would go to heaven?

    b. If you were to stand before God and he were to say to you, 'Why should I let you into my heaven?' what would you say?

        (1) If our trust is in ourselves we must be regarded as lost, no matter how worthy we feel ourselves or our works to be.

        (2) If our hope is in the blood of Christ, we must be regarded as saved.

8. *There are two other doctrines that further uphold and drive home all the above:*

    a. The doctrine of eternal punishment (Matt. 25:41,46).

        (1) Take eternal punishment away from the concept of God's wrath and it loses its impact.

        (2) We must never apologise for what God declares is just (Gen. 18:25).

b. The universality of the atonement (that Christ died for all) (Heb. 2:9).
  (1) If Jesus did not die for all, how can I be so sure he died for me?
  (2) He died for all that we may say to everybody, 'Jesus died for you' (2 Cor. 5:15).

II. Understanding our responsibility

A. Soul-winning is everybody's business (Matt. 28:19).
  1. *It is the task of the church* (Rev. 22:17).
    a. Every church is called to be evangelistic (Acts 4:20).
      (1) The purpose of Pentecost was to witness (Acts 1:8).
      (2) The result of Pentecost was conversions (Acts 2:41).
    b. What makes a church a true church is five things:
      (1) The Word is faithfully preached.
      (2) The sacraments are faithfully administered.
      (3) Discipline is exercised.
      (4) Fellowship is enjoyed.
      (5) People are being converted.
    c. Are people being converted in your church?
    d. Note: it is a mistake to wait:
      (1) For Billy Graham to come to town.
      (2) For new slogans to motivate us!
  2. *It is the task of the minister, in three ways:*
    a. To preach evangelistically regularly (2 Tim. 4:5).
      (1) We should not wait for 'missions'.
      (2) The gospel should be preached weekly.
    b. To witness to others personally (Acts 17:17).
      (1) This was the genius of the apostle Paul.
      (2) We ministers should not ask our people to do what we haven't done ourselves!
      (3) Church leader, have you personally led a soul to Christ lately?
    c. To train others for the work of evangelism (Eph. 4:11-12).
      (1) People should not leave the job of evangelism to their ministers.
      (2) People need to be trained in order that they can do the job themselves.

(3) The minister's task: to train others to do the work of an evangelist.

3. *It is the task of every Christian* (Acts 8:1).

  a. All Christians are, in a sense, preachers (Acts 8:4).

    (1) Preaching is not limited to the pulpit!

    (2) Everyone must bear witness to what they know is true.

  c. There is nothing that will substitute for your own personal witnessing to others.

    (1) There is a spiritual gap in our lives that can only be filled by soul-winning.

    (2) Apart from what it does for others, consider what it will do for us!

  d. Do we know if our milkman is a Christian? Grocer? Postman?

    (1) Do we carry Christian tracts with us?

    (2) Do we know how to lead a soul to Christ?

    (3) Do we talk to people about Jesus? Why not?

    (4) Do we know people who, if we don't tell them, will probably not be witnessed to?

B. Here is a simple outline of the gospel (memorise it, use it).

1. *Grace*

  a. Heaven is a free gift (Rom. 6:23).

  b. It is not earned or deserved (Eph. 2:8-9).

2. *Man*

  a. Is a sinner (Rom. 3:23).

  b. Cannot save himself (Jas. 2:10; John 6:44).

3. *God – The Bible says essentially two things about God:*

  a. He loves us and doesn't want to punish us (2 Pet. 3:9).

  b. He is just and must punish sin (Ex. 34:7).

4. *Jesus Christ*

  a. Who he is (the God-man) (John 1:1).

  b. What he did (died on the cross for our sins) (Rom. 5:8).

5. *Faith*

  a. What it is not:

    (1) Intellectual faith (head knowledge) (Jas. 2:19).

    (2) Temporal faith ('crisis faith') (John 6:66).

  b. What it is: Trusting Jesus alone (Eph. 2:8).

C. Closing with Christ

1. A gift must be received (we don't have to accept a gift, do we?)

2. *Do we want to receive this gift?*

   a. If we had the choice, and we do, to live with Christ or without him, which would we choose?

   b. We can receive this gift by actually inviting Jesus to come and live in our heart.

3. *When Jesus comes into our hearts, he comes in a two-fold manner:*

   a. He comes in as Saviour.

     (1) This means trusting Jesus Christ alone.

     (2) This means *transferring our trust* from our good works to his death on the cross.

   b. He comes in as Lord.

     (1) This means repenting of our sins (a U-turn in our lives).

     (2) Asking him to rule our lives.

4. If you are ready to do this, pray this prayer:

Lord Jesus Christ, I need you. I want you. I am sorry for my sins. I believe that Jesus Christ is the Son of God. Wash my sins away by your blood. I welcome your Holy Spirit into my heart. As best as I know how, I give you my life. In Jesus' name. Amen.

III. INDISCRIMINATE INVOLVEMENT

A. If I had to summarise what the Holy Spirit has laid upon my heart as much as anything else he has taught me in recent years it is this:

1. A church, to be a true church, must be constituted of all kinds of people, not a concentration of a certain 'type'.

2. We must begin where Jesus began and where the New Testament church began – offering the gospel indiscriminately to all people.

3. If the type of people that Jesus attracted are not attracted to us we are not being led by the Holy Spirit (Matt. 9:10).

B. I equally have the conviction that were we to 'lose' ourselves for his sake we will 'find' ourselves in the end and gain a hundred times more than we would have had, had we been selective in our evangelism.

1. At the individual level, what a person loses for Christ's sake is compensated a hundred times (Matt. 19:29).

2. *At the level of the church, what we abandon in terms of so-called 'prestige' and influence will be compensated far beyond anything we could have envisaged* (Luke 14:11).

   a. This is why I do not want Westminster Chapel to be an 'elitist' church, a 'student' church, an 'intellectual' church, a 'middle class' church – or any of those things that seem so important to some people.

   b. I predict that we may well reach more of the educated and well-to-do people under God's blessing when we utterly forget them and reach out to those to whom Jesus reached out.

   c. William Booth said, 'When you go to the poor with the gospel, the rich join hands with you to take it there.'

C. God is for the 'underdog'

1. *There is a strain running right through the Bible which many of us have overlooked – that God defends the helpless* (Amos 2:6-7; Jas. 1:27).

   a. Who in the Bible are the helpless? Answer: the widow, the blind, the lame, the poor, the hungry.

   b. In the streets you will find the unemployed, those afflicted by racial prejudice, the alcoholic, the rejects of society.

2. *Why is it that the Holy Spirit does not appear to come to the rescue of people like this when in fact Jesus did?*

   a. Answer: we are not listening to the Holy Spirit.

   b. But the Bible calls us to come to the defence of those God promises to defend (Ps. 82:1-4).

   c. When we take this seriously we get God's attention.

      (1) In Isaiah chapter 58 there was the complaint of the pious that God did not take notice of them. 'Why have we fasted and you have not seen it?' (Is. 58:3).

      (2) The fast which God owns is a different kind of 'fast'. 'Is not this the kind of fasting I have chosen: to loose the chains of injustice and untie the cords of the yoke, to set the oppressed free and break every yoke? Is it not to share your food with the hungry and to provide the poor wanderer with shelter – when you see the naked, to clothe him, and not to turn away from your own flesh and blood?' (Isa. 58:6-7).

C. We please God by offering ourselves to those whom most people seem to want to have nothing to do with.

1. *To help such people is to minister directly to Jesus.*
   a. We, therefore, should *see Jesus* when we see the tramp, *see Jesus* when we see the hungry, etc..
   b. This way we will give far more attention to such people.
2. *The Judaeo-Christian tradition was the first enterprise in the history of mankind that had anything to offer to the poor.*
   a. Jesus' ministry made this clear.
   b. James and Paul agreed on this, whatever differences they had on other matters (Gal. 2:10).
   c. We have an opportunity to restore the honour of God's name by returning to this principle of indiscriminate involvement.

D. It is my view that two things have militated against indiscriminate involvement.

1. *The practice of catering for the middle class.*
   a. This is one of the curses of the modern church; it has become predominantly middle class and has tried to preserve this status.
   b. This is nothing new; it began in the early church (Jas. 2:1-16).
2. *The doctrine of limited atonement (claiming that Jesus did not die for all).*
   a. This is less serious than the above, but none the less tends to justify not trying too hard to reach all people.
   b. It is not essential that we reject limited atonement so long as we are like Jesus by being involved with others.

E. What are the consequences of trying mainly to reach the middle class, the rich or famous? Four things:

1. *We will alienate the poor man.*
   a. If we make it obvious we are trying to reach the rich we will most certainly lose the poor.
   b. The poor man can instinctively tell if we are aiming for the middle class; he will feel unwanted.
      (1) He will, therefore, conclude that God does not want him.
      (2) He will also reject us and may fall into the Marxist thinking that religion is only for the rich.
2. *We put any sense of spiritual discernment into chaos.*
   a. Something bad happens within our hearts; it diminishes our ability to know the Holy Spirit's impulse.

    (1) This is the meaning of James 2:4: 'Have you not discriminated among yourselves and become judges with evil thoughts?'

    (2) The Greek words suggest virtually an internal combustion that renders our discernment mechanism defective.

  b. When we ignore a certain type of person, we cut off the Spirit's supply to others and, alas, to ourselves.

    (1) It is a very serious matter deliberately to ignore a person God has put in our path.

    (2) God does not judge us by striking us down; but he withholds the Spirit's power from us.

3. *We throw the church into chaos.*

  a. There is nothing that will hasten church troubles like defective evangelism.

  b. Once a church fails in its mission to reach the lost, here is what will happen:

    (1) People turn on each other in the church; this is because the Spirit has been largely withdrawn.

    (2) The flesh soon dominates.

  c. A church that is involved in the work of evangelism according to New Testament principles will be a happy church.

    (1) This does not mean the devil will not fight; he will fight more than ever.

    (2) But the church generally will know an atmosphere of sweetness and glory.

4. *We fail to win the rich as well.*

  a. The point James makes is this: 'You have tried to reach the rich by catering for them. Has it worked? No, it has not. Do not rich men oppress you...' (Jas. 2:6).

  b. Try to reach the rich and not only will you scare them off, but also you will make enemies of them.

  c. Note: It is a curious phenomenon; aim for the rich and you will lose them; aim for the poor and you have the best chance of reaching the rich as well.

Conclusion

When we meet someone we like, we want to introduce him to our friends. Why then are we shy evangelists?

26

HOW TO RESIST TEMPTATION

A. Like so many of our practical studies, it may seem rather presumptuous to address a subject like this one.

    1. I come not as the expert (far from it) but none the less as one familiar with the scripture on this matter.

    2. *We all are still in the battle of overcoming.*

        a. Perhaps we can all say with John Newton: 'I'm not what I ought to be; I'm not what I want to be; I'm not what I hope to be; but, thank God, I'm not what I used to be.'

        b. There is more than one kind of temptation, and we are called to resist every single one!

B. This subject is obviously relevant and important but let us unpack why this is so:

    1. *We are all being tempted. James 1:13 assumes this.*

        a. NIV says: 'When tempted...'

        b. AV says: 'Let no man say when he is tempted...'

            (1) The assumption is that we will be tempted.

            (2) As long as we are in this world we will know trouble, trial, temptation (John 16:33).

    2. *We are called to holiness, or sanctification* (1 Pet. 1:16; 1 Thess. 4:3).

        a. Sanctification (def.): the process of being made holy.

            (1) It is not a once for all experience that prevents future falling into sin.

            (2) It is a process whereby more and more we deny the works of the flesh (Gal. 5:19ff) and manifest the fruit of the Spirit (Gal. 5:22ff).

        b. That which largely stands in the way of holiness is temptation.

            (1) If there were no temptation we would automatically become holy.

(2) But temptation has to be dealt with before we can make any progress in sanctification.

3. *We fall into sin because we give in to temptation.*

   a. No-one falls into sin by by-passing temptation.

     (1) We do not go backwards spiritually by falling directly from a state of holiness to sin.

     (2) If our spiritual state is good – A – and sin is C, we don't go from A to C but A to B, which is temptation.

   b. We need to understand therefore what temptation is and how to deal with it.

4. *Some people fall into sin because they have not been properly taught.*

   a. Conversion does not automatically lead to spiritual and theological maturity.

     (1) Why do we have the New Testament?

     (2) The New Testament was written to teach us how to live the Christian life.

   b. Not only are too many people theologically ignorant; they are equally ignorant as to how to live the Christian life.

     (1) This lesson is a step in that direction.

     (2) A good place to begin: temptation.

5. *This study is good 'preventive medicine'.*

   a. It is better to keep from getting ill than finding the medicine after we are ill.

   b. Perhaps there is a real need for a study on 'After you have sinned, what then?'; but this lesson is designed to avoid unnecessary spiritual sickness!

I. TEMPTATION (DEF.): BEING ATTRACTED TO DO SOMETHING WRONG OR UNWISE BY THE PROSPECT OF PLEASURE OR ADVANTAGE

A. Gr. *peirazo*: 'to test', which may refer to one or both of two things:

   1. *Trial* (Jas. 1:2).

     a. Trial (def.): a situation of hardship that tests our ability to cope or endure.

       (1) This is the meaning when used in Galatians 4:14; 1 Peter 1:6; 1 Peter 4:12; Revelation 3:10.

       (2) But it is the same exact Greek word that is used when *to tempt* is the obvious meaning.

    b. In trial we are also tempted, that is, attracted to the idea to give in.

      (1) It may refer to murmuring (grumbling).

      (2) It may refer to unbelief.

  2. *Temptation* (1 Tim. 6:9).

    a. This refers to a state of being attracted (tempted) to do something wrong.

      (1) This is the meaning when used in James 1:13; 1 Thessalonians 3:5; Galatians 6:1.

      (2) But note: it is still the same Greek word that is used when hardship is the obvious meaning.

    b. In a time of temptation we are also being tried, that is, tested as to whether or not we will give in to what is wrong or unwise.

      (1) It may refer to sexual sin.

      (2) But it also could refer to unbelief, or murmuring.

  3. *Thus the basic meaning of testing is the umbrella term that encompasses both (as does the original Greek word).*

    a. Any trial is a test; any temptation is a test.

    b. When the word appears in the Greek the translators have to decide which English word to use.

      (1) The context, or common sense, determines the sense or meaning of the word.

      (2) In James 1:2 it is trial; so too James 1:12, but 'tempted' is the obvious meaning in James 1:13-14.

    c. In 1 Corinthians 10:13 either meaning is intended; so too in Matthew 6:13.

B. The 'wrong' we are tempted to is sin.

  1. *Sin (def.): any thought, word or deed that falls short of the glory of God* (Rom. 3:23).

    a. The 'attraction' may not necessarily be pleasant.

      (1) Unbelief is not pleasant.

      (2) Murmuring is not pleasant.

    b. But when we opt for unbelief or murmuring it is because the attraction (drawing power) was greater than our ability to resist.

      (1) Hence some cave in to unbelief or murmuring.

      (2) It is not that they find it pleasant, but that it seems easier to do at the time.

2. *Lack of wisdom may not necessarily be sin. For example:*

 a. In 1 Corinthians 7 Paul gives his godly judgment regarding whether people who are single or widowed should marry. (It is a controversial chapter.)

 (1) He urges them not to marry (1 Cor. 7:8).

 (2) But if they do marry, they have not sinned (1 Cor. 7:36).

 b. In other words, we may not agree with advice given by a godly person.

 (1) Not taking the advice may be unwise but it is not necessarily sin.

 (2) Sin in this case would not be sin unless it breaks the Moral Law (the Ten Commandments).

3. *Sin is that which either grieves the Holy Spirit (Eph. 4:30ff) or brings dishonour to God's name* (Eph. 5:3-5).

 a. It is possible for us to grieve the Spirit (e.g. by bitterness) and it not necessarily be obvious (and therefore not bring disgrace upon the church).

 (1) But it is sin – and sin against God.

 (2) What is more, it is deadly to our spirituality and great usefulness to God.

 b. What most certainly *does* bring dishonour to the name of God is what causes *division* or *scandal*.

 (1) Gossip and slandering bring division.

 (2) Sexual immorality brings scandal.

4. *Any sin leads to regret.*

 a. Not necessarily repentance!

 (1) Repentance is 'change of mind'.

 (2) Only the Holy Spirit brings repentance.

 b. But sin most certainly leads to regret.

 (1) It is only a matter of time before we will be very, very sorry for any sin (whether secret bitterness or open immorality).

 (2) It all begins with temptation (Jas. 1:13ff).

II. Root, or origin, of temptation. How does it begin?

A. There are generally two origins of temptation.

 1. *Within* (Jas. 1:13ff).

 a. This refers to the flesh (carnal or sinful nature).

(1) We all live in the flesh to some degree (Rom. 7:18; Gal. 2:20).

(2) There is in all of us the potential for the greatest evil (Jer. 17:9).

b. We, therefore, are continual targets for temptation because of what we are (Matt. 15:19).

(1) We were born that way (Ps. 51:5).

(2) We did not need training on 'how to sin', which I would have thought is the greatest evidence, if not proof, of original sin (that we are born sinners).

c. From the flesh, therefore, proceeds what is evil because it is already there.

(1) Lust is in the heart like a powder keg waiting to be ignited. So too hate, greed, etc.

(2) Thus temptation is essential to the flesh, that is, it is a part of what we all are naturally.

2. *Without. Outside of us. This includes two further origins (or causes).*

a. The world (1 John 2:15-17).

(1) 'Don't let the world squeeze you into its mould' (Rom. 12:2) (Phillips).

(2) The world refers to people, places, things.

(a) People can tempt us, whether it be to sexual immorality or anger or something else.

(b) Places can tempt us because of the pleasures they promise.

(c) Things (e.g. money, material possessions) can tempt us because of the prestige they promise.

b. The devil (1 Thess. 3:5; Matt. 4:1).

(1) Satan's chief goal is to divert us from the glory of God.

(2) He knows us better than we know ourselves:

(a) Our weaknesses.

(b) Our temperaments.

(c) Our hearts.

(d) Our past sins.

(3) Each of us is earmarked by the devil for the 'evil day' (Eph. 6:13).

(4) He has a way of slipping in alongside us at the most unexpected moments.

(5) He works through people and circumstances when the opportunity arises.

B. We – not God – are responsible for our own temptation (Jas. 1:13ff).

1. *This is the most important point that can be made; God is not the one who tempts.*

   a. 'No-one should say, "God is tempting me".'

   b. Why did James say that?

      (1) It is the first thing we often think: God is tempting me.

      (2) It is also the suggestion of Satan: to blame God.

2. *Temptation always seems 'providential', that is, since it is convenient and timely with immediate circumstances, God is actually in and behind the very moment of temptation.*

   a. Jonah's backsliding appeared to be confirmed or endorsed by Providence (Jonah 1:3).

      (1) He determined to head for Tarshish, not Nineveh.

      (2) Lo and behold, a ship was available that was actually going to Tarshish!

   b. All temptation is characterised by the feeling, 'God is in it so it will be right to do in this case.'

      (1) When Satan tempted Eve it appeared to be God's own way of reasoning and speaking (Gen. 3:5).

      (2) She rationalised 'the fruit of the tree was good for food...' and took it and ate it (Gen. 3:6).

3. *True spirituality affirms that we are responsible for our temptation.*

   a. It is by our 'own evil desire' that we are 'dragged away and enticed' (Jas. 1:14).

      (1) What makes us do it comes from within.

      (2) We sin, therefore, because we choose to sin.

   b. Consequently we must deal with our evil desire in order that evil desire becomes a 'no go' area. That means:

      (1) We know ourselves and refuse to allow the desire to be increased.

      (2) We make a prior commitment not to sin, no matter how pressing the circumstances.

      (3) Temptation ceases to have the feeling of inevitability and inescapability and lacks the inner desire it once had.

         (a) Satan makes us feel that giving in to temptation is inevitable and inescapable.

    (b) What was once scary temptation becomes a mere suggestion – which we refuse to take on board.

  c. In a word: temptation is reduced to the level of suggestion.

    (1) It was once that which was almost 'too much to handle'.

    (2) It becomes instead a suggestion that can be ignored.

C. God only tests us by permitting trial or temptation.

  1. *God tested Abraham* (Gen. 22:1).

    a. All trials are in this sense 'from above'.

      (1) This is why James said, 'Consider it pure joy' (Jas. 1:2).

      (2) It is a sign God trusts you to be tried.

    b. The Lord left Hezekiah 'to test him and to know everything that was in his heart' (2 Chron. 32:31).

      (1) God decided to hide his face from Hezekiah.

      (2) But it was to test him – to see what he was really like!

  2. *God tested Job* (Job 1:8).

    a. God actually initiated Job's ordeal by inviting Satan to test him.

    b. All that Satan was allowed to do was under the direct supervision of God's sovereign will.

    c. Eventual result: Job saw what he himself was really like (Job 42:6).

III. Temptation and sin

A. There is a difference between temptation and sin.

  1. *Jesus was tempted – but he didn't sin* (Heb. 4:15).

    a. If Jesus was tempted we should not be surprised if we are.

    b. It is not sin to be tempted.

      (1) We must never let Satan claim a victory just because we are tempted.

      (2) There is a difference between being tempted and giving in to temptation.

  2. *Sin is only sin when we yield to the temptation.*

    a. It is when we say yes to temptation by giving into it.

      (1) That is when sin has been committed.

      (2) Until then it was not sin.

    b. But when we give in to the temptation we have sinned.

      (1) This is what Eve did (Gen. 3:6).

      (2) It is what David did (2 Sam. 11:2-4).

B. Temptation and trial (1 Cor. 10:13).

1. *Temptation is resistible.*
   a. In the heat of the moment it seems irresistible.
      (1) This is because the suggestion was not at once rejected.
      (2) Suggestion develops into fiery temptation if it is not rejected at once.
   b. But even when temptation sets in there is a way of escape.
      (1) We can still say no.
      (2) If we say yes we can only blame ourselves.
2. *Any trial can be dignified.*
   a. We dignify (show respect or honour) the trial by affirming God.
      (1) Recognising that he allowed it.
      (2) Realising it has come with a purpose.
   b. We dignify the trial further by:
      (1) Not grumbling when it comes.
      (2) Letting the trial continue as long as God allows it by not aborting it prematurely.
         (a) Every trial has a time limit.
         (b) All trials end.

C. Giving in to temptation – or not dignifying the trial – will only cause grief in due time.

1. *We will always be sorry after we sinned.*
   a. We would do anything to turn back the clock.
      (1) But after we have sinned, it is too late.
      (2) We can't pretend it didn't happen.
   b. When being tempted consider how we will feel later.
      (1) This may be how God stops us.
      (2) Consider the consequences of sin.
2. *We will be ashamed if we do not dignify the trial God ordained for us.*
   a. It is his way of enabling us to get closer to him.
      (1) That is the main purpose of a trial.
      (2) It is to get to know God better.
   b. When a trial is over, it is over.
      (1) We cannot turn the clock back.
      (2) We may never have a trial like that one again.
   c. When tempted to complain when we fall into a trial, think about how we will feel when it is over!

IV. How to resist temptation

A. Remember that we are responsible for our own temptation.
    1. Do not pass the buck to God.
    2. Do not say 'God is tempting me.'

B. Remember that this is a unique opportunity to show God how much he matters to us.
    1. *We don't really prove how much we love God:*
        a. By our worship.
        b. By our love for the Bible or theology.
    2. We prove our love for God by saying no to temptation.

C. Consider the consequences of sin.
    1. The sorrow we will feel.
    2. The chastening that will follow (2 Sam. 12:10-14).

D. Make no provision for the flesh (Rom. 13:14).
    1. The best way to avoid falling into sin is to avoid the temptation.
    2. Most of us have a fairly shrewd idea what will tempt us; we are fools to proceed where we know we will be tempted.

E. Take 'preventive medicine' all the time!
    1. 'Backsliding begins in the knees.' How much are you praying? The more, the better.
    2. Read no less than one chapter a day from the Bible. The more, the better.
    3. Be involved in the work of ministry. 'Idleness is the devil's workshop.'
    4. Avoid people and circumstances which you suspect will be tools of the devil.

F. Be aware of Satan's devices (schemes) (2 Cor. 2:11).
    1. *Unbelief.*
        a. This was how Satan approached Eve (Gen. 3:1).
        b. This was how Satan approached Jesus (Matt. 4:3).
    2. *Fear.*
        a. That there is nothing we can do but give in (1 Pet. 5:8-9).
        b. That God will desert us.

3. *Pride.*
  a. Appealing to our reputation, a self-esteem and desire for prestige.
  b. A lot of sexual temptation centres in pride.

4. *Sex.*
  a. Appealing to a God-given desire and making us think it is God's will for it to be gratified.
  b. Appealing to loneliness and self-pity, not to mention the need to be considered desirable.

5. *Deep hurt.*
  a. Calling attention to the unfairness of what has been done to us.
  b. Making us feel justified in our resentment.

6. *Coincidences.*
  a. Letting us think that the way circumstances have come together prove that we are the exception to the rule.
  b. Remember: temptation always appears 'providential'.

CONCLUSION

It is not a sin to be tempted. Remember also that temptation is resistible. Aim for reducing temptation to the level of mere suggestion.

27

HOW CAN SPIRIT-FILLED CHRISTIANS DISAGREE?

INTRODUCTION

A. This is certainly one of the more painful subjects we have dealt with.
   1. *We wish it were not true; that the 'best' of God's people disagree.*
      a. There are various levels of this disagreement.
      b. Sometimes it is doctrine, when there is no personal animosity.
         (1) Sometimes it becomes a heated debate.
         (2) Sadly, sometimes the debate involves personal or emotional feelings.
   2. *Jesus commanded his disciples to love one another.*
      a. He prayed, 'That all of them may be one' (John 17:21).
      b. He continued, 'May they be brought to complete unity to let the world know that you sent me' (John 17:23).
         (1) This could refer to the world being so 'impressed' with that unity that they would be without excuse.
         (2) It may also mean that the unity results in an anointing that would make it easier to convince people.
   3. *Paul also wanted unity. 'Whatever happens, conduct yourselves in a manner worthy of the gospel of Christ. Then, whether I come and see you or only hear about you in my absence, I will know that you stand firm in one spirit, contending as one man for the faith of the gospel'* (Phil. 1:27).
      a. This led him to exhort, 'Then make my joy complete by being like-minded, having the same love, being one in spirit and purpose' (Phil. 2:2).
      b. The way forward, says Paul, is for each to have the same mind or attitude as was in Christ Jesus (Phil. 2:5ff).
         (1) Jesus made himself nothing – of no reputation.
         (2) Unity is achieved when we are utterly unselfish.

B. There are two basic assumptions that lie behind this study.

  1. *The Holy Spirit is the only infallible interpreter of Scripture.*

    a. He is the author of Scripture:

      (1) 'All Scripture is God-breathed and is useful for teaching, rebuking, correcting and training in righteousness' (2 Tim. 3:16).

      (2) 'Above all, you must understand that no prophecy of Scripture came about by the prophet's own interpretation. For prophecy never had its origin in the will of man, but men spoke from God as they were carried along by the Holy Spirit' (2 Pet. 1:20-21).

    b. He alone knows the meaning and correct interpretation of what he wrote.

      (1) 'But the Counsellor, the Holy Spirit, whom the Father will send in my name, will teach you all things and will remind you of everything I have said to you' (John 14:26).

      (2) 'But when he, the Spirit of truth, comes, he will guide you into all truth. He will not speak on his own; he will speak only what he hears, and he will tell you what is yet to come' (John 16:13).

      (3) 'But God has revealed it to us by his Spirit. The Spirit searches all things, even the deep things of God. For who among men knows the thoughts of a man except the man's spirit within him? In the same way no one knows the thoughts of God except the Spirit of God. . . The man without the Spirit does not accept the things that come from the Spirit of God, for they are foolishness to him, and he cannot understand them, because they are spiritually discerned' (1 Cor. 2:10-11,14).

    c. It follows that the Spirit knows the meaning of all Scripture and has the full and ultimate understanding of it all; therefore he will interpret what he wrote infallibly.

      (1) He knows what he meant when he wrote it.

      (2) He will not interpret what he wrote in a contrary manner.

    d. For the Holy Spirit is the 'Spirit of truth' (John 14:17).

      (1) The Holy Spirit is God (2 Cor. 3:17. cf. Acts 5:3-4).

      (2) It is impossible for God to lie (Titus 1:2; Heb. 6:18).

  2. *The Holy Spirit is perfect love and therefore the fountainhead of all the fruits of the Spirit.* 'But the fruit of the Spirit is love, joy, peace, patience, kindness, goodness, faithfulness' (Gal. 5:22).

a. There is no fear in love (1 John 4:18): 'There is no fear in love. But perfect love drives out fear, because fear has to do with punishment. The one who fears is not made perfect in love.'
   (1) Anyone filled with the Spirit will be without fear.
   (2) Anyone filled with the Spirit will not punish another.
b. The Holy Spirit in a Christian will not oppose the Spirit in another Christian.
   (1) It is the same God and the same Spirit.
   (2) God will not oppose himself.
c. If two Christians are truly Spirit-filled there will be no antagonism between them.
   (1) There will be reciprocal love and compassion.
   (2) One will prefer the other's honour (Rom. 12:10).
d. In a word: there will be unity.
   (1) Unity of doctrine.
   (2) Unity of love.
   (3) It is what Paul calls the 'unity of the Spirit' (Eph. 4:3).

C. The problem:
1. *Differences have emerged over doctrine.*
   a. It first occurred in the book of Acts (Acts 15:1-2).
   b. Paul had to fight all his life for the integrity of the Gospel.
   c. In church history various problems developed:
      (1) The 2nd century Christians became moralistic and seemed to lose sight of the Gospel.
      (2) Christological controversies dominated.
      (3) Predestination versus free will became an issue.
      (4) Eastern and Western Christianity developed their own culture and theology.
2. *Personal feelings surfaced.*
   a. Grecian Jews felt neglected (Acts 6:1ff).
   b. Paul and Barnabas quarrelled (Acts 15:39-40).
   c. Paul opposed Peter over fraternising with Gentiles (Gal. 2:11).
   d. In church history personality clashes arose.
      (1) Name-calling became common during the Reformation.
      (2) Luther fell out with Zwingli in bitter disputes.
      (3) Wesley and Whitefield had serious problems.
      (4) Augustus Toplady got off his death-bed to fight rumours that he and John Wesley had come to terms.

D. What is obvious:

1. Not all could be faithfully interpreting Scripture.
2. Not all could be totally governed by the Holy Spirit.
3. But all (presumably) sincerely felt that God was on their side.
4. Party lines developed.
5. There are more movements and denominations today than can be counted – but all believing they faithfully represent God and truth!

E. Why is this lesson important?

1. *The world loves to criticise Christians because they 'can't get together'.*
   a. We will never be able to stop them saying this.
   b. We can however be informed about how this has happened in the church from earliest times.
2. *It is surely reasonable to ask, why hasn't Jesus' prayer in John 17 been answered?*
   a. Is it our fault?
   b. If he prayed with a perfect faith, why hasn't his prayer been answered?
3. *There are so many people who stress being Spirit-filled today and yet they have as much dissension and lack of unity as anyone else.*
   a. Charismatics quarrel with Pentecostals.
   b. Charismatics quarrel with charismatics.
   c. Pentecostals quarrel with Pentecostals.
4. *We should ask ourselves if we are contributing to the problem.*
   a. Do we have quarrels with another believer?
   b. Why are we so sure we are right?
5. *It is our duty to make every effort to ensure that any continuing division is not because of us.*
   a. I must ask, do I love as I should?
   b. I must ask, am I truly Spirit-filled?

I. JESUS IS THE ONLY PERSON EVER TO HAVE THE HOLY SPIRIT WITHOUT LIMIT (John 3:34).

A. This shows that there are degrees of being 'filled' with the Spirit.

1. *John the Baptist was filled with the Holy Spirit from birth* (Luke 1:15).

a. But this does not mean that John the Baptist was perfect.

b. He himself vacillated in his convictions about Jesus.

(1) On the one hand he boldly proclaimed that Jesus was God's Saviour. 'The next day John saw Jesus coming toward him and said, "Look, the Lamb of God, who takes away the sin of the world!"' (John 1:29).

(2) But later it turns out that John wasn't so sure, and needed reassurance. 'When John heard in prison what Christ was doing, he sent his disciples to ask him, "Are you the one who was to come, or should we expect someone else?"' (Matt. 11:2-3).

(3) Jesus gave that reassurance. 'Jesus replied, "Go back and report to John what you hear and see: The blind receive sight, the lame walk, those who have leprosy are cured, the deaf hear, the dead are raised, and the good news is preached to the poor"' (Matt. 11:4-5).

c. This shows that being Spirit-filled is by degree:

(1) It may be a temporary filling.

(2) It will never equal the level of Jesus' own filling of the Spirit.

2. *One crucial difference between Jesus' filling and ours:*

a. When the Holy Spirit came on Jesus like a dove the same Spirit 'remained'.

(1) 'Then John gave this testimony: "I saw the Spirit come down from heaven as a dove and remain on him. I would not have known him, except that the one who sent me to baptise with water told me, 'The man on whom you see the Spirit come down and remain is he who will baptise with the Holy Spirit'"' (John 1:32-33).

(2) This continued without any break or diminishing from that moment.

b. When the Holy Spirit comes down on us, he doesn't 'remain'.

(1) We have high moments when the Spirit witnesses with great power.

(2) But the next day we too are like John the Baptist; beset with doubt.

3. *Jesus' unlimited measure of the Spirit resulted in:*

a. A perfect, unbroken relationship with the Father.

(1) 'Jesus gave them this answer: "I tell you the truth, the

Son can do nothing by himself; he can do only what he sees his Father doing, because whatever the Father does the Son also does"' (John 5:19).

(2) 'By myself I can do nothing; I judge only as I hear, and my judgment is just, for I seek not to please myself but him who sent me' (John 5:30).

(3) 'I always do what pleases him' (John 8:29).

b. A perfect faith.

(1) Jesus had faith. 'I will put my trust in him,' said Jesus (Heb. 2:13).

(2) Because he had the Spirit without limit he had a perfect faith.

(3) Our faith in his faith is what saves us (Rom. 1:17; 3:22; Gal. 2:16,20). (Sadly, the NIV translators do not render xristos pisteo 'faith of Christ' as the Authorised Version bears out.)

c. A perfect love.

(1) God is love (1 John 4:16).

(2) Jesus is God (John 1:1).

(3) Jesus loved his disciples with the perfect love of God (John 13:1,34).

B. Jesus is the truth. 'Jesus answered, "I am the way and the truth and the life. No one comes to the Father except through me"' (John 14:6).

1. He not only spoke the truth; being God he is the truth.

2. Therefore as the Spirit is the 'Spirit of truth' so Jesus was and is the man of truth. 'He who speaks on his own does so to gain honour for himself, but he who works for the honour of the one who sent him is a man of truth; there is nothing false about him' (John 7:18).

3. *To the degree we reflect Jesus in our words and behaviour we will:*

a. Be sound in our thinking.

b. Be like him in our language and attitude.

II . ALL CHRISTIANS ARE GIVEN A 'MEASURE' OF THE HOLY SPIRIT

A. Since Jesus was the only person to have no limit or measure of the Holy Spirit, it follows that our own possession of the Spirit is in measure.

   1. 'For by the grace given me I say to every one of you: Do not think of yourself more highly than you ought, but rather think of yourself with sober judgment, in accordance with the measure of faith God has given you' (Rom. 12:3).

   2. *'But to each one of us grace has been given as Christ apportioned it'* (Eph. 4:7).

   a. This principle is implicit in Paul's prayer. 'Now to him who is able to do immeasurably more than all we ask or imagine, according to his power that is at work within us' (Eph. 3:20).

   b. The power in us is of God – we can take no credit for this.

B. The 'measure' – or limit set – that we have is our anointing.

   1. Not all of us have the same measure – or extent – of the Spirit, therefore not all have the same anointing.

   2. *What may be your anointing will not be mine; what may be mine may not be yours.*

   a. It is our task to discover our anointing:

   (1) To come to terms with it.

   (2) To live within it. Cf. 'Peter principle'.

   b. We likewise must respect another's anointing.

   (1) We must not expect others to be like us.

   (2) We should set others free to be themselves.

C. The 'measure' of the Spirit in us also implies a 'gap' in us.

   1. *Gap (def.): something lacking.*

   a. There may be, for example, a gap in our learning.

   b. There may be a gap in our understanding; we all have 'blind spots'.

   2. *That 'gap' is therefore an imperfection.*

   a. All have sinned and (continue to) 'fall short' of God's glory (Rom. 3:23).

   b. That imperfection will be present until the day we die and are glorified.

   (1) Until then we will be 'prone to wander'.

(2) Until then we will be vulnerable to criticism and praise.

3. *The result: we are all sinners.*

    a. We naturally think of ourselves first.

        (1) Whose picture do you look for in a photograph?

        (2) Whose name do you look for in an article if you think you might be mentioned?

        (3) Do you ever ask, 'Did they mention me?' 'Did they say anything about me?'

    b. We are naturally threatened by:

        (1) Another person's anointing.

        (2) Another person's success or popularity.

        (3) Another person's blessing – whether being blessed or being a blessing to others.

III. The 'best' of times do not prohibit misunderstanding or a sense of threat

A. God manifested the glory of his Son on the Mount of Transfiguration.

    1. 'There he was transfigured before them. His face shone like the sun, and his clothes became as white as the light. Just then there appeared before them Moses and Elijah, talking with Jesus' (Matt. 17:2-3).

    2. *We might expect that the effect of this would be an immediate impartation of lucidity and clear understanding of God's purpose.*

        a. But no; 'Peter said to Jesus, "Lord, it is good for us to be here. If you wish, I will put up three shelters – one for you, one for Moses and one for Elijah"' (Matt. 17:4).

        b. This shows that in the best of times – undoubted manifestation of God's glory – we are capable of error and folly.

            (1) We may well expect this in Revival.

            (2) Revival will not be a cure-all for our foolish tendencies.

B. In the earliest church there was the paradox of some having a complete detachment from material things and others feeling neglected.

    1. In Acts 4:32: 'All the believers were one in heart and mind. No one claimed that any of his possessions was his own, but they shared everything they had.'

2. In Acts 6:1: 'In those days when the number of disciples was increasing, the Grecian Jews among them complained against the Hebraic Jews because their widows were being overlooked in the daily distribution of food.'

3. *Does this mean that some were Spirit-filled but the Grecian Jews were not?*

    a. There is no way of knowing whether some were walking in the Spirit more than others.

    b. What is certain: in the 'best' of times – when there was an obvious Revival situation – problems emerged.

C. The 'best' of God's people needed to be corrected.

  1. *Peter was prejudiced against Gentiles.*

    a. It took a supernatural revelation of the Spirit combined with the Spirit falling on Cornelius before his mind was changed (Acts 10).

    b. Peter was willing to sit with Gentile believers until Jews from Jerusalem appeared; then he quickly excused himself (Gal. 2:12ff).

      (1) That could not be right, but this was the same Peter who preached on the Day of Pentecost!

      (2) Paul said, 'I opposed him to his face' for this, 'because he was clearly in the wrong' (Gal. 2:11).

  2. *The church that gathered in Jerusalem for the first council meeting met because of division over Gentiles being baptised without first being circumcised.*

    a. 'Then some of the believers who belonged to the party of the Pharisees stood up and said, "The Gentiles must be circumcised and required to obey the law of Moses"' (Acts 15:5).

    b. After much discussion they compromised, claiming, 'It seemed good to the Holy Spirit and to us' (Acts 15:28).

      (1) Many have since questioned whether this was truly the wisdom of God.

      (2) But at the time 'it seemed good' – which is the best they could come up with.

    c. All this was carried out by the 'best' of God's people with the best of intentions.

  3. *Paul and Barnabas fell out over the issue of John Mark being worthy to continue to travel with them.*

    a. 'Barnabas wanted to take John, also called Mark, with them, but Paul did not think it wise to take him, because he had deserted them in Pamphylia and had not continued with them in the work' (Acts 15:37-38).

    b. The matter became very serious. 'They had such a sharp disagreement that they parted company. Barnabas took Mark and sailed for Cyprus, but Paul chose Silas and left, commended by the brothers to the grace of the Lord' (Acts 15:39-40).

        (1) Paul later said, 'Only Luke is with me. Get Mark and bring him with you, because he is helpful to me in my ministry' (2 Tim. 4:11).

        (2) This may mean that Paul changed his mind; or that Mark changed in the meantime.

    c. What is the explanation?

        (1) Was Barnabas Spirit-filled? Yes.

        (2) Was Paul Spirit-filled? Yes.

        (3) Even if one was in the wrong, it all worked out; Silas and Paul did well together.

CONCLUSION

The 'gap' that exists in all of us means that none of us is perfect in judgment or attitude, and that personal feelings – including envy – sooner or later emerge. This accounts for the 'best' of God's people disagreeing. Only Jesus was perfect. In the meantime, we must all lower our voices: 'Therefore judge nothing before the appointed time; wait till the Lord comes. He will bring to light what is hidden in darkness and will expose the motives of men's hearts. At that time each will receive his praise from God' (1 Cor. 4:5).

28

HOW TO COPE WITH GRUDGES

A. In the whole of my ministry I have never known the kind of response I get when I preach along the lines of 'total forgiveness'.

    1. This is an expression I got from Josif Tson: 'R.T., you must totally forgive them; until you totally forgive them, you will be in chains. Release them, and you will be released.'

    2. No-one had ever talked to me like that. 'Wounds from a friend can be trusted' (Prov. 27:6).

B. We all have a story to tell regarding some mistreatment:

    1. Betrayal by one we fully trusted.

    2. Someone lied about us.

    3. Someone kept us from getting that job, or promotion.

    4. Abuse by an authority figure.

    5. *Someone mistreated one of our children or close friends.*

        a. The list is endless.

        b. There is no-one who has not been hurt, deeply hurt, by people in the past.

C. The natural reaction: to hold a grudge.

    1. Grudge (def.): a feeling of resentment or ill-will.

    2. *It is the most natural feeling in the world.*

        a. Nobody needs to take a course on 'How to hold a grudge.'

        b. It is neither taught nor is there need of a role model so that we may know how to feel resentment.

            (1) Children feel it; as they get older he or she may begin to repress the feeling; that is, to deny it to oneself.

            (2) Many times a grudge is pushed down into our subconscious; we deny what is painful.

D. New Testament words:

1. *Gogguzo (Gr.), usually translated 'to murmur' (AV), 'to grumble' (NIV).*

   a. It comes from a root word that means 'to express dissatisfaction'; it may mean 'grumbling at disappointed hopes'.

   b. It is used eight times in the New Testament: Matthew 20:11; Luke 5:30 ('complained'); John 6:41,43,61; John 7:32 ('whispering'); 1 Corinthians 10:10.

2. *Goggusmos (Gr.), a participle of the same verb.*

   a. In the Septuagint it is used to sum up the murmurings of the Children of Israel in the wilderness. E.g., Exodus 16:7,8; Numbers 17:5,10.

   b. It is used four times in the New Testament: John 7:12; Acts 6:1; Phillipians 2:14; 1 Peter 4:9 (AV 'grudging').

   c. Cf. *Goggustes* (Gr. noun). Jude 16 ('grumblers').

3. *Pikria* (Gr. noun), *pikraivo* (Gr. verb), usually translated 'bitterness' or 'to be bitter'.

   a. From a root word denoting what is sharp to the senses, a pervasive smell; 'shrill' of noise; 'painful' to the feelings.

   b. The word or its equivalent is used 12 times in the New Testament, e.g., Colossians 3:19 ('harsh'); Acts 8:23; Romans 3:14; Ephesians 4:31; Hebrews 12:15 ('bitter root'); James 3:14; Matthew 26:75.

4. *Acharistos (Gr.), 'ungrateful' (Luke 6:35; 2 Tim. 3:2).*

   a. It is the opposite of graciousness.

   b. In a word: the opposite of a forgiving spirit; therefore, an unforgiving spirit.

5. Note: the word 'grudge' does not appear in the NIV although it does in the AV, but it is a common word today in any case and encompasses the meaning expressed in the words above.

E. Why is this study important?

1. It gets close to the bone, where we all live.

2. It is relevant to the work of the Holy Spirit, for holding a grudge grieves the Spirit.

3. It is relevant to theology because we cannot proceed in fresh theological thinking when we hold grudges!

4. It shows how holding a grudge displeases God.

5. It touches the very heart of Jesus' own theology.

I. IT IS THE VERY HEART OF THE **L**ORD'S **P**RAYER

A. Two things bear our immediate attention:
1. *The petition, 'Forgive us our debts, as we also have forgiven our debtors'* (Matt. 6:12).
   a. Gr. *opherlema,* when you owe someone a sum.
   b. We owe God perfection; the imperfection is sin.
2. *The 'P.S.' that immediately follows the Lord's Prayer:* 'For if you forgive men when they sin against you, your heavenly Father will also forgive you. But if you do not forgive men their sins, your Father will not forgive your sins' (Matt. 6:14-15).
   a. The word 'For' which introduces these two verses implies the rationale for the Lord's Prayer in the first place.
   b. This is the only part of the Prayer Jesus picked up on, and implies that it is the most important part of the Prayer.

B. How many of us have made liars of ourselves by repeating this Prayer when in fact we hold a grudge toward someone?
1. *Note: our forgiving others in order to be forgiven is not a condition for being saved.*
   a. If it were, salvation would be by works and not grace.
   b. If it were, who is saved?
2. It refers rather to our inheritance (reward) in the Kingdom, and closeness to God here below.
   a. The Sermon on the Mount is chiefly our Lord's spiritual interpretation of the Law and what the Kingdom of Heaven is.
   b. In a word: it refers to our way forward in fellowship with the Father and enjoying intimacy with him (1 John 1:7).
3. *It should not be surprising that this would be the heart of the Lord's Prayer; the whole of Jesus' teachings could be summed up in one word: love (Gr. agape).*
   a. 'But I tell you: Love your enemies and pray for those who persecute you' (Matt. 5:44).
   b. 'A new command I give you: Love one another. As I have loved you, so you must love one another. By this all men will know that you are my disciples, if you love one another' (John 13:34-35).

II. It is the primary sin that grieves the Holy Spirit

A. **Having said,** 'Do not grieve the Holy Spirit of God, with whom you were sealed for the day of redemption,' (Eph. 4:30), the next thing Paul says is, 'Get rid of all bitterness, rage and anger, brawling and slander, along with every form of malice. Be kind and compassionate to one another, forgiving each other, just as in Christ God forgave you' (Eph. 4:31-32).

  1. *As Jesus gave forgiving one another to be the main reason for the Lord's Prayer so Paul virtually repeats the same thing with regard to how we grieve the Holy Spirit.*

    a. Note the words:

      (1) Bitterness.

      (2) Rage and anger.

      (3) Brawling (noisy quarrels, shouting).

      (4) Slander.

      (5) Every form of malice (desire to harm others).

    b. Put positively:

      (1) Be kind.

      (2) Be compassionate.

      (3) Forgiving each other, just as in Christ God forgave you.

    c. Question: how deeply, how far do you suppose God has forgiven us?

      (1) He does not tell what he knows; it is forgotten (Heb. 8:12).

      (2) He does not want us to fear (Rom. 8:15).

      (3) He does not count our sins against us (2 Cor. 5:19).

      (4) He does not want us to feel guilty (Ps. 103:12).

  2. *Note: grieving the Spirit does not mean we lose our salvation because Paul said we are sealed with the Holy Spirit for the day of redemption – nothing could be clearer than that!*

    a. This coheres with Matthew 6:14-15, which points to our inheritance (reward) in the Kingdom.

    b. Paul also comes to this in Ephesians 5:5 ('For of this you can be sure: No immoral, impure or greedy person – such a man is an idolater – has any inheritance in the kingdom of Christ and of God.') which shows there are sins that militate against the reward and fellowship in the Spirit – but do not threaten our security as saved people.

B. What are examples of holding a grudge?

1. *Murmuring, or grumbling, a sin of the Children of Israel which caused them to forfeit their inheritance* (I Cor. 10:1-12).

    a. Complaining (Jas. 5:9).

    b. Not dignifying the trial God gives (Jas. 1:2).

2. *Jealousy* (James 3:14).

    a. The sin nobody talks about and yet which we can see in others but rarely in ourselves.

    b. It is when we resent another person's:

        (1) Success.

        (2) Achievement.

        (3) Personality.

        (4) Good looks.

        (5) Money.

        (6) Class.

        (7) Friends.

        (8) Gifts.

        (9) Connections.

        (10) Reputation.

3. *Judging another* (Matt. 7:1-2).

    a. Jesus stated this as a promise! 'Do not judge, and you will not be judged. Do not condemn, and you will not be condemned. Forgive, and you will be forgiven. Give, and it will be given to you. A good measure, pressed down, shaken together and running over, will be poured into your lap. For with the measure you use, it will be measured to you' (Luke 6:37-38).

    b. Consider the blessing that is promised purely on the basis of:

        (1) Not judging.

        (2) Not condemning.

        (3) Forgiving.

        (4) Giving.

    c. All the above is reciprocated: 'For with the measure you use, it will be measured to you.'

III. THE ULTIMATE OBJECT AND OBLIGATION OF GRUDGES

A. All grudges are ultimately directed at God himself.

1. *At first we may not realise this.*

    a. We feel angry toward another person.

    b. We are usually not aware at first where this anger is ultimately traceable.

2. *We are really holding a grudge against God.*

    a. He is the one who allowed it to happen!

      (1) We feel, 'How could this person do this to me?'

      (2) We are actually saying, 'How could God let this happen to me?'

      (3) When the Children of Israel were angry with Moses their grudge was actually against God (Ex. 16:7).

    b. He is the one who said, 'Forgive.'

      (1) Not to do this is to sin against him.

      (2) We may well be sinning against another person, yes.

      (3) But our sin is against God (Ps. 51:4).

B. God does not hold grudges against us.

1. When we confess our sin, he forgives (1 John 1:9).

2. *Chastening is not measured out toward sin which has been confessed and repented of.*

    a. Had David repented Nathan would not have come to him (2 Sam. 12).

    b. Had they repented, and not lied, Ananias and Sapphira would have lived (Acts 5:1-10).

    c. Chastening is also designed to reveal sin we had not been conscious of.

      (1) It shows we are saved (Heb. 12:6-7).

      (2) It is because God isn't finished with us (Heb. 12:10).

      (3) It is preparation – to make us holy (Heb. 12:10-11).

C. Our obligation: make it God's problem.

1. *Only God has the right to bring vengeance upon those who have hurt us.*

    a. This is his ancient promise and warning:

      (1) 'It is mine to avenge; I will repay' (Deut. 32:35).

      (2) 'Do not take revenge, my friends, but leave room for God's wrath, for it is written: "It is mine to avenge; I will repay," says the Lord' (Rom. 12:19).

    (3) 'For we know him who said, "It is mine to avenge; I will repay"' (Heb. 10:30a).

  b. This is a promise many of us forget.

    (1) We take vengeance into our own hands – by malice, slander, judging, making people fear. 'There is no fear in love. But perfect love drives out fear, because fear has to do with punishment. The one who fears is not made perfect in love' (1 John 4:18).

    (2) This only grieves the Holy Spirit and forfeits the promise.

2. *When we take vengeance into our own hands we rob God.*

  a. There are two ways we rob God:

    (1) Withholding tithes (Mal. 3:8-10).

    (2) Usurping his prerogative to avenge.

  b. We are utterly impoverished when we hold a grudge – in two ways:

    (1) We hurt ourselves – it causes sleeplessness, ageing, making us more irritable, even affecting us physically (e.g., high blood pressure, arthritis).

    (2) We forfeit God's brilliant means of dealing with those who hurt us.

  c. Note the story of Joseph.

    (1) God dealt with Joseph for his arrogance.

    (2) God dealt with Joseph's brothers for what they did.

IV. How to cope when you hold a grudge

A. Recognise it.

1. *Admit that this is what it is that has a hold on you.*

  a. Do not explain it away – or play games with yourself.

  b. Face it in yourself, when:

    (1) You feel hurt.

    (2) You feel resentment.

    (3) You feel mistreated.

    (4) You feel 'It's not fair'.

    (5) You want to point the finger. Isa. 58:9.

    (6) You feel threatened when you hear someone's name mentioned.

      (7) You want to 'put the record straight'.

      (8) You start to make another look less credible.

      (9) Another 'gets your goat'.

      (10) You have conversations (in your mind) regarding someone.

      (11) You want them punished and exposed.

      (12) You cannot genuinely pray for them.

2. *Admit that this is sin against God.*

    a. Never mind that the other person may have sinned.

    b. Your grudge is as heinous in God's sight as their mistreatment is to you!

      (1) Don't ask God what will happen to the next person (John 21:21). It's none of your business; face your sin and acknowledge it to God.

B. Analyze it.

1. *Consider how it is hurting you – not them.*

    a. When we refuse to forgive it is largely because we think the other will get away with it.

      (1) This is God's problem.

      (2) Have *you* ever got away with any sin? (Ezra 9:13; Ps. 103:12).

    b. We are the total losers when we don't forgive.

      (1) We do damage to ourselves.

      (2) We forfeit seeing God do 'his thing'.

2. *Consider how it grieves the Holy Spirit* (Eph. 4:30).

    a. You lose 'presence of mind'.

    b. You forfeit the promises of the Holy Spirit in John 14-16:

      (1) Making Jesus real (John 14:16).

      (2) Reminding you of what you learned (John 14:26).

      (3) Being led into more truth (John 16:13).

    c. You will not know God's will (Eph. 5:17).

    d. You lose communion and assurance of your own forgiveness (Matt. 6:14-15; 1 John 1:7).

C. If necessary, share it with one other person.

1. *This person should not be one who is in any way involved in your hurt.*

    a. It could be a subtle way of sending a signal to one who has hurt you.

    b. Share it with a person who is totally detached from the situation, so that nobody will know.

  2. *This is partly what is meant by 'Therefore confess your sins to each other and pray for each other so that you may be healed'* (Jas. 5:16).

    a. This is in the context of the anointing with oil.

    b. A grudge can delay healing (it *could* be the cause of the sickness), therefore, confess it – it shows you mean business.

D. Pray for the person who has hurt you and caused the damage.

  1. This is the hardest thing of all to do.

  2. *Ask yourself:*

    a. 'Would I want God to judge me every time I hurt another?'

    b. 'Would I want the one I hurt to pray for me?'

  3. *Your prayer should be for God to bless them* (Matt. 5:44).

    a. Don't pray, 'Punish them, Lord.' (That does not take one ounce of love and grace.)

    b. Pray along the lines of the Golden Rule: that God will bless them as you would want to be blessed if you should (for whatever reason) hurt another.

E. Remember that there are, almost certainly, those *you* have hurt who are having to cope with you! 'Do not judge, or you too will be judged. For in the same way as you judge others, you will be judged, and with the measure you use, it will be measured to you' (Matt. 7:1-2).

  1. *In many (if not all) cases, those you have to forgive feel innocent.*

    a. Don't go to them and say, 'I forgive you for what you did.'

      (1) They will say, 'What have I done?'

      (2) You might also be doing it just to point the finger a bit!

      (3) The situation will worsen and possibly get out of hand.

    b. The forgiveness must be in the *heart*.

      (1) Refuse to tell others what they did.

      (2) Make them feel at ease when you see them.

      (3) Pray for them.

  2. *Are you not aware there are those who could say to you, 'I have forgiven you,' and your reaction would be, 'Whatever for?'*

    a. And yet the other person feels it deeply.

b. It is best that this matter is not brought out in the open *unless you know it really will help.*

(1) Be very careful here.

(2) You will have a fairly shrewd idea whether it will do good to say, 'I forgive you.'

(3) Apply the Golden Rule: 'Do to others as you would have them do to you' (Luke 6:31).

CONCLUSION

The way to cope with grudges is to deal with them by forgiving totally and refusing to be bitter. Remember the promises of Luke 6:38: blessing will be poured out in proportion to your (1) withholding judging, (2) withholding condemnation, (3) forgiving, and (4) giving. That is a fairly good benefit! Most of all, think of the blessing of the Holy Spirit when he resides in you ungrieved!

29

HOW TO COPE WITH GUILT

INTRODUCTION

A. This subject is perhaps one of the 'unmentionable' subjects – both in theology and in Christian living.

    1. *At the theological level, many are opposed to the very notion of guilt.*

        a. It conjures up the idea of an angry God who wants people to be fearful and guilty.

        b. It also brings up the notion that Christ bore our guilt on the cross, something many theologians dismiss out of hand.

    2. *At the practical level, most of us are hesitant to admit to any problem of guilt.*

        a. For those who are not Christians, guilt is often as alien as the very idea of sin.

            (1) This is despite the fact that many psychiatrists and psychologists say that guilt is usually the chief problem with their patients and clients.

            (2) Humanistic psychologist Frederick Perls said he could cure all psychopathology in one hour if he could get his clients not to feel guilty.

        b. For those who are Christians, guilt is unmentionable since we are taught that we should not feel guilty since Christ has taken away our sins.

            (1) Hence we feel guilty about feeling guilty, though we hate to admit it.

            (2) The truth is, most Christians (I suggest) feel guilt, consciously or not, most of the time.

B. Guilt (def.): the feeling that we are to be blamed; a sense of shame.

    1. *Generally speaking, there are two aspects of guilt:*

        a. Objective guilt, when one has committed an offence.

      (1) The person in this case may or may not have a 'feeling' of guilt.

      (2) Guilt in this case refers to the fact that we have broken some established law or principle.

   b. Subjective guilt, when we have a feeling of guilt, or shame.

      (1) In this case we may not have committed an offence; but we feel a sense of shame as though we were truly guilty.

      (2) Guilt in this case refers to *feeling*.

2. *There are three Greek words that bear the meaning of our term and may be translated 'guilt'.*

   a. *Hydodikos,* used only once in the New Testament; Romans 3:19: '..the whole world held accountable (AV: guilty) to God.'

      (1) It means culpable, the idea that one must be brought to trial; that one can in no way escape condemnation.

      (2) It describes the state of an accused person who cannot reply at the trial initiated against him because he has exhausted all possibilities of refuting the charge against him and averting the condemnation and its consequences which inescapably follow.

   b. *Enochos,* used ten times in the New Testament; e.g., Matthew 5:21-22, when it is translated 'subject' ('danger' AV); Matthew 26:66, where it is translated 'worthy'; Mark 3:29, where it is translated 'guilty'; James 2:10 where it is translated 'guilty'.

      (1) It means 'to be subject', i.e., legally subject; guilty.

      (2) It can also mean 'deserved punishment'.

   c. *Opheilema,* used twice (although the verb form is used thirty-six times), translated 'debts', e.g., Matthew 6:12. Similar to this is *opheila*, used twice, translated 'debt', e.g. Matthew 18:32.

      (1) These words denote the sense of what is owed; one is 'obligated' to obey the whole law (Gal. 5:3).

      (2) The meaning is, the guilty person is a 'debtor'.

3. *There is another word, translated as 'shame; or 'disgrace', that may be partly related to this study.*

   a. But this word may have no bearing whatever on guilt.

      (1) 'The apostles left the Sanhedrin, rejoicing because they had been counted worthy of suffering disgrace for the Name' (Acts 5:41).

(2) 'Let us fix our eyes on Jesus, the author and perfecter of our faith, who for the joy set before him endured the cross, scorning its shame, and sat down at the right hand of the throne of God' (Heb. 12:2).

b. The sense of shame may be what others ascribe to us; in their minds we are guilty, but we feel no sense of shame since we have violated no valid principle. It's their problem, not ours.

    (1) The disgrace or shame that the disciples experienced was in fact a feeling of enormous joy; they felt no guilt whatever.

    (2) Jesus hated the shame but felt no guilt.

c. And yet a sense of shame should come as a result of true guilt, e.g. Philippians 3:19; Revelation 3:18; Luke 14:9.

C. Why deal with this subject? Why is it important?

1. As a theological issue we need to be reminded of the ABC of the Gospel.

2. We need to see the distinction between true guilt and pseudo (false) guilt.

3. Many of us feel guilty but shouldn't; what can we do about it?

4. Often we will say: 'I know God forgives me, but I can't forgive myself'.

5. If we could be truly set free from any sense of guilt it would revolutionise our outlook and attitude.

I. TRUE GUILT

A. True guilt is valid – because it is against God.

1. *Any sin against God is true guilt.*

    a. It does not follow that we 'feel' guilty.

        (1) All have sinned and fall short of the glory of God (Rom. 3:23).

        (2) God has declared the whole world 'guilty' (Rom. 3:19 AV).

    b. Those who are guilty in God's eyes don't necessarily feel guilty.

        (1) We can tell people, 'You have sinned against God' and they may reply, 'So?'

      (2) We can be objectively guilty (that is, there is true guilt – because it is against God) and feel no subjective guilt (that is, feel nothing in our conscience).

2. *One of the Old Testament offerings was the 'guilt offering'* (Lev. 5:14-6:7).

  a. A guilt offering had to be offered whether or not the person felt what he had done was wrong.

    (1) 'If a person sins and does what is forbidden in any of the LORD's commands, even though he does not know it, he is guilty and will be held responsible. He is to bring to the priest as a guilt offering a ram from the flock, one without defect and of the proper value. In this way the priest will make atonement for him for the wrong he has committed unintentionally, and he will be forgiven. It is a guilt offering; he has been guilty of wrong-doing against the LORD' (Lev. 5:17-19).

    (2) It is a case of God imputing (charging) the person with guilt.

  b. The modern equivalent of this is 'paying our due to society'.

    (1) Sometimes a person will plead 'not guilty' because he is unconvinced he has done wrong.

    (2) But the law of the land must be upheld.

3. *True guilt is what God imputes (charges) to us. See Romans 4:8: 'Blessed is the man whose sin the Lord will never count against him.'*

  a. God may say we are guilty, but we feel 'no guilt'.

  b. The guilt is there but we may feel absolutely nothing, just like a hardened criminal who has no remorse for what he has done.

4. *Only the Holy Spirit can make a person see that there is real guilt.*

  a. Until then he is 'dead' (Eph. 2:1).

    (1) This means he is unashamed; he feels nothing.

    (2) There is no use trying to convince him if the Holy Spirit does not come alongside to show him.

  b. But once the Holy Spirit has arrested him he becomes sorry.

    (1) It is like the Prodigal Son (Luke 15:17-18).

    (2) In this case what one feels is valid, true guilt.

5. *In a word: true guilt is when there is sin against God.*

    a. This is when his law has been violated (1 John 3:4).

    b. We should 'feel guilty' when there has been a transgression (sin) against the moral law (which is the Ten Commandments).

B. Christ fulfilled the Law for us (Matt. 5:17).

    1. *His death on the cross was for our sins* (1 Cor. 15:3; 1 Pet. 2:24).

        a. His offering on the cross was the ultimate fulfilment of all the sacrificial offerings of the Old Testament, including the guilt offering (Heb. 10:1-10).

        b. Objectively, Christ bore the guilt of our sins.

            (1) Without the Holy Spirit's enlightening this will mean no more to us than the fact that we are sinners will convict us.

            (2) But by the Holy Spirit not only showing us our sins and leading us to Christ's righteousness we know we have a Perfect Saviour (John 16:8-10).

        c. We are 'in Christ Jesus, who has become for us wisdom from God – that is, our righteousness, holiness and redemption' (1 Cor. 1:30).

    2. *In Christ, God says we are 'not guilty'.*

        a. The Holy Spirit pronounces us 'guilty', then 'not guilty' in two stages:

            (1) He convicts us of our sins; the result: we are sorry and we confess them (1 John 1:9).

            (2) He points us to the Lamb of God who takes away our sins (John 1:29).

        b. It is by faith that we believe the promise: that God will forgive us for our sins (Heb. 8:12).

            (1) Christ takes away all past sin (Rom. 3:25).

            (2) The blood cleanses all present sin as we walk in the light (1 John 1:7).

    3. *There is no basis of true guilt left when the blood of Christ cleanses from all sin.*

        a. If there is a 'feeling' of guilt it is because we have not held on to the promise of forgiveness.

        b. What follows, then, is not true guilt but pseudo (false) guilt.

II. PSEUDO GUILT

A. Pseudo (false) guilt (def.): a feeling of shame for which there is no valid basis, either because (i) the blood of Christ has cleansed the sin, or (ii) because it is not a case of sin.

   1. *It is entirely subjective, i.e., it is an emotional feeling that has no objective basis in reality.*

      a. We may imagine it, truly believe it.

      b. But there is no good reason for it.

   2. *The guilt feels very real.*

      a. It is like a psychosomatic (mind over body) illness; the illness is very real, although it is mainly caused by what we think (e.g., a headache may be brought on by worry or pressure).

      b. Pseudo guilt is a very real feeling; it is horrible and can be more tantalising than if caused by true guilt.

   3. *It is false guilt because God did not put it there.*

      a. Therefore it is to be seen for what it is – and rejected.

      b. What God is not in, we must reject.

         (1) Our giving in to pseudo guilt does not honour God.

         (2) God never, never, never wants us to feel any shame from pseudo guilt.

B. What are the origins of pseudo guilt?

   1. *The flesh: the weakness that flows from human nature* (Heb. 4:15; 2 Cor. 12:9-10).

      a. Blaming ourselves when God doesn't.

         (1) This assumes we have applied 1 John 1:9: 'If we confess our sins, he is faithful and just and will forgive us our sins and purify us from all unrighteousness.'

         (2) If we have repented, God isn't blaming us.

      b. Not forgiving ourselves when God has.

         (1) This is a spiritual problem, because it is competing with God; he forgives us but we don't forgive ourselves. We must beware of a subtle form of self-righteousness creeping in.

         (2) And yet this is pseudo guilt; when God isn't blaming us but we blame ourselves, we are heaping pain on our own consciences that God hasn't put there.

      c. Psychological weaknesses. Note: we all have emotional or psychological weaknesses that have their origin in the past;

they will compete with what God has done for us and lead us to false shame. For example:

(1) Perfectionism: imposing an unrealistic standard on ourselves – which God hasn't put there.

    (a) None of us is perfect (Ps. 130:3).

    (b) God's commands are not burdensome (1 John 5:3).

(2) Inferiority complex: a feeling of worthlessness.

    (a) This is a very, very common feeling (Ex. 4:10).

    (b) This feeling often works against a feeling that we are okay – which we are (1 Cor. 5:7).

(3) Sexual fears: any hang-up regarding sexuality which almost certainly stems from bad past experiences or some degree of deprivation of genuine love.

    (a) Sexual abuse often leaves the victim feeling guilty as if he or she were to blame!

    (b) Many cannot shake off this feeling, even though they see the unreasonableness of it.

(4) Anxiety or depression: anxiety is the common denominator of all psychopathology.

    (a) Anxiety leads to depression, and other emotional problems.

    (b) This weakness parallels a spiritual desire to please God and often competes with it so that the person never feels spiritual enough; it is not a spiritual problem in such a case.

2. *The devil: our arch-enemy who will ruthlessly seize upon any of the above to keep us feeling guilty.*

  a. He is called the 'accuser' (Rev. 12:10).

    (1) He knows every sin in our past, and will throw them at us at the worst possible time!

    (2) He knows every weakness we have, and will make us feel totally unworthy.

  b. The devil will work through these with relentless vigour:

    (1) Blaming ourselves.

    (2) Not forgiving ourselves – despite 1 John 1:9.

    (3) Emotional weakness.

3. *Failure to see what Christ has done for us, and what the blood of Christ means to God the Father.*

  a. In a sense this is (obviously) a spiritual problem – we could argue that we should feel guilty over not having enough faith.

b. But often a person is weak in faith because of:

    (1) A psychological problem.

    (2) Lack of good teaching.

III. WE ALL HAVE PROBLEMS OF GUILTY FEELINGS

A. None of us is perfect psychologically (Ps. 103:14).

1. We all have got imperfect parents.

2. We all had negative childhood experiences to some degree – it's a wicked world!

B. None of us is perfect spiritually (1 Kings 8:46).

1. Most of us have skeletons in the cupboard – the devil knows them all.

2. *We all have a sense of failure – to some degree.*

    a. Failure to overcome temptation.

    b. Failure after having overcome, then slipping again.

    c. Failure to be the best possible parents.

    d. Failure to heed God's warnings.

    e. Failure to walk in the light.

    f. Failure to spend time properly – whether regarding work, time with family or time with God.

IV. HOW TO COPE WITH GUILT

A. Make a distinction between true guilt and pseudo guilt.

1. True guilt stems from sin which remains unconfessed to God.

2. False guilt stems from blaming ourselves even when we have confessed our sin.

B. Understand what the blood of Christ does for the Father.

1. The Father has never forgotten the pain his Son had to bear.

2. He honours that blood to the hilt! Believe that – and we are free.

C. Refuse to let Satan cast us down when we know we have repented over the past.

1. We know in our heart of hearts whether we have come clean with God.

2. If we have, then we remember this line from John Newton's hymn 'Approach, my soul, the mercy-seat':

Be Thou my shield and hiding-place,
That, sheltered near thy side,
I may my fierce accuser face,
And tell him thou hast died.

CONCLUSION

If we have begun to grasp the principles in this chapter, it may turn out that we will be able to see pseudo guilt for what it is – and not let it bother again. The only guilt that should weigh us down is true guilt – and that can be dealt with at once!

30

HOW TO COPE WITH AMBITION

INTRODUCTION

A. The Glory of God.
 1. The nearest we get to the 'essence' of God.
 2. It is the sum total of all his attributes.

B. But what about *our* glory?
 1. *What about our desire for glory?*
  a. Granted, God desires glory.
  b. So do we; is this desire for glory legitimate or is it a wicked desire?
 2. What is the glory of man?

C. Ambition.
 1. *Ambition (def.): a strong desire to achieve something.*
  a. It is a word that comes from the Latin *ambitio*, 'a going around, especially of candidates for office in Rome, to solicit votes'.
  b. Hence it means the desire for office or honour.

  "Cromwell, I charge thee, fling away ambition;
  By that sin fell the angels."
  Shakespeare

 2. It is a word that can mean the object of desire. E.g.: 'It is my ambition to be Prime Minister'.

D. Relevant Greek words:
 1. Kenodoxos. *Literally, 'empty glory'; it is used in two places:*
  a. Galatians 5:26: 'Let us not become *conceited*, provoking and envying each other.'
  b. Philippians 2:3: 'Do nothing out of selfish ambition or vain *conceit*, but in humility consider others better than yourselves.'

2. Eritheia. *It means baseness; self-interest, ambition, contention, those who think only of immediate gain.*

    a. Paul had rivals who preached Christ 'out of selfish ambition' (Phil. 1:17).

    b. James uses it twice, showing that it is wisdom that has its origins from below not from above (Jas. 3:14,16).

E. Why deal with this subject? Why is it important?

    1. It will help us to come to terms with our personalities and (perhaps) our feelings.

    2. It helps expose (at least for some of us) our hearts (Jer. 17:9).

    3. It brings us face to face with our motivation; why are we *really* motivated to do this or that?

    4. It makes us face the question: Is there such a thing as a pure, unmixed motive?

I. AMBITION: A NATURAL TENDENCY

A. Martin Luther: 'God uses sex to drive a man to marriage, ambition to drive a man to service, fear to drive a man to faith.'

    1. *This assumes that ambition is wholly natural.*

        a. We know that sex is natural; it is a God-given urge – it is biological – the way God made us.

            (1) 'Sex was not born in Hollywood but at the Throne of Grace.' – Clyde Narramore.

            (2) Were it not for the sexual urge people would not want to marry.

        b. Luther's statement however assumes that ambition is as natural as the sexual urge.

            (1) I believe this is true.

            (2) Dale Carnegie said that the two strongest urges in the world are the sex urge and the desire to feel important.

    2. *But either of these urges can become unbalanced, not to mention perverted.*

        a. The Christian faith should teach us that the sexual urge must wait for gratification – until marriage.

            (1) Sex outside marriage is wrong.

            (2) The person who cannot control his or her sexual appetite will eventually be sorry.

    b. Sometimes the sexual urge gets completely out of control, the result being:

      (1) Perversion, the unnatural desire.

      (2) Infidelity in marriage.

    c. So too with ambition: it can lead to a person's downfall.

3. *As for fear, there are two kinds:*

    a. Natural fear, which may not necessarily lead to faith.

    b. Supernatural fear, which is brought on by the power of the Holy Spirit, and which does lead to faith.

> 'Twas grace that taught my heart to fear
> And grace my fears relieved;
> How precious did that grace appear
> The hour I first believed.'
> *John Newton (1725-1807)*

    c. In this case Luther's statement would not refer necessarily to what is natural, because natural fear does not necessarily lead to faith.

B. Given that ambition is a natural tendency, some have a higher level of ambition than others.

  1. *Leaders, for example, are highly motivated people.*

    a. It may be a good question:

      (1) Are leaders leaders because they are already highly motivated?

      (2) Or do they become like that?

    b. However, not all highly motivated people are leaders.

      (1) Some highly motivated people are reclusive and shun the public eye but excel in their chosen career.

      (2) Many writers, scientists and musicians are highly motivated – but have no leadership gifts.

  2. *Ambition has its origin partly in the influences of the past.*

    a. At the natural level:

      (1) Our parental relationships.

      (2) Our peer relationships.

      (3) Authority figures.

      (4) Deprivations, such as poverty, social class.

      (5) Traumas.

b. At the spiritual level:

    (1) God uses some or all of the above.

    (2) God may infuse motivation either at the level of common grace or special grace.

       (a) Common grace: God's goodness to all men (whether or not they are saved).

       (b) Special grace: when a saved person is given something unusual to live for (e.g., a prophetic word, a vision).

3. *There are degrees of ambition; some have a lot, some very little.*

    a. Those who have a lot of ambition tend to see it as a good thing.

       (1) They feel it is quite right to be ambitious.

       (2) They tend to look down on those who are not so ambitious.

    b. Those who are not so ambitious tend to be suspicious of those who are ambitious.

       (1) They are not so sure it is good to be ambitious.

       (2) They tend to look down on those who are like that.

    c. Most of us like ourselves the way we are!

C. The truth is, generally speaking, ambitious people are the achievers in this world: the movers and shakers.

    1. *They are the ones who tend to make a difference in others' lives and in history.*

       a. By their inventions (whether the light bulb or small gadgets).

       b. By their research and discoveries (whether science, medicine, etc.).

       c. By their oratory (whether for good or ill).

       d. By their leadership (whether in church or politics).

       e. By their composition (whether literary or music).

    2. *Whether ambition is good or bad is not always the issue; the fact is, ambitious people are almost always the ones who make a difference.*

       a. This is true in society.

       b. This is true in the church.

       c. Don't forget: there is such a thing as being ambitious for the glory of God only!

II. NOW FOR THE BAD NEWS: AMBITION IS LARGELY MOTIVATED BECAUSE IT MAKES OTHERS JEALOUS.

'And I saw that all labour and all achievement spring from man's envy of his neighbour. This too is meaningless, a chasing after the wind' (Eccl. 4:4).

A. There are three kinds of ambition:
  1. *Authentic ambition: what all should wish for.*
    a. It is natural, part of being human.
    b. We should not be ashamed of it.
      (1) We grow up wanting to please our parents.
      (2) Along the way we develop rival relationships with peers and the best of friends.
    c. After conversion we develop an ambition to glorify God. For example, here is the children's equivalent:
  2. *Ambiguous ambition: Some want to be great but in the name of God!*
    a. They are anxious for their career and future.
    b. God's name is eventually brought in, as if to justify the desire for greatness (cf. Jas. 1:8).
    c. Those who go into the ministry but for whom preaching the gospel is not the main thing after a while.
    d. But they continue to tell themselves and the world 'It's all for God'. Really?
  3. *Arrogant ambition: shameful bending of the rules to achieve a goal.*
    a. Sometimes this is by sheer fraud.
    b. Sometimes it is done by name-dropping, or being seen with the right people.
    c. At bottom, people like this want to make others stand in awe of them.

B. But, according to Ecclesiastes 4:4, this is the only kind of motivation that gets things done!
  1. *In other words, if we knew that nobody would ever discover it, would we:*
    a. Want to be photographed with a famous person?
    b. Accept a knighthood or an honour from the Queen?

2. *To put it another way:*

    a. Could we turn down tea with the Queen and keep quiet about it?

    b. Could we turn down any honour and keep quiet about it?

3. *And if you have been saying, 'This sort of thing never matters to me anyway', why must you take the time to think or say* that?

    a. Is it important to you to let others know that you are not bothered by that sort of thing?

    b. If you think it is an accomplishment of some sort that you have no desire to be honoured, why do you let anybody know that, unless this too is so that you are admired?

4. *The truth is, very little in this world is accomplished if there isn't some sort of recognition:*

    a. This is just as true (sadly) for most things that happen at church.

    b. Without recognition (or someone saying, 'Thank you') we aren't going to be highly motivated.

C. Nothing we do that appears to be for God is with totally pure and unmixed motives. For example:

    1. Being one of the twelve disciples.

    2. Accepting the call to the ministry.

    3. Being a pilot light.

    4. Being an intercessor in prayer (and nobody, absolutely nobody, ever knowing that you pray for them).

III. BUT ARE WE TO BELIEVE THAT ECCLESIASTES 4:4 IS THE ULTIMATE MOTIVATION FOR THE CHRISTIAN IN THIS LIFE? NO.

A. Recalling Luther's statement we know:

    1. *The fear that leads to faith does not remain the same.*

        a. As John Wesley put it, the faith of a slave becomes the faith of a son.

        b. The fear that gives rise to faith becomes that by which we say 'Abba Father'.

    2. *The sexual love that makes people want to get married is not the love that will sustain that marriage.*

        a. *Eros* love must become *agape* love – a love that casts out fear and keeps no record of wrongs.

    b. *Eros* love was used of God but, sooner or later, there must be a parallel *unselfish* love – or that marriage will fall apart.

B. Are we to believe, then, that the ambition which God uses to drive us to service must also be changed? Yes.

  1. This is what Peter learned (John 21:18-19).

  2. This is what James and John learned (Matt. 20:20-28).

  3. *Sooner or later, if we continue to make spiritual progress, we must, as it were, attend our own funeral.*

    a. We all must *die*:

      (1) To the things that had been so important to us.

      (2) To the things that motivated us.

      (3) To the desire for success and honour.

    b. This comes as we walk in the light and are 'transformed into his likeness with ever-increasing glory' (2 Cor. 3:18; cf. 1 John 1:7).

      (1) Every process of change is painful.

      (2) Every elevation to a higher level of glory almost always brings its own experience of suffering.

      (3) But the fresh increment of grace is worth it!

C. What is the new motivation that transcends the old ambition to service? Answer: a love for God's glory.

'How can you believe if you accept praise from one another, yet make no effort to obtain the praise that comes from the only God?' (John 5:44).

  1. *Recall: a love for the glory of God is what Satan cannot successfully counterfeit.*

    a. If we have a love for the glory of God, this, we may be sure, is a religious affection that only God put there.

    b. It is perhaps the highest spiritual plateau there is.

  2. *What, then, is a love for the glory of God?*

    a. A contentment that he alone knows about so that you get your joy:

      (1) Not from telling others (which is the honour that comes from 'one another').

      (2) But just knowing that *he* knows (the honour from God only)!

b. Abandonment of any success that God has not ordained.

    (1) This means forfeiting our own plans.

    (2) It is waiting on his manner of doing things plus his timing.

c. Getting our joy by doing things for those who cannot pay us back. (Luke 14:12-14).

    (1) The honour of man is: 'What will this person do for me?'

    (2) The honour of God is: 'Who can I help who cannot possibly return the favour?'

d. Refusal to vindicate ourselves.

    (1) If I try to 'clear my name' I get honour from you.

    (2) If I refuse to clear my name I get honour from God.

e. It is the refusal to point the finger.

    (1) Pointing the finger is keeping a record of wrongs, that I might be exalted over you.

    (2) The honour of God is that I will be self-effacing and let him do the judging (1 Cor. 4:5).

f. It is, when it comes to honour, preferring one another (Rom. 12:10; Phil. 2:1-5).

CONCLUSION

Many Christians (sadly) will never know what it would have been like had they postponed the honour that comes from one another and waited for the honour that comes only from God. The exaltation God has in mind for us is worth waiting for (1 Pet. 5:6). The root of our problem is often unsanctified ambition. Who knows what God will do with us if love for his glory be our chief motivation?

31

HOW TO OVERCOME FEAR

INTRODUCTION

A. Our subject is of a practical nature.
    1. In some ways I am loathe to present 'how to' talks.
    2. *It may imply that I myself have 'arrived'.*
        a. I am on a pilgrimage; I am not 'there' yet, and God isn't finished with me yet!
        b. The last thing I should want to convey is the impression that I am the perfect example of my subject!

B. Our subject is connected to the Fear of God.
    1. *I certainly don't mean overcoming the Fear of God!*
        a. The more we fear God and experience what is truly the fear of God the more we will overcome fear.
        b. We are therefore talking about a different kind of fear.

C. Fear (def.): an attitude of being continually anxious.
    1. *By fear we really mean what the apostle Paul meant by a 'spirit of fear'.*
        a. 'For God did not give us a spirit of timidity, but a spirit of power, of love and of self-discipline' (2 Tim. 1:7).
        b. Gr. *phobos*, fear or timidity, from which we get the word 'phobia'.
            (1) Phobia (def.): a lasting abnormal fear.
            (2) There are neurotic states of mind, as claustrophobia (abnormal fear of being in a closed space); hydrophobia (abnormal fear of water), and many others.
        c. This study does not intend to deal with neuroses, although they are not entirely disconnected from our subject.
            (1) Neurosis (def.): a mental disorder producing depression or abnormal behaviour, sometimes with physical symptoms but with no evidence of disease.

(2) All of us have experienced neurotic tendencies to some degree at one time or other.
- **d.** At the psychological level, anxiety is the common denominator of all psychopathology.
  - (1) Anxiety (def.): the state of being troubled or worried.
  - (2) Psychopathology (def.): mental illness.
- **e.** This study does not intend to cure mental illness.
  - (1) It *could* turn out to be the best *preventive* to mental illness!
  - (2) To the extent we apply the spiritual principles suggested below, we *may* find great relief from mental disturbances.

2. *A spirit of fear is mainly an attitude, but sometimes a* spirit.
- **a.** By 'attitude' we mean:
  - (1) Governed by anxiety (Judg. 6:15).
  - (2) Being controlled by timidity (easily alarmed, or shy).
- **b.** By 'spirit' we mean the devil (2 Tim. 2:26. cf. 1 Sam. 16:14).
  - (1) This may be demonic oppression (the devil weighing us down from *without*).
  - (2) It could be demon possession (the devil controlling from *within*).
- **c.** In either case we are confident that a spirit of fear or timidity is not the heritage of the Christian.
  - (1) God gives love, power and clear thinking.
  - (2) Any other motivation comes either from the flesh (what we are like without the Holy Spirit) or the devil.
  - (3) As Dr Lloyd-Jones put it, 'God never oppresses us'.

3. *We are not talking merely about natural fear.*
- **a.** Natural fear (def.): a God-given instinct that protects us from danger. For example:
  - (1) Walking too close to the edge of a cliff.
  - (2) Walking into a busy street without looking both ways.
- **b.** Natural fear, as with a small measure of anxiety, will keep us from trouble.
- **c.** And yet the devil can play into our natural fears. '"If you are the Son of God," he said, "throw yourself down. For it is written: 'He will command his angels concerning you, and they will lift you up in their hands, so that you will not strike your foot against a stone'"" (Matt. 4:6).

D. The purpose of this study is to set us free from counter-productive anxiety.

   1. *There is a 'creative anxiety'; God has used this endlessly in the lives of people* (Heb. 11:7).

      a. To get things done; to meet deadlines.

      b. To invent things for the good of society.

   2. *Counter-productive anxiety: fear that brings the opposite effect to what we desire.*

      a. It keeps us from getting things done.

      b. It works against the possibilities that faith can achieve.

   3. God wants to set us free from counter-productive fear.

E. Why is this study important?

   1. Many Christians are governed by a spirit of fear. This is not the best way to live. It keeps us from living productive lives.

   2. Fear is the opposite of faith and love and we are called to exemplify the latter.

   3. Being cowardly is put alongside sins that are heinous in the sight of God (Rev. 21:8).

   4. Being set free from fear will lead us to see the hidden potential within us with the Holy Spirit's power.

   5. Fear is the devil's best weapon against us; overcoming fear puts us in the best position to resist the devil.

I. FEARS THAT SHOULD BE OVERCOME

A. Note: we pass over neurological fears.

   1. *Not that this is totally irrelevant for such a discussion.*

      a. We all have certain neurotic fears that stem from past experiences.

      b. God can and has helped many people in this area:

         (1) Through counselling.

         (2) Through self-understanding.

         (3) Through the Holy Spirit.

   2. *I do not feel this book is the place to tackle this subject.*

      a. Admittedly, some fears overlap with those that were born or nurtured from past traumas.

      b. But as we truly come to terms with what follows it may be surprising how far we can come in overcoming many such fears.

B. The chief fear: the fear of man (Ps. 27:1).

  1. *Self-consciousness* (John 5:44).

    a. This comes from the fear of 'what they will think'.

    b. Peter and Barnabas gave in to this fear (Gal. 2:12-13).

    c. This is what keeps many from witnessing to people.

      (1) To the general public.

      (2) To their friends.

    d. This is what keeps many from taking a stand for what they know is right.

      (1) If many join them, they are all right about this.

      (2) But if they must stand alone – never.

    e. This keeps many from worshipping in freedom.

      (1) They are at home as long as they are in a company of those who enjoy liberty in worship.

      (2) But they 'freeze' elsewhere.

  2. *Being ashamed* (Mark 8:38).

    a. This comes from fear of the 'offence'.

    b. This is what governed Peter when he denied knowing Jesus (Matt. 26:69-75).

      (1) As long as Jesus was performing miracles and walking on water, Peter was all right.

      (2) But when Jesus was arrested and things did not go 'according to plan', Peter caved in.

    c. This fear obviously overlaps with the fear of self-consciousness.

  3. *Persecution* (Matt. 13:21).

    a. Persecution may be of two kinds:

      (1) Verbal – what people say to us or about us.

      (2) Non-verbal – what people do to us or behind our backs.

    b. Persecution is the inevitable lot of the godly (2 Tim. 3:12).

      (1) It may come from non-Christians, who make us suffer – whether at work or within the family.

      (2) It may come from fellow Christians (very common).

C. Unbelief (Mark 6:6).

  1. *Fear that God will not keep his word* (Ps. 12:6).

    a. Financial problems (Phil. 4:19).

    b. Leave us unvindicated (Rom. 12:19).

    c. Blessing on evangelistic efforts (Acts 18:10).

      d. Prophetic utterances (1 Thess. 5:20).

      e. Using our gift (1 Cor. 12:11).

      f. Fear of growing old.

  2. *Fear of the future* (Matt. 6:34).

      a. That we will be deserted (Heb. 13:5).

      b. That we will miss God's will (Phil. 1:6).

      c. That our past sins will be found out (Ps. 103:10).

      d. That we will fall into sin (1 Cor. 10:12).

      e. That we will lose our good health (3 John 2).

II. Overcoming fear

A. Fearlessness: being at ease; like being 'at home'.

  1. *Paul prayed for fearlessness in preaching. 'Pray also for me, that whenever I open my mouth, words may be given me so that I will fearlessly make known the mystery of the gospel, for which I am an ambassador in chains. Pray that I may declare it fearlessly, as I should'* (Eph. 6:19-20).

      a. This was not merely praying for courage.

        (1) Courage and real fearlessness are not the same thing.

        (2) Courage is needed when we are afraid – but we still press on.

      b. Fearlessness is when there is no fear.

        (1) Peter had this on the day of Pentecost (Acts 2).

        (2) Stephen had this before the Sanhedrin (Acts 6-7).

  2. *Fearlessness is a special anointing whereby the presence of God enters our being.*

      a. In this case we are as relaxed before a thousand hostile people as if we were relaxed at home.

      b. It is that which Paul wanted chiefly.

  3. *This is an anointing that is given for special times.*

      a. Obviously Paul didn't have it at all times.

      b. But when he had it he was calmly confident (Acts 27:24-25).

      c. It is a sovereign anointing.

        (1) It may be 'emergency grace'.

        (2) Sometimes it comes without any advanced notice.

      d. If God gave it to us at all times we would not need this lesson!

B. Apart from the special anointing of God's presence, is there that which we can do to reach a state of fearlessness? Yes.

1. *Perfect love. 'There is no fear in love. But perfect love drives out fear, because fear has to do with punishment'* (1 John 4:18).

   a. This is an attainable state, otherwise John would not mock us by putting before us an unachievable goal.

   b. However, how long we hold on to this lofty height is determined by our love.

     (1) Many have experienced it for moments, then they lose it.

     (2) Why? They discontinue walking in love.

2. *How do we know we are not walking in perfect love? Answer: when we punish.*

   a. 'Fear has to do with punishment'. When we punish it is because we are afraid:

     (1) That God won't take over soon enough.

     (2) That someone who has hurt us isn't going to get what is coming to him.

   b. How do we punish?

     (1) By threatening, 'emotional blackmail'; making someone feel guilty.

     (2) By judging – calling attention to another's wrongs; by keeping a record of wrongs (1 Cor. 13:5).

     (3) By telling another what we know about the one who hurt us.

     (4) By discrediting another person.

     (5) By vindicating ourselves instead of letting God do it.

   c. When we utterly refuse to punish we are approaching the fearlessness John promises.

     (1) Peter exhorted the same thing. 'Who is going to harm you if you are eager to do good?' (1 Pet. 3:13).

     (2) What, then, is doing good? 'Finally, all of you, live in harmony with one another; be sympathetic, love as brothers, be compassionate and humble. Do not repay evil with evil or insult with insult, but with blessing, because to this you were called so that you may inherit a blessing. For, "Whoever would love life and see good days must keep his tongue from evil and his lips from deceitful speech. He must turn from evil and do good;

he must seek peace and pursue it. For the eyes of the Lord are on the righteous and his ears are attentive to their prayer, but the face of the Lord is against those who do evil"' (1 Pet. 3:8-12).

3. *Our model is Jesus. 'To this you were called, because Christ suffered for you, leaving you an example, that you should follow in his steps'* (1 Pet. 2:21).

a. Jesus was the perfect fearless man.

b. We begin to experience his fearlessness when we behave as he did. 'When they hurled their insults at him, he did not retaliate; when he suffered, he made no threats. Instead, he entrusted himself to him who judges justly' (1 Pet. 2:23).

c. A state of fearlessness becomes a conscious feeling of sheer joy.

(1) There is inner peace and calm.

(2) The fear of man subsides.

(3) God's ungrieved Spirit begins to govern (Eph. 4:30).

(4) The special anointing (as above) comes on us.

4. *There is an intimate connection between praying in faith and totally forgiving those who have hurt us.*

a. Jesus said, 'I tell you the truth, if anyone says to this mountain, "Go, throw yourself into the sea," and does not doubt in his heart but believes that what he says will happen, it will be done for him' (Mark 11:23).

b. We are to believe that we have received what we ask for (Mark 11:24).

c. But most people forget an attached condition: 'And when you stand praying, if you hold anything against anyone, forgive him, so that your Father in heaven may forgive you your sins' (Mark 11:25).

(1) Faith is the opposite of fear just as love is.

(2) In both cases it comes to the same thing: total forgiveness – refusing to punish the one who has hurt us.

5. It is surprising (perhaps it shoudn't be) how our fears – virtually all of them – dissolve into nothing when we have hearts utterly devoid of bitterness.

C. None of us is perfect; and perfect, permanent fearlessness is what we will have when we are glorified (1 John 3:3).

1. But what is sadly underestimated is how much we can overcome fear – daily – by applying these principles.

2. *God does not want us to be afraid.*

    a. 'Fear not' or its equivalent is found 366 times in the Bible.

    b. (One for every day of the year and one for a leap year, according to Josif Tson.)

3. The above principles are beyond doubt the best 'preventive medicine' against psychopathology.

4. *These principles of total forgiveness are the best remedy against the fears listed above; perfect love casts out fear:*

    a. That God will not keep his word.

    b. Of the future.

5. *Most people I know have a problem with bitterness – which* always *grieves the Spirit and therefore militates against simple trust in God* (Eph. 4:30ff).

    a. The way forward is perfect love.

    b. The way forward is refusing to punish.

    c. How do we know if we have totally forgiven either our enemies or those who have hurt us? (See Genesis 45.)

        (1) Refuse to tell what you know about them.

        (2) Don't let them be afraid of you.

        (3) Don't let them be angry with themselves.

        (4) Let them save face.

        (5) Protect them from their greatest fear.

        (6) Keep on forgiving after we've done it once; make it a total lifestyle (Gen. 50:21).

CONCLUSION

The more unbelief, the more fear; the more faith, the less fear. Perfect love drives out fear. When the fear of man is gone, many of the other fears go away as well. The more we fear God, the less we fear humans (John 5:44). The fear of God is evident by our walking in the light (1 John 1:7). This engenders an ever-increasing faith in his Word and his promises, and leads to the experience of his presence.

32

HOW TO COPE WITH DELAY

INTRODUCTION

A. Langston Hughes, the black American poet whose time came after he died, wrote:

> What happens to a dream deferred?
> Does it dry up
> Like a raisin in the sun?
> Or fester like a sore -
> And then run?
> Does it stink like rotten meat?
> Or crust and sugar over -
> Like a syrupy sweet?
> Maybe it just sags
> Like a heavy load?
> Or does it explode?

B. A dream deferred – having to cope with delay.
    1. To cope (def.): to manage successfully; to cope with (def.): to deal successfully with.
    2. *'You have need of patience'* (Heb. 10:36 AV).
        a. Do we? The Hebrew Christians did.
        b. Do we know what it means to cope with delay?

C. The need of patience
    1. *But what if we ourselves are at the other end of that wait?*
        a. What are we to do when nothing is happening?
        b. What are we to do 'between the times' when there is a delay:
            (1) In the answering of prayer?
            (2) In the fulfilment of the prophetic word?
    2. *Patience (def.): the ability to wait before speaking or acting.*
        a. In our case it means the ability to wait without complaining
          – without trying to make things happen.

D. Why is this lesson important?

1. We have all experienced the pain of delay or disappointment; is there a way to cope with delay that is productive?

2. *Most of the Christian life is 'between the times'.*

    a. It is what follows a 'high water mark' – that is, a happy experience.

    b. It is the time during which we are waiting for something to happen.

    c. We need to learn the most productive way to live in the uninteresting times of life.

3. *One of the fruits of the Spirit is patience* (Gal. 5:22).

    a. It surely follows that we should seek such a fruit.

    b. Does this fruit flow automatically, just because we are Christians?

4. Since patience is one of God's attributes (characteristics) it follows that patience is an evidence of godliness.

    a. If we seek to be godly we should seek to be patient.

    b. Patience exhibited is a sign of being godly.

5. We should learn what we can do during the time God delays his answer to our prayer.

I. OLD TESTAMENT EXAMPLES OF BEING FORCED TO WAIT

A. Abraham.

1. *At the age of 75, with no heir and an ageing wife, God told Abraham that his seed would be as numerous as the stars in the heavens* (Gen. 15:5).

    a. Abraham believed that word; such faith was 'credited to him as righteousness' (Gen. 15:6).

    b. That became Paul's chief illustration for his doctrine of justification by faith alone (Rom. 4).

2. *With nothing happening and no hope (humanly speaking), Abraham agreed to Sarah's suggestion that he lie with her maidservant Hagar* (Gen. 16:1-4).

    a. He did; Ishmael was born (Gen. 16:15).

    b. For thirteen years Abraham assumed that Ishmael was the fulfilment of God's promise.

3. *God then said that Sarah would conceive* (Gen. 17:16).

    a. She did; Isaac was born (Gen. 21:1-5).

      b. Isaac was in fact the promised son and the covenant was carried on through Isaac's seed (Gen. 17:4).

   4. *God wanted to fulfil his own word in a manner that defied a natural explanation.*

      a. Ishmael's birth was a result of Abraham's impatience.

      b. Isaac's birth was the result of what God did.

         (1) The lesson: God will honour what he promised.

         (2) When we try to nudge the arm of Providence we will find grief (cf. Gen. 16:5ff; 21:8-14).

B. Joseph

   1. *Joseph was given prophetic dreams that indicated that his eleven brothers would bow down to him.* (Gen. 37:5-9).

      a. Joseph foolishly shared these dreams with his brothers.

      b. There was nothing wrong with Joseph's gift; but there was a lot wrong with Joseph.

   2. *Joseph waited 22 years for the fulfilment of his dreams.*

      a. In the meantime he learned to forgive.

      b. Lesson: 'The worst thing that can happen to a man is to succeed before he is ready.' Dr Lloyd-Jones.

C. Moses

   1. Moses thought he would endear himself to his fellow Israelites by killing an Egyptian. (Ex. 2:11-14).

   2. God put Moses on the far side of the desert for 40 years.

      a. Lesson: when we have to prove ourselves we aren't ready for usefulness.

      b. The greatest freedom is having nothing to prove.

D. Job

   1. *As far as we know, Job had been given no promise that his trial would ever end.*

      a. He did not know what was happening in the heavenlies. (Job 1:6-12; 2:1-7).

      b. He lost everything and was in great physical pain.

   2. *Job's 'friends' accused him of covering up sin.*

      a. They presented general principles that were widely accepted at the time.

      b. In the meantime Job became as self-righteous as his accusers!

   3. *Job's trial ended and his 'patience' became legendary.* 'As you know, we consider blessed those who have persevered. You have heard of Job's perseverance and have seen what the Lord finally brought about. The Lord is full of compassion and mercy' (Jas. 5:11).

a. Job's lessons:

(1) Though 'blameless and upright' he had to come to terms with the sinfulness of his self-righteousness. 'I am unworthy – how can I reply to you? I put my hand over my mouth' (Job 40:4. cf. Job 42:6).

(2) 'I know that you can do all things; no plan of yours can be thwarted' (Job 42:2).

b. Sometimes God's delays are designed to show us what we are really like – which is never pleasant!

E. Habakkuk

1. *The prophet Habakkuk began by crying out, 'How long, O LORD, must I call for help, but you do not listen? Or cry out to you, "Violence!" but you do not save?'* (Hab. 1:2).

a. He could not understand why God tolerated evil and injustice. 'Why do you make me look at injustice? Why do you tolerate wrong? Destruction and violence are before me; there is strife, and conflict abounds' (Hab. 1:3).

b. He was given a promise – and with it a warning that its fulfilment was a long way off:

(1) 'For the revelation awaits an appointed time; it speaks of the end and will not prove false. Though it linger, wait for it; it will certainly come and will not delay' (Hab. 2:3).

(2) He gained a great insight: to live by God's faithfulness (Hab. 2:4), a word that was quoted three times in the New Testament (Rom. 1:17; Gal. 3:11; Heb. 10:38).

2. *The end of the prophecy shows that the delay continued.*

a. But Habakkuk came to terms with it: 'Though the fig-tree does not bud and there are no grapes on the vines, though the olive crop fails and the fields produce no food, though there are no sheep in the pen and no cattle in the stalls, yet I will rejoice in the LORD, I will be joyful in God my Saviour' (Hab. 3:17-18).

b. Lesson: we must learn to trace the rainbow through the rain.

II. NEW TESTAMENT EXAMPLES OF BEING FORCED TO WAIT

A. Simeon (Luke 2:25-32)

1. Almost certainly an old man, he was told by the Holy Spirit that he would not die before he had seen the Lord's Messiah.

2. *When he saw baby Jesus he praised God and said, 'Sovereign Lord, as you have promised, you now dismiss your servant in peace. For my eyes have seen your salvation'* (Luke 2:29-30).

    a. Lesson: sometimes the Lord fulfils his word when we have almost given up hope.

    b. When God makes a promise it is his honour that is at stake, not ours.

B. The disciples' theological prejudice

1. Even after Jesus' death and resurrection the followers of Jesus believed that the purpose of his coming was to restore the ancient glory to Israel. 'So when they met together, they asked him, "Lord, are you at this time going to restore the kingdom to Israel?"' (Acts 1:6).

2. Jesus' reply: 'It is not for you to know the times or dates the Father has set by his own authority. But you will receive power when the Holy Spirit comes on you; and you will be my witnesses in Jerusalem, and in all Judea and Samaria, and to the ends of the earth' (Acts 1:7-8).

    a. This meant an indefinite delay to their hope!

    b. Lesson: sometimes what we wait for isn't on God's agenda after all.

        (1) We must be certain we have truly heard from God.

        (2) His honour is not at stake when it comes to our biases and prejudices!

C. Paul and Silas in jail (Acts 16:16-40)

1. *They had been put in jail because Paul cast a demon out of a slave girl* (Acts 16:18).

    a. The result: those who used her lost income (Acts 16:19).

    b. It caused a riot which made everyone turn on Paul and Silas; any plans they had were delayed – they were imprisoned! (Acts 16:22-24).

2. *Paul and Silas used the time to pray and sing hymns to God!* (Acts 16:25).

    a. At this time an earthquake caused everyone's chains to be broken (Acts 16:26).

    b. Instead of fleeing prison Paul led the jailer to Christ (Acts 16:31-34).

    c. Lesson: 'While we wait, we can worship.' Donald Gray Barnehouse.

        (1) Praise to God is like the mist that ascends and forms clouds that bring showers.

        (2) 'May the peoples praise you, O God; may all the peoples praise you. Then the land will yield its harvest, and God, our God, will bless us' (Ps. 67:5-6).

D. Paul in Athens (Acts 17:16-34)

    1. *Paul was waiting for Silas and Timothy to join him* (Acts 17:16).

      a. He decided to use the time to witness in the synagogue 'as well as in the market place day by day with those who happened to be there' (Acts 17:17).

      b. As a result he was invited to address a group of philosophers at the Areopagus (Acts 17:19-22ff).

        (1) This was a prestigious platform.

        (2) Had Paul tried on his own he would never have been invited!

    2. *There he preached one of the most famous sermons in the New Testament.*

      a. Not all believed, but some did (Acts 17:32-34).

      b. Lesson: While we wait, we can witness!

D. Discouraged Hebrew Christians

    1. *The epistle to the Hebrews was written to discouraged Christians* (Heb. 10:32-39).

      a. They were discouraged because:

        (1) Signs and wonders had apparently discontinued (Heb. 2:4).

        (2) Old friends had fallen away (Heb. 6:4-6; 10:25).

        (3) The temple was still standing, which meant that they remained unvindicated in their stand.

      b. The remnant of Christian Jews who had not abandoned the faith (that is, the Christian faith) were on the edge.

        (1) This is one of the main reasons for the epistle.

        (2) The writer urges them not to give up (Heb. 6:9-20).

1

2. *The delay was two-fold:*
- **a.** God coming to their rescue by a renewal of power was promised but had not come.
- **b.** Vindication by Jesus' prophecy of the temple in Jerusalem being destroyed (Matt. 24:1-2,34; Luke 19:41-44).
  - **(1)** The truth: the temple was destroyed in AD 70, probably only five or six years after this epistle was written.
  - **(2)** Lesson: How sorry these Hebrew Christians would have been after AD 70 had they too given up!

III. HOW TO COPE WITH DELAY

A. Remember that we are in good company.
- **1.** *All those people described in Hebrews 11 had in common the fact of delay of what they hoped for.*
  - **a.** 'These were all commended for their faith, yet none of them received what had been promised' (Heb. 11:39).
  - **b.** 'For I tell you the truth, many prophets and righteous men longed to see what you see but did not see it, and to hear what you hear but did not hear it' (Matt. 13:17).
- **2.** *John encourages us in this same manner.* 'I, John, your brother and companion in the suffering and kingdom and patient endurance that are ours in Jesus, was on the island of Patmos because of the word of God and the testimony of Jesus' (Rev. 1:9).
  - **a.** When we suffer and have to wait on and on, we are getting an invitation to join the Big League.
  - **b.** 'Blessed is the man who perseveres under trial, because when he has stood the test, he will receive the crown of life that God has promised to those who love him' (Jas. 1:12).

B. Do something good while we wait! 'Trust in the LORD and do good.' (Ps. 37:3).
- **1.** *This word came in the context of possible fretting over evil men who were successful* (Ps. 37:1).
  - **a.** When we are having to wait while others seem to be on top, do we wallow in self-pity?
  - **b.** No. Do something good.
    - **(1)** While we wait, we can worship.
    - **(2)** While we wait, we can witness.

2. *Waiting on God doesn't mean doing nothing.*

    a. Idleness is the devil's workshop.

    b. 'Between the times' can be the most productive era of all.

C. Ask God to show us what lesson we are to learn during the time of God's delay.

    1. Joseph had to learn to forgive before God could trust him with success.

    2. Job had to learn about his own sinfulness of which he had not been aware; his situation did not change moreover until he prayed for his friends (Job 42:10).

    3. Habakkuk had to learn to get his joy from within and not to derive it from happy circumstances. Some things just don't change.

    4. The disciples had to learn that what was on God's agenda was far more wonderful than God restoring Israel's earthly glory (Acts 2).

    5. Paul prayed three times for his 'thorn in the flesh' to be removed but God said, 'My grace is sufficient for you, for my power is made perfect in weakness' (2 Cor. 12:7-9).

D. Remember that there is an intelligent, coherent and most wise reason for every delay.

    1. The better we know God, and the longer we wait without complaining, the more we see how right he was to hold up things where we are concerned.

    2. We will learn to thank God for unanswered prayer.

    3. *We will learn to thank God for the closed door.*

        a. All that pertains to us is 'lavished' with 'all wisdom and understanding' (Eph. 1:8).

        b. God has a plan and he therefore 'works out everything in conformity with the purpose of his will' (Eph. 1:11).

E. Consider God's patience with us! 'God is patient with you' (2 Pet. 3:9).

    1. This is why Peter said, 'The Lord is not slow in keeping his promise, as some understand slowness. He is patient with you, not wanting anyone to perish, but everyone to come to repentance' (2 Pet. 3:9).

2. *When we are having to exercise patience try and consider that the real factor is that God is being patient with us!*

   a. We say, 'Why do you take so long?'

   b. He says to us, 'Why do you take so long?'

      (1) He is often sorting us out.

      (2) He may be waiting for us to walk in the light at last.

3. *We may not be as teachable, open or ready as we may suppose.*

   a. Jesus said, '"Can you drink the cup I am going to drink?" "We can," they answered' (Matt. 20:22).

   b. We tend to say 'We can,' having no more objectivity about ourselves than the disciples did.

      (1) When Jesus said, 'I have much more to say to you, more than you can now bear,' (John 16:12), it would not have been surprising had they said, 'We can receive it – tell us now.'

      (2) Why the delay? We are not as teachable as we tend to think!

F. God's delay will last no longer than we can bear.

   1. Every trial has its time limit (James 1:2-4).

   2. God is never too late, never too early; always just on time. 'No temptation has seized you except what is common to man. And God is faithful; he will not let you be tempted beyond what you can bear. But when you are tempted, he will also provide a way out so that you can stand up under it' (1 Cor. 10:13).

CONCLUSION

Exercising patience increases more patience (Luke 21:19; Rom. 5:3). What happened to Habakkuk is what the writer of the Epistle to the Hebrews puts before us: 'We do not want you to become lazy, but to imitate those who through faith and patience inherit what has been promised' (Heb. 6:12). That is what happened to those who entered the Big League.

33

HOW TO SUBMIT

A. **In this chapter we deal with a subject which has both theological and practical implications.**

1. *Theological: what are the biblical principles that lie behind submission?*

   a. To whom do we submit – if to anybody?

   b. If so, does the Bible make things clear?

2. *Practical: how is submission carried out?*

   a. Is submission to God alone? If so, how do we do it?

   b. How else does this subject relate to our lives?

   (1) Church leadership

   (2) Marriage and the family

   (3) To one another

B. **Submission (def.): to yield oneself voluntarily to the authority or control of another; to surrender.**

1. Greek: *hupotasso*: 'to place under, to subordinate, to subject oneself'; used as a verb or noun 40 times in the New Testament.

2. Greek: *hupakoe*: 'to obey'; used as a verb or noun 36 times in the New Testament.

3. *Note: there is a slight difference between 'submission' and 'obedience', although sometimes they are used as if interchangeably.*

   a. In the Old Testament the common Hebrew word for 'obedience' is a root which means 'hear'.

   b. Translators are continually faced with the problem of when to translate *shamar* by 'hear' and when to translate it by 'obey'.

   c. The Greek *hupakoe* reflects the Hebrew understanding.

   (1) When Jesus said, 'He who has ears, let him hear' (e.g. Matt. 13:9), the word 'hear' has the full meaning of *shamar* in the Old Testament.

   (2) He was asking not only for hearing in the physical sense,

but for acceptance of his word as a word from God and obedience to it.

(3) E.g., 'Therefore everyone who hears these words of mine and puts them into practice is like a wise man who built his house on the rock' (Matt. 7:24).

4. Greek: *peitho*, to persuade; *pistis* (faith) comes from this; therefore the idea of trust, or obedience, is sometimes meant and is so translated.

  a. 'You were running a good race. Who cut in on you and kept you from obeying the truth?' (Gal. 5:7).

  b. 'Obey your leaders and submit to their authority. They keep watch over you as men who must give an account. Obey them so that their work will be a joy, not a burden, for that would be of no advantage to you' (Heb. 13:17).

C. Sometimes submission is involuntary; that is, we are in submission to a higher authority whether we like it or not.

1. 'The seventy-two returned with joy and said, "Lord, even the demons submit to us in your name"' (Luke 10:17). 'However, do not rejoice that the spirits submit to you, but rejoice that your names are written in heaven' (Luke 10:20).

2. 'For he "has put everything under his feet". Now when it says that "everything" has been put under him, it is clear that this does not include God himself, who put everything under Christ. When he has done this, then the Son himself will be made subject to him who put everything under him, so that God may be all in all' (1 Cor. 15:27-28).

3. 'And God placed all things under his feet and appointed him to be head over everything for the church' (Eph. 1:22).

4. 'Who, by the power that enables him to bring everything under his control, will transform our lowly bodies so that they will be like his glorious body' (Phil. 3:21).

5. 'It is not to angels that he has subjected the world to come, about which we are speaking' (Heb. 2:5. cf. Heb. 2:8).

6. Note: *hupotasso* is used in each of these verses.

D. This lesson however is about voluntary submission.

1. *One day all men will submit, whether they like it or not. 'The sea gave up the dead that were in it, and death and Hades*

gave up the dead that were in them, and each person was judged according to what he had done' (Rev. 20:13).

    a. The dead will be raised – without our help.

    b. All will stand before God – like it or not.

2. We are going to discuss mainly the act of voluntary submission.

E. Why is this study important?

1. Submission to God and his Word is of paramount importance.

2. Any word that is used 40 times in the New Testament must demand our attention.

3. God extends the matter of submission beyond just yielding to himself – but to others.

4. How far are we to carry the idea of submission to a church leader?

5. How far are we to carry the idea of submission to one's husband?

6. Cannot the concept of submission be abused?

7. In a day in which authority generally has been undermined – whether in the world, the church or the home – some sanity and balance must return.

I. SUBMISSION TO GOD

A. Our ultimate submission must be to God.

1. *He is our creator* (1 Pet. 4:19; Ps. 100:3).

    a. It is he who chose our parents as well as place and date of birth (Acts 17:26).

    b. We were created for a purpose (Acts 17:27).

2. *He is our Redeemer and Saviour* (Isa. 43:1; 45:17).

    a. He sent his Son into the world (John 3:16-17).

    b. He died on the cross for our sins (1 Cor. 15:3).

3. *He knows everything about us* (Ps. 139:1-4).

    a. He knows what we have need of before we ask him (Matt. 6:8).

    b. All things are 'uncovered and laid bare before the eyes of him to whom we must give account' (Heb. 4:13).

4. *He has dealt with us in all wisdom and understanding* (Eph. 1:8).

    a. He therefore knows what is best for us (Ps. 84:11).

    b. He has never let anybody down who put him first (Ps. 37:25-28).

5. Those who fear God have wisdom (Prov. 1:7).

    a. This fear begins with submission to him (Jas. 4:7).

        (1) 'If any of you lacks wisdom, he should ask God, who gives generously to all without finding fault, and it will be given to him' (Jas. 1:5).

        (2) That wisdom is 'first of all pure; then peace-loving, considerate, submissive, full of mercy and good fruit, impartial and sincere' (Jas. 3:17).

    b. The purpose of being disciplined is to learn submission to God. 'Moreover, we have all had human fathers who disciplined us and we respected them for it. How much more should we submit to the Father of our spirits and live!' (Heb. 12:9).

B. God has deposited his Word with the church and this Word is to be obeyed as absolutely and fearfully as we would obey God himself; there is no difference.

    1. This is where submission (*hupotasso*) and obedience (*hupakoe*) are used interchangeably.

    a. God's Word may be understood four ways:

        (1) The Scriptures.

            (a) 'All Scripture is God-breathed and is useful for teaching, rebuking, correcting and training in righteousness' (2 Tim. 3:16).

            (b) 'Above all, you must understand that no prophecy of Scripture came about by the prophet's own interpretation. For prophecy never had its origin in the will of man, but men spoke from God as they were carried along by the Holy Spirit.' (2 Pet. 1:20-21).

        (2) The gospel.

            (a) 'He will punish those who do not know God and do not obey the gospel of our Lord Jesus.' (2 Thess. 1:8. cf. Rom. 1:5; Acts 6:7).

            (b) 'But thanks be to God that, though you used to be slaves to sin, you wholeheartedly obeyed the form of teaching to which you were entrusted.' (Rom. 6:17. cf. Rom. 10:3; 10:16).

        (3) The person or word of Jesus (John 1:1).

            (a) 'And, once made perfect, he became the source of eternal salvation for all who obey him' (Heb. 5:9).

      (b) 'We demolish arguments and every pretension that sets itself up against the knowledge of God, and we take captive every thought to make it obedient to Christ' (2 Cor. 10:5).

   (4) Apostolic authority.

      (a) 'If anyone does not obey our instructions in this letter, take special note of him. Do not associate with him, in order that he may feel ashamed' (2 Thess. 3:14).

      (b) 'If anybody thinks he is a prophet or spiritually gifted, let him acknowledge that what I am writing to you is the Lord's command' (1 Cor. 14:37).

2. *The first thing mentioned of the earliest church after the coming of the Holy Spirit is that they 'devoted themselves to the apostles' teaching' which was the same thing as God's word.* (Acts 2:42).

  a. For many years all the church had was the Old Testament scriptures.

  b. What did they do in the meantime, that is, before the New Testament canon (rule) of scriptures became available? They adhered to apostolic teaching.

C. Submission to the Holy Spirit.

  1. *The Holy Spirit is God.*

    a. When Ananias 'lied to the Holy Spirit' (Acts 5:3) he was then declared to have lied to God (Acts 5:4).

    b. The Lord is the Spirit (2 Cor. 3:17).

  2. *The Holy Spirit is the Spirit of Jesus.*

    a. 'If anyone does not have the Spirit of Christ, he does not belong to Christ' (Rom. 8:9).

    b. The disciples were forbidden of the Holy Spirit from preaching the word in Asia; when they tried to enter Bithynia 'the Spirit of Jesus would not allow them to' (Acts 16:6-7).

  3. God gives the Holy Spirit to those who obey him. 'We are witnesses of these things, and so is the Holy Spirit, whom God has given to those who obey him' (Acts 5:32).

    a. This could refer to obedience to God.

    b. This could refer to obedience to the Holy Spirit.

    c. It would not matter which; obedience to the Spirit is obedience to God.

4. Not to obey the Spirit is to test or tempt him (Acts 5:9).
5. The Holy Spirit can give direct and immediate guidance.
   a. 'The Spirit told Philip, "Go to that chariot and stay near it"'
   (Acts 8:29).
   b. Philip obeyed at once and a remarkable conversion followed
   (Acts 8:30-39).
   c. This same thing happened with Peter (Acts 10:19).
      (1) This incident was referred to again: 'The Spirit told me
      to have no hesitation' (Acts 11:12).
      (2) This obedience to the Spirit was also seen in Acts 16:7.
   d. Agabus prophesied 'through the Spirit' (Acts 11:28).
   e. The Holy Spirit spoke directly (possibly prophetically)
   concerning Barnabas and Saul (Acts 13:2).
   f. The early church acted on what 'seemed good to the Holy
   Spirit' (Acts 15:28).
   g. Ordinary Christians urged Paul 'through the Spirit' (Acts
   21:4).

D. How then do we submit to God, the Word and the Spirit?

1. *Remember that God is our Father; he will do us no harm.*
   a. He will only permit what is good and right for us.
      (1) No good thing will he withhold (Ps. 84:11).
      (2) What he has in mind will be greater than our own idea.
   b. God owns us in the first place; we are bought by the blood
   of his Son (1 Cor. 6:20).
      (1) We have no right to ourselves. 'Submit yourselves, then,
      to God' (Jas. 4:7a).
      (2) By our submission we release God to do what he pleases.
2. *The word is a mirror of his will for us* (Ps. 19:7-11).
   a. All our plans and ideas must come under his word.
      (1) No matter what we may feel, we must let his word judge
      us (Ps. 119:11).
      (2) Any 'leading' we may have must be put to one side if it
      conflicts with his word.
   b. God's word is magnified above his name (Ps. 138:2 AV).
      (1) His integrity is more important to him than his reputation
      (what his name partly means).
      (2) We therefore esteem the Bible above our convictions;
      the Bible is God's integrity on the line.

3. We surrender to the Holy Spirit by offering God a signed, blank and open contract.

    a. To yield ourselves to the Spirit is to trust the Spirit to give us what the Father has willed.

        (1) The Holy Spirit is God; there will be no contradiction between the Father's will and the will of the Spirit.

        (2) We literally put our whole lives – mind, will and body – in the Spirit's hands.

    b. If there is a fear that any spirits other then the Holy Spirit will enter us, we should always pray 'Lord Jesus, cover me by your blood.'

        (1) Only what is warranted by the Spirit will get past the blood.

        (2) Anything that is warranted by the Spirit, therefore, we must welcome.

II. Submission to God's ordained authorities

A. Government (Rom. 13:1-7; 1 Pet. 2:13-17; Titus 3:1).

    1. *This submission does not mean uncritical approval of the political party that may be in power.*

    a. The earliest church hardly approved of Caesar and all he stood for!

    b. It was however a great testimony to the Christian faith at the time that Christians turned out to be the most exemplary citizens. 'For it is God's will that by doing good you should silence the ignorant talk of foolish men.' (1 Pet. 2:15).

    2. *'Submission' in this case means 'respect'.* 'Everyone must submit himself to the governing authorities, for there is no authority except that which God has established. The authorities that exist have been established by God' (Rom. 13:1).

    a. God has ordained government; it exists for our good.

    b. What would things be like without a measure of law and order?

        (1) The one in authority is 'God's servant to do you good' (Rom. 13:4).

        (2) The obedience, then, is to God. 'Therefore, it is necessary to submit to the authorities, not only because of possible punishment but also because of conscience' (Rom. 13:5).

    c. One practical consequence is that we pay taxes! (Rom. 13:6-7).

  3. *In a word: we don't do it because we 'feel' like it or because we like it; but because it is right to do.*

    a. God can remove existing authorities (Ps. 75:6-7).

    b. In the meantime we show a certain respect because God's honour is at stake. 'Honour the king' (1 Pet. 2:17).

    c. The possible exception: when government imposes laws that violate our relationship with Christ.

      (1) That is why there were martyrs in the early church; they put Christ first and lost their lives.

      (2) They were good citizens; in fact Christians were the best citizens.

      (3) But when required to deny Christ they refused to give in.

B. Church leadership.

  1. *Note: see study on ecclesiology (Understanding Theology I*, ch 27, p 200).

    a. There is more than one form of church government; each (congregational, episcopal, presbyterian) has some warrant in Scripture.

    b. What follows below will vary from person to person, depending upon the kind of ecclesiastical structure of our own places of worship.

      (1) Some are under the authority of a bishop.

      (2) Some are under the authority of a council, like a presbytery.

      (3) Some are under the authority of a pastor.

      (4) Some churches recognise apostles and therefore adhere to apostolic leadership as in New Testament times.

  2. *Leadership is both a position and a gift.*

    a. Position: God has created leadership structures.

      (1) God has appointed apostles, prophets and teachers (1 Cor. 12:28).

      (2) God has appointed pastors and teachers as well (Eph. 4:11).

      (3) The purpose of such leadership: 'To prepare God's people for works of service, so that the body of Christ may be built up' (Eph. 4:12).

(4) Such leadership is also referred to as 'elders' and they are to be held in high esteem. 'The elders who direct the affairs of the church well are worthy of double honour, especially those whose work is preaching and teaching' (1 Tim. 5:17).

b. Gift: being equipped with certain leadership abilities.

    (1) 'We have different gifts, according to the grace given us .... if it is leadership, let him govern diligently' (Rom. 12:6,8).

    (2) It seems to be called 'gifts of administration' (1 Cor. 12:28).

    (3) Elders are described as 'shepherds of God's flock' (1 Pet. 5:2).

    (4) They speak the word of God (Heb. 13:7).

c. Such leadership is male.

    (1) Note: see study on the role of women in the church (*Understanding Theology II*, Chapter 31, page 316).

    (2) 'Now I want you to realise that the head of every man is Christ, and the head of the woman is man, and the head of Christ is God' (1 Cor. 11:3).

        (a) The Greek *kephale* means 'head' rather than 'source'.

        (b) This does not prohibit a woman from prophesying or preaching but it does not allow her to 'have authority over a man' (1 Tim. 2:12).

    (3) In the light of this it seems difficult to reconcile male members of a church being in submission to female leadership.

3. *Submission to church leadership.*

    a. 'Now we ask you, brothers, to respect those who work hard among you, who are over you in the Lord and who admonish you. Hold them in the highest regard in love because of their work. Live in peace with each other' (1 Thess. 5:12-13).

    b. 'Obey your leaders and submit to their authority. They keep watch over you as men who must give an account. Obey them so that their work will be a joy, not a burden, for that would be of no advantage to you' (Heb. 13:17).

    c. To summarise:

        (1) Respect those who are in positions of church leadership.

        (2) They are 'over you in the Lord'.

        (a) God put them there.

        (b) They are to be submitted to because you are obeying the Lord.

    (3) They are to be held in the highest regard.

    (4) This is done 'in love', that is, unselfishly.

    (5) They are to be obeyed since they speak God's word, not their own (1 Pet. 4:11).

    (6) We submits to their authority.

        (a) We trust that God put them there and is guiding them.

        (b) We respect their position and honour what they say since God told us to.

        (c) They must give account of the way they lead; all they do and say will be judged (Jas. 3:1).

    (7) Make their job easy by submitting with joy.

4. Note: this authority can be abused.

    a. As secular government is not to be obeyed if it contradicts our relationship with God, so church leadership is to be obeyed as it is building up our relationship to God.

    b. Only in matters of heresy (false teaching) or moral scandal should one refuse to submit to such leadership.

        (1) Obedience is not to be slavish, oppressive or legalistic.

        (2) If anyone objects to the leadership he should leave rather than stay and protest; let God deal with any church leader who abuses his authority.

C. Marriage and family relationships (Eph. 5:22-6:4; Col. 3:18-21).

1. The pattern of the man being the head is passed on to the marital relationship (Eph. 5:23).

    a. 'Wives, submit to your husbands as to the Lord' (Eph. 5:22).

        (1) The wife must yield to her husband's authority.

        (2) Why?

            (a) She does it for the Lord.

            (b) The husband is 'head of the wife as Christ is the head of the church' (Eph. 5:23).

    b. This assumes that, as with secular government and leadership, such authority is not abused.

        (1) Mental and physical cruelty constitute abuse.

        (2) The Lord does not abuse us; the abusive husband must not expect submission.

2. The husband's responsibility: to love his wife 'just as Christ loved the church' (Eph. 5:25).

   a. Loving authority is not likely to meet with a wife objecting to submission.

   b. The husband's duty is to love (*agape* – as in 1 Cor. 13).

3. The bottom line: 'Each one of you also must love his wife as he loves himself, and the wife must respect her husband' (Eph. 5:33).

4. The parental relationship.

   a. Children are to obey their parents (Eph. 6:1).

   b. Fathers are particularly admonished not to 'exasperate' their children (Eph. 6:4).

D. Other relationships.

1. *Employee relationship* (1 Pet. 2:18ff. cf. Col. 3:22ff).

   a. These passages of course refer to a culture that fortunately does not exist today, at least in the West.

   b. But the principle is the same: we should work for our boss or company, so making great testimony to our faith.

2. Young people should show respect 'to those who are older' (1 Pet. 5:5).

3. We should submit to one another (Eph. 5:21; 1 Pet. 5:5).

   a. This means 'consider others better than yourselves' (Phil. 2:3).

   b. We all need each other; we can learn from one another.

CONCLUSION

We must respect the divine order of things. All submission here below is done as to God – who gave us his Word. When I submit to those God said to yield to, I am doing it to God. That is good enough reason to do it!

347

34

HOW TO SURVIVE IN THE NON-CHRISTIAN WORLD

INTRODUCTION

A. This is one of the most practical (and most difficult) subjects we have dealt with.

    1. *Theology is of two kinds, generally speaking:*

        a. The theoretical, the intellectual, the cerebral.

        b. The application of theology; how it works in our lives.

    2. *The purpose of studying theology is to change lives.*

        a. Some (I fear) are only interested in the cerebral side.

        b. Theology is of little value if it does not affect the way we live.

B. There may be a place for dealing with the subject: 'Surviving in the Christian world'!

    1. For many Christians the real problem is Christians!

    'Dwelling with the saints above – oh, that will be glory.
    Dwelling with the saints below – well, that's another story!'

    2. *One of the greatest shocks for every new Christian is to discover the imperfections of Christians.*

        a. They naively assume that those already in the church are so mature and gracious.

        b. There is a rude shock for every new Christian.

        c. It is not unlike what Moses felt when he revealed himself to his people.

            (1) He assumed that they would be so glad to have him around – that they would cheerfully welcome him.

            (2) But no. 'Moses thought that his own people would realise that God was using him to rescue them, but they did not' (Acts 7:25).

C. This lesson, however, will focus on the Christian in the world.

    1. *The world is essentially non-Christian.*

        a. When Jesus said that we are the salt of the earth it was a sure indication that Christians would be a minority.

        b. Even though Christ was sent into the world not to condemn it but to save it (John 3:17), there was never a realistic expectation that the entire world would actually be saved.

           (1) His death was sufficient for the world.

           (2) But only believers would be saved (John 3:16).

    2. *Even where there is a Bible belt, the world is not only non-Christian but also very ungodly.*

        a. In America, where church attendance is high (compared with Britain), the effect of Christianity on society is not as great as one might suppose.

        b. The media, Hollywood and the world of politics all show how godless the atmosphere is in the US.

    3. *All efforts to save the world by political power have failed.*

        a. Constantine 'Christianising' the Roman Empire did not make people Christians.

        b. The theocracy which some appeared to espouse after the Great Reformation did not mean the conversion of the lost.

           (1) Theocracy (def.): the rule of God in government.

           (2) Some wanted to make a modern nation under the rule of law as ancient Israel was.

           (3) Even in Israel, 'not all who are descended from Israel are Israel' (Rom. 9:6).

        c. The non-Christian world is here to stay.

           (1) We may well wish that the Great Revival for which we pray will convert the world.

           (2) It may awaken the world, it may well mean a larger number are converted.

           (3) It would be wrong to assume that the Garden of Eden will be restored this side of the Second Coming.

D. Why is this lesson important?

    1. *We need all the help we can get in learning how to live the Christian life in the real world.*

        a. Living the Christian life in the church – or among Christian friends and relations is one thing (and that isn't easy).

      b. Living the Christian life in a godless world is quite another thing.

  2. *The world has a fairly shrewd suspicion that Christians are to be different from non-Christians.*

      a. We have an obligation to meet those expectations.

      b. We must leave the non-Christian without excuse.

        (1) True, all people are already without excuse by virtue of creation and conscience. 'For since the creation of the world God's invisible qualities – his eternal power and divine nature – have been clearly seen, being understood from what has been made, so that men are without excuse' (Rom. 1:20).

        (2) How much more ought people who are born again to live lives that leave people without excuse?

  3. *Our witness in the world should reflect the God who saved us.*

      a. The God of the Bible is a God of glory.

        (1) The glory of God is the sum total of all his attributes.

        (2) These attributes include holiness.

      b. We therefore must see ourselves as representatives of the true God.

  4. *Is there more than one way to witness?*

      a. Is it only by our lives – as examples?

      b. When and where do we actually talk about our faith and make efforts to lead people to Christ?

  5. *How do we cope when Christian principles conflict with the demands of one's job?*

      a. What about the Christian doctor or nurse who is obliged to be involved in abortions?

      b. What about the Christian who sees things happen in the office that are flagrantly contrary to the Christian faith – or even the laws of the land?

I. THE WORLD, THE FLESH, THE DEVIL

A. The world

1. *The created order of things.*

      a. God made the world and all who dwell in it.

      b. In this world there is a certain order.

        (1) This is because of common grace – God's goodness to all people – what Calvin called 'special grace within nature'.

(2) This refers not only to gifts and talents in non-Christians, but also to the reason the world is no worse than it is!

(3) Common grace serves as a restraint over the world, keeping wicked people from being as evil as they might be (otherwise all men would be Hitlers).

2. *A fallen race.*

  a. All of us have this in common: we are a fallen people.

    (1) We are not born before the Fall as Adam was.

    (2) We inherited the condition thrust on Adam after the Fall (Rom. 5:12).

  b. Everybody we meet has this in common with us: they are sinners.

    (1) 'What shall we conclude then? Are we any better? Not at all! We have already made the charge that Jews and Gentiles alike are all under sin. As it is written: "There is no one righteous, not even one; there is no one who understands, no one who seeks God. All have turned away, they have together become worthless; there is no one who does good, not even one." "Their throats are open graves; their tongues practice deceit." "The poison of vipers is on their lips." "Their mouths are full of cursing and bitterness." "Their feet are swift to shed blood; ruin and misery mark their ways, and the way of peace they do not know." "There is no fear of God before their eyes"' (Rom. 3:9-18).

    (2) 'For all have sinned and fall short of the glory of God' (Rom. 3:23).

B. The flesh

1. *This refers to our sinful nature: why it is easier to do wrong than to do right.*

  a. We came from our mothers' wombs speaking lies (Ps. 58:3).

  b. No child needs to be taught how to lie.

2. *For this reason we should not expect non-Christians to behave like Christians.*

  a. We should expect people to do wrong.

  b. A Christian is a person who learns not to be surprised at anything.

> **(1)** We know what we ourselves are capable of; for being Christians gives us objectivity about ourselves.
>
> **(2)** We therefore should never be surprised at anything!
>
> **3.** *In a word: people give in to the flesh.*
>
> > **a.** Things which pertain to the ego; pride, jealousy, hate, gossip, vengeance, holding grudges.
> >
> > **b.** Things which pertain to the sensuous: sexual lust.

C. The devil

> **1.** All the above surely serve to explain mankind.
>
> **2.** *But as well as that there is the devil.*
>
> > **a.** He keeps people from becoming Christians. 'The god of this age has blinded the minds of unbelievers, so that they cannot see the light of the gospel of the glory of Christ, who is the image of God' (2 Cor. 4:4).
> >
> > **b.** He keeps people from believing that he himself exists.
>
> **3.** *The devil is the embodiment of evil.*
>
> > **a.** He is a literal person.
> >
> > **b.** He is capable only of evil.
>
> **4.** *He builds strongholds – in two ways:*
>
> > **a.** He moves into strategic places
> >
> > > **(1)** Government, making decisions often anti-God.
> > >
> > > **(2)** The media, feeding into the selfishness of people.
> > >
> > > **(3)** Education, ensuring that unbiblical principles are taught.
> > >
> > > **(4)** Financial world, where ethics often count for nothing.
> > >
> > > **(5)** Business, where honesty is exceedingly rare.
> > >
> > > **(6)** The family unit, where infidelity is so common where children suffer – passing it on to the next generation.
> > >
> > > **(7)** The church, where leaders no longer believe the Bible.
> >
> > **b.** In people's minds.
> >
> > > **(1)** We are intimidated and assume there is no hope.
> > >
> > > **(2)** We imbibe the spirit of the world and become no better than what we say we despise.
> > >
> > > **(3)** We fall into the love of money (1 Tim. 6:10).

II. THE CHRISTIAN: SALT AND LIGHT

A. Jesus: 'You are the salt of the earth. But if the salt loses its saltiness, how can it be made salty again? It is no longer good for anything, except to be thrown out and trampled by men' (Matt. 5:13).

1. *Salt is used for:*
   a. Seasoning food (Job 6:6).
   b. Seasoning sacrifices (Lev. 2:13; Ezek. 43:24).
   c. Ratifying covenants (Num. 18:19; 2 Chron. 13:5).
   d. Strengthening new-born infants (Ezek. 16:4).
   e. Preserving food.
2. If we are not salt we are good for nothing.

B. Jesus: 'You are the light of the world. A city on a hill cannot be hidden. Neither do people light a lamp and put it under a bowl. Instead they put it on its stand, and it gives light to everyone in the house. In the same way, let your light shine before men, that they may see your good deeds and praise your Father in heaven' (Matt. 5:14-16).
   1. *God is light.* 'This is the message we have heard from him and declare to you: God is light; in him there is no darkness at all' (1 John 1:5).
      a. Light is essential to God's very nature.
      b. Satan is thus the prince of darkness (John 12:31; Eph. 6:12).
   2. *Jesus is light* (John 1:9; 9:5).
      a. Jesus is the image of the glory of God (Heb. 1:1-3).
      b. The result: people hate Jesus Christ. 'This is the verdict: Light has come into the world, but men loved darkness instead of light because their deeds were evil. Everyone who does evil hates the light, and will not come into the light for fear that his deeds will be exposed. But whoever lives by the truth comes into the light, so that it may be seen plainly that what he has done has been done through God' (John 3:19-21).

C. As Christians we have come to the light, having been turned 'from darkness to light, and from the power of Satan to God.' (Acts 26:18).
   1. *As a consequence these things characterise the Christian:*
      a. We have a sense of sin (John 16:7-9; 1 John 1:8).
      b. We have the Holy Spirit (Rom. 8:9).
      c. We are called to obedience, namely, to walk in the light (1 John 1:7).
   2. *Consequently we are different from the world.*

       a. Not that we are not tempted.

       b. But we are called to mirror the likeness of God and his Son.

D. We are called to make ethical and moral decisions that will not be popular in a fallen world.

    1. *No one said it would be easy.*

       a. 'Then he called the crowd to him along with his disciples and said: "If anyone would come after me, he must deny himself and take up his cross and follow me. For whoever wants to save his life will lose it, but whoever loses his life for me and for the gospel will save it"' (Mark 8:34-35).

       b. 'I have told you these things, so that in me you may have peace. In this world you will have trouble. But take heart! I have overcome the world' (John 16:33).

    2. *Jesus said he would always be with us* (Matt. 28:20).

       a. This is by the Holy Spirit, the Spirit of truth (John 14:16-17).

       b. When the Holy Spirit came the disciples had Jesus back with them!

III. Hard decisions

A. In our personal lives

    1. We cannot survive in the non-Christian world without a close personal relationship with God.

    2. *Personal, private worship is essential.*

       a. Thirty minutes per day alone with God in prayer.

       b. Reading at least one chapter from the Bible every day.

    3. *Church involvement.*

       a. We should be church members and remain committed to one local church, not going from one to another.

       b. We should play a vital part in the church's life if we expect to have a solid witness before non-Christians.

B. Our witness to the Gospel

    1. *There is more than one way to be a witness to the Gospel.*

       a. When involved in the evangelistic outreach of our church we have every right to be bold.

         (1) When knocking on doors – e.g. Evangelism Explosion.

         (2) When witnessing on the streets – e.g. Pilot Lights.

b. A softer approach is being used of the Lord these days –
e.g. Alpha.

   (1) This is inviting people to our homes, for a meal.

   (2) A presentation of the Gospel with discussion and answering questions may be effective.

2. *In the public arena we must win the right to present the Gospel.*

  a. Making friends and living a godly life without pointing the finger.

   (1) Being friendly.

   (2) Being faithful in what we are employed to do.

  b. Bringing in the content of the Gospel must be done in the power of the Spirit, with wisdom (Acts 6:10).

   (1) This is done when we are put on the spot, as Stephen was.

   (2) This is done when we are not violating company policy.

   (3) This is done when we know in our hearts it is what is required of us.

   (4) Note: unnecessarily and prematurely confronting people with the Gospel may bring unnecessary offence – and can do damage to Christ's name.

C. At work

1. *When we are in charge.*

  a. As Christians we will be watched; remember that most people have a fairly shrewd idea how a Christian is to behave.

  b. It follows then that we:

   (1) Speak honestly.

   (2) Carry out work with transparent integrity.

   (3) Are blameless in money matters.

   (4) Pay fairly, providing fair working conditions.

   (5) Watch our conduct when any sexual implications could be anticipated.

   (6) Do not lose our tempers.

   (7) Listen to complaints with sympathetic understanding.

  c. Note: those in other managerial roles also note the above.

2. *When we work for someone else:*

  a. As Christians we will be watched.

  b. It follows that we:

      (1) Put in a good day's work.

      (2) Are careful to observe the policy of the company, government, hospital, office, etc. where we work.

      (3) Never steal.

      (4) Don't complain.

      (5) Are pleasant and likeable.

      (6) Develop trust by those over us and around us.

      (7) Live a life centred on biblical principles.

  c. Note: a person who violates the above forfeits the right to talk about Christ and will hurt the Christian witness.

3. *When we have to make difficult decisions.*

  a. When we work for someone we know is being dishonest, breaking the law or going against Christian principles.

    (1) We will have to decide early on, if we discover we are a part of a set-up that is wrong, whether to:

      (a) Say something to the person over us.

      (b) Keep quiet as though we know nothing.

      (c) Quietly resign.

    (2) There are two Scriptures that must be applied, above and below:

      (a) 'Therefore, my dear friends, as you have always obeyed – not only in my presence, but now much more in my absence – continue to work out your salvation with fear and trembling' (Phil. 2:12).

      (b) 'Let us therefore make every effort to do what leads to peace and to mutual edification' (Rom. 14:19).

  b. When we are forced to participate in what may be legal but contrary to our biblical convictions.

    (1) Medical ethics, e.g.:

      (a) Abortion.

      (b) Euthanasia.

    (2) Legal ethics, e.g.:

      (a) Divorce.

      (b) A Christian suing a fellow-Christian.

    (3) Politics, e.g.:

      (a) Pushing for unjust laws.

      (b) Upholding laws that are contrary to the Christian faith.

    (4) Education, e.g.:

(a) Teaching what is unbiblical.

(b) Not teaching what is biblical.

(5) Sales clerk, e.g.:

(a) Selling what is not honouring to God.

(b) Selling what is overpriced.

(6) Financial matters, e.g.:

(a) Unjust interest, taking unfair advantage.

(b) Forcing to bankruptcy.

C. The issues

1. Sometimes we know in advance that a compromise with Christian principles will be inevitable.

2. Many times we discover later that this compromise will be required if we are to survive.

3. *We have to work to live.*

a. Do we take a job, assuming it is the only way forward?

b. What if you are a doctor or nurse?

(1) Does one refuse to study medicine in the first place?

(2) Or do you adhere to the law in order to keep your job (as in performing abortions)?

(3) What if you have no choice: perform the abortion or lose your job?

CONCLUSION

We should be very sympathetic with those who are in these awkward positions. God will never lead us to do what will violate our inner peace (Rom. 14:19). When I know I'm in God's will I have inner peace. If I lose that inner peace, I have to do what will restore it.

35

HOW TO DEAL WITH JEALOUSY

INTRODUCTION

A. This is a painful subject – but always a timely one.
   1. *It is painful because we tend to resist the thought that we ourselves are jealous.*
   a. We may admit to a problem generally.
   b. We tend to deny that it is at work at a given moment.
      (1) 'I am not jealous in this particular case.'
         'Oh, beware of jealousy, it is the green-eyed monster, which doth mock the meat it feeds on.'
            William Shakespeare (1564-1616)
         'Jealousy is the injured lover's hell.' *John Milton (1608-74)*
      (2) 'I am not jealous of him – or her.'
   c. It is embarrassing to be jealous.
      (1) It betrays our insecurity.
      (2) We tend not to admit to being jealous.
   d. It hurts our pride to admit to being jealous.
      (1) We rather hope people will think we are beyond such a weakness. 'Tis a monster begat upon itself, born on itself.' *Shakespeare.*
      (2) It is the last thing we often admit to. 'In jealousy there is more of self-love, than of love to another.' *Francois Rochefoucauld (1630-80).*
   2. *It is timely because chances are it is a problem which we all are trying to cope with at any given moment.*
   a. Why should we deny it? After all:
      (1) It is a work of the flesh (Gal. 5:20).
      (2) We are all sinners; why pretend this is something we are not bothered with?
   b. It is clearly akin to an unforgiving spirit.
      (1) Totally forgiving people is probably the hardest thing in the world to do.

     (2) To the minutest degree we struggle to forgive, to that degree will we be governed by jealousy.

3. *It is the easiest thing to see in another person, the hardest to see in ourselves!*

  a. The reason we can see it in others is because we are detached from the personal pain of having to see it in ourselves.

    (1) We are like David when hearing Nathan's parable (2 Sam. 12:1-10); when we have no idea that we are part of the problem we can see clearly what justice is.

    (2) We therefore can detect it in another person in an instant.

  b. We want people to put the most noble motive on our decisions.

    (1) We may wish to fancy that we are upholding the honour of God and are being led by the Holy Spirit when the truth is, we are jealous.

    (2) We would rather die a thousand deaths than admit that our most grandiose plans and decisions were in fact traced to jealousy.

B. Jealousy is the cause of the ever-increasing fragmentation within the church.

1. It is usually why new churches are started.

2. It is usually why new committees are formed.

3. It is usually why new publishers are conceived.

4. It is usually why Christians fall out with each other.

5. It is usually why theological controversies emerge (and has almost nothing to do with theology at all!).

6. It is usually the reason a book gets a bad review.

7. *It is usually the reason we don't recognise an author's success.*

  a. This is why we are jealous of excellence.

  b. This is why the greatest opposition to what God is doing today comes from those who were at the centre of what God was doing yesterday. 'He who is next heir to supreme power, is always suspected and hated by him who actually wields it.' *Tacitus (55-120).*

C. Etymological background.

1. *Greek:* phthonos, *used 9 times in the New Testament; often translated 'envy', e.g.:*

    a. 'For he knew it was out of envy that they had handed Jesus over to him' (Matt. 27:18. cf. Mark 15:10).

    b. 'They have become filled with every kind of wickedness, evil, greed and depravity. They are full of envy, murder, strife, deceit and malice' (Rom. 1:29).

    c. 'And envy, drunkenness, orgies, and the like. I warn you, as I did before, that those who live like this will not inherit the kingdom of God' (Gal. 5:21).

2. *Gr. zeelos, used 17 times in the New Testament, translated either 'envy' or 'jealousy', e.g.:*

    a. 'Because the patriarchs were jealous of Joseph, they sold him as a slave into Egypt. But God was with him' (Acts 7:9).

    b. 'But the Jews were jealous; so they rounded up some bad characters from the market-place, formed a mob and started a riot in the city. They rushed to Jason's house in search of Paul and Silas in order to bring them out to the crowd' (Acts 17:5).

    c. 'Idolatry and witchcraft; hatred, discord, jealousy, fits of rage, selfish ambition, dissensions, factions' (Gal. 5:20).

3. *Note: there does not seem to be any etymological difference between envy and jealousy, although some have sought to find one.*

    a. 'Jealousy is the fear or apprehension of superiority, envy our uneasiness under it.' *William Shenstone (1714-63).*

    b. It is possible that our English usage may be summarised:

        (1) Jealousy is what makes us act in a certain way.

        (2) Envy is what we may passively feel.

    c. But at the end of the day the two are the same; envy and jealousy can be used interchangeably.

        (1) 'And I saw that all labour and all achievement spring from man's envy of his neighbour. This too is meaningless; a chasing after the wind' (Ecc. 4:4).

        (2) Gr. *zeelos* translates Hebrew *gin'ah* ('jealousy' or 'envy').

D. Why is this lesson so important?

1. *It is important that we develop an acute sense of sin generally.*

    a. The evidence that we have seen the glory of God is partly shown by consciousness of sin (Is. 6:1-6).

    b. 'If we claim to be without sin, we deceive ourselves and the truth is not in us' (1 John 1:8).

2. *It is important that we learn to recognise jealousy in ourselves.*

    a. It is one thing to say, 'I know I am not perfect.'

    b. It takes deep conviction by the Holy Spirit to admit:

        (1) I have a problem with jealousy.

        (2) I am experiencing jealousy with this or that person – now.

3. *We need to learn how to recognise jealousy in ourselves.*

    a. It takes no grace to see it in others; even the non-Christian can do that!

    b. It takes a lot of grace to see it and admit to it in ourselves.

4. We must discover how Satan provokes our sin of jealousy and uses it for his wicked purposes.

5. There is a positive side: how God uses it to accomplish his purposes.

II. How Satan uses jealousy

A. It is listed as a work of the flesh (Gal. 5:19-20).

1. *This means we have the problem before the devil gets involved.*

    a. It is a result of the Fall (Rom. 5:12).

    b. It is part of dying (Gen. 2:17).

2. *It is not dealt with automatically by salvation.*

    a. God chose to deal with sin in two stages:

        (1) By his Son's death (Rom. 5:8-9).

        (2) By his Second Coming when we are glorified (Rom. 8:30; 1 John 3:2).

    b. Our conversion does basically two things:

        (1) It saves us from all our sins (1 John 1:9).

        (2) We have the Holy Spirit by whom we do not fulfil the desires of the flesh (Gal. 5:16,22ff).

    c. The flesh in us will be there until we die.

        (1) Therefore the works of the flesh will be with us (Gal. 5:19-21).

        (2) The potential for all those listed must be acknowledged and dealt with. 'The acts of the sinful nature are obvious: sexual immorality, impurity and debauchery; idolatry and witchcraft; hatred, discord, jealousy, fits of rage, selfish ambition, dissensions, factions and envy; drunkenness, orgies, and the like. I warn you, as I did before, that those who live like this will not inherit the kingdom of God' (Gal. 5:19-21).

3. *It is our task to do three things:*

    a. Acknowledge our sin generally and those works of the flesh to which we happen to be more vulnerable.

    b. Admit to our weakness and sin as soon as it appears.

    c. Determine to walk in the Spirit.

        (1) 'So I say, live by the Spirit, and you will not gratify the desires of the sinful nature' (Gal. 5:16).

        (2) 'But the fruit of the Spirit is love, joy, peace, patience, kindness, goodness, faithfulness, gentleness and self-control. Against such things there is no law. Those who belong to Christ Jesus have crucified the sinful nature with its passions and desires. Since we live by the Spirit, let us keep in step with the Spirit. Let us not become conceited, provoking and envying each other' (Gal. 5:22-25).

B. How the devil uses jealousy: to kill

1. *Jealousy of another's righteousness.*

    a. The first case of jealousy was that of Cain.

        (1) He was jealous that God accepted Abel's sacrifice and not his (Gen. 4:3-5).

        (2) The result: Cain killed Abel (Gen. 4:6-8).

    b. Jealousy will be dealt with one of two ways:

        (1) From without: when that person ceases to be a problem to us.

            (a) Cain dealt with Abel by murder.

            (b) We may do it by killing another's reputation; this way they are out of the way.

        (2) From within: when we get an internal victory.

            (a) We do this by walking in the Spirit.

            (b) We do this by total forgiveness.

2. *Threatened by the popularity of a 'rising star'.*

    a. After David killed Goliath:

        (1) 'As they danced, they sang: "Saul has slain his thousands, and David his tens of thousands"' (1 Sam. 18:7).

(2) 'Saul was very angry; this refrain galled him. "They have credited David with tens of thousands," he thought, "but me with only thousands. What more can he get but the kingdom?" And from that time on Saul kept a jealous eye on David' (1 Sam. 18:8-9).

  b. King Saul was consumed with the fear of David.

    (1) He was more threatened by David than the ancient enemy of Israel – the Philistines.

    (2) It led to his downfall.

      (a) He lost integrity, not even keeping an oath (1 Sam. 19:6,9,10).

      (b) He ceased to hear God speak (1 Sam. 28:15).

3. *Sibling rivalry.*

  a. Jacob (a loving father) preferred Joseph over the rest of his sons.

    (1) He gave Joseph a 'coat of many colours' (AV); 'a richly ornamented robe' (Gen. 37:3).

    (2) 'When his brothers saw that their father loved him more than any of them, they hated him and could not speak a kind word to him' (Gen. 37:4).

  b. On top of this Joseph was given supernatural dreams (Gen. 37:5-9).

    (1) He was unwise to tell them to his brothers.

    (2) They sold Joseph to slavery. 'Because the patriarchs were jealous of Joseph, they sold him as a slave into Egypt. But God was with him' (Acts 7:9).

4. *Jealousy of another's leadership.*

  a. Miriam and Aaron did not like Moses' Cushite wife, they said, '"Has the LORD spoken only through Moses?" they asked. "Hasn't he also spoken through us?" And the LORD heard this' (Num. 12:2).

  b. Korah led a rebellion against Moses and Aaron. 'They came as a group to oppose Moses and Aaron and said to them, "You have gone too far! The whole community is holy, every one of them; and the LORD is with them. Why then do you set yourselves above the LORD's assembly?"' (Num. 16:3).

5. *Jealousy of Jesus.*

  a. King Herod was threatened by the news that one had been born King of the Jews – and sought to kill him (Matt. 2).

    b. A later King Herod joined in the conspiracy to crucify Jesus for one reason; Pontius Pilate knew the real reason: 'For he knew it was out of envy that they had handed Jesus over to him' (Matt. 27:18).

6. *When there is opposition to the success of the gospel.*

    a. 'When the Jews saw the crowds, they were filled with jealousy and talked abusively against what Paul was saying' (Acts 13:45).

    b. 'But the Jews were jealous; so they rounded up some bad characters from the market-place, formed a mob and started a riot in the city. They rushed to Jason's house in search of Paul and Silas in order to bring them out to the crowd' (Acts 17:5).

    c. Note: this was what really lay behind the Judaizers' efforts to undermine the apostle Paul (2 Cor. 10–11).

7. *Even minsters of the gospel were jealous of Paul. 'It is true that some preach Christ out of envy and rivalry, but others out of goodwill'* (Phil. 1:15).

    a. Sadly this is common to the present day.

    b. But Paul could say: 'But what does it matter? The important thing is that in every way, whether from false motives or true, Christ is preached. And because of this I rejoice. Yes, and I will continue to rejoice' (Phil. 1:18).

        (1) Church splits often spring out of envy.

        (2) New movements often spring out of envy.

8. Theological controversies often originate out of envy (Acts 11:1-2).

    a. This was true of the Judaizers (Gal. 6:12-13).

    b. This was true of the gnostics (Jude 11,16).

    c. John said of one of his rivals 'I wrote to the church, but Diotrephes, who loves to be first, will have nothing to do with us' (3 John 9).

9. It is what causes division in churches. 'For where you have envy and selfish ambition, there you find disorder and every evil practice' (James 3:16).

10. *It lies behind the worst sins. 'You want something but don't get it. You kill and covet, but you cannot have what you want. You quarrel and fight. You do not have, because you do not ask*

God' (Jas. 4:2). Note: 'what you want' is translated from the Greek verb for being jealous.

   a. 'A heart at peace gives life to the body, but envy rots the bones' (Prov. 14:30).

   b. There may be more to this verse than meets the eye: envy can affect our health, there being a connection between our mental attitude and the marrow in the bones!

II. THE POSITIVE SIDE: HOW GOD USES JEALOUSY

A. The movers and shakers of this world are highly motivated people.

   1. A soul-searching verse: 'And I saw that all labour and all achievement spring from man's envy of his neighbour. This too is meaningless; a chasing after the wind' (Ecc. 4:4).

   2. *Why do we want to excel?*

      a. To make people admire us.

      b. To make people a little jealous. 'Eat your heart out,' we say – joking or not!

   3. *But God uses this too.*

      a. 'God uses sex to drive a man to marriage; ambition to drive a man to service; fear to drive a man to faith.' *Martin Luther.*

      b. This ambition – to glorify God – must ultimately be transcended by a desire to receive honour from God only (John 5:44).

B. Paul expressed the hope this would motivate Jews to accept the gospel.

   1. 'Again I ask: Did Israel not understand? First, Moses says, "I will make you envious by those who are not a nation; I will make you angry by a nation that has no understanding"' (Rom. 10:19).

   2. 'Again I ask: Did they stumble so as to fall beyond recovery? Not at all! Rather, because of their transgression, salvation has come to the Gentiles to make Israel envious' (Rom. 11:11).

C. Paul could speak of godly jealousy.

   1. This lay behind his motives to spare the Corinthians from the Judaizers' onslaught. 'I am jealous for you with a godly jealousy. I promised you to one husband, to Christ, so that I might present you as a pure virgin to him' (2 Cor. 11:2).

2. *He applied this to those who might be jealous for spiritual gifts; he used the Greek verb 'to be jealous' in the following verses:*

a. 'But eagerly desire the greater gifts. And now I will show you the most excellent way' (1 Cor. 12:31).

b. 'Follow the way of love and eagerly desire spiritual gifts, especially the gift of prophecy' (1 Cor. 14:1).

c. 'Therefore, my brothers, be eager to prophesy, and do not forbid speaking in tongues' (1 Cor. 14:39).

3. *Jesus used this word to the Laodiceans: 'Those whom I love I rebuke and discipline. So be earnest, and repent'* (Rev. 3:19).

a. When the word is used for a godly jealousy, it means to let the natural jealousy we all have be as intense as our seeking of God.

b. This is when we want God's honour as we once wanted the honour of people.

D. The first church quarrel apparently sprang from jealousy.

1. 'In those days when the number of disciples was increasing, the Grecian Jews among them complained against the Hebraic Jews because their widows were being overlooked in the daily distribution of food' (Acts 6:1).

2. *The result: God raised up deacons* (Acts 6:2-4).

a. The eventual result: 'So the word of God spread. The number of disciples in Jerusalem increased rapidly, and a large number of priests became obedient to the faith' (Acts 6:7).

b. God turned a bad situation to his glory.

E. All of the above examples of wicked jealousy were turned to good.

1. Abel was the church's first martyr (Heb. 11:4).

2. David was spared despite Saul's jealousy, and became Israel's greatest king.

3. Joseph became Prime Minister of Egypt and saved his family from starvation.

4. Moses became all the stronger, eventually becoming the greatest leader in history.

5. Satan overreached himself in planning Jesus' crucifixion (1 Cor. 2:8).

III. Recognising jealousy

A. We don't need help in recognising it in others.

1. Even at the natural level, it is recognised that people are jealous of another person's class.

2. *The most intense jealousy is toward the class nearest you.*

    a. The middle class are jealous of the upper middle class.

    b. The upper middle class are jealous of aristocracy.

    c. The lower middle class are not jealous of the aristocracy, generally speaking, but of the middle class.

    d. The working class are jealous of the lower middle class.

    Class; Jilly Cooper (1979)

B. But how can I recognise jealousy in myself?

1. When someone 'gets my goat', I am probably jealous.

2. If I get a sinking feeling over someone's success, it is probably jealousy.

3. If I feel threatened by someone's promotion, it is probably jealousy.

4. If I feel good when someone falls, it is probably jealousy.

5. If I feel good when someone gets caught, it is probably jealousy.

6. If I feel good when someone has bad news, it is probably jealousy.

7. If I am threatened by someone's popularity, it is probably jealousy.

8. If I am threatened by someone's good performance, it is probably jealousy.

9. If I am threatened by someone's good looks, it is probably jealousy.

10. If I am unhappy about someone's property, it is probably jealousy.

11. When I look for a valid criticism that will not let someone look quite so good, it is probably jealousy.

12. When I criticise someone at all, it is probably jealousy.

13. When I damn with faint praise, it is probably jealousy.

C. How do I overcome jealousy?

1. Admit it to myself when I feel any of the above.

2. Confess it to God.

3. Share it openly with at least one other person (if I am truly serious about dealing with it).

4. *Be sure there is no unforgiving spirit:*
   a. Toward the person.
   b. Toward God for blessing this person.

5. Rejoice with those who rejoice (harder to do than weeping with those who weep).

CONCLUSION

Jealousy is the sin seldom preached about or admitted to. But remember that Jesus is touched with the feeling of our weaknesses (Heb. 4:15). He accepts us and works to change us.

36

HOW TO DEAL WITH PREJUDICE

A. When you think of the word 'prejudice' what kind of prejudice first comes to your mind? For some:

  1. *Racial prejudice, when people avoid you or isolate you because of:*

    a. The colour of your skin.

    b. Your nationality.

  2. *Cultural prejudice, when people feel:*

    a. They are a cut above you because of their culture.

      (1) The English have their Irish jokes (and vice versa).

      (2) The Polish have their Russian jokes (and vice versa).

    b. You feel others put you down because you are deprived, owing to:

      (1) Education.

      (2) Social standing – who one knows and mixes with.

  3. *Political prejudice.*

    a. When Christians insist there is a 'Christian' view that justifies one particular party.

      (1) Some provide a theological rationale for Labour, or Socialism.

      (2) Some provide a theological rationale for being Tory, or Conservative.

    b. When Christians divide merely on the basis of political preference.

  4. *Theological prejudice.*

    a. When Christians do not isolate one another merely over essentials of the faith but divide over non-essential issues.

    b. When a 'party line' becomes more important than true Christian unity.

  5. *Other examples:*

    a. When we are threatened by another person and allow a prejudice to emerge – which means we are going to keep him in his place.

    b. When it is jealousy but we don't have sufficient objectivity about ourselves to it or its cause.

    c. When we hastily 'categorise' people and isolate them before we know the whole story.

B. Prejudice (def.): When our minds are made up although we don't know the whole story.

    1. *It is when we 'pre-judge' – we pass a sentence before we have heard the evidence.*

        a. What a pity when a judge is like this.

        b. What a pity when a jury is like this. Illustration: O J Simpson.

    2. *We can do this in human relationships and miss an opportunity to have a true friend.*

        a. We may be biased against their looks or appearance.

        b. We may be biased against a certain type of personality.

C. Why is this study important?

    1. *All of us have been hurt as a result of people being prejudiced against us.*

        a. When they don't know us.

        b. We need to come to terms with this – and try not to take it too personally.

    2. *We have hurt others for the same reason.*

        a. We can feel the pain when people are prejudiced against us.

        b. Can we see it in ourselves – when we hurt others even though we may not have meant to?

    3. All great people in the Bible knew what it was like to be either prejudiced – or to be the object of prejudice.

    4. Israel missed their promised Messiah because of prejudice.

    5. *People refuse to become Christians partly because of their prejudices:*

        a. Against the Bible.

        b. Against the Church.

        c. Their accepting 'science' uncritically.

    6. The greatest object of prejudice that ever was, is God.

I. THE ORIGIN OF PREJUDICE

A. Fear.

1. *In the south of the USA racial prejudice stemmed largely from fear.*
   a. Black people were afraid of the white man's power – and consequently were afraid to trust white people.
   b. White people were afraid of the black people's anger and physical power – and consequently worked to keep them 'in their place.'
2. *Theological prejudice is based largely on fear.*
   a. We fear having our own view undermined, or fear that people will adopt a view other than our own – to leave us outside the comfort zone of the larger community.
   b. Beneath this fear is pride; rather than admit we are wrong we defend what we hope is true.

B. Jealousy (see previous study on this subject).

1. *We are jealous that deprived or isolated people will get recognition.*
   a. We tell ourselves 'It's not good for them to get this recognition.'
   b. We hate to admit we are jealous.
2. If a person we don't like is vindicated we find this threatening – but never do we admit it's jealousy!

C. 'Positive' prejudice (irrational in fact): having a prejudice in a person's favour but without knowing the whole story.

1. We may like a person because they remind us of someone we like!
2. People will vote for a person owing to his or her good looks!
3. People will prefer a political party in a foreign country but know little about the background or situation.
4. Some choose a church because of its architecture or music!
5. *Note: I call this 'positive' but it can backfire (it often does), which means it is not so positive after all.*
   a. It is irrational; it is not based on reason or evidence.
   b. It is when we go by a feeling – that can be misleading.

Understanding Theology

II. OLD TESTAMENT EXAMPLES

A. Abraham

1. *Abraham was prejudiced against the Egyptians, assuming they would kill him in order to get his wife Sarah.* 'As he was about to enter Egypt, he said to his wife Sarai, "I know what a beautiful woman you are. When the Egyptians see you, they will say, 'This is his wife.' Then they will kill me but will let you live. Say you are my sister, so that I will be treated well for your sake and my life will be spared because of you"' (Gen. 12:11-13).
   a. He was wrong.
   b. His prejudice was based on fear.
2. *Abraham did not want Isaac but Ishmael to be the child of promise.* 'And Abraham said to God, "If only Ishmael might live under your blessing!"' (Gen. 17:18).
   a. This, too, probably stemmed from fear.
   b. He was comfortable with things as they were and didn't want to adjust to a major upheaval in his old age!

B. Isaac and Rebekah

1. Isaac was prejudiced on behalf of Esau, his first-born.
2. Rebekah was prejudiced on behalf of Jacob (Gen. 25:28), although God's promise may have had something to do with this (Gen. 25:22-23).

C. Jacob

1. *Jacob was prejudiced in favour of Joseph, the son of his beloved Rachel* (Gen. 30:22ff) *and because Joseph 'had been born to him in his old age'* (Gen. 37:3).
   a. Note: one would think Jacob, having been prejudiced against by his own father, would have wanted to avoid this pitfall when he became a father.
   b. Isn't it amazing how we repeat the sins of our parents!
2. *Jacob was prejudiced for Rachel and against Leah – apparently for one reason: their appearance.* (Gen. 29:16-18).
   a. This was 'positive' (irrational) prejudice.
   b. Jacob never appreciated Leah whose children turned out to mean much to the Kingdom of God in the long run (she bore Judah and Levi).

3. *Jacob played into Pharaoh's prejudice (at Joseph's suggestion) against shepherds* (Gen. 46:31–47:6).

    a. This shows how God can use people's prejudices to achieve a positive end.

    b. The land of Goshen is what Joseph wanted for his family in the first place!

    c. Note: God will use every prejudice against you for his glory, it is his way of 'gaining glory'!

D. David

    1. As we saw from an earlier lesson, Saul was prejudiced against David out of jealousy (1 Sam. 18:9).

    2. *Hanun, King of the Ammonites, was so prejudiced against King David that he misjudged David's motive which, in fact, was to show kindness to them* (2 Sam. 10:2).

        a. 'The Ammonite nobles said to Hanun their lord, "Do you think David is honouring your father by sending men to you to express sympathy? Hasn't David sent them to you to explore the city and spy it out and overthrow it?" So Hanun seized David's men, shaved off half of each man's beard, cut off their garments in the middle at the buttocks, and sent them away' (2 Sam. 10:3-4).

        b. Their prejudice sprang from fear; they paid dearly for this (cf. 2 Sam. 10:7-19).

E. Jonah

    1. Jonah was prejudiced against the Ninevites and resented God showing mercy to them. 'He prayed to the LORD, "O LORD, is this not what I said when I was still at home? That is why I was so quick to flee to Tarshish. I knew that you are a gracious and compassionate God, slow to anger and abounding in love, a God who relents from sending calamity" ' (Jonah 4:2).

    2. This is a demonstration of how God can use us in spite of our being full of prejudice (an encouraging thought).

III. New Testament examples

A. Jesus.

    1. *Prejudice against his background.*

        a. His place of upbringing.

(1) '"Nazareth! Can anything good come from there?" Nathanael asked. "Come and see," said Philip' (John 1:46).

(2) 'They replied, "Are you from Galilee, too? Look into it, and you will find that a prophet does not come out of Galilee"' (John 7:52).

b. His (lack of) education. 'The Jews were amazed and asked, "How did this man get such learning without having studied?"' (John 7:15).

c. His parentage. 'They said, "Is this not Jesus, the son of Joseph, whose father and mother we know? How can he now say, 'I came down from heaven'?"' (John 6:42).

2. *Prejudice over his views of the Sabbath.*

    a. Jesus again and again healed on the Sabbath (John 5:9ff; 9:14. cf. Luke 6:6-11).

    b. God may mock our prejudices by doing things deliberately that play into them!

3. *Prejudice over doctrine.*

    a. The Sadducees were prejudiced because Jesus believed in the resurrection of the body (Matt. 22:23-33).

    b. The Pharisees were prejudiced because all Jesus taught seemed to go against their theological biases (cf. Matt. 22:15ff; 41-46).

4. *The chief priests were threatened by his authority and maintained prejudices to the end* (Matt. 21:23-27).

    a. The miracle of Jesus' raising Lazarus from the dead did not eliminate their prejudice. 'Then the chief priests and the Pharisees called a meeting of the Sanhedrin. "What are we accomplishing?" they asked. "Here is this man performing many miraculous signs. If we let him go on like this, everyone will believe in him, and then the Romans will come and take away both our place and our nation"' (John 11:47-48).

    b. This is a warning to us: our prejudice can cause us to miss the manifestation of God's glory, that is, miss the benefit that would be ours.

5. *The bottom line*: 'As he approached Jerusalem and saw the city, he wept over it and said, "If you, even you, had only known on this day what would bring you peace – but now it is hidden from your eyes. . . . because you did not recognise the time of God's coming to you"' (Luke 19:41-42,44).

   a. Prejudice prevented Israel from seeing their own promised Messiah.

   b. Prejudice can prevent us from recognising the Holy Spirit at work today.

   c. The chief priests rejected a 'second chance' to confess Jesus when the guards at the empty tomb reported what happened (Matt. 28:11).

      (1) They knew the guards weren't making up the story.

      (2) Yet, 'When the chief priests had met with the elders and devised a plan, they gave the soldiers a large sum of money, telling them "You are to say, 'His disciples came during the night and stole him away while we were asleep.' If this report gets to the governor, we will satisfy him and keep you out of trouble"' (Matt. 28:12-14).

6. Remember: Jesus knew prejudice, and as our high priest sympathises: 'For we do not have a high priest who is unable to sympathise with our weaknesses, but we have one who has been tempted in every way, just as we are – yet was without sin' (Heb. 4:15).

B. Stephen

   1. *No greater man in church history than Stephen.*

      a. He was among the first deacons, and was a man 'full of faith and of the Holy Spirit' (Acts 6:5).

      b. His countenance was memorable. 'All who were sitting in the Sanhedrin looked intently at Stephen, and they saw that his face was like the face of an angel' (Acts 6:15).

   2. *This however did not stop their prejudice.*

      a. 'Then they secretly persuaded some men to say, "We have heard Stephen speak words of blasphemy against Moses and against God." So they stirred up the people and the elders and the teachers of the law. They seized Stephen and brought him before the Sanhedrin. They produced false witnesses, who testified, "This fellow never stops speaking against this holy place and against the law. For we have heard him say that this Jesus of Nazareth will destroy this place and change the customs Moses handed down to us"' (Acts 6:11-14).

b. After his brilliant defence (Acts 7:1-53), 'When they heard this, they were furious and gnashed their teeth at him. But Stephen, full of the Holy Spirit, looked up to heaven and saw the glory of God, and Jesus standing at the right hand of God. "Look," he said, "I see heaven open and the Son of Man standing at the right hand of God." At this they covered their ears and, yelling at the top of their voices, they all rushed at him, dragged him out of the city and began to stone him. Meanwhile, the witnesses laid their clothes at the feet of a young man named Saul. While they were stoning him, Stephen prayed, "Lord Jesus, receive my spirit." Then he fell on his knees and cried out, "Lord, do not hold this sin against them." When he had said this, he fell asleep' (Acts 7:54-60).

(1) It is incredible that prejudice would override such a testimony.

(2) But it eventually was overruled in Saul of Tarsus! (Acts 9:1-9).

C. Paul (see previous lesson on Jealousy).

IV. OVERCOMING PREJUDICE

A. Jephthah: prejudiced against by his family.

1. *Jephthah had many things working against him.*

a. His mother was a prostitute (Jud. 11:1).

b. His parents drove Jephthah away and he was disinherited (Jud. 11:2).

2. *And yet Jephthah earned a place in the great Faith Chapter of the Bible* (Heb. 11:32).

a. God's hand was on him and he waited for his time to come; he became a 'mighty warrior' (Jud. 11:1).

b. Israel came begging for his help – and offered him the rank of commander (Jud. 11:6).

(1) He negotiated a deal with Israel (Jud. 11:9-10).

(2) The result: Jephthah by his learning and shrewdness led Israel to an astonishing victory (Jud. 11:29-33).

c. Note: this is proof that the worst possible circumstances and background can be overcome; stay true to God and one day the very people who ignored you will come begging! 'I will make those who are of the synagogue of Satan, who claim to be Jews though they are not, but are liars – I will make them come and fall down at your feet and acknowledge that I have loved you' (Rev. 3:9).

B. Gideon: the man who was prejudiced against himself!

1. *God said to him: 'The LORD is with you, mighty warrior'* (Jud. 6:12).
  a. Gideon didn't feel like a mighty warrior; but that is the way God saw him.
  b. '"But Lord," Gideon asked, "how can I save Israel? My clan is the weakest in Manasseh, and I am the least in my family" (Jud. 6:15).

2. *God prepared Gideon one step at a time.*
  a. Then came a supernatural manifestation (Jud. 6:21-22).
  b. Gideon's famous 'fleece' (Jud. 6:36-40).
  c. Learning of the Midiantes' fear of him (Jud. 7:13-15).
  d. The eventual result: a mighty victory (Jud. 7:16-25).
    (1) Note: many of us are prejudiced against ourselves (inferiority complex).
    (2) God knows our frame and he will lead us also one step at a time.

C. Job: prejudiced against by friends.

1. *God raised up three 'friends' to tantalise Job* (Job 2:11-13).
  a. Job underwent extreme suffering (Job 1-2).
  b. Job's friends were totally convinced that Job had covered up some sin or else God wouldn't have permitted such suffering (Job 4-37).
  c. Job became extremely self-righteous in the process.

2. *Job was taken through a process that led him to complete vindication (despite his self-righteousness)* (Job 42:7-17).
  a. God stepped in and reached him (Job 38-39).
  b. Job repented (Job 42:6).
  c. He prayed for his friends (Job 42:10).

D. Peter: prejudiced against Gentiles.

1. It took a major spiritual experience to change him (Acts 10:9-20).

2. He was forced to conclude: God was no respecter of persons (Acts 10:34).

CONCLUSION

We can learn to see prejudices in our own hearts and in the hearts of others. But we can take courage in the knowledge that God can use prejudices against us for his glory. One day God will expose the folly of prejudices against himself – and will gloriously clear his own Name!

37

HOW TO OVERCOME SELF–PITY

INTRODUCTION

A. We have all fallen into the pit of self-pity; I am the world's expert!
    1. *Some, of course, are more prone to this than others; this may be due to:*
        a. Temperament and background; deprivation and childhood experiences.
        b. Satan taking advantage of any weakness, especially unbelief.
    2. *But all of us – sooner or later – find ourselves in this state.*
        a. The psalmist must have felt something of this:
            (1) 'Surely in vain have I kept my heart pure; in vain have I washed my hands in innocence. All day long I have been plagued; I have been punished every morning' (Ps. 73:13-14).
            (2) 'Will the Lord reject for ever? Will he never show his favour again? Has his unfailing love vanished for ever? Has his promise failed for all time? Has God forgotten to be merciful? Has he in anger withheld his compassion?' (Ps. 77:7-9).
        b. Self-pity sometimes sets in when God hides his face – what some call the 'dark night of the soul'.
            (1) 'How long, O LORD? Will you forget me for ever? How long will you hide your face from me?' (Ps. 13:1).
            (2) 'For troubles without number surround me; my sins have overtaken me, and I cannot see. They are more than the hairs of my head, and my heart fails within me' (Ps. 40:12).

B. Self-pity (def.): feeling sorry for yourself.
    1. I have not found any simple Greek word that encompasses what we tend to mean by self-pity.

    2. *But we know it when we see it – and we should be able to see it in ourselves; but when we are wallowing in it:*

      a. We are often unteachable and tend to deny it.

      b. We tend to justify it in any case.

C. Self-pity is a sin; it is self-righteousness.

    1. It will not do to blame one's temperament, personality or circumstances, even if these are not unrelated.

    2. *Self-pity is, at bottom, anger towards God.*

      a. We feel sorry for ourselves because God has allowed a situation that seems to make no sense.

      b. We feel sorry for ourselves because God seems to have deserted us – and there seems no way out.

        (1) It is sulking before God, almost demanding that he either explain himself or step in.

        (2) Sulking, which is anger, gets us nowhere with God. 'For the wrath of man worketh not the righteousness of God' (Jas. 1:20 AV).

    3. *But it is sin.*

      a. It is anger – toward God.

      b. It is self-righteousness – claiming it isn't fair, that we do not deserve this to have happened.

        (1) It is sometimes a case of not forgiving ourselves, which is a form of self-righteousness; it is focusing on ourselves.

        (2) If we admit to God's forgiveness but not to forgiving ourselves, it is because we are not content with his forgiveness but are trying to atone for our folly some other way.

D. Sometimes self-pity is traceable to pseudo-guilt (false guilt).

    1. True guilt: when we have sinned against God.

    2. *Pseudo-guilt: when we impose guilt on ourselves which God didn't put there.*

      a. It is charging ourselves when God doesn't.

      b. It is upstaging God, if not playing God, which is sin; a subtle form of self-righteousness.

E. Why is this study important?

1. *We all know what it is to wallow in self-pity.*
  a. It is good to know we are not alone.
  b. 'No temptation has seized you except what is common to man. And God is faithful; he will not let you be tempted beyond what you can bear. But when you are tempted, he will also provide a way out so that you can stand up under it' (1 Cor. 10:13).
    (1) Satan says: 'You are the only one to experience this.'
    (2) Satan says: 'God has forgotten you.'

2. *It will hopefully give us a better understanding of ourselves.*
  a. Socrates said: 'Know thyself.'
  b. The Bible alone leads us to true self-understanding.

3. *We need to see the subtlety of sin in self-pity:*
  a. That it is anger towards God.
  b. It is self-righteousness, self-centredness.
  c. It is also unbelief – accusing God of forgetting us.

4. *It will show that God's greatest servants have experienced this.*
  a. Not only do others experience this.
  b. But God's 'best' do as well!

5. *There is a way forward: we all can overcome self-pity.*
  a. We will see how God's servants did.
  b. If they overcame it, so can we.

I. BIBLICAL EXAMPLES

A. Jacob, focusing upon himself.

1. *When Jacob concluded that Joseph had been torn to pieces by some wild animal, he felt sorry for himself and refused help.*
  a. 'All his sons and daughters came to comfort him, but he refused to be comforted. "No," he said, "in mourning will I go down to the grave to my son." So his father wept for him' (Gen. 37:35).
  b. Self-pity is quickly identified when we don't want help.
    (1) We prefer to wallow in melancholy rather then accept a way out.
    (2) A distinguishing mark of self-pity: unteachableness.

2. *When there was a way forward Jacob blamed others rather than listen to them.*

    a. 'But Jacob said, "My son will not go down there with you; his brother is dead and he is the only one left. If harm comes to him on the journey you are taking, you will bring my grey head down to the grave in sorrow"' (Gen. 42:38).

    b. Self-pity became so self-centred in Jacob that he was insensitive to his remaining sons.

        (1) Benjamin was *not* the only one left; there were ten others!

        (2) Jacob became so defensive that he was ready to blame them for his never-ending sorrow.

B. Joseph

  1. Now in prison, having been accused of trying to rape Potiphar's wife, Joseph's self-pity emerged.

  2. 'But when all goes well with you, remember me and show me kindness; mention me to Pharaoh and get me out of this prison. For I was forcibly carried off from the land of the Hebrews, and even here I have done nothing to deserve being put in a dungeon' (Gen. 40:14-15).

    a. This was not Joseph's finest hour.

    b. It was God who put him there; it was all part of the divine strategy.

    c. Joseph *had* done wrong; he made his brothers jealous (Gen. 37:5-11).

  3. *God kept him in prison until Joseph was ready.*

    a. He had to forgive his brothers.

    b. He had to wait until nothing but God could change things.

C. Moses, focusing on the negative.

  1. He challenged God's wisdom in choosing him (Ex. 3:11).

  2. He lamented his lack of gifts (Ex. 4:10).

  3. He complained over slowness of positive results (Ex. 5:22-23).

D. Job, focusing on his personal righteousness.

  1. He cursed the day of his birth (Job 3:1-3).

  2. He challenged God to discern any fault (Job 10:2,7,14).

  3. *He also challenged his friends* (Job 13:2-3,23).

    a. He challenged God's justice (Job 27:2).

    b. He became blatantly self-righteous (Job 27:5-6).

E. David, before and after he became king.

    1. *After running from Saul for so long he came to the conclusion he would never make it.* 'But David thought to himself, "One of these days I shall be destroyed by the hand of Saul. The best thing I can do is to escape to the land of the Philistines. Then Saul will give up searching for me anywhere in Israel, and I will slip out of his hand"' (1 Sam. 27:1).

        a. He had been anointed by Samuel (1 Sam. 16:13ff).

        b. He had been reassured by Jonathan (1 Sam. 20).

    2. There was almost certainly a touch of self-pity over the failure of his attempt to bring the Ark to Jerusalem (2 Sam. 6:8-9).

    3. *He blamed himself for Absalom's death.* 'The king was shaken. He went up to the room over the gateway and wept. As he went, he said: "O my son Absalom! My son, my son Absalom! If only I had died instead of you – O Absalom, my son, my son!"' (2 Sam. 18:33).

        a. His mourning was out in the open (2 Sam. 19:1-4).

        b. Joab rebuked him, lest his self-pity cause all his men to forsake him (2 Sam. 19:7).

F. Elijah, running from Jezebel.

    1. *He prayed that he might die.* 'I have had enough, LORD. . . . Take my life; I am no better than my ancestors.' (1 Kings 19:4).

        a. Whoever thought he was better than his ancestors?

        b. This shows a fundamental flaw in Elijah's perception of himself all along.

    2. *Not only that; he perceived himself as the only true prophet left!*

        a. He said this to the angel (1 Kings 19:14).

        b. He said it before the prophets of Baal! (1 Kings 18:22).

        c. This shows another flaw in Elijah's self-understanding.

G. Naaman, when Elisha gave him instructions and refused to meet him.

    1. 'Elisha sent a messenger to say to him, "Go, wash yourself seven times in the Jordan, and your flesh will be restored and you will be cleansed" ' (2 Kings 5:10).

    2. 'But Naaman went away angry and said, "I thought that he would surely come out to me and stand and call on the name of the LORD his God, wave his hand over the spot and cure me of my leprosy. Are not Abana and Pharpar, the rivers of Damascus, better than any of the waters of Israel? Couldn't I wash in them and be cleansed?" So he turned and went off in a rage' (2 Kings 5:11-12).

H. Jeremiah, who stood alone.
1. 'O LORD, you deceived me, and I was deceived; you overpowered me and prevailed. I am ridiculed all day long; everyone mocks me' (Jer. 20:7).
2. 'Cursed be the day I was born! May the day my mother bore me not be blessed! Cursed be the man who brought my father the news, who made him very glad, saying, "A child is born to you – a son!"' (Jer. 20:14-15).

I. Jonah, who was embarrassed over his unfulfilled prophecy.
1. He clearly prophesied, 'Forty more days, and Nineveh will be overturned' (Jonah 3:4).
2. *They took Jonah seriously and repented* (Jonah 3:5-9).
   a. God had compassion on Nineveh (Jonah 3:10).
   b. Did this make Jonah happy? 'Now, O LORD, take away my life, for it is better for me to die than to live' (Jonah 4:3).

J. Some New Testament examples:
1. The man at the Pool of Bethesda, whose excuse for being an invalid for thirty-eight years was: 'I have no-one to help me into the pool when the water is stirred. While I am trying to get in, someone else goes down ahead of me' (John 5:7).
2. *Mary and Martha.*
   a. Jesus deliberately let Lazarus die; he arrived four days after the funeral.
      (1) 'When Martha heard that Jesus was coming, she went out to meet him, but Mary stayed at home' (John 11:20).
      (2) When Mary did meet him she said, 'Lord, if you had been here, my brother would not have died' (John 11:32).
   b. But Martha was capable of self-pity:
      (1) Mary sat at Jesus' feet while Martha did the work.
      (2) Martha came to him and asked, 'Lord, don't you care

that my sister has left me to do the work by myself?'
(Luke 10:40).

II. Some observations about self-pity

A. It is counter-productive.
1. This means it doesn't do any good; it gets us nowhere.
2. *It never achieves its goals; we only hurt ourselves.*
   a. Jacob seemed willing to let his family die rather than urge them to do the right thing and go to Egypt where they could get food.
   b. Job only made himself look more ridiculous by being so defensive.
      (1) Had he kept quiet, his friends would have had no further basis to accuse him.
      (2) His self-righteousness found him out.
   c. David appeared more willing to pander to his sorrow than to be the strong leader he was.
   d. Naaman risked missing one of the great miracles of the Old Testament.

B. It gives the devil a greater opportunity to walk over us and defeat us.
1. The devil loves it when we feel sorry for ourselves.
2. *It is no threat to him; he welcomes it with both hands.*
   a. Satan got nowhere as long as Job kept quiet.
   b. After Job became defensive he showed himself to be as self-righteous and self-centred as anyone else.
      (1) The tongue is so often the devil's instrument whereby the situation becomes worse then ever (Jas. 3).
      (2) The tongue not only conveys to others what we feel, but God and the angels are listening! (Ps. 39:1).
3. *The devil's aim is to get us to grieve the Holy Spirit.*
   a. It is one thing to feel sorry for ourselves.
   b. It is worse to verbalise it unless we are confessing it as a shameful sin (Jas. 5:16).
      (1) If we are complaining, it is sin.
      (2) If we are confessing it as something we are sorry about, it may be how we are set free.

385

C. It is a convenience to avoid responsibility.

    1. It is self-defeating, keeping us in a rut.

    2. It is self-deceiving, giving us a feeling that we are quite right to be in this state.

    3. *It is a convenient way of reasoning with ourselves and telling ourselves there is no way out!*

        a. Convenience (def.): that which is always accessible.

            (1) We don't need a theology course on how to feel sorry for ourselves.

            (2) No exam is needed in order to pass!

            (3) It is following a voice inside that says, 'What's the use?'

        b. The man at the Pool of Bethesda had the most convenient excuse that ever was: 'I have no-one to help me into the pool when the water is stirred' (John 5:7).

            (1) This convenience lasted thirty-eight years!

            (2) It took no effort to feel as he did.

        c. Jesus had one comment to him: 'Do you want to get well?' (John 5:6).

            (1) Self-pity is more interested in defending itself than looking for a solution.

            (2) We don't want the problem solved; we want it understood!

D. It is a choice.

    1. Jacob 'refused to be comforted' (Gen. 37:35). 'No,' he said, 'in mourning I will go down to the grave to my son.'

    2. *We may not think it fair, but it is a voluntary condition.*

        a. Rather than recognising it and resisting it, we welcome it.

        b. It is *not* a condition over which we have no control.

    3. *It is a choice we make in anger.*

        a. The ultimate object of all anger is God.

        b. We may not have thought it through at first, but our anger is toward God for allowing a situation to occur.

            (1) Faith says, 'God let this happen for a reason.'

            (2) Unbelief gives way to anger which always seems right at the time!

III. How to overcome self-pity

A. Recognise it as a sin.
   1. *When we see it as a sin we have no option but to deal with it.*
      a. As long as we see it as a temperamental weakness, we will excuse it every time.
      b. If it isn't sin, we tell ourselves, it can't be too serious.
         (1) We postpone dealing with it.
         (2) We prefer the understanding of others rather then their warnings.
   2. *When we see it as sin we must confess it* (1 John 1:9).
      a. Confessing it means saying to God, 'I'm sorry.'
      b. Confessing it to another person means 'I'm ashamed of it and I want to do something about it.'

B. Listen to those who want to help, whoever they are.
   1. *Jesus wanted to help the man at the Pool of Bethesda.*
      a. Jesus said to him, 'Get up! Pick up your mat and walk.'
      b. The man listened and was cured; he picked up his mat and walked (John 5:9).
   2. *Jacob wouldn't listen to those who wanted to help. 'All his sons and daughters came to comfort him, but he refused to be comforted'* (Gen. 37:35).
      a. Had he listened, God might have begun to speak to him as he once did.
      b. It would be another twenty-two years before Jacob had further communication with God (Gen. 46:1-2).
   3. *'Wounds from a friend can be trusted'* (Prov. 27:6).
      a. I myself was wallowing in self-justifying self-pity when Joseph Tson said, 'You must totally forgive them.'
      b. Listening to him was the best thing I ever did (with regard to the kindest but hardest word I ever received).

C. Admit that you are no better off to continue in this state.
   1. Recognise that it is a cul-de-sac, self-defeating and self-deceiving!
   2. *You are only hurting yourself, things will not change until you snap out of it.*
      a. Self-pity is a choice, coming out of it is a choice.

     b. Don't pray about it – do it!

       (1) Praying can be a cop-out.

       (2) You shouldn't pray over whether to be obedient!

D. Consider that God permitted the situation that gave rise to self-pity for a better purpose than you are allowing for.

    1. In Jacob's case, there was no objective basis for his sorrow at all – Joseph was actually alive!

    2. In any case, God's purpose was far more wonderful than Jacob dreamed! (Rom. 8:28).

CONCLUSION

Self pity is a cancer that eats at the Christian's life. Recognising it for what it is – a perverted form of self love – puts it in its sinful place. The Bible is full of important teaching on the subject. The fact that God was able to use such men as Jacob, Joseph and Job, even though at times they indulged in self-pity, should inspire us and encourage us.

38

HOW TO AVOID GREED

A. The main thing to remember about theology generally is that there is a biblical, intelligent and relevant balance between the extremes.
   1. We have seen that doctrine must be balanced by experience.
   2. *In all areas of theology we must be careful to see the need of balance – e.g.:*
      a. Jesus is God and man; the emphasis of one without the other gives a wrong impression.
      b. God is sovereign in salvation but commands us to preach the gospel to every creature.
   3. We, therefore, need to warn regarding the perils of being greedy.

B. Greed (def.): the excessive desire for more.
   1. Various Hebrew words denote greed: covetousness, dishonest or unjust gain.
   2. The Greek *pleonexia* essentially means wanting more, used ten times in the New Testament.
      a. It is translated 'greed'; *pleonektes* (greedy) is used four times in the New Testament.
      b. It is translated 'covetousness' or 'covetous' in the AV.
      c. In ancient Hellenistic literature it often signified an excessive longing for food or wealth:
         (1) Hungry for power.
         (2) To take a greater share.
         (3) To seek aggrandisement (increase of wealth or importance).
         (4) To outdo in something.
         (5) To forge ahead at the expense of others.
   3. It is the opposite of contentment (being satisfied with what one has).

4. *It is regarded by God as serious sin.*
  a. Jesus put it alongside sexual immorality and murder (Mark 7:21-22).
  b. Paul put it alongside sexual sin, robbery and drunkenness (1 Cor. 6:9-10. cf. Rom. 1:29).

C. Why is this subject important?

1. The less greedy we are, the more we will recognise good theology and put it into practice.
2. It is a warning to those who uphold the 'prosperity gospel' or 'health and wealth gospel'.
3. It focuses on how God regards greed.
4. It should help us to see our own greed and what we can do about it.

I. GREED IN THE OLD TESTAMENT

A. The tenth commandment: 'You shall not covet your neighbour's house. You shall not covet your neighbour's wife, or his manservant or maidservant, his ox or donkey, or anything that belongs to your neighbour' (Ex. 20:17).

1. *The apostle Paul felt good about himself with regard to the first nine commandments.*
  a. It was when he analysed the command 'You shall not covet' that he realised what a sinner he was (Rom. 7:7-11).
  b. We might keep the nine commandments so that we appear blameless to others.
  c. The tenth commandment makes us see what we are in our hearts – that we are guilty of breaking those commandments we thought we had kept.
2. *Greed, therefore, is a condition of the heart.*
  a. It must be brought under control or it will destroy us.
  b. Many of the Old Testament laws were given in order that man's greed should not destroy himself or others, e.g.:
    (1) 'Do not go over your vineyard a second time or pick up the grapes that have fallen. Leave them for the poor and the alien. I am the LORD your God' (Lev. 19:10).
    (2) 'Do not defraud your neighbour or rob him. Do not hold back the wages of a hired man overnight' (Lev. 19:13).

(3) 'Do not use dishonest standards when measuring length, weight or quantity. Use honest scales and honest weights, an honest ephah and an honest hin. I am the LORD your God, who brought you out of Egypt' (Lev. 9:35-36).

B. The sin of greed was intolerable in the priesthood.

1. *The sons of Eli 'had no regard for the LORD.'* (1 Sam. 2:12).

    a. The sacrifices were to be cooked before being eaten.

    b. A practice developed whereby the priests, to keep more meat for themselves, would take a three-pronged fork and plunge it into the pan or kettle and keep whatever the fork brought up (1 Sam. 2:13–14).

        (1) 'But even before the fat was burned, the servant of the priest would come and say to the man who was sacrificing, "Give the priest some meat to roast; he won't accept boiled meat from you, but only raw"' (1 Sam. 2:15).

        (2) 'If the man said to him, "Let the fat be burned up first, and then take whatever you want," the servant would then answer, "No, hand it over now; if you don't, I'll take it by force"' (1 Sam. 2:16).

2. *This was sin these priests were getting away with, but the Lord took notice;* they were 'treating the Lord's offering with contempt' (1 Sam. 2:17).

    a. God held Eli responsible for what his sons were doing.

    b. Their sin was greed. 'Why do you scorn my sacrifice and offering that I prescribed for my dwelling? Why do you honour your sons more than me by fattening yourselves on the choice parts of every offering made by my people Israel?' (1 Sam 2:29).

        (1) God decreed their death and the end of Eli's house (1 Sam. 2:31-36).

        (2) After their death the wife of one of the priests gave birth to a son she named Ichabod ('No glory'), saying, 'The glory has departed from Israel' (1 Sam. 4:21).

C. Jeremiah regarded the greediness of the people as a principal cause of their decline and impending subjectivity to Babylon.

1. 'From the least to the greatest, all are greedy for gain; prophets and priests alike, all practise deceit' (Jer. 6:13).

2. 'Therefore I will give their wives to other men and their fields to new owners. From the least to the greatest, all are greedy for gain; prophets and priests alike, all practise deceit' (Jer. 8:10. cf. Jer. 22:17).

    a. Greed is a serious sin in God's sight.

        (1) We all think we will get away with it.

        (2) God takes notice; it is only a matter of time before it will catch up with us.

    b. 'I was enraged by his sinful greed; I punished him, and hid my face in anger, yet he kept on in his wilful ways' (Isa. 57:17).

        (1) God warns, we continue on.

        (2) But there will be 'pay day, some day.'

        (3) 'A greedy man brings trouble to his family' (Prov. 15:27).

        (4) 'I gave you over to the greed of your enemies' (Ezek. 16:27).

        (5) 'These men lie in wait for their own blood; they waylay only themselves! Such is the end of all who go after ill-gotten gain; it takes away the lives of those who get it' (Prov. 1:18-19).

II. GREED IN THE NEW TESTAMENT

A. What Jesus said about greed.

1. It is set alongside the worst sins. 'For from within, out of men's hearts, come evil thoughts, sexual immorality, theft, murder, adultery, greed, malice, deceit, lewdness, envy, slander, arrogance and folly' (Mark 7:21-22).

2. *We should beware of 'all kinds of greed' because our life does not consist in the abundance of possessions* (Luke 12:15).

    a. He gave the parable of the rich fool (Luke 12:16-21).

    b. The one who was greedy and felt he would live on and on was suddenly called to account: 'But God said to him, "You fool! This very night your life will be demanded from you. Then who will get what you have prepared for yourself?" This is how it will be with anyone who stores up things for himself but is not rich towards God' (Luke 12:20-21).

B. What Paul said about greed.
  1. He placed it alongside the sins of those God had given over to a depraved mind (a mind devoid of judgement) (Rom. 1:28-29).
  2. He warned that we should not keep company with greedy people (1 Cor. 5:10-11).
  3. *The greedy will not have an inheritance in God's kingdom* (1 Cor. 6:9-10). *This means two things:*
    a. God will not use the greedy effectively in the Kingdom.
    b. The greedy will receive no reward at the Judgement Seat of Christ.
  4. There should not be even a hint of greed among God's people (Eph. 5:3. cf. Col. 3:5).

C. Peter said that greed was the earmark of the false teachers who tried to influence God's people for evil (2 Pet. 2:3. cf. Jude 11).
  1. These men were 'experts in greed' (2 Pet. 2:14).
  2. They were like Balaam, the false prophet who 'loved the wages of wickedness' (Num. 22-24. cf. Rev. 2:14).

III. THE RESULT OF GREED: THE OPPOSITE TO BEING CONTROLLED BY THE HOLY SPIRIT

A. Regarding time
  1. *With greed, we never have enough time* (Ps. 37:7).
    a. The tendency is to panic to get things done.
      (1) Irritability – impatience with others.
      (2) Fear – of not meeting deadlines.
    b. The fear of not accomplishing goals.
      (1) Generally, that life is passing us by; we are not seeing things happen as we thought we would.
      (2) Particularly, that there is 'too much on our plate'.
  2. *With the Holy Spirit, we know we do have enough time* (Ecc. 3:1-11).
    a. There is no need to panic; we will get done what God has ordained to get done by us (Ps. 90:10-12).
      (1) A sweet spirit prevails; we are easy to have around.
      (2) There is faith that God has given us all the time we need.

b. There is contentment with life (Is. 26:3).

  (1) We know God will accomplish in us what he has raised us up for and has been preparing us for.

  (2) We take one day at a time; our strength will be equal to our days (Deut. 33:25).

B. Regarding money

1. *With greed, we never have enough* (1 Tim. 6:10).

  a. We justify all our wishes and call them needs.

  (1) Result: pride of life (1 John 2:15-16).

  (2) We become obsessed with material things.

  b. The fear is that we will never have enough (1 Tim. 6:9).

  (1) We have set goals for ourselves that God didn't set.

  (2) The result: continual frustration and the desire for more and more.

2. *With the Holy Spirit, we are content with what we have* (1 Tim. 6:6).

  a. We come to terms with our true needs.

  (1) We know God will always supply our needs (Phil. 4:19).

  (2) Therefore we realise that what we do not have we did not really need after all.

  b. The Holy Spirit whets our appetite for valid desires (Ps. 37:4).

  (1) We find our interest in things that previously did not charm us – more anointing, more love.

  (2) The peace of the Holy Spirit compensates for everything (Phil. 4:7).

C. Regarding relationships

1. *With greed, we crave to know people God has not intended for us* (Gen. 34:1ff).

  a. The tendency is to seek out the wrong kind of people.

  (1) Those who have money, so we can feel we are moving in higher circles.

  (2) Those who are well known, so we can feel prestigious and can 'name drop'.

  b. The root of much sexual immorality is not being content with where we are or who we are; e.g.:

  (1) Looking for an extra-marital relationship (2 Sam. 11:1-5).

  (2) Justifying our sin because of a bad situation where we are.

2. *With the Holy Spirit, we allow him to choose our friends and arrange events for us to find them* (Ps. 37:23).

    a. The Holy Spirit knows the type of people who are right and best for us (Jer. 29:11).

        (1) Their monetary or social standing will not be the governing motivation.

        (2) God wants us to know people, and to have mutually beneficial friendships.

    b. The Holy Spirit will never lead us to a relationship with the opposite sex that is unbiblical (Gal. 5:16).

        (1) The Holy Spirit will lead us to those we will bless and make feel at ease, when there is no 'angle' in the developing relationship.

        (2) The Holy Spirit will provide a relationship where there is godly freedom; where the Spirit of the Lord is, there is liberty (2 Cor. 3:17).

D. Regarding ambition

1. *Ambitious for position.*

    a. With greed, we want a job beyond the level of our competence. Illustration: the Peter Principle.

        (1) If we got it, we wouldn't know how to cope.

        (2) This is what causes fatigue, nervous breakdowns, bitterness.

    b. With the Holy Spirit, we want him to do the promoting (Ps. 75:6-7).

        (1) The Lord never promotes us to the level of our incompetence.

        (2) We will be at ease – at home – with the position to which he himself has called us.

2. *Ambitious for knowledge.*

    a. With greed, we are not content with what we know.

        (1) We become insatiable and frustrated.

        (2) We are always learning but never able to affirm the truth (2 Tim. 3:7).

    b. God has promised to fill those who hunger and thirst for righteousness (Matt. 5:6).

        (1) It is good to have a desire to know more and more of God and about God.

    (2) But if we are obedient we will always know exactly what he wants us to know (2 Pet. 1:8. cf. Phile. 6).

  3. *Ambitious for recognition.*

    a. With greed, we are insatiable in wanting people to like us.

      (1) We will go to great pains to be liked and known as a good person.

      (2) We will find ourselves not being true to ourselves, going over the top to be seen and known.

    b. With the Holy Spirit, we want God to control what is thought of us (2 Cor. 12:6).

      (1) Our real concern: what does God think of me?

      (2) Best advice: be gripped by, 'How can you believe if you accept praise from one another, yet make no effort to obtain the praise that comes from the only God?' (John 5:44).

E. The melancholy effects of greed

  1. *Sheer frustration – night and day.*

    a. Whether it be with regard to time, money, unfulfilled ambition – whatever – one is, simply, not a happy person.

    b. The only answer: a quest for true godliness. 'But godliness with contentment is great gain. For we brought nothing into the world, and we can take nothing out of it. But if we have food and clothing, we will be content with that' (1 Tim. 6:6-8).

      (1) The Holy Spirit never leads us to sin. 'So I say, live by the Spirit, and you will not gratify the desires of the sinful nature' (Gal. 5:16).

      (2) The fruit of the Spirit is the answer. 'But the fruit of the Spirit is love, joy, peace, patience, kindness, goodness, faithfulness, gentleness and self-control. Against such things there is no law. Those who belong to Christ Jesus have crucified the sinful nature with its passions and desires' (Gal. 5:22-24).

  2. *Marriage breakdown.*

    a. We will be preoccupied with our personal goals and ambitions – and forget what is essential.

      (1) Time with God goes down the drain.

      (2) Time with family takes second place.

b. The Holy Spirit shows us our priorities.

   (1) To love our spouses.

   (2) The happiest marriage: when the husband and wife love God more than they love each other. They end up loving each other more than ever.

3. *Playing the lottery.*

   a. Greed lies behind the lottery; it would fail overnight if all citizens became Spirit-filled Christians.

   b. Rule Number One for every Christian: never play the lottery or buy anything that offers hope of making quick money.

4. *Arrested development in spiritual growth.* 'The one who received the seed that fell among the thorns is the man who hears the word, but the worries of this life and the deceitfulness of wealth choke it, making it unfruitful' (Matt. 13:22).

   a. Riches are 'deceitful'.

   b. Those who seek such end up in disaster. 'People who want to get rich fall into temptation and a trap and into many foolish and harmful desires that plunge men into ruin and destruction' (1 Tim. 6:9).

5. *Neglect of poor.*

   a. Those in the early church who welcomed only prestigious people to church neglected the poor (James 2:1-6).

   b. The Holy Spirit is always prejudiced for the poor and to those who are truly spiritual the poor will be a priority. 'Religion that God our Father accepts as pure and faultless is this: to look after orphans and widows in their distress and to keep oneself from being polluted by the world' (Jas. 1:27).

CONCLUSION

There is one kind of greed, or covetousness, that the Holy Spirit welcomes: 'But eagerly desire [AV – covet earnestly] the greater gifts. And now I will show you the most excellent way' (1 Cor. 12:31). There follows the best way to show our desire for the greater gifts: the quest for love (1 Cor. 13). The more we seek to love, the less greedy we will be!

39

WOULD GOD TELL US TO LIE?

A. This question must – on the surface – appear to be the most ridiculous question ever asked!

1. Would God tell us to do what he has already forbidden?
2. If we are to be godly, and that means being like God who does not lie, would God ask us to lie?

B. Why deal with this subject?

1. *There are sovereign vessels in the Bible who not only appeared to lie but were none the worse for it.*
   a. Not only were they not punished.
   b. Not only were they no worse off.
   c. They seemed to be blessed.
   d. They seemed to be commended, especially Rahab (Jas. 2:25).
2. *People are sometimes put in awkward situations in which telling the whole truth could be hurtful if not damaging.*
   a. People could be hurt if the truth were known.
   b. Do you tell a lie to keep a person from being hurt?
3. *The Bible nowhere tells us to be dishonest; on the contrary, we are admonished to be honest.* 'Therefore each of you must put off falsehood and speak truthfully to his neighbour, for we are all members of one body' (Eph. 4:25).
   a. 'Honesty is the best policy,' as it is often said.
   b. A person who tells the truth doesn't have to have a good memory (that is, to remember what lie he told and to whom).
   c. Jesus said, 'Then you will know the truth, and the truth will set you free' (John 8:32).
4. *The matter of truth, truthfulness and honesty is apparently perishing from the earth.*
   a. This is seen in business, government and many institutions.
   b. Should not the church stand tall by upholding the truth, thereby standing against the trend of the times?

5. *'Situation ethics' is a concept that was particularly popularised in the 1960's, threatening traditional moral values.*
   a. Some people made a case for breaking any of the Ten Commandments under certain circumstances – depending on the 'situation'.
   b. If God would ever tell a person to lie, is this not playing right into the proposition posed by situation ethics?
6. *Some people are extremely conscientious and fear the wrath of God on them for the slightest deviation from his high standard.*
   a. Is this healthy? Is this Christian maturity?
   b. Should not the person with an overly scrupulous conscience be commended?
   c. Or is there another way to look at some of these things without grieving the Holy Spirit or compromising the eternal standards of Holy Scripture?

C. Definitions
   1. Truth: what is genuine, faithful and in accordance with fact.
   2. Lie: a statement known to be false made with intent to deceive.
   3. Promise: the declaration that one will do or not do a certain thing, sometimes subject to certain conditions.
   4. Oath: a solemn undertaking to do something, appealing to a greater witness – e.g. God.

I. INTEGRITY AND THE BIBLE

A. The integrity of Scripture
   1. 'All Scripture is God-breathed and is useful for teaching, rebuking, correcting and training in righteousness' (2 Tim. 3:16).
   2. 'Above all, you must understand that no prophecy of Scripture came about by the prophet's own interpretation. For prophecy never had its origin in the will of man, but men spoke from God as they were carried along by the Holy Spirit' (2 Pet. 1:20-21).
   3. 'Heaven and earth will pass away, but my words will never pass away' (Matt. 24:35).
   4. 'Jesus answered, "My teaching is not my own. It comes from him who sent me"' (John 7:16).

5. 'The Scripture cannot be broken' (John 10:35).
6. 'I tell you the truth, until heaven and earth disappear, not the smallest letter, not the least stroke of a pen, will by any means disappear from the Law until everything is accomplished. Anyone who breaks one of the least of these commandments and teaches others to do the same will be called least in the kingdom of heaven, but whoever practices and teaches these commands will be called great in the kingdom of heaven' (Matt. 5:18-19).
7. 'All your commands are true' (Ps. 119:151).
8. 'Your word, O LORD, is eternal; it stands firm in the heavens' (Ps. 119:89).
9. 'And the words of the LORD are flawless, like silver refined in a furnace of clay, purified seven times' (Ps. 12:6).
10. 'Man does not live on bread alone but on every word that comes from the mouth of the LORD' (Deut. 8:3).

B. The integrity of God
1. God 'does not lie' (Titus 1:2).
2. 'God did this so that, by two unchangeable things in which it is impossible for God to lie, we who have fled to take hold of the hope offered to us may be greatly encouraged' (Heb. 6:18).
   a. What are the two unchangeable things? (1) Promise. (2) Oath.
   b. Either of these is backed by God's integrity.
3. 'I the LORD do not change' (Mal. 3:6).
4. 'He who is the Glory of Israel does not lie or change his mind; for he is not a man, that he should change his mind' (1 Sam. 15:29).
5. 'God, who has called you into fellowship with his Son Jesus Christ our Lord, is faithful' (1 Cor. 1:9).

C. The command for people to be truthful.
1. *Two of the Ten Commandments touch on this.*
   a. 'You shall not misuse the name of the LORD your God, for the LORD will not hold anyone guiltless who misuses his name' (Ex. 20:7).
      (1) This does not primarily refer to bad language.
      (2) This refers to swearing by God's name when making a promise (or declaring what is true) and one being insincere.

b. 'You shall not give false testimony against your neighbour' (Ex. 20:16).

(1) This primarily refers to being a witness in a court of law.

(2) The punishment for being a false witness was severe. 'If the witness proves to be a liar, giving false testimony against his brother, then do to him as he intended to do to his brother. You must purge the evil from among you. The rest of the people will hear of this and be afraid, and never again will such an evil thing be done among you. Show no pity: life for life, eye for eye, tooth for tooth, hand for hand, foot for foot' (Deut. 19:18-21).

c. It could be argued that both of these commands refer not to everyday conversation but to the oath.

(1) People appeal to the oath when they are afraid they won't be believed.

(2) In a court of law the oath is assumed.

(3) The warning was to one who broke the oath. 'When a man makes a vow to the LORD or takes an oath to obligate himself by a pledge, he must not break his word but must do everything he said' (Num. 30:2).

2. *Although the Law may have primarily referred to keeping one's oath, everyday honesty and integrity were assumed as the way godly people behaved.*

a. 'Here I stand. Testify against me in the presence of the LORD and his anointed. Whose ox have I taken? Whose donkey have I taken? Whom have I cheated? Whom have I oppressed? From whose hand have I accepted a bribe to make me shut my eyes? If I have done any of these, I will make it right' (1 Sam. 12:3).

b. 'They did not require an accounting from those to whom they gave the money to pay the workers, because they acted with complete honesty' (2 Kings 12:15. cf. 2 Kings 22:7).

c. 'The integrity of the upright guides them, but the unfaithful are destroyed by their duplicity' (Prov. 11:3).

d. 'Better a poor man whose walk is blameless than a fool whose lips are perverse' (Prov. 19:1).

3. *In the New Testament this behaviour continued to be assumed among believers.*

a. Jesus said, 'But I tell you, Do not swear at all: either by heaven, for it is God's throne; or by the earth, for it is his footstool; or by Jerusalem, for it is the city of the Great King. And do not swear by your head, for you cannot make even one hair white or black. Simply let your 'Yes' be 'Yes,' and your 'No,' 'No'; anything beyond this comes from the evil one' (Matt. 5:34-37).

(1) It would seem that people under the Law could not always be trusted to tell the truth – unless they swore an oath.

(2) Jesus is saying that his followers need not swear they are telling the truth every time they open their mouths, they should tell the truth anyway.

b. 'Finally, brothers, whatever is true, whatever is noble, whatever is right, whatever is pure, whatever is lovely, whatever is admirable – if anything is excellent or praiseworthy – think about such things' (Phil. 4:8).

c. 'Therefore each of you must put off falsehood and speak truthfully to his neighbour, for we are all members of one body' (Eph. 4:25).

d. 'But I tell you that men will have to give account on the day of judgment for every careless word they have spoken' (Matt. 12:36).

D. The warning regarding lying.

1. *Aggravated forms of lying.*

a. That which perpetuates a fraud, such as deceiving one's neighbour about something trusted or left in one's care – 'or if he cheats him' – or 'finds lost property and lies about it, or if he swears falsely. . . and becomes guilty. . . he must make restitution in full, add a fifth of the value to it' (Lev. 6:1-5).

b. That which secures a false condemnation (see above) (Deut. 19:16).

c. Testimony of false prophets (Jer. 14:14).

d. A false witness (Prov. 6:19).

e. 'Better be poor than a liar' (Prov. 19:22).

f. The Lord hates 'a lying tongue' (Prov. 6:17).

2. *In the New Testament*

a. 'Do not lie to each other, since you have taken off your old self with its practices' (Col. 3:9).

b. Jesus said that Satan is the father of lies (John 8:44).

c. Ananias and Sapphira were struck dead for lying to the Holy Spirit (Acts 5:1-11).

d. 'Who is the liar? It is the man who denies that Jesus is the Christ. Such a man is the antichrist – he denies the Father and the Son' (1 John 2:22).

e. All liars have their place in the 'fiery lake of burning sulphur' (Rev. 21:8).

f. Anyone who does what is 'deceitful' will be kept out of the New Jerusalem (Rev. 21:27).

II. PEOPLE OF GOD WHO LIED

A. Abraham lied about his wife, claiming she was his sister.

1. Abraham told Sarah to lie (Gen. 12:13).

2. Abraham said the same thing of Sarah again (Gen. 20:2).

3. However, there was a further clarification. 'Besides, she really is my sister, the daughter of my father though not of my mother; and she became my wife' (Gen. 20:12).

B. Isaac did the same thing (Gen. 26:7).

1. He too was found out and was also treated mercifully.

2. His rationale: 'I thought I might lose my life' (Gen. 26:9).

C. Jacob deliberately lied to his father.

1. 'Jacob said to his father, "I am Esau your firstborn. I have done as you told me. Please sit up and eat some of my game so that you may give me your blessing"' (Gen. 27:19).

2. Esau is called 'godless' (Heb. 12:16).

3. God said, 'I have loved Jacob, but Esau I have hated' (Mal. 1:2-3).

D. Rahab (Josh. 2)

1. *This is probably the case we most readily think of when dealing with our present subject.*

a. Joshua sent two spies to Jericho.

b. They ended up in the house of a prostitute named Rahab.

c. The King of Jericho ordered a search of Rahab's house.

d. Her reply: 'But the woman had taken the two men and hidden them. She said, "Yes, the men came to me, but I did not know where they had come from. At dusk, when it was time to close the city gate, the men left. I don't know which way they went. Go after them quickly. You may catch up with them." (But she had taken them up to the roof and hidden them under the stalks of flax she had laid out on the roof.) So the men set out in pursuit of the spies on the road that leads to the fords of the Jordan, and as soon as the pursuers had gone out, the gate was shut' (Jos. 2:4-7).

e. Her rationale for this deception was stated to the two spies: 'I know that the LORD has given this land to you' (Josh. 2:8).

f. She made a plea to the spies: 'Now then, please swear to me by the LORD that you will show kindness to my family, because I have shown kindness to you. Give me a sure sign that you will spare the lives of my father and mother, my brothers and sisters, and all who belong to them, and that you will save us from death" ' (Jos. 2:12-13).

g. The spies agreed to her plea. '"Our lives for your lives!" the men assured her. "If you don't tell what we are doing, we will treat you kindly and faithfully when the LORD gives us the land" ' (Jos. 2:14).

h. She enabled them to escape (Josh. 2:15-16).

i. The ultimate result: She was spared when the Israelites conquered Jericho (Josh. 6:25).

2. *Rahab is mentioned in the New Testament.*

a. The Messianic line is traced through her (Matt. 1:5).

b. She is mentioned in the great 'faith' chapter in the Bible. 'By faith the prostitute Rahab, because she welcomed the spies, was not killed with those who were disobedient' (Heb. 11:31).

(1) Her lie to the King of Jericho is not explicitly mentioned.

(2) She is said to have acted in faith by welcoming the spies.

c. James implicitly mentions her deceit and commends this. 'In the same way, was not even Rahab the prostitute considered righteous for what she did when she gave lodging to the spies and sent them off in a different direction?' (Jas. 2:25)

(1) Her sending the spies off in a different direction refers to her deceit, although it is not mentioned explicitly.

(2) In any case, she is 'considered righteous for what she did.'

(3) What she did: lied.

3. *God did not tell Rahab to lie; this must not be forgotten.*

   a. What she did, she did on her own.

   b. But after it was done, it is rather obvious:

      (1) She greatly encouraged Joshua; increasing his faith (Josh. 2:24).

      (2) She saved her own life as well as the lives of her family (Josh. 6:25).

      (3) She is said to have acted 'by faith' (Heb. 11:31).

      (4) She was 'considered righteous for what she did' (Jas. 2:25).

   c. Was she not justified for lying? James uses Rahab's ordeal as an example of what he calls justification by deeds (cf. Jas. 2:21).

      (1) John the Baptist said, 'A man can receive only what is given him from heaven' (John 3:27).

      (2) What Rahab was given: faith to do what she did.

      (3) Did this not come from God?

      (4) Although she acted on her own was she not under an anointing of the Spirit?

E. Samuel was instructed to go to the house of Jesse to anoint David as the next king – although Saul was still wearing the crown (1 Sam. 16:1).

   1. Samuel's reaction: 'But Samuel said, "How can I go? Saul will hear about it and kill me." The LORD said, "Take a heifer with you and say, 'I have come to sacrifice to the LORD'"' (1 Sam. 16:2).

   2. *The Lord did not tell Samuel to lie, rather he had to withhold the entire truth for the time being.* 'Invite Jesse to the sacrifice, and I will show you what to do. You are to anoint for me the one I indicate' (1 Sam. 16:3).

      a. This was the Lord's own word – not to divulge the real purpose of the visit at first.

      b. This was not lying but concealing the whole truth.

F. Jonathan deliberately lied to his father, King Saul (1 Sam. 20).

   1. *Jonathan and David made a covenant.*

      a. Both knew that Saul was determined to kill David.

     b. Jonathan swore an oath to protect David (1 Sam. 20:16-17).

2. *Although David was hiding in a field, Jonathan claimed that David was in Bethlehem.*

     a. The King asked of David's whereabouts (1 Sam. 20:27).

     b. 'Jonathan answered, "David earnestly asked me for permission to go to Bethlehem. He said, 'Let me go, because our family is observing a sacrifice in the town and my brother has ordered me to be there. If I have found favour in your eyes, let me get away to see my brothers.' That is why he has not come to the king's table'" (1 Sam. 20:28-29).

3. *Note: Jonathan swore an oath to David but not to his father.*

     a. There is nothing, strictly speaking, Jonathan did wrong according to the Law.

       (1) There was no oath to Saul.

       (2) Jonathan was not a witness in a court of law.

     b. Jonathan kept his oath to David.

4. *It apparently saved David's life at the time.*

     a. God did not tell Jonathan to lie.

     b. But what he did was to preserve the man who had been anointed by Samuel and who was a man after God's 'own heart' (1 Sam. 13:14).

     c. One concludes that what Jonathan did was right.

G. David pretended to be insane before Achish, King of Gath.

1. He fled to Achish to escape Saul.

2. *David could see that Achish was suspicious.*

     a. Achish had heard too much about David! (1 Sam. 21:11).

     b. David suddenly feared for his life. 'So he pretended to be insane in their presence; and while he was in their hands he acted like a madman, making marks on the doors of the gate and letting saliva run down his beard' (1 Sam. 21:13).

3. This was not verbal lying or going against an oath but none the less was deliberate deceit on David's part.

4. It worked; it saved his life. 'Achish said to his servants, "Look at the man! He is insane! Why bring him to me? Am I so short of madmen that you have to bring this fellow here to carry on like this in front of me? Must this man come into my house?"' (1 Sam. 21:14-15).

a. God did not tell David to do this.

b. And yet he had the presence of mind – almost certainly traceable to his anointing – to do this.

H. David's return to Jerusalem after his exile was ensured by a lie.

1. Ahithophel, whose advice was 'like that of one who inquires of God' (2 Sam. 16:23), had sided with Absalom (2 Sam. 15:12, 31).

2. *This was devastating news for David who prayed, 'O Lord, turn Ahithophel's counsel into foolishness'* (2 Sam. 15:31).

   a. Ahithophel gave counsel to Absalom that probably was militarily wise and would have kept Absalom in power (2 Sam. 17:1-3).

   b. Just before acting upon Ahithophel's advice Absalom turned to Hushai – who actually lied to Absalom twice:

   (1) First, he claimed to be on Absalom's side when in fact he was David's true friend (2 Sam. 16:18).

   (2) He later said to Absalom, 'The advice Ahithophel has given is not good this time' and counselled Absalom to take a course that led directly to his downfall (2 Sam. 17:7-13; 18:1-15).

   (3) The upshot was: 'Absalom and all the men of Israel said, "The advice of Hushai the Arkite is better than that of Ahithophel." For the Lord had determined to frustrate the good advice of Ahithophel in order to bring disaster on Absalom' (2 Sam. 17:14).

3. *It is noteworthy that the Lord determined to frustrate the advice of Ahithophel.*

   a. God did not order Hushai to lie.

   b. But it was none the less the way God apparently answered David's prayer.

I. God apparently permitted a subterfuge (a trick to avoid blame) in order that his righteous judgment be enacted upon Ahab.

1. A 'spirit' came forward and stood before the Lord and proceeded to lure Ahab by being a lying spirit in the mouths of all his prophets (1 Kings 22:22).

2. God said, 'Go and do it.' 'So now the Lord has put a lying spirit in the mouths of all these prophets of yours. The Lord has decreed disaster for you' (1 Kings 22:23).

III. Some observations about those who lied

A. God never ordered anybody to tell a lie.
1. *Jacob, though loved by God, followed his mother Rebekah's idea to lie to Isaac, who was by then blind* (Gen. 27:1-17).
    a. Rebekah was told prophetically that Esau would be subservient to Jacob (Gen. 25:23).
    b. She apparently felt she had to make this prophecy happen.
        (1) Who knows what would have ensued had Jacob not lied?
        (2) The lie only appears to be justified.
2. *Rahab did what she did to save her own skin as well as that of her family.*
    a. Her faith was that she saw how God was with Israel.
    b. Her lie in this case was the result of that faith.
    c. But she acted on her own.
3. Samuel was not ordered to lie but not tell all he was doing.
4. *Jonathan followed the 'lesser of two evils'.*
    a. He lied to his father – but not under oath.
    b. He kept his oath to David.
5. David saved his own life by feigning insanity – which he did on his own.
6. Hushai was not under oath when he lied to Absalom – who virtually upstaged David for a time.

B. None of the people of God who lied broke the oath.
1. *The Law was predominantly concerned with a person's truthfulness under oath.*
    a. This may well have led to people feeling the need to swear an oath nearly every time they opened their mouths.
    b. Lying not under oath, unless it had to do with another's property, was not severely punished (Cf. Lev. 6:1-7).
2. Rahab's lie did not break the Mosaic Law.
3. None of those covered above broke the Mosaic Law.

C. The New Testament presents a much higher standard than that of the Law (cf. Matt. 5:34; Eph. 4:25; Col. 3:9).
1. We are to speak the truth all the time without the oath.
2. What was oath level honesty in the Old Testament becomes everyday honesty for the Christian.

D. Question: is there any justification for a Christian telling a lie?

1. Under oath in a court of law, no.

2. *We can imagine some instances in which God would not hold us responsible for lying.*

    a. To protect another person's life or possessions.

    b. To protect another person's reputation.

    c. To preserve another person's peace of mind.

    d. To protect one's own life or possessions from danger.

        (1) I myself was mugged in Green Park a few years ago.

        (2) They asked for my credit cards; I said, 'I don't have any on me, only this fiver.' (Fortunately, they didn't take my wallet but only the fiver I handed over.)

CONCLUSION

One day every secret will be revealed (Matt. 10:26ff; Rom. 2:16). But that is not entirely true! 'As far as the east is from the west, so far has he removed our transgressions from us' (Ps. 103:12). The blood of Christ overrules the word about all secrets being revealed.

God may have other principles – not clear to us now – by which he leads and judges the affairs of men and women. '"For my thoughts are not your thoughts, neither are your ways my ways," declares the LORD. "As the heavens are higher than the earth, so are my ways higher than your ways and my thoughts than your thoughts"' (Isa. 55:8-9). As Abraham put it, 'Will not the Judge of all the earth do right?' (Gen. 18:25).

40

DO WE MAKE GOD'S PROMISES HAPPEN?

<small>INTRODUCTION</small>

A. The Bible is God's integrity on the line.
1. *He claims it to be his own Word.*
   a. The New Testament claims this for the Old Testament.
   (1) 'All Scripture is God-breathed and is useful for teaching, rebuking, correcting and training in righteousness' (2 Tim. 3:16).
   (2) 'Above all, you must understand that no prophecy of Scripture came about by the prophet's own interpretation. For prophecy never had its origin in the will of man, but men spoke from God as they were carried along by the Holy Spirit' (2 Pet. 1:20-21).
   b. The New Testament claims this for itself.
   (1) 'If anybody thinks he is a prophet or spiritually gifted, let him acknowledge that what I am writing to you is the Lord's command' (1 Cor. 14:37).
   (2) 'He [Paul] writes the same way in all his letters, speaking in them of these matters. His letters contain some things that are hard to understand, which ignorant and unstable people distort, as they do the other Scriptures, to their own destruction' (2 Peter 3:16).
2. *God magnifies his Word above all his name* (Ps. 138:2 AV).
   a. He certainly magnifies his name, which refers basically to:
   (1) Reputation (Josh. 2:8-11).
   (2) Power (Ex. 15:1-18).
   b. He regards his personal integrity to be of greater importance than his power and reputation.
   (1) He cares more about what he says than what people say about him.
   (2) He has avowed: he cannot lie (Titus 1:2; Heb. 6:18).

B. The contents of the Bible could be summarised like this (cf. Luke 24:44).

    1. *History.*

        a. Genesis: account of Creation and the Fall.

        b. Exodus: account of Israel's emancipation from Egypt.

        c. Books which depict the rise of the kingship and the prophets, as well as Israel's history.

    2. *The Law: moral, civil, ceremonial.*

        a. Giving of the Law at Sinai.

        b. Detailed rules of the Law.

    3. *The worship of God.*

        a. Ceremonial Law, e.g. Leviticus.

        b. The praise of God, e.g. Psalms.

    4. *The promises of God.*

        a. Some are attached to the Mosaic Law.

        b. Some come from the prophets, called prophecy.

C. Definitions:

    1. Promises of God: what he says he will do.

    2. *Prophecy: what God claims through the mouth of a prophet.*

        a. It may refer to present or past situations.

        b. It may refer to the future.

    3. Making promises happen: making sure that what God promised truly comes to pass.

D. Why is this study important?

    1. With the rise of the prophetic in recent years, the question arises whether or not a prophetic word is reliable without our help.

    2. With the desire for people to be healed, do we require the sick person to be responsible for his or her divine healing?

    3. With a widespread hope for Revival, can we hasten it?

    4. We need to face openly the danger of overclaiming and hype that Revival is here or there.

    5. We need to examine the nature of a promise from God.

    6. We need to see the difference between the promise and the oath.

    7. The sovereignty and power of God are at stake in this issue.

I. THE PROMISES OF GOD

A. The kinds of things promised.
    1. Health (Prov. 3:8).
    2. Prosperity (Prov. 3:2).
    3. Longevity (Ex. 20:12. cf. Prov. 3:2).
    4. Usefulness (Prov. 2:6-7. cf. 2 Tim. 2:21).
    5. Protection (Prov. 2:8).
    6. Guidance (Prov. 3:6).
    7. Eternal life (John 3:16).
    8. Inheritance or reward (1 Cor. 3:14).
    9. Spirit of glory (1 Pet. 4:14).
    10. The Holy Spirit (John 14:16; Luke 11:13).
    11. God's rest (Heb. 4:1-11).
    12. Wisdom (Jas. 1:5).
    13. Healing (Is. 58:8).
    14. Vindication (Ps. 37:6).
    15. Power (Acts 1:8; Luke 24:49).

B. There are basically two kinds of promise:
    1. *Conditional.*
        a. Definition: something required before the promise is fulfilled.
        b. Every single one of the above promises is conditional:
            (1) Health is promised to the one who fears the Lord and shuns evil (Prov. 3:7).
            (2) Prosperity is promised to the one who keeps God's commands in his heart (Prov. 3:1).
            (3) Longevity is promised to the one who honours his parents (Eph. 6:1-2).
            (4) Usefulness is promised to the one who finds the knowledge of God (Prov. 2:5).
            (5) Protection is promised to the one who is just and faithful (Prov. 2:8).
            (6) Guidance is promised to the one who acknowledges God in all his ways (Prov. 3:6).
            (7) Eternal life is promised to the one who believes in God's Son (John 3:16).
            (8) A reward is promised to the one who builds a superstructure of gold, silver, precious stones (1 Cor. 3:10-15).

    (9) A Spirit of glory comes to the persecuted who bear up (1 Pet. 4:12-14).

    (10) The Holy Spirit is given to those who persevere in prayer (Luke 11:9-13).

    (11) God's rest is given to those who believe and persevere (Heb. 4:3-11).

    (12) Wisdom is promised to the one who asks without doubting (Jas. 1:5-6).

    (13) Healing is promised to the one who fasts in line with God's will (Is. 58:1-11).

    (14) Vindication is promised to the one who delights himself in the Lord (Ps. 37:4-6).

    (15) Power is promised to the one who tarries (Luke 24:49).

  2. *Unconditional.*

    a. Definition: nothing on our part to make it happen.

    b. If God says it will happen, it will happen; nothing can or will stop it from happening.

C. Kinds of things promised unconditionally:

  1. *The death and resurrection of Christ.*

    a. First promise of this: 'And I will put enmity between you and the woman, and between your offspring and hers; he will crush your head, and you will strike his heel' (Gen. 3:15).

    b. Isaiah 53, noting especially verse 6: 'We all, like sheep, have gone astray, each of us has turned to his own way; and the LORD has laid on him the iniquity of us all.'

      (1) Isaiah saw Israel's unbelief – that they would not accept Messiah and would see his death as a sign he deserved God's punishment.

      (2) Nothing could stop this from happening, nothing did.

    c. The resurrection and ascension were seen by David.

      (1) 'I have set the LORD always before me. Because he is at my right hand, I shall not be shaken' (Ps. 16:8. cf. Acts 2:25-28).

      (2) 'The LORD says to my Lord: "Sit at my right hand until I make your enemies a footstool for your feet"' (Ps. 110:1. cf. Acts 2:34).

2. *The coming of the Spirit on the Day of Pentecost.*

    a. Pentecost commemorated the giving of the Law at Sinai.

      (1) We fulfil the Law by walking in the Spirit (Gal. 5:16-18).

      (2) Looking back, it is no surprise that this was when God foresaw the coming of the Spirit.

    b. Jesus' forecast of the Spirit required no condition on the part of the disciples.

      (1) He plainly said that the Spirit would come (John 14:16; 15:26; 16:6-8,13; Acts 1:8; Luke 24:49).

      (2) There was no condition attached, only that the disciples should not leave Jerusalem (Acts 1:4).

    c. This fulfilled Joel's prophecy as well (Joel 2:28ff).

3. *The Second Coming of Christ.*

    a. It is a fixed date in history, known only to the Father. 'No one knows about that day or hour, not even the angels in heaven, nor the Son, but only the Father' (Matt. 24:36. cf. Mark 13:32).

    b. There are no conditions required to make this come to pass.

    c. There are only warnings that we should be ready:

      (1) 'So you also must be ready, because the Son of Man will come at an hour when you do not expect him' (Matt. 24:44).

      (2) 'The master of that servant will come on a day when he does not expect him and at an hour he is not aware of' (Matt. 24:50).

4. *The salvation of God's elect.*

    a. All those who are predestined to be saved will be saved.

      (1) 'All that the Father gives me will come to me, and whoever comes to me I will never drive away' (John 6:37).

      (2) 'And those he predestined, he also called; those he called, he also justified; those he justified, he also glorified' (Rom. 8:30).

    b. Nothing can stop this; however, God who predestined the end also predestined the means.

      (1) He will raise up people to preach the Gospel.

      (2) God's elect will, in his time, hear the Word and be saved.

    c. This also means that the elect are eternally saved.

      (1) When they believe they are adopted into God's family – never to be 'unadopted'.

      (2) It is absolutely true: once saved, always saved.

5. *The survival of the church.*

    a. God has never left himself without a witness; he never will.

    b. He has always had a people: 'called out'.

      (1) Gr. ecclesia (church) means 'called out'.

      (2) The church, then, is the people of God.

    c. Jesus said, 'I will build my church, and the gates of Hades will not overcome it' (Matt. 16:18).

II. THE PROMISE AND THE OATH

A. The writer of Hebrews says there are 'two unchangeable things' – the promise and the oath (Heb. 6:18).

    1. *As we saw, there are two kinds of promise:*

      a. Conditional.

      b. Unconditional.

    2. *The oath is much like an unconditional promise.*

      a. If God swears an oath, it will happen.

      b. If he makes a promise, we must look to see whether or not there are conditions attached.

B. The oath (def.): a solemn declaration – by swearing – that one will do or not do a certain thing.

    1. *It is unusual for God to do this.*

      a. After all, his promise can be believed.

      b. God cannot lie; if he promises something, he will keep his word.

      (1) If however there is an attached condition, he is set free from keeping his promise if we don't obey.

      (2) But if we obey his word, he will keep his promise.

    2. *The oath is God's extraordinary way of communicating with us; he doesn't do this every day.*

      a. He did it to Abraham. 'And said, "I swear by myself, declares the LORD, that because you have done this and have not withheld your son, your only son, I will surely bless you and make your descendants as numerous as the stars in the sky and as the sand on the seashore. Your descendants will take possession of the cities of their enemies, and through your offspring all nations on earth will be blessed, because you have obeyed me"' (Gen. 22:16-18).

b. Abraham then knew that this was as good as done – although it was still future.

(1) Nothing would stop it.

(2) Nothing did.

C. Purpose of the oath: to put an 'end to all argument' (Heb. 6:16).

1. If it is a promise, there will be a debate as to whether it is conditional or unconditional.

2. *If God swears an oath there is no argument – no further discussion; it is as good as done.*

a. The five aforementioned examples of unconditional promises had been preceded by God's oath.

b. That is what guaranteed their happening.

(1) Nobody said, 'We must make this happen.'

(2) God saw to that.

III. Our response to the promises of God

A. Legitimate response

1. *Even if we know God has given an oath, we must still react most responsibly.*

a. God swore an oath to David that his line would be established forever.

(1) 'You said, "I have made a covenant with my chosen one, I have sworn to David my servant, 'I will establish your line for ever and make your throne firm through all generations'"' (Ps. 89:3-4).

(2) 'The LORD declares to you that the LORD himself will establish a house for you. . . . Your house and your kingdom shall endure forever before me; your throne shall be established forever' (2 Sam. 7:11,16).

b. Yet David admonished the young Solomon:

(1) Observe what God requires; walk in his ways, obey his decrees and commands (1 Kings 2:3).

(2) Reason. 'And that the LORD may keep his promise to me: "If your descendants watch how they live, and if they walk faithfully before me with all their heart and soul, you will never fail to have a man on the throne of Israel'" (1 Kings 2:4).

   c. Bathsheba and Nathan the prophet (who gave the oath to David, 2 Sam. 7:11-16), acted responsibly when it appeared that Adonijah rather than Solomon would be the next king.

     (1) David had sworn an oath to Bathsheba that Solomon would be the next king (1 Kings 1:17).

     (2) She, then Nathan, stepped in and reminded the ailing King David of this (1 Kings 1:18-27).

   d. Joseph and Mary acted responsibly concerning the child Jesus when Herod determined to kill all baby boys (Matt. 2).

     (1) They might have said, 'We won't worry – nothing can happen to the Son of God.'

     (2) No; they acted immediately and responsibly, as though all depended on them.

     (3) Note: this is precisely how all evangelism should be carried out; as if all depended on us.

2. *Examples of legitimate response to God's promises (and oaths):*

   a. Prayer (Luke 18:1-8).

     (1) Prayer preceded the coming of the Messiah. Anna 'worshipped night and day, fasting and praying' (Luke 2:37).

     (2) Prayer preceded the coming of the Spirit: 'They all joined together constantly in prayer' (Acts 1:14).

   b. Faith.

     (1) 'We do not want you to become lazy, but to imitate those who through faith and patience inherit what has been promised' (Heb. 6:12).

     (2) 'Yet he did not waver through unbelief regarding the promise of God, but was strengthened in his faith and gave glory to God, being fully persuaded that God had power to do what he had promised' (Rom. 4:20-21).

   c. Obedience.

     (1) 'We must obey God rather than men' (Acts 5:29).

     (2) This is called 'walking in the light' (1 John 1:7).

   d. Expectancy.

     (1) 'So do not throw away your confidence; it will be richly rewarded' (Heb. 10:35).

     (2) 'We do not lose heart' (2 Cor. 4:1).

B. Illegitimate response

1. *Even if one is conscious of God's promise, one may act in unbelief by trying to make things happen.*

   a. Abraham slept with Hagar, fearing that he had to help God keep his word (Gen. 16:4).
      (1) Ishmael was born.
      (2) God later disclosed that he wanted the child to come through Sarah (Gen. 17:19).
   b. Moses thought he would become Israel's leader by doing what would convince them (Ex. 2:11-12).
      (1) It completely backfired on Moses (Ex. 2:14).
      (2) 'Moses thought that his own people would realise that God was using him to rescue them, but they did not' (Acts 7:25).

2. *Examples of an illegitimate response:*

   a. Overclaiming (def.): claiming more than is true.
      (1) King Saul claimed he had carried out God's word – but he hadn't (1 Sam. 15:15).
      (2) Hananiah claimed to have heard from God – but he hadn't (Jer. 28:1-4. cf. Jer. 28:17).
   b. Running ahead of God.
      (1) Joseph and Mary proceeded without Jesus but assumed that he was with them (Luke 2:41-44).
      (2) Joseph in prison tried to manipulate his way out of prison (Gen. 40:14-15).
   c. Working things up.
      (1) Since nothing appeared to be happening – Moses was absent – Aaron participated in worshipping a golden calf and called it 'a festival to the LORD' (Ex. 32:5).
      (2) King Saul grew impatient in waiting for Samuel, so he took upon himself the responsibility for the burnt offering (1 Sam. 13:8-9).
   d. Pressuring people.
      (1) King Saul kept his men in distress because of his oath that nobody could eat (1 Sam. 14:24).
      (2) King Rehoboam tried to show his strength by engendering fear. 'My father laid on you a heavy yoke; I will make it even heavier. My father scourged you with whips; I will scourge you with scorpions' (1 Kings 12:11).

CONCLUSION

It is difficult to know whether a prophetic word given by someone today is at a promise level or oath level. The same is true regarding healing; only God can heal. Overclaiming regarding healing does damage to God's name. If God makes a promise he will keep it – or make it absolutely clear what we are to do.

41

DOES GOD APPEAL TO OUR SELF–INTEREST?

A. Motivation
1. *What motivates us?*
    a. Motivation (def.): when we have been given an incentive to do or say something.
    b. Incentive (def.): something that arouses or energises us to act or to make an effort.
2. *What makes a person want to do something? For example:*
    a. What makes us get up to go to work? Answer:
        (1) To keep our jobs.
        (2) To get paid.
        (3) To appear responsible before others.
    b. What motivates us to achieve? Answer:
        (1) Pride, we will look good for what we achieved.
        (2) Ambition, that springs from 'man's envy of his neighbour' (Eccl. 4:4).
3. *Some people are more motivated than others. Why?*
    a. At the natural level we are born with certain drives:
        (1) Hunger and thirst, so we will eat and drink to stay alive.
        (2) Sex, so the race will be procreated.
        (3) The desire to feel important, which, according to Dale Carnegie (*How to Win Friends and Influence People*), is one of the strongest urges we have.
        (4) The desire to stay alive (or fear of death).
        (5) The desire to avoid pain: physical pain, mental pain, the fear of embarrassment.
    b. Some are more ambitious than others. Why?
        (1) The drive that sometimes comes from sibling rivalry.
        (2) The desire to please parents.
        (3) The drive that comes from strong parents.
        (4) The hurt as a child that we want to compensate for throughout life.

(5) A competitive spirit that springs from peer pressure.

4. *All the above is set in a context apart from our relationship with God.*

  a. Some are more motivated than others, whether or not they become Christians.

  (1) That they are motivated by self-interest goes without saying.

  (2) Man is born selfish. Ecclesiastes 4:4 sums it up: 'And I saw that all labour and all achievement spring from man's envy of his neighbour. This too is meaningless, a chasing after the wind.'

  b. Some people do not get sufficiently motivated to do much of anything until they are Christians; we must therefore ask:

  (1) What motivated them to become Christians in the first place?

  (2) Why has Christianity set them free to do things they had not been interested in before?

B. Therefore the question follows: does God appeal to our self-interest?

  1. *Self-interest (def.): one's own personal advantage.*

  a. Being motivated to do or say something because it is to our own personal advantage (benefit, or profit).

  b. It means we will get on with something because we will be better off personally by doing so, and worse off by not doing so.

  2. *Does God appeal therefore to our self-interest – our selfish nature – to motivate us?*

  a. Some say yes because the Scriptures support this.

  b. Some say no because our obedience should flow out of love for God alone and not out of any self-interest.

  c. It is true, there are those who are noble at heart and want to do something valiant.

  (1) Rarely will one die for a righteous man (Rom. 5:7).

  (2) Paul was willing to be cursed for his people (Rom. 9:3).

  d. But by and large we are weak human beings who need to be motivated along lines of self-interest.

C. Why is this study important?

1. It faces embarrassing things about our human nature.

2. It examines the Scriptures that seem to suggest God appeals to our self-interest.

3. It touches on profound theological issues, such as the work of the Holy Spirit, and the Spirit's role in motivating us.

4. It should help us to understand ourselves better.

5. It should help us to appreciate God who 'knoweth our frame (AV), he remembereth that we are dust' (Ps. 103:14).

I. STATEMENTS OF COMMAND AND PROMISE IN THE OLD TESTAMENT

A. The first command with promise: 'And the LORD God commanded the man, "You are free to eat from any tree in the garden; but you must not eat from the tree of the knowledge of good and evil, for when you eat of it you will surely die"' (Gen. 2:16-17).

1. The command: you must not eat from the tree of the knowledge of good and evil.

2. *The promise which was a warning: when you eat of it you will surely die.*

a. This was before the Fall – man without sin.

b. And yet God appealed to man's self-interest by showing the negative consequence of disobedience: death.

(1) This disobedience was called sin. 'Therefore, just as sin entered the world through one man, and death through sin, and in this way death came to all men, because all sinned – for before the law was given, sin was in the world' (Rom. 5:12,13a).

(2) Summed up: 'The wages of sin is death' (Rom. 6:23).

3. *This is significant: before sin came into the world, God appealed to Adam's self-interest.*

a. Adam at that time had no fallen, sinful nature.

b. Yet God appealed to Adam's self-interest.

4. *Note: the first command to man (mankind) that had no attached promise was in Genesis 1:28:* 'God blessed them and said to them, "Be fruitful and increase in number; fill the earth and subdue it."'

a. But God provided the motivation to carry out this promise: the sexual urge.

    b. Without the natural sexual urge in man there would be no population on the earth.
5. After the Fall God removed from Adam the possibility of eating from the tree of life. 'And the LORD God said, "The man has now become like one of us, knowing good and evil. He must not be allowed to reach out his hand and take also from the tree of life and eat, and live for ever"' (Gen 3:22).
    a. God knew Adam might well be motivated by self-interest to eat of this tree.
    b. God however made this an impossibility (Gen. 3:24).
    c. God would decide who would be given eternal life.
        (1) This would come as a result of faith (Rom. 3:26).
        (2) God alone would give faith (Eph. 2:8-9).
        (3) God would take the responsibility for motivating man to want eternal life (Ex. 33:19).
        (4) The Holy Spirit would be behind the motivation (John 6:63).

B. Cain and Abel
    1. Cain was angry that Abel's offering was accepted.
    2. *God gave Cain a second chance.* 'If you do what is right, will you not be accepted? But if you do not do what is right, sin is crouching at your door; it desires to have you, but you must master it' (Gen. 4:7).
    a. The promise: you will be accepted.
    b. The command: do what is right.

C. Noah.
'By faith Noah, when warned about things not yet seen, in holy fear built an ark to save his family. By his faith he condemned the world and became heir of the righteousness that comes by faith' (Heb. 11:7).
    1. *God told Noah to build an ark.*
    a. He promised to destroy the earth.
    b. The exception: Noah and his family.
    2. *Noah had a two-fold motivation; though it was by faith:*
    a. Fear.
    b. Saving himself and his family.

D. Abraham (Gen. 12:1-3; Heb. 11:8-10)

1. The command: 'The LORD had said to Abram, "Leave your country, your people and your father's household and go to the land I will show you"' (Gen. 12:1).

2. The promise: 'I will make you into a great nation and I will bless you; I will make your name great, and you will be a blessing. I will bless those who bless you, and whoever curses you I will curse; and all peoples on earth will be blessed through you' (Gen. 12:2-3).

  a. Abraham did what he did by faith.

  b. But God motivated Abraham none the less by the promise of greatness – the desire to feel important.

E. Moses

1. He left the palace of Pharaoh and chose to be treated with cruelty along with God's people.

2. But there was a motivation behind this, even though he did it all by faith. 'He regarded disgrace for the sake of Christ as of greater value than the treasures of Egypt, because he was looking ahead to his reward' (Heb. 11:26).

F. The Law given at Sinai

1. *The reasons people were motivated to keep the Law were fear of punishment and the promise of blessing:*

  a. 'If you obey' (from Deuteronomy 28:1-14):

    (1) You will be blessed in the city and blessed in the country.

    (2) The fruit of your womb will be blessed.

    (3) Your enemies will be defeated.

    (4) You will be blessed with food.

  b. 'If you do not obey' (from Deuteronomy 28:15-25):

    (1) You will be cursed in the city and cursed in the country.

    (2) The fruit of your womb will be cursed.

    (3) You will be plagued with diseases.

    (4) You will be defeated before your enemies.

    (5) (Many more punishments are listed, vv26-68.)

2. *The Law, however, was not of faith* (Gal. 3:12).

  a. Why? The blessings of the Law come by doing. 'All who rely on observing the law are under a curse, for it is written: "Cursed is everyone who does not continue to do everything written in the Book of the Law"' (Gal.3:10).

b. No-one ever kept the Law (Acts 15:10).

G. Wisdom, begun by the fear of the Lord (Prov. 1:7; 9:10).

1. *By rejecting God's wisdom:*

    a. God will laugh at us in the day of disaster (Prov. 1:26).

    b. God will not answer when we call to him (Prov. 1:28).

    c. The result: dread, hardship, folly. Proverbs, *passim.*

2. *By accepting God's wisdom:*

    a. You will live in safety (Prov. 1:33).

    b. God will direct your paths (Prov. 3:6).

    c. The result: happiness, prosperity, blessing. Proverbs, *passim.*

H. Giving (or tithing).

1. *This was begun by Abraham, four hundred years before the Law came.*

    a. Abraham did what he did voluntarily (Gen. 14).

    b. The Law made it mandatory (Lev. 27:30).

2. *This shows that giving is done by faith.*

    a. 'Honour the LORD with your wealth, with the firstfruits of all your crops; then your barns will be filled to overflowing, and your vats will brim over with new wine' (Prov. 3:9-10).

    b. 'Bring the whole tithe into the storehouse, that there may be food in my house. Test me in this,' says the LORD Almighty, 'and see if I will not throw open the floodgates of heaven and pour out so much blessing that you will not have room enough for it' (Mal. 3:10).

II. STATEMENTS OF COMMAND AND PROMISE IN THE GOSPELS

A. The preaching of John the Baptist.

1. The command to repent (Matt. 3:2).

2. The warning of God's coming wrath (Matt. 3:7).

B. The command and consequences of secret righteousness.

1. 'Be careful not to do your "acts of righteousness" before men, to be seen by them. If you do, you will have no reward from your Father in heaven' (Matt. 6:1).

   a. Command: Do not be righteous to be seen.

   b. Consequence: There will be no reward from the Father.

2. 'But when you pray, go into your room, close the door and pray to your Father, who is unseen. Then your Father, who sees what is done in secret, will reward you' (Matt. 6:6).

   a. Command: pray in secret.

   b. Promise: the Father will reward you.

C. The command and promise with regard to prayer generally.

1. 'Ask and it will be given to you; seek and you will find; knock and the door will be opened to you. For everyone who asks receives; he who seeks finds; and to him who knocks, the door will be opened' (Matt. 7:7-8).

   a. Further results: good gifts (Matt. 7:11).

   b. Ultimate result: the Holy Spirit (Luke 11:13).

2. *Jesus urged that we pray and not give up* (Luke 18:1).

   a. Parable of the unjust judge (Luke 18:2-5).

   b. The motivation to persistent prayer. 'And will not God bring about justice for his chosen ones, who cry out to him day and night? Will he keep putting them off? I tell you, he will see that they get justice, and quickly' (Luke 18:7-8a).

D. The command to be ready for the Lord's appearing, or manifesting his glory.

1. *Why be ready?*

   a. We do not know when he will come (Matt. 24:42-44).

   b. The consequence of not being ready: 'The master of that servant will come on a day when he does not expect him and at an hour he is not aware of. He will cut him to pieces and assign him a place with the hypocrites, where there will be weeping and gnashing of teeth' (Matt. 24:50-51).

2. *The command to be ready for service* (Luke 12:35ff).

   a. Result if you are found watching: 'It will be good for those servants whose master finds them watching when he comes. I tell you the truth, he will dress himself to serve, will have them recline at the table and will come and wait on them' (Luke 12:37).

   b. The consequence of not watching: assignment of a place with the unbelievers (Luke 12:46).

E. Motivation to believe the Gospel.

1. 'Whoever believes and is baptised will be saved, but whoever does not believe will be condemned' (Mark 16:16).

2. 'For God so loved the world that he gave his one and only Son, that whoever believes in him shall not perish but have eternal life' (John 3:16).

3. 'Whoever believes in the Son has eternal life, but whoever rejects the Son will not see life, for God's wrath remains on him' (John 3:36).

F. Motivation to accept the Holy Spirit (in the light of Jesus' departure).

1. 'It is for your good that I am going away. Unless I go away, the Counsellor will not come to you' (John 16:7).

2. 'He will teach you all things and will remind you of everything I have said to you' (John 14:26).

3. 'He will guide you into all truth' (John 16:13).

4. 'Your grief will turn to joy' (John 16:20).

III. GENERAL MOTIVATIONAL TEACHING IN THE NEW TESTAMENT

A. The benefit of personal righteousness in the Beatitudes (Matt. 5:1-12).

1. Each description is followed by a promise.

2. *Jesus goes from the first level to the highest.*

　　a. Being poor in spirit results in possessing the Kingdom.

　　b. Being persecuted means a 'great' reward in heaven.

B. How to protect ourselves from being judged and condemned.

1. *Command is followed by promise:*

　　a. 'Do not judge, and you will not be judged' (Luke 6:37).

　　b. In other words, the way to avoid the pain of a guilt trip is never to point the finger.

2. *This is a direct appeal to our self-interest.*

　　a. But the result is greater than merely not being judged.

　　b. We develop into mature Christians; yet Jesus gained our attention by self-interest.

C. How to avoid humiliation (Luke 14:8-11).

1. Take the lowest seat at a banquet.

2. *If you go to the top table, you may find that it has been reserved for someone more important:*
    a. 'Then, humiliated, you will have to take the least important place.'
    b. Jesus appeals to our self-esteem; none of us enjoys unnecessary public humiliation.

D. The principle of giving.
    1. The more we get here below (generally speaking): 'Remember this: Whoever sows sparingly will also reap sparingly, and whoever sows generously will also reap generously' (2 Cor. 9:6).
    2. The greater our reward in heaven: what can be credited to our account (Phil. 4:17).

E. Jesus motivates us to love with a view to what will give us 'credit'.
    1. *'We love because he first loved us.'* (1 John 4:19).
        a. God took the initiative, sent his Spirit.
        b. But the Spirit always motivates in the light of what the promise and warning is!
    2. *Three times the word 'credit' is used in Luke 6:32-34:*
        a. 'If you love those who love you, what credit is that to you?'
        b. 'If you do good to those who are good to you, what credit is that to you?'
        c. 'If you lend to those from whom you expect repayment, what credit is that to you?'
        d. The point: God notices and keeps records (Mal. 3:16-18).

CONCLUSION

God openly and unashamedly appeals to our self-interest. He knows our frame, we were made this way, even before the Fall. Yet when we have done everything we were told to do, we should say, "We are unworthy servants; we have only done our duty"' (Luke 17:10).

42

HOW TO BE GRATEFUL

A. One of the greatest open secrets of the Bible is that of God's own pleasure regarding gratitude.

   1. *This gratitude refers to two things:*

      a. Our gratitude toward others.

      b. Our gratitude toward God himself.

   2. *There are two kinds of secret:*

      a. Closed secret: when it will never be known.

         (1) There are secrets, or mysteries of God, that he does not reveal – at least for a while.

         (2) There is the mystery of evil; how God can be just and merciful but allow sin and suffering.

            (a) That will not be revealed this side of heaven.

            (b) One day God will clear his name and explain the reason for sin and suffering.

         (3) There is the mystery of providence; when God eventually lets it be known what his plans were.

            (a) The way he governs our lives.

            (b) His purpose in redemption (1 Cor. 2:7-8).

      b. Open secret: when information is available but which we sometimes take so long to discover.

         (1) This is when something is plainly revealed in God's Word.

         (2) But we are so loathe to experience it, owing to the hardness of our hearts.

            (a) It is there all the time for us to see.

            (b) We are so slow to delve into it.

   3. One such open secret is God's feelings regarding gratitude.

B. Gratitude: showing that we are thankful.

   1. *There are three stages in this connection.*

      a. When we don't feel grateful.

      b. When we feel grateful.

      c. When we show gratitude.

  2. *When we don't feel grateful it is probably because:*

      a. We are hurt or disappointed, hence feel virtually justified for that hurt.

      b. We have not come to see that behind the disappointment is a loving God who has permitted something for our good (but which we have not seen yet).

      c. We are full of self-pity.

C. There are three principles worth memorising:

  1. God loves gratitude.

  2. God hates ingratitude.

  3. *Gratitude must be taught.*

      a. There are generally two types of gratitude:

        (1) When it is spontaneous; we feel it to our fingertips.

        (2) When it is a matter of discipline; when we force ourselves to show thankfulness.

D. There are three passages in the Bible which the Holy Spirit has used to wake me up in this matter:

  1. 'Do not be anxious about anything, but in everything, by prayer and petition, with thanksgiving, present your requests to God' (Phil. 4:6).

  2. 'Jesus asked, "Were not all ten cleansed? Where are the other nine?"' (Luke 17:17).

  3. 'For although they knew God, they neither glorified him as God nor gave thanks to him, but their thinking became futile and their foolish hearts were darkened' (Rom. 1:21).

E. Why is this lesson important?

  1. It could easily be the greatest spiritual breakthrough some have had in years and years.

  2. There is a way forward that brings incalculable blessing.

  3. It touches on the very character of God.

  4. It touches on the doctrine of sanctification.

  5. *It is a secret the devil does not want us to discover.*

      a. The more ungrateful we are, the better Satan loves it.

      b. The more thankful we are, the more Satan hates it.

      c. Satan would keep us blind to this wonderful secret.

I. THE NATURE OF GOD: HE IS A GOD OF GLORY

A. Stephen, one of the first Deacons, was described as 'full of faith and of the Holy Spirit' (Acts 6:5).

   1. When he faced the Sanhedrin, Stephen's opening line referred to God as a God of glory. 'To this he replied: "Brothers and fathers, listen to me! The God of glory appeared to our father Abraham while he was still in Mesopotamia, before he lived in Haran"' (Acts 7:2).

   2. This indicates that when we are truly full of faith and of the Holy Spirit we will have an understanding of God that is:

     a. Theologically and biblically sound.

     b. Pleasing to God himself.

   3. *What is so thrilling:*

     a. At the beginning of Acts 7 Stephen reveals his love for God as a God of glory.

     b. At the end of Acts 7 he actually sees the glory of God. 'But Stephen, full of the Holy Spirit, looked up to heaven and saw the glory of God, and Jesus standing at the right hand of God' (Acts 7:55).

       (1) If we are unashamed of God as a God of glory, we too may well see his glory!

       (2) True, Stephen was fiercely persecuted; but any opportunity to see the glory of God is worth it!

B. Glory of God (def.): the sum total of all his attributes (characteristics); it is the sum total of all he is.

   1. Hebrew *kabodh* means weightiness, honour.

   2. Greek *doxa* means praise, but it comes from a root word that means opinion.

   3. *God's glory is the dignity of his will.*

     a. His will is weighty.

     b. His opinion is weighty.

   4. God therefore wants his glory to be recognised and praised.

II. SANCTIFICATION IS THE DOCTRINE OF GRATITUDE

A. This concept of sanctification is essential to the Gospel.

   1. *Sanctification (def.): the process of being made holy.*

a. It does not come at once, except by imputation.

    (1) Imputation (def.): what God puts to our credit.

    (2) When we believe, God imputes sanctification to us. 'It is because of him that you are in Christ Jesus, who has become for us wisdom from God – that is, our righteousness, holiness and redemption' (1 Cor. 1:30).

b. It is erroneous teaching to suppose that we can be sanctified in actual experience all at once.

    (1) I wish it were true.

    (2) But the Bible consistently shows that sanctification is a process, that is, something which happens little by little.

2. *Sanctification is the process between justification and glorification.* *'And those he predestined, he also called; those he called, he also justified; those he justified, he also glorified'* (Rom. 8:30).

a. Had sanctification been seen as an instant happening in the Christian life, Romans 8:30 would have been where Paul would put it.

b. Justification and glorification are each instantaneous.

    (1) We are justified by faith; as soon as we believe our faith counts for righteousness (Rom. 4:5).

    (2) We are glorified by God's own act, which takes place on entering heaven (1 John 3:2).

B. We are not saved by sanctification.

1. *We are saved by faith in the sacrifice of Christ.*

a. This comes as a result of two things:

    (1) Hearing the Gospel (Rom. 10:14).

    (2) Believing the Gospel (Rom. 10:17).

b. It is by grace, through faith, that we are saved (Eph. 2:8).

2. *Sanctification does not precede conversion but follows it.*

a. If it preceded it, it would then follow that we must begin to become holy before we believe.

b. This would be the same thing as salvation by works.

c. The Big Question would be: at what point would we be sufficiently holy that we could feel ready to believe the promise?

    (1) We would never feel ready.

    (2) We would never know for sure we were saved.

C. After we are saved we are commanded to be holy.

1. 'It is God's will that you should be sanctified: that you should avoid sexual immorality' (1 Thes. 4:3).

2. 'Therefore do not let sin reign in your mortal body so that you obey its evil desires. Do not offer the parts of your body to sin, as instruments of wickedness, but rather offer yourselves to God, as those who have been brought from death to life; and offer the parts of your body to him as instruments of righteousness' (Rom. 6:12-13).

3. 'Therefore, I urge you, brothers, in view of God's mercy, to offer your bodies as living sacrifices, holy and pleasing to God – this is your spiritual act of worship. Do not conform any longer to the pattern of this world, but be transformed by the renewing of your mind. Then you will be able to test and approve what God's will is – his good, pleasing and perfect will' (Rom. 12:1-2).

D. Sanctification is gratitude.

1. We do not show gratitude in order to be saved.

2. *We show gratitude because we have been saved.*

   a. God puts us on our honour.

   b. We, therefore, must show our gratitude for such a wonderful salvation.

III. TEACHING GRATITUDE

A. This is the responsibility of a leader.

1. *It is the responsibility of parents.*

   a. Children must be taught to be thankful.

      (1) Most of us don't appreciate our parents for many years, often years after we ourselves become adults.

      (2) As we grow up we tend to resent our parents; when we are older we can see their frailties and good points.

   b. The sooner children are taught gratitude, the better.

      (1) They are made to see things for which they ought to be thankful.

      (2) If it is not pointed out, it is likely not to cross their minds what they should be thankful for.

   c. The fifth commandment is this: 'Honour your father and your mother, so that you may live long in the land the Lord your God is giving you' (Ex. 20:12).

    (1) Paul referred to this as 'the first commandment with a promise' (Eph. 6:2).

    (2) This means that God provided a motivation (appealing to our self-interest) for showing gratitude to our parents.

2. *It is the responsibility of a spiritual leader.*

    a. We must risk teaching gratitude.

        (1) It may backfire.

        (2) People may resent this teaching.

    b. And yet it shows that we truly respect those we teach.

        (1) We do not want to withhold what will do them good.

        (2) It gives them dignity and self-worth.

B. Examples of teaching gratitude.

1. *Moses, who gave the Ten Commandments.*

    a. The Ten Commandments taught Israel how to worship.

    b. The Ten Commandments equally taught Israel how to be thankful.

    c. 'Only be careful, and watch yourselves closely so that you do not forget the things your eyes have seen or let them slip from your heart as long as you live. Teach them to your children and to their children after them' (Deut. 4:9).

2. *Joshua, who would not let Israel forget.*

    a. He instructed a representative of each tribe to take a large stone from the river Jordan.

        (1) This is when God miraculously cut off the Jordan so the people could walk across on dry land.

        (2) Theses stones were erected and formed an instant memorial.

    b. Joshua anticipated that future generations would ask the meaning of this monument.

        (1) 'To serve as a sign among you. In the future, when your children ask you, "What do these stones mean?" tell them that the flow of the Jordan was cut off before the ark of the covenant of the LORD. When it crossed the Jordan, the waters of the Jordan were cut off. These stones are to be a memorial to the people of Israel forever' (Josh. 4:6-7).

(2) In a word: to teach Israel to be thankful for what God did.
3. Samuel, who taught Israel to remember God's deliverance over the Philistines at a critical time. 'Then Samuel took a stone and set it up between Mizpah and Shen. He named it Ebenezer, saying, "Thus far has the LORD helped us"' (1 Sam. 7:12).
4. *David, who taught the fear of the Lord.*
   a. Sometimes the fear of the Lord, like gratitude, is spontaneous.
      (1) 'Everyone was filled with awe, and many wonders and miraculous signs were done by the apostles' (Acts 2:43).
      (2) 'Great fear seized the whole church and all who heard about these events' (Acts 5:11).
   b. In the meantime, it must be taught. 'Come, my children, listen to me; I will teach you the fear of the LORD' (Ps. 34:11).
5. *Jesus, who showed his disappointment that only one healed leper bothered to come back and say, 'Thank you.'*
   a. Ten lepers called out in a loud voice, 'Jesus, Master, have pity on us' (Luke 17:13).
   b. Jesus answered their request. 'When he saw them, he said, "Go, show yourselves to the priests." And as they went, they were cleansed' (Luke 17:14).
      (1) 'One of them, when he saw he was healed, came back, praising God in a loud voice. He threw himself at Jesus' feet and thanked him – and he was a Samaritan' (Luke 17:15-16).
      (2) 'Jesus asked, "Were not all ten cleansed? Where are the other nine?"' (Luke 17:17).
   c. In that comment Jesus gave no small hint how much God loves gratitude and hates ingratitude.
6. *Paul, who taught gratitude continually.*
   a. To show gratitude when we ask for things. 'Do not be anxious about anything, but in everything, by prayer and petition, with thanksgiving, present your requests to God' (Phil. 4:6).
   b. To show gratitude in all situations. 'Give thanks in all circumstances, for this is God's will for you in Christ Jesus' (1 Thess. 5:18).
7. James, who taught us to dignify every trial. 'Consider it pure joy, my brothers, whenever you face trials of many kinds' (Jas. 1:2).

8. *The writer to the Hebrews spoke of gratitude as being a sacrifice.*

    a. 'Through Jesus, therefore, let us continually offer to God a sacrifice of praise – the fruit of lips that confess his name' (Heb. 13:15).

    b. 'And do not forget to do good and to share with others, for with such sacrifices God is pleased' (Heb. 13:16).

IV. LEARNING GRATITUDE

A. Gratitude must be taught but also 'caught'.

    1. This means we have taken gratitude on board.

    2. This means we have absorbed the importance of being grateful.

    3. This means it has become a part of our lives.

    4. This means it has become a part of our worship.

B. There are likely to be stages we will go through.

    1. We agree we need to be grateful.

    2. We discipline ourselves to be grateful. 'Christians bent on maturity must work hard on gratitude.' Don Carson.

    3. We keep it up as a disciplined habit, whether we feel like it or not.

    4. It becomes a joy – we are thankful for the privilege.

    5. *It becomes almost selfish – we can't express our gratitude as we see its benefits.*

        a. God loves praise; he inhabits the praises of his people.

        b. Paul Cain speaks of a hydrological cycle:

            (1) The mist going upwards forms clouds that come down as rain.

            (2) Our praise is like mist that goes to heaven; God comes down with blessing. 'May the peoples praise you, O God; may all the peoples praise you. Then the land will yield its harvest, and God, our God, will bless us' (Ps. 67:5-6).

C. Learning gratitude is basically remembering to be thankful.

    1. Part of the purpose of the Lord's Supper is this. 'And when he had given thanks, he broke it and said, "This is my body, which is for you; do this in remembrance of me." In the same way, after supper he took the cup, saying, "This cup is the new covenant in my blood; do this, whenever you drink it, in remembrance of me." For whenever you eat this bread and drink this cup, you proclaim the Lord's death until he comes' (1 Cor. 11:24-26).

2. *We therefore must discipline ourselves to remember.*

    a. We remember to be at work on time.

    b. We remember to pay our bills.

    c. We remember to plan for a holiday.

    d. When we truly feel gratitude, we will remember that too.

3. *The reward can be beyond our greatest dreams.*

    a. Ancient Israel was in a great battle with Moab and Ammon.

    b. An unusual weapon emerged! 'After consulting the people, Jehoshaphat appointed men to sing to the Lord and to praise him for the splendour of his holiness as they went out at the head of the army, saying: "Give thanks to the LORD, for his love endures forever"' (2 Chron. 20:21).

    c. God himself stepped in and granted victory. 'As they began to sing and praise, the LORD set ambushes against the men of Ammon and Moab and Mount Seir who were invading Judah, and they were defeated' (2 Chron. 20:22).

D. Practical ways that show we have learned to be grateful.

    1. *Tell people who have been a blessing to you.*

        a. Call your parents on the phone (if possible).

        b. Tell your pastor or church leader (Gal. 6:6).

        c. Tell your friends.

        d. Tell your boss when he or she is good to you; if you are a manager, tell your staff when they are being particularly helpful.

        e. Show appreciation to anyone for whom you are thankful.

    2. *Count your blessings to God* (Phil. 4:6).

        a. Recall yesterday's good things.

        b. Recount blessings from God over the years.

            (1) Illustration: recently Louise and I drove through the Cotswolds back to London and enumerated seventy-five things for which we were grateful over the past forty years.

            (2) Some of them – I am almost ashamed to admit it – I fear had never been mentioned before, even the most obvious!

    c. Think of things about God and his Word:

      (1) Thank him for being as he is.

      (2) Thank him for Jesus and his blood.

      (3) Thank him for the Holy Spirit.

      (4) Thank him for the Bible.

      (5) Thank him for saving you.

CONCLUSION

It may be years since we last sang the old hymn, but it says it all:

Count your blessings, name them one by one,
Count your blessings, see what God has done.
Count your blessings, name them one by one
And it will surprize you what the Lord has done.

43

WHAT ABOUT SEX,
SINGLENESS AND MARRIAGE?

INTRODUCTION

A. More and more young people are either postponing or rejecting marriage. Why?
  1. Living together as husband and wife is an easier option than commitment with its legal implications.
  2. It is easier to dissolve living together than to dissolve a marriage.
  3. Living together is fashionable, largely devoid of much stigma, and is rapidly becoming a part of today's culture. In 1993 the number of marriages in the UK fell to its lowest level for 50 years, and one in five unmarried men and women were cohabiting. The stigma attached to cohabiting in the 1990s is far less than it was two or three decades ago.
  4. Couples who live together do not need marriage ('a piece of paper', some would say) to prove commitment to each other. By the 1990s about 70% were cohabiting prior to marriage. Of women marrying a second time in the 1990s, about 90% will cohabit before their second marriage.

B. There are some couples who have professed faith in Christ who do not believe they need to get married. Why?
  1. They are part of the culture referred to above.
  2. They do not believe a marriage ceremony is necessary.
  3. They believe that since sleeping together makes them 'one flesh' they are married in the sight of God.

C. There are also those who do not believe that pre-marital sexual intercourse is sinful. Why?
  1. They say it is promiscuity that the Bible condemns; that if they are in love it is not promiscuity.

2. They think there is no explicit biblical injunction that says, 'Do not have sexual intercourse before marriage.'

3. There is nothing in the Bible that says there must be a civil or Christian marriage ceremony before one can engage in sexual intercourse.

D. There are homosexual people who want to 'Christianise' their sexual intercourse and believe it is not sinful. Why?

1. They say the Bible was written during a different period and culture from ours.

2. They say the Bible is not infallible and therefore not unchanging in what it teaches.

3. They say God made us with our sexual proclivity; they have a right to express their sexuality as much as the heterosexual.

4. They say, 'We have a right to get married as much as a heterosexual couple.'

E. Definitions:

1. Sex: sexual intercourse.

2. Singleness: remaining unmarried.

3. Marriage: the state in which a man and a woman are formally united for the purpose of living together (usually in order to procreate children) and with certain legal rights and obligations towards each other.

'Marriage is an exclusive heterosexual covenant between one man and one woman, ordained and sealed by God, preceded by a public leaving of parents, consummated by sexual union, issuing in a permanent mutually supportive partnership, and normally crowned by the gift of children.' John Stott.

4. Heterosexual: physical attraction to the opposite sex.

5. Homosexual: physical attraction to the same sex.

6. Monogamy: having one partner.

7. Heterosexual monogamy: man and woman committed only to each other.

F. Why is this lesson important?

1. We need to address the relevance of the Bible for these issues.

2. We must face squarely whether a marriage ceremony is to precede sleeping together.

3. Does the Bible explicitly forbid pre-marital intercourse?

4. Can couples who sleep together and claim to be committed truly be regarded as Christians?

5. Should a church accept such couples into church membership?

6. Is there a case for homosexual marriage?

7. What constitutes marriage?

I. THE BIBLE AND MARRIAGE

A. Mankind is male and female.

  1. 'So God created man in his own image, in the image of God he created him; male and female he created them.' (Gen. 1:27).

  2. *This means that God made people one sex or the other – either male or female.*

    a. The distinction between the sexes was therefore God's idea.

    b. He decreed this by creation.

B. Marriage is heterosexual monogamy.

  1. *'The LORD God said, "It is not good for the man to be alone. I will make a helper suitable for him"'* (Gen. 2:18).

    a. God's general will for all men and women is that they should not live alone.

    b. When God said 'It is not good' for the man to live alone, it was because:

      (1) He knew the basic sexual desires with which he endowed his creation.

      (2) He knew the pain and frustration of loneliness.

    c. He did not create another person of the same sex for Adam.

      (1) This does not mean we should not enjoy the friendship and company of others of the same sex.

      (2) But when it comes to sexual desire the opposite sex was the only thing God had in mind for his creation.

  2. *God instituted marriage in the Garden of Eden before the Fall* (Gen. 2:19-24).

    a. He made woman for the man (1 Cor. 11:9).

    b. Marriage was to be heterosexual. 'For this reason a man will leave his father and mother and be united to his wife, and they will become one flesh' (Gen. 2:24).

   (1) It was monogamous; a commitment to each other.

   (2) Sexual intercourse made man and woman 'one flesh'.

C. The ceremony: an assumption. "'Haven't you read," he (Jesus) replied, "that at the beginning the Creator 'made them male and female', and said, 'For this reason a man will leave his father and mother and be united to his wife, and the two will become one flesh'? So they are no longer two, but one. Therefore what God has joined together, let man not separate'" (Matt. 19:4-6).

  1. *Jesus' words above show:*

    a. There is a leaving: a public act of lifelong exclusive commitment.

    b. There is a uniting of the man and the woman; they are 'glued together' (Nicky Gumbel; *Searching Issues*).

    c. This union is sexual.

  2. *Jacob loved Rachel and said to her father Laban, 'I'll work for you seven years in return for your younger daughter Rachel'* (Gen. 29:18).

    a. The assumption was that sexual intercourse was unthinkable without a ceremony.

    b. The marriage was called a 'feast' (Gen. 29:22).

      (1) True, Jacob found out that he had Leah with him the next morning.

      (2) But there was obviously a public acknowledgement that preceded any sleeping together.

  3. *A 'pledge' to be married was a commitment but it was assumed (see Deuteronomy 22:13-30) that:*

    a. There must be a ceremony to make it 'marriage'.

    b. There was no sexual intercourse during the engagement (cf. Matt. 1:18; Luke 1:34).

  4. *Jesus affirmed the wedding ceremony.* 'On the third day a wedding took place at Cana in Galilee. Jesus' mother was there, and Jesus and his disciples had also been invited to the wedding' (John 2:1-2).

    a. This is profound and significant.

      (1) It shows they had weddings! Why?

        (a) It was a celebration.

        (b) It is what sanctified sexual intercourse.

      (2) Jesus' presence was his own affirmation of the wedding.

> **(3)** This account is incorporated in the traditional wedding ceremony: 'This holy estate Jesus adorned and beautified with his presence and first miracle that he wrought, in Cana of Galilee.'

b. He even chose the event to perform his first miracle!

> **(1)** 'When the wine was gone, Jesus' mother said to him, "They have no more wine"' (John 2:3).
>
> **(2)** 'Jesus said to the servants, "Fill the jars with water"; so they filled them to the brim. Then he told them, "Now draw some out and take it to the master of the banquet"' (John 2:7-8).
>
> **(3)** 'And the master of the banquet tasted the water that had been turned into wine. He did not realise where it had come from, though the servants who had drawn the water knew. Then he called the bridegroom aside and said, "Everyone brings out the choice wine first and then the cheaper wine after the guests have had too much to drink; but you have saved the best till now"' (John 2:9-10).

c. 'This, the first of his miraculous signs, Jesus performed at Cana in Galilee. He thus revealed his glory, and his disciples put their faith in him' (John 2:11).

5. *The church is called the bride of Christ.* (Rev. 21:2; 22:17. cf. Eph. 5:23,32).

a. Jesus is called the bridegroom (Mark 2:18-20).

b. The wedding ceremony has not yet taken place.

> **(1)** We are engaged to Christ the bridegroom.
>
> **(2)** The wedding takes place after the Second Coming of Jesus – when the church is glorified.

II. SEX AND SINGLENESS

A. The assumption throughout the Bible is that as long as we are single we go without sex.

1. *Virginity in Jewish maidens was an assumption.*

a. If a man found that his bride was not a virgin he could divorce her (Deut. 22:13-19).

b. Proof of her virginity could even be required were there any doubt (Deut. 22:17).

2. If a man slept with a virgin, even though they were not engaged, he had to marry her. 'If a man seduces a virgin who is not pledged to be married and sleeps with her, he must pay the bride-price, and she shall be his wife' (Ex. 22:16).

    a. The father of the young lady could step in and stop the marriage.

    b. But the point is this: sexual intercourse was not done in ancient Israel unless the couple were married.

3. *If a young woman married who turned out not to be a virgin,* 'she shall be brought to the door of her father's house and there the men of her town shall stone her to death. She has done a disgraceful thing in Israel by being promiscuous while still in her father's house. You must purge the evil from among you' (Deut. 22:21).

    a. We can be thankful we are not under the Law today!

    b. But the assumption of a girl remaining a virgin until she was married:

        (1) Governed the concept of sex and singleness in the Old Testament.

        (2) There is nothing that changed this in the New Testament.

4. *The matter of rape shows the same principles.*

    a. 'If a man happens to meet a virgin who is not pledged to be married and rapes her and they are discovered, he shall pay the girl's father fifty shekels of silver. He must marry the girl, for he has violated her. He can never divorce her as long as he lives' (Deut. 22:28-29).

    b. The point: virginity was a thing both taken for granted and cherished if one was not married.

        (1) Isaac's wife Rebekah was 'very beautiful, a virgin; no man had ever lain with her' (Gen. 24:16).

        (2) Tamar was a virgin (2 Sam. 13:2).

        (3) The virgin daughters of the king wore special garments. (2 Sam. 13:18).

        (4) One of the rules for the priests: 'The woman he marries must be a virgin' (Lev. 21:13).

5. *If sexual temptation gets very severe, assuming you are engaged, you should push forward the wedding date!* 'If anyone thinks he is acting improperly towards the virgin he is engaged to, and if she is getting on in years and he feels he ought to marry, he should do as he wants. He is not sinning. They should get married' (1 Cor. 7:36).

a. Note: Paul clearly says they are engaged.

b. And if they were engaged they should still 'marry' – a ceremony is assumed – before they have sexual intercourse.

c. When Amnon was in love – it was in fact lust – with Tamar, he tried to force her to have sex with him. Her reply:

    (1) '"Don't, my brother!" she said to him. "Don't force me. Such a thing should not be done in Israel! Don't do this wicked thing. What about me? Where could I get rid of my disgrace? And what about you? You would be like one of the wicked fools in Israel. Please speak to the king; he will not keep me from being married to you"' (2 Sam. 13:12-13).

    (2) The point: they should not do this unless they were married.

    (3) The proof it was lust; after he raped her, 'Then Amnon hated her with intense hatred. In fact, he hated her more than he had loved her. Amnon said to her, "Get up and get out!"' (2 Sam. 13:15).

6. *Love is the fulfilling of the Law* (Rom. 13:8).

  a. 'The commandments, "Do not commit adultery," "Do not murder," "Do not steal," "Do not covet," and whatever other commandment there may be, are summed up in this one rule: "Love your neighbour as yourself." Love does no harm to its neighbour. Therefore love is the fulfilment of the law' (Rom. 13:9-10).

  b. Love that is true, will mean:

    (1) No premarital sex; if someone loves, they will respect the one they love, knowing that the highest road will be most appreciated later on.

      (a) Those who engage in sexual intercourse apart from marriage will eventually wish they hadn't.

      (b) Those who are engaged but have sexual intercourse will wish they had waited until after they got married.

      (c) True love will postpone sexual gratification.

      (d) Note: statistics have shown that those who slept together (or lived together) before they got married ended up divorced as often as those who had not lived together. This refutes the idea that they should 'try it out' and see if they will be sexually adjusted to each other before they get married. Data from the General Household Survey show that a couple who cohabit before marriage are, on average, twice as likely to divorce as a couple who do not cohabit before marriage. For example, among women aged between 40 and 50 who married when they were in their early twenties (20-24) and who cohabited before marriage, 39% were divorced compared to 21% of those who did not. Taking all age groups, the ratio of divorce between couples who premaritally cohabited and couples who did not cohabit, is 1.8 to 1, showing an 80% greater likelihood of divorce among those who cohabited before marriage. Studies show that cohabiting women are more irritable, worried and depressed than those who are married.

c. There will be no adultery.

d. There will be no sexual immorality.

B. The Bible and homosexuality

1. *The apostle Paul calls the practice of homosexuality 'against nature'.* 'Because of this, God gave them over to shameful lusts. Even their women exchanged natural relations for unnatural ones. In the same way the men also abandoned natural relations with women and were inflamed with lust for one another. Men committed indecent acts with other men, and received in themselves the due penalty for their perversion' (Rom. 1:26-27).

    a. The reason: God by creation decree made mankind male and female; by his own plan any sexual attraction was heterosexual.

        (1) In man's pre-fallen state there was no confusion regarding sexual attraction.

        (2) Since the Fall, owing to man's fallen and sinful condition, sexual proclivity (orientation of sexual desire) sometimes becomes confused.

    b. The homosexual person may say, 'My orientation is natural to me,' meaning that it is surely not unnatural to have a sexual attraction for the same sex.

        (1) One sympathises with people's feelings.

(2) But the Word of God must set an objective standard; therefore homosexual desire is regarded by God as unnatural.

c. Note: Romans 1:26 explicitly refers to lesbian practice.

2. *There is a difference between homosexual proclivity and homosexual practice.*

   a. Having an inclination or desire for the same sex is one thing; this is not sin; there is a difference between temptation and sin.

   b. Homosexual practice is another thing; this the Bible calls sin.

      (1) There are many people who have a desire for the same sex but would never dream of carrying out the actual practice.

      (2) Likewise there are heterosexual people who would not dream of indulging in pre-marital sex or adultery.

3. *Homosexuality is dealt with explicitly nine times in the Bible.*

   a. The men of Sodom who tried to have sex with Lot's guests (angels) (Gen. 19:1-11).

   b. Leviticus 18:22: 'Do not lie with a man as one lies with a woman; that is detestable.'

   c. Leviticus 20:13: 'If a man lies with a man as one lies with a woman, both of them have done what is detestable. They must be put to death; their blood will be on their own heads.'

   d. When 'wicked men' insisted on having sex with a man (Judges 19:22-24).

   e. Romans 1:26-27 (quoted above).

   f. What some Corinthians were before they were converted: 'homosexual offenders' (1 Cor. 6:9-11).

   g. Referred to as 'perverts' in 1 Timothy 1:9-10.

   h. Referring to Sodom and Gomorrah (2 Pet. 2:6-7).

   i. Called 'perversion' in Jude 7.

4. In a word: there is a difference between temptation and sin.

   a. It is not a sin to be tempted.

   b. Sin is not in the proclivity but the practice.

III. SEX AND MARRIAGE

A. Martin Luther: 'God uses sex to drive a man to marriage, ambition to drive a man to service, fear to drive a man to faith.'
  1. *There are three ancient Greek words for love:*
    a. Eros – physical love.
      (1) Sex was not born in Hollywood but at the throne of grace.
      (2) God made sexual love pleasurable.
    b. Philia – brotherly love.
    c. Agape – unselfish love (cf. John 3:16).
  2. *The irony: the love that makes people want to get married (eros) is not the love which will sustain the marriage.*
    a. Not that eros is replaced.
    b. Agape love must parallel physical love.
      (1) Keeping no record of wrongs.
      (2) Loving Jesus Christ more than you love each other.

B. We should not marry entirely for sex, neither should we marry hoping to avoid it.
  1. Sexual union consummates a marriage.
  2. *Sexual union is an assumption in marriage.*
    a. Paul acknowledges this is partly why people marry. 'But since there is so much immorality, each man should have his own wife, and each woman her own husband' (1 Cor. 7:2).
    b. This continued sexual union must be mutual. 'The husband should fulfil his marital duty to his wife, and likewise the wife to her husband. The wife's body does not belong to her alone but also to her husband. In the same way, the husband's body does not belong to him alone but also to his wife' (1 Cor. 7:3-4).

C. The seventh commandment and its continued relevance in the New Testament is for our good: 'You shall not commit adultery' (Ex. 20:14).
  1. Adultery destroys the foundation of all that marriage is.
  2. Love will prevent us from committing adultery (Rom. 13:8-10).

3. God will judge the adulterer (Heb. 13:4).

4. *Fidelity in marriage helps ensure the stability of the family.*

   a. When infidelity occurs its effect reaches the children.

   b. God instituted sexual purity in marriage partly for the stability of the family.

5. Infidelity in marriage, with or without children, breaks down trust.

IV. THE CASE FOR REMAINING SINGLE **(I COR. 7:25-40).**

A. You avoid 'many troubles in this life' (I Cor. 7:28).

   1. Some feel pressured to get married; they've been told by their friends they must get married and often panic as they grow older at the thought of remaining single.

   2. Some say how terrible to go throughout life without some sex; Paul says this is nonsense, and his appeal is that no unmarried person should feel second class.

   3. Paul bestows great dignity upon those who remain single.

B. The 'troubles' that emerge in marriage, for example, are:

   1. Surrender of independence; never again can we take a decision ourselves.

   2. Discovery of tensions in life we never knew existed – after the honeymoon is over; faults in the other we hadn't seen; problems of possessiveness and insecurity; illness.

   3. The care of children; they involve time and money; we must make room for them.

   4. Competition with 'the Lord's affairs'. 'I would like you to be free from concern. An unmarried man is concerned about the Lord's affairs – how he can please the Lord. But a married man is concerned about the affairs of this world – how he can please his wife – and his interests are divided' (1 Cor. 7:32-34a).

C. Marry if you must, although you are better off if you don't (1 Cor. 7:38-40).

   1. 'If anyone thinks he is acting improperly towards the virgin he is engaged to, and if she is getting on in years and he feels he ought to marry, he should do as he wants. He is not sinning. They should get married' (1 Cor. 7:36).

2. 'A woman is bound to her husband as long as he lives. But if her husband dies, she is free to marry anyone she wishes, but he must belong to the Lord' (1 Cor. 7:39).

CONCLUSION

Marriage is for life. The only thing worse than being unhappily unmarried is being unhappily married.

44

WHAT ABOUT MARRIAGE AND DIVORCE

INTRODUCTION

A. Marriage (def.): the state in which a man and a woman are formally united for the purpose of living together (usually in order to procreate children) and with certain legal rights and obligations towards each other.

1. *The purpose of living together is partly for sexual union.*
    a. The reason for '*usually* in order to procreate children' is added because:
       (1) Some may not be able to have children but still wish to marry.
       (2) The procreation of children would therefore follow the 'living together' having been formalised.
    b. The assumption is that this union will necessarily follow not precede the formality.
       (1) This rules out the sleeping together of a man and woman without the relationship being formalised.
       (2) The formality is what makes the sexual union legal and also holy (Heb. 13:4).
2. *Marriage therefore is exclusively heterosexual: for 'man and woman'.*
    a. This rules out a so-called 'homosexual marriage'.
    b. Homosexuality is categorically condemned and forbidden in scripture (Lev. 18:22).
       (1) A homosexual proclivity is not condemned, only the practice.
       (2) There is no biblical justification for homosexual practice or marriage.

B. Divorce (def.): the legal termination of a marriage.
1. *This is not necessarily the same as separation.*
    a. A married couple may live separately, or even be legally separated, without divorce.

b. Divorce is when the marriage is legally ended.

2. Divorce may set one free to remarry, depending on the willingness of the church or state to formalise such a marriage.

C. Why is this study important?

1. Many Christians assume what the Bible teaches on these matters, but often don't really know it; we want to get to the bottom of the matter if possible.

2. Marriages are breaking up more rapidly than ever; we need to ask why and whether we can do anything about this.

3. Fewer couples are getting married than in previous times; couples sleeping together without marriage is common; we need to ask, is this right?

4. As more and more Christian couples, sadly, are being divorced; the question inevitably follows, are they free to remarry?

5. This subject causes problems for many people, and it must be examined.

I. THE BIBLICAL VIEW OF MARRIAGE

A. The record of the creation of Eve indicates the unique relationship of husband and wife (Gen. 2:18-24).

1. *Marriage is God's idea.* 'The LORD God said, "It is not good for the man to be alone. I will make a helper suitable for him"' (Gen. 2:18).

   a. 'So the LORD God caused the man to fall into a deep sleep; and while he was sleeping, he took one of the man's ribs and closed up the place with flesh. Then the LORD God made a woman from the rib he had taken out of the man, and he brought her to the man' (Gen. 2:21-22).

   b. 'The man said, "This is now bone of my bones and flesh of my flesh; she shall be called 'woman', for she was taken out of man"' (Gen. 2:23).

2. *God ordained marriage in the Garden of Eden.* 'For this reason a man will leave his father and mother and be united to his wife, and they will become one flesh' (Gen. 2:24).

   a. Sex was not born in Hollywood but at the Throne of Grace.

   b. God ordered that man and woman should have children. 'God blessed them and said to them, "Be fruitful and increase in number; fill the earth and subdue it. Rule over the fish of the sea and the birds of the air and over every living creature that moves on the ground"' (Gen. 1:28).

B. Marriage is regarded as normal.
1. There is no word for 'bachelor' in the Old Testament.
2. *The relationship of husband and wife serves as a picture of the relationship between God and his people* (Jer. 3; Ezek. 16; Hosea 1-3).
  a. It is a picture of the relationship between Christ and his church (Eph. 5:22-33).
   (1) Jeremiah's call to remain unmarried is a unique prophetic sign (Jer. 16:2).
   (2) In the New Testament celibacy was God's call to some Christians for specific purposes (Matt.19:10-12. cf. 1 Cor. 7:7-9).
  b. Marriage and family life are the normal calling (John 2:1-11; Eph. 5:22-6:4; 1 Tim. 3:2; 4:3; 5:14).

C. Monogamy (def.: being married to only one person at a time) is implicit in the story of Adam and Eve, since God only created one wife for Adam.
1. *However, polygamy (def.: having more than one wife at a time) is not forbidden in the Old Testament.*
  a. It was adopted from the time of Lamech (Gen. 4:19).
  b. Some have offered the opinion that God left it to man to discover by experience that his original institution of monogamy was the proper relationship.
   (1) It is shown that polygamy brings trouble, and often results in sin (Gen. 21; Judges 8:29-9:57; 2 Sam. 11; 13; 1 Kings 11:1-8).
   (2) In view of oriental customs Hebrew kings are warned against it (Deut. 17:17).
   (3) Family jealousies arise from it, as with Elkanah's two wives, one of whom is an adversary to the other (1 Sam. 1:6. cf. Lev. 18:18).
2. *It is difficult to know how far polygamy was practised, but on economic grounds it is probable that it was found more among the wealthier than among ordinary people.*

  a. Jacob was tricked into polygamy, and loved Rachel more than Leah (Gen. 29).

  b. Elkanah preferred Hannah in spite of her having no children (1 Sam. 1:1-8).

  c. A woman having more than one husband at the same time was apparently out of the question, insofar as biblical approval goes (cf. John 4:16-18).

 3. *The return to monogamy is assumed for Christians in the New Testament. 'But since there is so much immorality, each man should have his own wife, and each woman her own husband'* (1 Cor. 7:2).

  a. He who loves his *wife* loves himself' (Eph. 5:28).

  b. 'For this reason a man will leave his father and mother and be united to his *wife*, and the two will become one flesh' (Eph. 5:31).

  c. 'However, each one of you also must love his *wife* as he loves himself, and the wife must respect her husband' (Eph. 5:33).

  d. The standard of monogamy is explicit for those holding office in the church:

   (1) 'Now the overseer must be above reproach, the husband *of but one wife*, temperate, self-controlled, respectable, hospitable, able to teach' (I Tim. 3:2).

   (2) 'A deacon must be the husband *of but one wife* and must manage his children and his household well' (I Tim. 3:12).

D. The wedding ceremony

 1. *The purpose of the ceremony was to sanctify sexual union.*

  a. It was assumed that intercourse before marriage was out of the question.

  b. Before coming together, for which the Hebrew uses the idiom 'to know', prayer was offered by husband and wife.

  c. The assumption that the wife is to be a virgin is evident by the display of a blood-stained cloth as proof of the bride's virginity (Deut. 22:13-21).

 2. *An important feature of the ceremony was the public acknowledgement of the marital relationship.*

  a. Special garments for the bride and groom.

   (1) The bride sometimes wore embroidered garments (Ps.

45:13-14), jewels (Is. 61:10), ornaments (Jer. 2:32) and a veil (Gen. 24:65).

    (2) The groom might wear a garland (Is. 61:10).

  b. Wedding attendants:

    (1) Bridesmaids and friends (Ps. 45:14).

    (2) The groom had his companions (Judges 14:11; Matt. 9:15).

  c. The procession.

    (1) Sometimes the bridegroom and his friends went in procession to the bride's house (Gen. 29:22; Judges 14).

    (2) The procession might be accompanied by singing, music and dancing (Jer. 7:34) and by lamps at night (Matt. 25:7).

  d. The marriage feast.

    (1) Usually held at the house of the groom (Matt. 22:1-10; John 2:9).

    (2) It was often at night (Matt. 22:13; 25:6).

    (3) Many relatives and friends attended, so the wine might well run out (John 2:3).

    (4) A steward or friend supervised the feast (John 2:9-10).

    (5) To refuse an invitation to the wedding feast was an insult (Matt. 22:7).

    (6) The guests were expected to wear festive clothes (Matt. 22:11-12).

  e. Covering the bride.

    (1) The man covers the woman with his garment, perhaps a sign that he takes her under protection (Ruth 3:9; Ezek. 16:8).

    (2) The implication of this was, 'From now on, nobody but me will cover you.'

  f. Blessing. Parents and friends blessed the couple and wished them well (Gen. 24:60; Ruth 4:11).

E. Covenant

  1. *Another solemn element of the ceremony was the covenant of faithfulness. The content was implied in:*

    a. 'It will save you also from the adulteress, from the wayward wife with her seductive words, who has left the partner of her youth and ignored the covenant she made before God' (Prov. 2:16-17).

    b. 'Later I passed by, and when I looked at you and saw that you were old enough for love, I spread the corner of my garment over you and covered your nakedness. I gave you my solemn oath and entered into a covenant with you, declares the Sovereign LORD, and you became mine' (Ezek. 16:8).

    c. 'You ask, "Why?" It is because the LORD is acting as the witness between you and the wife of your youth, because you have broken faith with her, though she is your partner, the wife of your marriage covenant' (Mal. 2:14).

  2. In some cases the father of the bride drew up a written marriage contract.

  3. *This covenant is upheld by the seventh commandment: 'You shall not commit adultery'* (Ex. 20:14).

    a. Marriage was for life. 'For example, by law a married woman is bound to her husband as long as he is alive, but if her husband dies, she is released from the law of marriage. So then, if she marries another man while her husband is still alive, she is called an adulteress. But if her husband dies, she is released from that law and is not an adulteress, even though she marries another man' (Rom. 7:2-3).

    b. Jesus said, 'I tell you that anyone who divorces his wife, except for marital unfaithfulness, and marries another woman commits adultery' (Matt. 19:9).

F. The apostle Paul gives his advice on marriage (cf. I Cor. 7:6).

  1. *In general, people should remain as they are.*

    a. If they are married, stay married (1 Cor. 7:10).

      (1) Full conjugal rights are to be carried out (1 Cor. 7:3-4).

      (2) But what they do in this way must be by mutual consent (1 Cor. 7:5).

    b. If they are unmarried, stay unmarried (1 Cor. 7:8).

      (1) This is best for virgins (1 Cor. 7:25ff).

      (2) So too with widows (1 Cor. 7:40).

  2. *People should get married to avoid immorality* (1 Cor. 7:2).

    a. This shows two important principles:

      (1) Sex outside of marriage is immoral.

      (2) Sex is an essential ingredient in marriage. 'But if they cannot control themselves, they should marry, for it is better to marry than to burn with passion' (1 Cor. 7:9).

    b. Paul does not say, 'Let them sleep together,' but 'They should marry' – showing a formalising ceremony.

3. *Celibacy (staying unmarried) is a gift of God* (1 Cor. 7:7).

    a. This means it comes easily.

    b. If one does not have this gift he or she should hope to be married.

4. *Marriage is for life.*

    a. 'To the married I give this command (not I but the Lord): A wife must not separate from her husband' (1 Cor. 7:10).

    b. But if she does separate she has one of two options:

        (1) Stay unmarried.

        (2) Be reconciled to her husband (1 Cor. 7:11).

    c. A husband must not divorce his wife (1 Cor. 7:11).

        (1) This is the case, even if she is not a Christian (1 Cor. 7:12).

        (2) So too with the wife whose husband is not a Christian (1 Cor. 7:13).

5. *The case for remaining single* (1 Cor. 7:25-40).

    a. You avoid 'many troubles in this life' (1 Cor. 7:28).

        (1) Some feel pressured to get married; they've been told by their friends they must get married and often panic as they grow older with the thought of remaining single.

        (2) Some say how terrible to go throughout life without some sex; Paul says this is nonsense and his appeal is that no unmarried person should feel second class.

        (3) Paul bestows great dignity upon those who remain single.

    b. The 'troubles' that emerge in marriage, for example, are:

        (1) Surrender of independence; never again can we take a decision by ourselves.

        (2) Discovery of tensions in life we never knew existed – after the honeymoon is over; faults not seen before; problems of possessiveness and insecurity; illnesses.

        (3) The care of children; they involve time and money; we must make room for them.

        (4) Competition with 'the Lord's affairs'. 'I would like you to be free from concern. An unmarried man is concerned about the Lord's affairs – how he can please the Lord.

But a married man is concerned about the affairs of this world – how he can please his wife – and his interests are divided' (1 Cor. 7:32-34a).

6. *Marry if you must, although you are better off if you don't* (1 Cor. 7:38-40).

    a. 'If anyone thinks he is acting improperly towards the virgin he is engaged to, and if she is getting on in years and he feels he ought to marry, he should do as he wants. He is not sinning. They should get married' (1 Cor. 7:36).

    b. 'A woman is bound to her husband as long as he lives. But if her husband dies, she is free to marry anyone she wishes, but he must belong to the Lord' (1 Cor. 7:39).

II. DIVORCE

A. The Old Testament.

1. *Moses did not command divorce but regulated an existing practice.*

    a. 'If a man marries a woman who becomes displeasing to him because he finds something indecent about her, and he writes her a certificate of divorce, gives it to her and sends her from his house, and if after she leaves his house she becomes the wife of another man, and her second husband dislikes her and writes her a certificate of divorce, gives it to her and sends her from his house, or if he dies, then her first husband, who divorced her, is not allowed to marry her again after she has been defiled. That would be detestable in the eyes of the LORD. Do not bring sin upon the land the LORD your God is giving you as an inheritance' (Deut. 24:1-4).

    b. From this we may gather that divorce was practised.

      (1) A form of contract was given to the wife.

      (2) She was free to remarry.

2. *The grounds of divorce were in such general terms that no precise interpretation can be given.*

    a. What the NIV calls 'indecent' the AV calls 'unclean' in (Deut. 24:1).

    b. Shortly before the time of Christ there were two schools of thought:

(1) The School of Shammai interpreted it by unfaithfulness only.

(2) The School of Hillel extended it to mean anything unpleasant to the husband.

3. *There were two situations in which divorce was forbidden:*

    a. When a man has falsely accused his wife of pre-marital unfaithfulness (Deut. 22:13-19).

    b. When a man had pre-marital relations with a woman and was forced to marry her (Deut. 22:28-29).

4. *On two exceptional occasions divorce was insisted upon:*

    a. When the returned exiles had married pagan wives (Ezra 9 and 10; Neh. 13:23ff).

    b. When some men had put away their Jewish wives so as to marry pagans (Mal. 2:10-16).

5. *In Malachi 2:16 God said, 'I hate divorce.'*

    a. This gives us God's view of marriage and divorce.

    b. Jesus said that Moses permitted divorce 'because your hearts were hard' (Matt. 19:8).

B. The New Testament.

1. *Matthew's gospel.*

    a. 'But I tell you that anyone who divorces his wife, except for marital unfaithfulness, causes her to become an adulteress, and anyone who marries the divorced woman commits adultery' (Matt. 5:32).

    b. 'I tell you that anyone who divorces his wife, except for marital unfaithfulness, and marries another woman commits adultery' (Matt. 19:9).

        (1) Marital unfaithfulness (AV: 'fornication') is given as the only ground on which a man may divorce his wife.

        (2) The Greek word *porneia* may refer to any kind of sexual immorality.

2. *Mark 10:11-12 and Luke 16:18 do not include the reference to infidelity, thus allowing no exceptions.*

    a. The reason could be that no Jew, Roman or Greek ever doubted that adultery constituted grounds for divorce.

    b. Hence Mark and Luke took this for granted.

3. Matthew 19:9 allows for remarriage after divorce, given the grounds of marital unfaithfulness.

4. *Note: among Jews there was no such custom as separation without permission to remarry.*

    a. A Jewish wife could not normally divorce her husband.

    b. But a wife could appeal to the court against her husband's treatment of her, and the court could compel the husband to divorce her.

    c. Hence Jesus may have had Greek and Roman law in mind in Mark 10:12, which states the woman's initiative.

5. *The 'Pauline privilege': on grounds of desertion* (1 Cor. 7:15).

    a. 'But if the unbeliever leaves, let him do so. A believing man or woman is not bound in such circumstances; God has called us to live in peace' (1 Cor. 7:15).

      (1) When the non-Christian spouse leaves, release him or her.

      (2) Don't *you* leave him/her; don't initiate it.

      (3) But if they initiate it, then let them go.

    b. Paul has no right, save his apostolic authority, to say this.

      (1) It wasn't taught by Jesus.

      (2) Paul makes this concession.

    c. The Big Question: can the divorced person remarry?

      (1) Remarriage is implied, since remarriage was forbidden when one does the deserting (1 Cor. 7:11).

      (2) But if one didn't take the initiative remarriage is implied. One is 'not bound in such circumstances' (1 Cor. 7:15).

    d. Note: Paul envisaged an extreme situation; when one tried to hold the marriage together – but failed.

Conclusion

The New Testament presents a much higher standard than is seen in Deuteronomy 24:1-4. A husband did not have to look too hard if he wanted to divorce his wife, under the Mosaic law. The New Testament only allows two exceptions: unfaithfulness and desertion by the unbelieving spouse. Some say that in either case remarriage was still not allowed. My own view is that the purpose of divorce was largely to set one free to remarry. Today, as Christians, we have this tension we face: to maintain the high standard of Christian marriage and yet show compassion to those who suffer irretrievable marriage breakdown. We can only do this with fear and trembling.

45

THE MINISTRY OF HEALING TODAY

INTRODUCTION

A. Today we have become increasingly interested in the ministry of divine healing.

  1. *By 'divine' I mean: what God does.*

   a. God may use medicine and qualified medical practitioners.

   (1) This is from God.

   (2) It is an example of common grace: God's goodness to all men, that is quite apart from saving grace.

   b. But I refer mainly to what God does apart from what can be explained at the natural level.

   (1) So much 'healing' that is claimed these days either didn't happen at all − or it had a medical or scientific explanation.

   (2) Those who make such claims do not really bring honour to God's name.

  2. *We long to see the 'real thing' − that which defies a natural, medical or scientific explanation.*

   a. We want to see the kind of healing which can be verified at the empirical level.

   (1) Empirical (def.): proof of healing not by hearsay but what is based on observation or experiment.

   (2) When records − e.g. x-rays -- prove a healing that medicine had no bearing upon.

   b. It is true that sometimes there can be an overlap between the natural and the supernatural.

   (1) If one has been taking medicine and healing follows, it is possible that the healing was supernatural, but there could be some doubt.

   (2) Medical authorities often remain sceptical when an obvious healing or miracle has taken place.

   c. It is also true that sometimes a person knows he or she has

461

been healed and it will not be provable at the empirical level.

    (1) This has happened many times.

    (2) We must not take this lightly.

  d. We long to see the undoubted healing that cannot be explained except in terms of God's supernatural overruling.

    (1) That is what we pray for.

    (2) That is what this lesson is about.

B. Why is this lesson important?

  1. With the rise of Pentecostalism and the charismatic movement there has been an emphasis on healing.

  2. There have been a number of claims of people being healed.

  3. Too often these claims do not match the facts.

  4. Overclaiming is not good for the testimony of Jesus Christ.

  5. It is important to ask: Does God heal? If so, why?

I. THE MINISTRY OF JESUS

A. A part of Jesus' ministry was healing.

  1. *Why did Jesus heal people?*

    a. He cared about people.

      (1) When Jesus saw a large crowd, 'he had compassion on them, because they were like sheep without a shepherd' (Mark 6:34).

      (2) Jesus looked at a man 'and loved him' (Mark 10:21).

    b. He knew what the people's needs were.

      (1) "'I have no husband," she replied. Jesus said to her, "You are right when you say you have no husband. The fact is, you have had five husbands, and the man you now have is not your husband. What you have just said is quite true"' (John 4:17-18).

      (2) The person who had been delivered from demon possession begged to stay with Jesus. 'Jesus did not let him, but said, "Go home to your family and tell them how much the Lord has done for you, and how he has had mercy on you"' (Mark 5:19).

    c. Jesus fulfilled Messianic expectations.

      (1) 'When evening came, many who were demon-possessed

were brought to him, and he drove out the spirits with a word and healed all the sick. This was to fulfil what was spoken through the prophet Isaiah: "He took up our infirmities and carried our diseases"' (Matt. 8:16-17).

(2) 'Surely he took up our infirmities and carried our sorrows' (Isa. 53:4).

d. Jesus validated forgiving people of their sins.

(1) 'Which is easier: to say, "Your sins are forgiven," or to say, "Get up and walk"? But so that you may know that the Son of Man has authority on earth to forgive sins. . . ." Then he said to the paralytic, "Get up, take your mat and go home"' (Matt. 9:5-6).

(2) This implicitly showed Jesus' deity since they asked, 'Who can forgive sins but God alone?' (Luke 5:21).

c. It vindicated Jesus' ministry.

(1) As Peter later said, 'You know what has happened throughout Judea, beginning in Galilee after the baptism that John preached – how God anointed Jesus of Nazareth with the Holy Spirit and power, and how he went around doing good and healing all who were under the power of the devil, because God was with him' (Acts 10:37-38).

(2) Nicodemus said, 'We know you are a teacher who has come from God. For no-one could perform the miraculous signs you are doing if God were not with him' (John 3:2).

2. *The kinds of healing Jesus did: 'Every disease and sickness'* (Matt. 4:23).

a. Leprosy. (Matt. 8:2-4; Luke 17:11-19).

b. Paralysis (Matt. 8:5-13; 9:1-8; John 5:1-15).

c. Fever (Matt. 8:14-15).

d. Demon-possession (Matt. 8:28-34; Mark 1:23-26).

e. Haemorrhage (Matt. 9:20-22).

f. Raising the dead (Matt. 9:23-26; John 11).

g. Blindness (Matt. 9:27-31).

h. Dumbness (Matt. 9:32-33).

i. Epilepsy (Matt. 17:14-18).

j. Restoration of an ear which had been cut off (Luke 22:50-51).

B. The ways Jesus chose to heal.

1. By his physical touch (Matt. 8:3; 8:15; 9:29).
2. By remote control (Matt. 8:5-13).
3. By his word: 'Go!' (Matt. 8:32). 'Lazarus, come out!' (John 11:43).
4. By forgiving sin (Matt. 9:1-8).
5. *When one touched his garment.*
   a. Jesus said it was her faith (Matt. 9:22).
   b. Yet power went out from him (Luke 8:46).
6. *By spitting and laying on of hands.*
   a. He did this in two stages.
      (1) 'He looked up and said, "I see people; they look like trees walking around" ' (Mark 8:24).
      (2) 'Once more Jesus put his hands on the man's eyes. Then his eyes were opened, his sight was restored, and he saw everything clearly' (Mark 8:25).
   b. Note: the man who had a 'legion' of devils was not delivered the first time Jesus approached him. 'For Jesus had said to him, "Come out of this man, you evil spirit!"' (Mark 5:8).
7. With mud and saliva, followed by the command to wash in the pool of Siloam (John 9:6-7).

C. Jesus did not wish to keep the healing ministry to himself.

1. He gave the disciples authority 'to drive out evil spirits and to cure every kind of disease and sickness' (Matt. 10:1).
2. He appointed seventy-two others with authority (Luke 10:1-20).
3. He said that after his ascension those who believe would drive out demons and make sick people well by the laying on of hands (Mark 16:15-18).

II. THE MINISTRY OF HEALING AFTER JESUS WENT TO HEAVEN

A. The Holy Spirit continued the healing ministry of Jesus (John 14:16).

1. God testified to salvation by 'signs, wonders and various miracles, and gifts of the Holy Spirit distributed according to his will' (Heb. 2:4).
2. By his Holy Spirit, God showed that as well as people being saved, healing was to continue.

B. God did this to vindicate his Son, thus showing the ongoing manifestation of the supernatural, by:

1. *Signs*

    a. Greek *semeion*, used 77 times in the New Testament, e.g. Matthew 12:38-39; Matthew 16:1-4; 1 Corinthians 1:22. Note: it usually appears alongside the other two words: wonders and miracles.

    b. In ancient Hellenistic literature it meant 'sign', 'characteristic', 'mark'.

      (1) There were sometimes two characteristics: prominence and visibility.

      (2) It was often a pointer to something beyond itself.

    c. The Hebrew equivalent is found 79 times in the Old Testament, e.g. Psalm 86:17: 'Give me a sign of your goodness, that my enemies may see it and be put to shame, for you, O LORD, have helped me and comforted me.'

      (1) The rainbow was a sign in Genesis 9:12ff.

      (2) Gideon's 'fleece' was a sign (Judg. 6:36-40).

2. *Wonders*

    a. Greek *teras*, used 16 times in the New Testament, e.g., Matthew 24:24; John 4:48; Acts 2:19. It is usually accompanied by 'signs', if not also 'miracles', e.g. Acts 2:22; 4:30; Romans 15:19; 2 Corinthians 12:12.

    b. In ancient Hellenistic literature it was used to describe anything awesome, if not terrible or terrifying, like a clap of thunder in a clear sky.

      (1) They were thought to be associated with the gods, as if of divine origin.

      (2) A mysterious element was usually associated with teras.

    c. Its equivalent in Hebrew occurs 46 times in the Old Testament, e.g., Exodus 15:11; Psalm 105:5; 1 Chronicles 16:12.

3. *Miracles*

    a. Greek *dunamis*, used 120 times in the New Testament, e.g., Matthew 7:22; 11:20; Luke 8:46 ('power'); Acts 1:8 ('power'). It is often translated 'power'.

    b. It is clearly connected to the idea of potency or 'possibility', 'capacity' or 'ability'.

    c. It is translated 'miracles', e.g. in Matthew 7:22 and Galatians

3:5; the context would indicate whether dunamis be translated 'power' or 'miracles'.

d. It is seen as an extension of the operation of the Holy Spirit.

4. Note: these words can be used interchangeably. For example, semeion (signs) is translated 'miracles' throughout the Gospel of John in the NIV.

5. *Whichever word is used, it is to be seen as:*

   a. What God does, not what man does.

   b. That which is supernatural, that is, 'beyond nature'.

6. *Gifts.*

   a. *Charisma*, used 17 times in the New Testament, but not the word used in Hebrews 2:4, which is *merismos* (a rarely used word).

   b. It means 'grace-gift', e.g. 1 Corinthians 12:4,9,28,30,31.

C. These were seen in the book of Acts.

1. *The healing of the forty-year-old man who had never walked* (Acts 3:1-10).

   a. Peter stepped in and asked, 'Why does this surprise you?'

   b. The explanation was simple: 'The God of Abraham, Isaac and Jacob, the God of our fathers, has glorified his servant Jesus. You handed him over to be killed, and you disowned him before Pilate, though he had decided to let him go' (Acts 3:13).

      (1) This was a demonstration that the healing ministry of Jesus was to go on after his death, resurrection and ascension.

      (2) Whereas Jesus did it by being physically present, it was now done 'By faith in the name of Jesus, this man whom you see and know was made strong. It is Jesus' name and the faith that comes through him that has given this complete healing to him, as you can all see' (Acts 3:16).

2. *There was so much power present in the early church that* 'people brought the sick into the streets and laid them on beds and mats so that at least Peter's shadow might fall on some of them as he passed by' (Acts 5:15).

   a. It brought crowds from the towns around Jerusalem.

   b. People brought their sick and those tormented by evil spirits, as in Jesus' day, 'and all of them were healed' (Acts 5:16).

3. *Simon Peter was powerfully used in this way.*

    a. A man paralysed for eight years was healed (Acts 9:32-34).

    b. A lady was raised from the dead (Acts 9:36-42).

4. *The apostle Paul was powerfully used in this way.*

    a. A man who was crippled from birth was healed (Acts 14:8-10).

    b. A girl who was demon possessed was delivered (Acts 16:16-18).

    c. A young man was raised from the dead (Acts 20:9-12).

    d. All the sick in the island of Malta were cured (Acts 28:7-10).

D. Two of the gifts of the Spirit are healing and miracles (1 Cor. 12:9-10).

1. *Healing (def.): when disease or defect in a body is removed and the natural process of cure is restored.*

    a. This is usually a gradual process although sometimes it comes suddenly.

    b. The gift (anointing) of healing is distinguished from ordinary medical skill.

    c. The value of healing.

        (1) It gives relief of pain and/or the prolonging of life.

        (2) It demonstrates the power of Jesus' name.

2. *Miracles (def.): extraordinary occurrences that cannot be explained naturally.*

    a. This is an instantaneous healing.

    b. It may be an instantaneous deliverance (from demonic possession or oppression).

        (1) Possession: when an evil spirit comes inside a person and holds virtual control.

        (2) Oppression: when an evil spirit comes from without yet appears to have the upper hand on a person.

    c. The value of miracles.

        (1) Instant relief.

        (2) Honour to God's name.

E. The anointing of oil (Jas. 5:13-16).

1. *This would appear to involve the elders of the church.*

    a. The word 'elder' literally means an older man.

    b. It came to refer to a wiser person, and eventually became a function or office in the church.

467

2. *If someone is sick he or she should call for the elders.*

    a. This means the sick person initiates the process.

    b. The elders 'pray over' and 'anoint' with oil.

3. *'And the prayer offered in faith will make the sick person well; the Lord will raise him up. If he has sinned, he will be forgiven'* (Jas. 5:15).

    a. There is a big 'if' here; not all sickness, therefore, is a sign of sin or disobedience.

    b. If there is reason to believe that the sick person has sinned so as to bring this illness, he or she should confess the sins. 'Therefore confess your sins to each other and pray for each other so that you may be healed. The prayer of a righteous man is powerful and effective' (Jas. 5:16).

III. HEALING TODAY

A. Why should we want it?

    1. People who are in pain want a better quality of life.

    2. This brings honour to Jesus' name.

    3. It provides a greater platform for preaching the Gospel.

B. Principles of healing today.

    1. *God can use anyone in the ministry of healing.*

        a. Structural authority has been given to the church.

            (1) The apostles largely had this power in the New Testament (Acts 8:14-17).

            (2) The sick would call for the elders of the church (Jas. 5:14ff).

        b. Spiritual authority has been given to the body of Christ.

            (1) The gift of healing was apparently available to many.

            (2) 'God can use little old me,' says Randy Clark.

    2. *We have a right, if not a mandate, to pray for the sick.*

        a. The right lies in the tone of Scripture generally.

            (1) The ministry of healing didn't stop when Jesus ascended (Eph. 4:8-11).

            (2) The ministry of healing did not end with the early church (Heb. 13:8).

        b. I believe there is a real sense in which we are called to pray for the sick.

(1) People in pain want to be touched by God.

(2) If not us, who will pray for them?

3. *No case is too difficult for God.*

  a. God can cure cancer as easily as he can heal a cold.

  b. What Jesus did in person the Holy Spirit can do in person (John 14:12).

  c. 'For nothing is impossible with God' (Luke 1:37).

4. *If we don't pray for the sick, we will probably never see people healed.*

  a. God can sovereignly heal – in more ways than one.

    (1) He can use common grace – doctors and medicine.

    (2) He can heal during the preaching of the Gospel.

  b. But if we don't make prayer for healing available, we will not see people healed.

5. *Only God heals.*

  a. It is not the laying on of hands or the oil which heals.

  b. It is God who steps in.

    (1) By a healing presence (Luke 5:17).

    (2) By granting the prayer of faith (Jas. 5:15).

  c. We must not have faith in our faith or in our gift – only in God.

6. *We must overcome the fear of failure (people not getting healed).*

  a. God is sovereign; we cannot make him heal anybody.

  b. But if we don't pray for people, they probably won't be healed.

  c. What keeps people from praying for the sick:

    (1) Fear of being emotionally involved.

    (2) Pride – fear of failure and not having answers.

7. *We must never make people feel guilty if they are not healed.*

  a. Jesus never rebuked the afflicted person for his or her lack of faith.

  b. He only rebuked those who prayed for not having more faith (Mark 9:19).

8. *Affirm the least thing God does.*

  a. Forget the critics if only a back pain or headache is healed.

    (1) After all, to the one who has suffered this is no small healing.

    (2) Thank God for anything – whatever it is – that he does.

  b. God may later trust us with extraordinary healings.

9. *Pray for anybody who asks to be prayed for.*

    a. Whether or not they are saved.

        (1) God may heal them before they are converted.

        (2) This will almost certainly lead them to Christ.

    b. Whether or not you have prayed for them previously.

        (1) God may be testing you and them.

        (2) Their time may come this time!

    c. Whether or not you 'feel' faith.

        (1) It is not faith in your faith.

        (2) Faith in a big God is what is needed.

10. *Remember that nobody ever truly deserves to be healed.*

    a. We are all unworthy.

    b. The gift of healing – charismata – is a grace-gift.

        (1) Sin may be a cause of sickness (Jas. 5:14-15).

        (2) It is for the sick person not you to determine this.

C. Practical suggestions: when people request prayers for healing

    1. *Interview them.*

        a. Try to get them to open up – what is wrong?

        b. The purpose of this: to have some diagnosis of their problem.

    2. *Welcome the Holy Spirit when you pray.*

        a. Invite him to come.

        b. If you feel his presence, say so and thank him.

    3. *Feel compassion for the person.*

        a. This will increase your own faith.

        b. This will make the person feel loved – and not rejected.

    4. *Be open for a sure word of knowledge.*

        a. If you discern something and pray accordingly, this increases faith.

        b. The purpose of a word of knowledge: it releases the gift of faith (Randy Clark).

    5. *Speak to the condition, being specific.*

        a. Pray that God will deal with the very cause (if you know what it is).

        b. The Holy Spirit may lead you to pray in surprising detail.

    6. *Don't try to make the correct use of words with a magic formula.*

        a. If you think you've come up with a formula, it probably won't work.

        b. Pray with spontaneity in the Spirit.

    7. *Ask them if they are feeling anything.*

    a. This may mean God is at work.

    b. They may feel a sensation that doesn't relate to the pain they wanted to be relieved of; if so, pray in the way God leads you.

8. *If there is a sense of God, keep praying.*

    a. God often touches people gradually, in stages or 'waves'.

    b. If you sense God has stopped answering, then you stop praying.

9. Always thank God for the least thing he does.

10. *Be open to further learning of God's ways.*

    a. Be willing to say, 'I don't know.'

    b. We all see through a glass darkly.

CONCLUSION

Faith is not the absence of doubt, but facing doubt and praying anyway. God may use you to see healings that defy a natural or medical explanation. It's not you who heals but God's power; never get proud if God uses you. In the meantime, be willing to endure the pain of failure.

46

OVERCOMING DEPRESSION

A. One of the severest forms of suffering is depression.

1. *For those who have never experienced this there may be a lack of sensitivity and tolerance.*

   a. It is hard to sympathise with another's weakness if you yourself have not experienced that weakness.

   b. One reason for suffering generally is that we can learn to sympathise. 'If we are distressed, it is for your comfort and salvation; if we are comforted, it is for your comfort, which produces in you patient endurance of the same sufferings we suffer' (2 Cor. 1:6).

2. *But for those who have experienced this, there will not only be sympathy – but also questions:*

   a. Why does God allow depression?

   b. Is it the consequence of sin?

   c. Is there a meaningful purpose in it?

B. Depression (def): a feeling of having nothing to live for.

1. The Oxford dictionary defines it as a state of excessive sadness or hopelessness, often with physical symptoms.

2. *It is a condition marked by feelings of worthlessness, dejection (lowness of spirit) and worry.*

   a. The depressed person is an unhappy individual with a pessimistic outlook on life.

   b. He (or she) is vulnerable, even minor frustrations may cause increased feelings of depression.

      (1) He thinks that all he does results in failure.

      (2) He feels inadequate and unworthy of the love and respect of others.

   c. In a word: he has an inadequate self-image (or self-concept).

3. In more serious forms, depression may result in suicide attempts.

C. The person suffering from depression has strong feelings of guilt.

1. *He feels unworthy and thinks he is in need of punishment because of failures, sins and inadequacies.*

   a. He may worry constantly over some deed committed many years before.

   b. He is unable to remove the feelings of guilt and concern.

2. *When this person is a Christian, because he feels unworthy and sinful he often misinterprets God's Word:*

   a. By giving attention only to those verses which judge and condemn.

   b. By ignoring verses that affirm and encourage.

D. Why is this subject important?

1. *The best of Christians suffer from depression from time to time.*

   a. We can see this in the best of God's people in the Bible.

   b. History and experience reveal the same thing.

2. *We need to know the answer to questions such as:*

   a. Can a truly converted person suffer from depression?

   b. Can a truly godly person suffer from depression?

   c. Is depression the result of God's displeasure?

   d. Is it a sign of disobedience?

3. *We need to examine the causes of depression.*

   a. Is it spiritual?

   b. Or are there other causes?

4. *Is there a place for counselling when a person is depressed?*

   a. Should such counselling always come from a Christian?

   b. Is there a case to be made for psychiatry?

5. Is there a cause for depression?

6. How does one overcome depression?

7. Why does God allow depression?

8. Is there a valid theology that will uphold a person suffering from depression?

I. KINDS OF DEPRESSION

A. Emotional depression.

1. *Neurotic depression (def.): a nervous condition that produces symptoms for which there is no evidence of disease. For example:*

    a. Anxiety reaction: varying degrees of dread, worry and apprehension for which there is no objective cause.

      (1) Anxiety is often the common denominator of psychopathology.

      (2) It is what leads to more serious mental disorders.

    b. Hypochondria: characterised by excessive preoccupation with health without accompanying organic pathology.

      (1) Sufferers may complain of aches and pains for which the physician can find no organic basis.

      (2) They often spend time reading health journals and newspaper articles on disease.

  2. *Psychotic depression (def.): a mental state in which one is detached from reality. For example:*

    a. Manic depressive reaction: characterised by moods of elation and depression, which may last from a few days to many months.

    b. Melancholia: characterised by a hopeless outlook, often by the fear of having committed the unpardonable sin.

    c. Postpartum depression: extreme depression connected with childbirth, which may occur any time during pregnancy and throughout the first year following the birth of a child.

B. Spiritual depression.

  1. *When God hides his face.* 'How long, O LORD? Will you forget me for ever? How long will you hide your face from me?' (Ps. 13:1).

    a. All Christians sooner or later experience the hiding of God's face.

      (1) Some saints have experienced what they call the 'midnight of the soul'.

      (2) The feelings produced overlap with some of the emotional disturbances described above.

    b. This is best explained as 'chastening' or 'being disciplined by the Lord.' 'And you have forgotten that word of encouragement that addresses you as sons: "My son, do not make light of the Lord's discipline, and do not lose heart when he rebukes you, because the Lord disciplines those he loves, and he punishes everyone he accepts as a son."' (Heb. 12:5-6).

(1) If anxiety is the common denominator of most psychopathology, the hiding of God's face is the common denominator of chastening.

(2) The cause: God's sovereign will in what he either causes or permits.

2. *Disobedience.* '*Against you, you only, have I sinned and done what is evil in your sight, so that you are proved right when you speak and justified when you judge*' (Ps. 51:4).

  a. When David sinned by adultery and murder, it is not surprising that he went into a depression – when he was exposed by Nathan the prophet (2 Sam. 12:7).

    (1) Nathan told him that his and Bathsheba's child would die (2 Sam. 12:14).

    (2) 'David pleaded with God for the child. He fasted and went into his house and spent the nights lying on the ground' (2 Sam. 12:16).

  b. Depression after wilful disobedience may be God's instrument to get our attention.

    (1) David apparently felt little guilt for his sin until rebuked by Nathan.

    (2) The cause of spiritual depression in some cases: wilful sin against God's known will.

II. Causes of depression

A. It may be physical.

  1. *A physical malady may be the chief reason for depression. We should always keep in mind, for example:*

    a. Diet

      (1) We should try to eat three times a day; lack of food may result in weakness and a depressed spirit.

      (2) We ought also to take seriously the quality of food; what is good and is not good to eat – which may vary from person to person.

    b. Sleep

      (1) We should come to terms with the need for the proper amount of time to sleep.

      (2) Sleeplessness can easily result in excessive anxiety and depression.

    c. Hormonal change

       (1) Menopause (termination of menstrual cycle), when the body loses oestrogen, often results in depression and the loss of self-esteem.

       (2) Chemical imbalance therefore is physical and we should not see adverse emotional behaviour as if spiritually derived.

    d. Glandular dysfunction: the endocrine glands produce hormones which affect both physiological and psychological development and functioning of a person; adverse effects come from over- or under-secretion of the hormones. For example:

       (1) Thyroid: this gland regulates the body's metabolism which may in turn affect one's emotional stability.

       (2) Adrenal: this gland regulates one's supply of extra energy in emergencies and the lack of adrenalin may result in depression.

  2. Many other physical conditions could be discussed which may be the chief cause of depression.

B. It may be emotional

  1. *Many emotional conditions can be traced to a trauma or some form of arrested development in childhood.*

    a. Arrested development: too little or too much gratification at a particular age, resulting in a fragile or potentially vulnerable state when it comes to a specific kind of stress.

       (1) Too much gratification (e.g. getting too much attention) may result in a person's immaturity, reflecting a particular emotional age.

       (2) A person may be forty years old but have the maturity of a fourteen year old.

       (3) Too little gratification may result in a person seeking attention which he or she never got, and may consequently reflect the emotional age when this was most keenly felt.

    b. Trauma: an emotional shock which produces a lasting effect on a person.

       (1) Child abuse is sadly a chief cause for such a condition, resulting in a feeling of utter worthlessness.

(2) Verbal abuse by a parent or authority figure may result in a feeling of guilt.

(3) A death or an accident may have the result of making a person afraid to be trusting.

2. *'All behaviour is caused.' says Dr Clyde Narramor.*

  a. 'Every person is worth understanding.' says Dr Clyde Narramor.

  b. If we knew the person's background we would be more sympathetic and less judgemental.

C. It may be spiritual

1. Not all causes of depression are spiritual, as we can see from above.

2. *But some are, and a good theological background is useful here; we should understand:*

  a. The need to be soundly converted (John 3:3).

  b. The importance of walking in the light (1 John 1:7).

  c. The ways of God, especially the hiding of God's face (Is. 45:15).

3. But if we can put our finger on an area of unconfessed sin, the cause of depression may emerge quickly.

4. We will spend most of our time with this below.

III. Overcoming depression

A. We should first seek to know the cause.

1. *If it is certainly a depression that is spiritually derived, we need look no further.*

  a. But the cause of the depression may be a mixture of spiritual, emotional and physical.

  b. If we have dealt with the matter as a spiritual malady, as best we can, and there is no improvement in the depression as a result, this leaves two other underlying causes:

    (1) Emotional, which may take some time.

    (2) Physical, which will require treatment.

2. *A good physical examination will do no harm.*

  a. Speak frankly and honestly with our doctor.

  b. A glandular or physiological disturbance will not be successfully dealt with without medical treatment – unless of course God intervenes miraculously.

3. *If the spiritual and physical diagnoses leave us in a continuing depressed state, the cause would appear to be emotional.*

    a. A good self-understanding as to why we are as we are can shed a good deal of light – and lead to a breakthrough.

    b. Christian counselling that is safe and competent is rare and (sadly) expensive.

        (1) Most ministers do not have the time, experience or training to deal with acute cases.

        (2) A good Christian counsellor should be sought.

4. *Psychiatry should be the last resort (short of God stepping in miraculously).*

    a. Most psychiatrists today:

        (1) Do little counselling, partly because of time.

        (2) Rush the patient through by prescribing medicine.

        (3) Are biased against Christians.

    b. On the other hand, a psychiatrist can often help deeply disturbed people and can be of benefit in the same way as a non-Christian doctor can practise medicine.

        (1) Most of us do not have Christian doctors.

        (2) Yet our doctors help us from time to time.

B. There are spiritual steps a depressed person can take, regardless of the cause, which will not militate against any medical treatment or psychotherapy, and which may indeed lead one out of depression.

    1. *Intimacy with God.*

    a. The general route to this is twofold:

        (1) Getting to know God through the Bible and good teaching (Ps. 119:11).

        (2) Consistent quiet times with God; I recommend a minimum of thirty minutes a day alone with God (Mark 1:35).

    b. The particular route:

        (1) Joy in the Holy Spirit (Gal. 5:22ff).

        (2) Experiencing the ungrieved Spirit (Eph. 4:30ff).

    c. Intimacy with God is getting to know him for his own sake – what he is like – and enjoying him without any ulterior motive regarding what he can do for us.

        (1) The Lord 'confides' in such people (Ps. 25:14). ('The secret of the Lord is with them that fear him' AV.)

(2) Abraham became God's friend (James 2:23).

(3) Moses entered into such intimacy at the Tent of Meeting that the Lord spoke to him 'face to face, as a man speaks with his friend' (Ex. 33:11).

2. *Getting our self-esteem from his glory* (John 5:44).

   a. For those who feel no sense of worth, God will make up for this.

   b. He says to us, 'If I alone approve of you, will I do – or do you want man's approval more?'

   c. Here are five principles that will work, if we really and truly are willing to be content with God's approval alone:

      (1) Remember that God, who is the righteous judge, knows everything.

      (2) He knows what is fair and just at the moment.

      (3) He is glorified when he is the only one to know the truth about what we are facing.

      (4) We make a choice: glory and recognition from God or glory and credit from man.

      (5) We get our satisfaction from knowing that he knows and approves of us.

3. *Refuse to keep a record of wrongs* (1 Cor. 13:5).

   a. Love keeps no record of wrongs.

      (1) This is how God deals with us (Ps. 103:12).

      (2) We are to treat others as we have been treated by God (Eph. 4:30-32).

   b. Why do we keep a record of wrongs?

      (1) The same reason we keep records of anything – to use them.

      (2) When we say 'I'll remember that' when someone mistreats us, we have decided to keep a record of wrongs.

   c. Being critical out of anger is the result of keeping a record of wrongs.

      (1) Instead of speaking blessings it is speaking evil (Col. 4:6).

      (2) A judgemental spirit never blesses anybody; it adds to their sadness – and ours.

   d. The absolute refusal to keep a record of wrongs, including during a time of stress, allows for the Holy Spirit to be himself in us.

    (1) Joy will become our experience.

    (2) Depression begins to melt away.

   e. This joy comes from 'letting the past be past.'

    (1) Forget what is behind (Phil. 3:13).

    (2) Keep your eyes on Jesus (Heb. 12:2).

4. *Believe 1 John 1:9 with all our heart: 'If we confess our sins, he is faithful and just and will forgive us our sins and purify us from all unrighteousness.'*

   a. God's Word is true – believe it!

    (1) Know what the blood of Christ does for the Father.

    (2) Rest our case in his blood.

   b. Forgive ourselves.

    (1) Some say, 'I know God forgives me, I just can't forgive myself.'

    (2) Are we wiser or better than God? Affirm what he says about us; we are forgiven!

   c. David prayed Psalm 51 after his sin; we need it too if it applies.

    (1) For all I know, this is what he penned when he fasted and prayed after Nathan's word.

    (2) What I do know: when David saw he could do no more, he stopped fasting and went about his business – and worshipped (2 Sam. 12:20).

   d. Life was not finished for David; life is not finished with us!

Conclusion

A Christian can be depressed. Both Job and Jeremiah cursed the day of their birth (Job 3:1ff; Jer. 20:14). Many of the psalms reflect a man who was in a depression to some degree. But there is a way forward. David was once in a very bleak situation; his two wives were kidnapped and his followers were on the brink of deserting him. But he 'found strength in the LORD his God' (1 Sam. 30:6). David once said, 'Trust in the LORD and do good' (Ps. 37:3). When depressed, don't wallow in self-pity; it only leads to evil (Ps. 37:8). When depressed, do something good!

SUBJECT INDEX

BIBLE PERSONS

PERSONS INDEX

SCRIPTURE INDEX